W9-DDW-273

Ethics and Politics
Cases and Comments

Ethics and Politics
Cases and Comments

Edited by
Amy Gutmann
and
Dennis Thompson

PRINCETON UNIVERSITY

Nelson-Hall Publishers nh Chicago

Library of Congress Cataloging in Publication Data
Main entry under title:

Ethics and politics.

   1. Political ethics—Addresses, essays, lectures.
I. Gutmann, Amy.   II. Thompson, Dennis F. (Dennis
Frank), 1940- .
JA79.E823   1984   172   83-24996
ISBN 0-8304-1090-2 cloth
ISBN 0-8304-1115-1 paper

Copyright ©1984 by Amy Gutmann and Dennis F. Thompson

All rights reserved. No part of this book may be reproduced in any form without permission in writing from the publisher, except by a reviewer who wishes to quote brief passages in connection with a review written for broadcast or for inclusion in a magazine or newspaper. For information address Nelson-Hall Inc., Publishers, 111 North Canal Street, Chicago, Illinois 60606.

Manufactured in the United States of America

10 9 8 7 6 5 4 3 2 1

The paper in this book is pH neutral (acid free).

Contents

Part Two: The Ethics of Policy

Acknowledgments

This book grew out of several courses we have taught at Princeton University during the past decade. We are grateful to our students who helped us recognize the importance of cases in understanding political ethics and who helped us choose (and in some instances write) the cases we present here. For able and creative research assistance, we are indebted to Mike Comiskey. Donald E. Stokes, Dean of the Woodrow Wilson School at Princeton, encouraged this project from the beginning, and we are grateful to him and to the School for their support.

Introduction

Dean Acheson, Secretary of State under President Truman, once described the place of morality in making foreign policy in this way: "Our discussions centered on the appraisal of dangers and risks, the weighing of the need for decisive and effective action against considerations of prudence.... Moral talk did not bear on the issue." When one of his colleagues objected to a course of action charging that it was morally wrong, Acheson's reply probably reflected the conventional wisdom of American policymakers at the time. He told his colleague that on the Day of Judgment his view might be confirmed and that he was free to go forth and preach the necessity of salvation, but that "it was not, however, a view which I would entertain as a public servant."

The public servants whose views are revealed in the Pentagon Papers and the Watergate Transcripts apparently accepted — with a vengeance — Acheson's view that ethics has no place in politics. One has to look long and hard to find any hint of "moral talk" in these or similar documents of government at that time. To preserve national honor or to keep a president in office seemed to be the noblest aims to which these officials aspired. And its use as a technique of public relations appeared to be the most important role for ethics. Certainly, many officials continued to serve conscientiously, and many policies fulfilled the public interest. But insofar as officials heeded ethics, they did so tacitly. They were, at best, closet moralists.

Partly because of public reaction to Vietnam and Watergate, times are changing. Public officials are less hesitant to raise moral questions and are less reluctant to accept ethical constraints on their conduct. In 1977, Congress passed the toughest code of ethics in its history. And in 1978, it imposed a strict code on the executive branch, setting up an Office of Government Ethics to enforce it. Several presidents and executive agencies have established commissions or councils to advise them on questions of ethics. Even more significantly, questions of undeniable moral content have captured a prominent place on the political agenda. Officials can hardly escape talking about ethics when they address, for example, issues of affirmative action or abortion.

One reason for some of these changes is, no doubt, that politicians have discovered that moral talk, and sometimes even moral action, help them win or stay in office. But there are also, as there have always been, good moral reasons for public officials to be guided by ethical considerations in making policy. The reasons are now even more compelling, because the scope and stakes of American politics are greater than ever.

Public officials use means—such as violence and the threat of violence—that affect the fate of all of us and future generations as well. And the goods that our political institutions distribute—such as health care and employment opportunities—are among those that people value the most. Because officials and institutions act in ways that seriously affect the well-being of many other people and societies, we want their actions to be guided by rules that prevent them from subordinating other people's interests to their own, or the interests of some people to those of others. Because in a democracy officials and institutions are supposed to act in our name and only on our authority, we want their actions to conform to the moral principles we share with each other.

Moral or ethical principles, broadly speaking, express the rights and duties that individuals should respect when they act in ways that seriously affect the well-being of other individuals and society, and the conditions that collective practices and policies should satisfy when these similarly affect the well-being of individuals and society. Those who reject the relevance of ethics to politics do not necessarily reject all principled approaches to politics. They often recommend that public officials use principles of prudence to tell them how to achieve their own goals, or the goals of their institutions, in the most efficient way possible. What distinguishes ethical principles is the disinterested perspective they embody. Prudence asks whether an action or policy serves the interests of some particular individual or group or nation. Ethics asks whether an action or policy could be accepted by anyone who did not know his or her particular circumstances (such as social class, race, or nationality).

When prudence opposes morality in politics, we sometimes describe this as a conflict between expedience and principle. In a conflict so described, almost no one wants to argue in favor of expedience over principle. But some may argue that the free pursuit of self-interest will contribute to the public interest—at least if social and political institutions are designed correctly. But this claim does not fundamentally challenge the relevance of morality to politics; it simply proposes a (supposedly) more effective means of achieving moral ends in politics. If there is a dispute, it is over the devices of moralists, not their desires.

Should we try to change the principles that motivate public officials, or should we try to restructure political institutions to elicit ethical behavior from those who are self-interested? Presumably we have to attempt both, and perhaps we should want to change the structures of power in government and society so that citizens and officials can live together in a genuinely moral community. Whatever ways we choose to realize morality in politics, we must understand the meaning, justification, and application of moral principles in political life. This is the subject of political ethics.

Discussions of political ethics are hard to find in the literature on American politics or moral philosophy. Texts in American government tend to concentrate on the mechanics of power. If they do not banish ethics from politics, they keep it safely segregated in a realm of ideals that rarely intrude into the real world of politics. The literature of moral philosophy often takes the opposite, equally mistaken, approach. It introduces the principles of ordinary morality into politics without change. It attends to none of the special features of political life — neither the necessities of politics in general nor the imperatives of democratic politics in particular. The moral values of the political process itself, so important in a democracy, usually meet with benign neglect.

Although political ethics must be consistent with a more general theory of ethics, it cannot be the same as ordinary ethics because political life differs in morally significant ways from private life. More than most citizens, public officials assume responsibility for protecting the rights and interests of all of us. They act in our name and on our behalf. And the environment in which they act is largely impersonal and intractable. Often it is populated with powerful people and institutions that are hostile, sometimes extremely hostile, to the purposes of public-spirited officials. These and other differences between public and private life do not make ethics irrelevant to politics. If anything they make it all the more important. But they do require us to take account of the special characteristics of politics as we frame our moral judgments.

We make these moral judgments about two different aspects of politics — the ethics of the process and the ethics of policy. The first part of this book considers the moral problems of the methods used to achieve political goals, while the second part examines problems of the content of the goals themselves. The cases focus on problems of public policy and the officials who make it. Public policy is not necessarily the most important part of politics, but it plays an increasingly important role in the modern state. Knowing how to think ethically about the means and ends of public policy is essential not only for officials but for all participants in the democratic process.

The moral problem of process is that politics often requires public officials to use bad means to achieve good ends — means, such as violence, that ordinary citizens may not use except under the most extraordinary circumstances. The moral demands of ordinary politics may include a willingness to use and threaten to use violence, to deceive and manipulate, to break promises and disobey orders — in short, to harm some people for the sake of helping more people or protecting the same people from even greater harm.

If we recognize that public officials cannot avoid using bad means to achieve good ends, we must seek moral limits on the use of these means. Machiavelli's advice to the Prince is inadequate: "He should not depart from the good if he can hold to it, but he should be ready to enter on evil *if he has to.*" Political necessity is at best a vague and at worst a misleading standard. We want to prevent public officials not only from pursuing their self-interest with impunity but also from unfairly sacrificing the interests of some people or societies for the sake of advancing the interests of others. To admit that politicians must get their hands dirty, therefore, is not to agree with Machiavelli that "when the effect is good . . . it always justifies the action." Both utilitarians and their critics agree that politicians cannot so easily or frequently justify using morally bad methods to achieve good ends. Utilitarians insist on a strict calculation of the costs and benefits of such means; politicians must employ only those means that maximize benefits to all people who are affected by their use. The leading critics of utilitarianism argue that some means, such as torturing innocent persons, are never justified, no matter how high the ratio of social benefits to costs.

The cases in the first three chapters of Part One invite you to examine the morally questionable means that are most commonly used in the political process: violence and the threat of violence, deception, manipulation, and promise-breaking. We encounter more rarely the method illustrated in chapter 4 in the protests by Daniel Ellsberg, Otto Otepka, and the sixty-five lawyers who worked for the Justice Department in the late 1960s. The occasion for "civil disobedience" by public officials is generally a governmental policy that they believe to be seriously unjust. But their decision to disobey is itself an instance of the problem of dirty hands. We (and they) must decide whether they are justified in doing wrong in order to do good. Should they overtly or covertly disobey rules while remaining in office, leave office silently or in protest, or comply with an unjust policy for the sake of furthering other just ones?

The cases in Part Two illustrate the ethical problems of determining the goals of public policy. In everyday life we must choose among the many things that we ideally would like to accomplish. But our choices generally do not raise the same difficult moral questions as in politics, because in private life we are not responsible for acting in the interests of so many other people and reconciling their conflicts over such a wide range of goods. Competing preferences, scarce resources, and stakes as high as life and death combine with the duties of office to make the choices among policy goals morally hard ones.

Utilitarianism is attractive as a theory for guiding hard choices in politics because it offers a single simple principle — maximize social happiness — by which to resolve all conflicts among policies. The first case in Part Two, which assesses the risks of nuclear power, suggests that, for both empirical and moral reasons, this hope of theoretical simplicity may be illusory. Even if the experts appointed by the Atomic Energy Commission had been able to estimate the level of risk accurately, they seemed to concede that they could not decide, by using a policy analysis (based on utilitarianism), whether that level was socially acceptable.

Critics question whether the utilitarian principle is a desirable standard for choosing among policy options even in theory. They take issue with two assumptions of policy analysis as it is commonly practiced: that all competing goods can be reduced to a common measure (generally money) and that justice entails maximizing social welfare rather than distributing goods in a fair way among individuals. But utilitarians, in turn, challenge their critics to supply a better principle or set of principles by which public officials can make hard choices among competing goods.

In the congressional debate over funding of renal dialysis (chapter 6), Senator Vance Hartke takes up the challenge with two questions that implicitly attack both assumptions: "How do we explain that the difference between life and death is a matter of dollars? How do we explain that those who are wealthy have a greater chance to enjoy a longer life than those who are not?" His own proposal, which would make treatment available to all citizens who suffer from kidney disease, suggests an alternative principle of distribution based upon need. But the implications of such a principle are more problematic than the Senator reveals. We may have to choose between providing treatment to those with kidney disease and those with other illnesses, and between funding health care and other important social needs.

Few people would apply the principle of need to jobs, where equal opportunity is commonly thought to be the proper standard of distribution. But in a society where past discrimination has prevented some minorities and women from developing their talents and obtaining the same jobs as equally talented white men, it is not obvious whether equal opportunity in employment requires nondiscrimination or preferential treatment. The cases in chapter 7 ask you to choose between competing views of what constitutes fair employment practices in industry and in government.

No choice is harder to justify in a liberal democracy than the choice between saving life and protecting liberty. The cases in chapters 8 and 9 illustrate two variations of this conflict. "Legalizing Laetrile" poses a problem of legislative paternalism: Should government restrict the liberty of some citizens for the sake of prolonging or saving their lives? Abortion poses the even more difficult problem of choosing between life and liberty when citizens disagree over what constitutes a human life. Joseph Califano's account of his own struggle with this dilemma while Secretary of Health, Education and Welfare does not merely exemplify a problem of hard choices. It also brings us back to the problem of dirty hands and with a new twist: should citizens accept a public office that requires them to pursue policies contrary to their own moral principles?

Califano gives an intricate account of his predicament, including a description of his Roman Catholic upbringing and the conversations he had before making his decision to accept office. Most cases in this book are similarly detailed, since they seek to represent, as far as possible, actual decisions and policies rather than hypothetical ones. The purpose of such cases is, first of all, to convey the complexity that confronts officials who make policy and citizens who assess it. One of the most difficult but least examined steps in political ethics is to identify and frame the ethical issues themselves. Issues do not usually announce themselves as moral dilemmas; they often lie buried in a mass of facts and a welter of claims and counterclaims. The cases offer an opportunity for some moral detective work to discover the ethical suspects among the many leads the facts may suggest.

The complexity of the cases also serves a second purpose. Moral principles in their pristine form often seem to have little critical force in politics. Either they are so general that everyone readily accepts them as truisms, or they are so extreme that almost no one takes them seriously. By trying to apply the principles to particular cases, we can begin to see exactly what difference which principles make in our political judgments. Finally, the complexity should remind us that context matters in political ethics. The cases, of course, cannot give a full account of the history of the events and institutions or the structures of social and economic power. But they provide enough information to prompt us to ask what more must be known about the context to reach ethical conclusions.

The subjects of some of the cases are officials at the highest levels of government, making decisions of great historical significance—as in the decision to use the atomic bomb against Japan. And some are statements of policies with far-reaching implications for society now and in the future—as in the reports on nuclear energy. We have included such cases because they raise important issues in themselves and because they illustrate principles that have wider application. But equally important are the cases that describe less famous and less momentous events in which lower level officials make decisions that directly affect relatively few people, such as the Denver Income Maintenance Experiment, which included fewer than two hundred families. Such cases represent the more typical moral world of politics. It is a world that both citizens and officials can more often influence because the scale of its problems is more manageable and because the patterns of its problems are more predictable. Though less dramatic than the once-in-a-lifetime dilemmas we more often hear about, these decisions of normal politics cumulatively affect at least as many people.

The range of cases is intended to indicate that ethical problems may appear almost any place in political life. Behind the tedious accounting practices in the New York City fiscal crisis were large questions of democratic accountability. In Califano's story of the abortion battles, the seemingly petty disputes over legislative language (for example, whether rape must be reported within thirty, sixty, or ninety days) actually affect the welfare of many citizens and reveal disagreements of fundamental principle. Ethical issues do not arrive only at great moments in history; they also dwell in the routine of everyday politics.

However valuable cases may be, they cannot stand alone. All of the selections in this book are meant to be read in conjunction with works in moral philosophy and political theory. Such works provide principles to help assess the cases, although the cases may sometimes suggest revisions in the principles to take account of the special features of politics. Recommended readings accompany each set of cases. The recommendations are neither exclusive nor exhaustive, and other works not mentioned may be equally appropriate. But without some substantial basis in theory, any analysis of the cases is likely to be superficial.

At the end of each set of cases are comments and questions designed to encourage discussions of the ethical issues that the cases raise. Since ethical analysis should be viewed as a process of deliberation, it is best conducted (at least in part) through discussion with other people. This is especially true for political ethics. In a democracy, it is only through persuading other citizens of the moral worth of our cause that we can legitimately win their support in the making of public policies.

Recommended Reading

The best brief introduction to moral philosophy is William K. Frankena, *Ethics*, 2d ed. (Englewood Cliffs, N.J.: Prentice Hall, 1973). Also see J. L. Mackie, *Ethics* (New York: Penguin, 1977), and Bernard Williams, *Morality* (New York: Harper and Row, 1972). More difficult but worthwhile for advanced students is Alan Donagan, *The Theory of Morality* (Chicago: University of Chicago Press, 1977). For some interesting applications of moral theory to a wide range of topics, see Jonathan Glover, *Causing Death and Saving Lives* (New York: Penguin, 1978). In *After Virtue* (South Bend, Ind.: Notre Dame University Press, 1981), Alasdair MacIntyre challenges the dominant approaches to ethics since the Enlightenment. For a critical approach sympathetic to Marxism, see Richard W. Miller, "Marx and Aristotle," in Kai Nielsen and Steven C. Patten (eds.), *Marx and Morality*, supp. vol. 7 of the *Canadian Journal of Philosophy* (Guelph, Ontario: 1981), pp. 323–52. Generally on political ethics, see Joel Fleishman et al. (eds.), *Public Duties: The Moral Obligations of Government Officials* (Cambridge, Mass.: Harvard University Press, 1981).

A general framework for questions about the ethics of process can be gleaned from the literature on the problem of dirty hands. The classic sources are Machiavelli, *The Prince* (New York: Random House, 1950), and Max Weber, "Politics as a Vocation," in H. H. Gerth and C. W. Mills (eds.), *From Max Weber* (New York: Oxford University Press, 1958). If you read only one modern work on the subject, it should be Michael Walzer, "Political Action: The Problem of Dirty Hands," *Philosophy & Public Affairs* 1 (Winter 1972), pp. 160–80; reprinted in Marshall Cohen et al. (eds.) *War and Moral Responsibility* (Princeton, N.J.: Princeton University Press, 1974). Some other contemporary discussions are the articles by Stuart Hampshire, Bernard Williams, and Thomas Nagel in Hampshire et al. (eds.), *Public and Private Morality* (New York: Cambridge University Press, 1978).

The ethics of policy has generated a large literature in recent years, in part stimulated by the revival of moral and political philosophy. For a provocative view, see Robert E. Goodin, *Political Theory and Public Policy* (Chicago: University of Chicago Press, 1982). A general approach is presented by Brian Barry and Douglas W. Rae, "Political Evaluation," in F. I. Greenstein and N. W. Polsby (eds.), *Handbook of Political Science* (Reading, Mass.: Addison Wesley, 1975), vol. I, pp. 337–401. For a defense of "normative policy analysis," see David E. Price, "Assessing Policy," in Joel Fleishman et al. (eds.), *Public Duties,* pp. 142–72. On the strengths and weaknesses of utilitarianism, the foundation of the dominant approach to policy analysis, see J. J. C. Smart and Bernard Williams, *Utilitarianism For and Against* (New York: Cambridge University Press, 1973).

The philosophical work that has been most influential on the study of the ethics of policy is John Rawls, *A Theory of Justice* (Cambridge, Mass.: Harvard

University Press, 1971). For commentaries on Rawls, see Norman Daniels (ed.), *Reading Rawls* (New York: Basic Books, 1976).

A selection of philosophical writing on particular policies appears in the readers compiled by the editors of *Philosophy & Public Affairs* and published by Princeton University Press. See Marshall Cohen et al. (eds.), *Equality and Preferential Treatment* (1978); *Medicine and Moral Philosophy* (1982); *Rights and Wrongs of Abortion* (1974); and *War and Moral Responsibility* (1974). Also see the valuable series, Maryland Studies in Public Philosophy, edited by the Center for Philosophy and Public Policy, University of Maryland, and published by Rowman and Allanheld.

Students can keep up with the latest work in this subject by regularly reading the journals *Ethics* (University of Chicago Press) and *Philosophy & Public Affairs* (Princeton University Press).

Part One

The Ethics of Process

1   Violence

Introduction

Violence violates the fundamental moral prohibition against harming persons, yet governments must sometimes use violent means to defend that same fundamental principle. The most dramatic instance of the use of violence is war, and the most terrifying kind of war is nuclear war. The cases in this chapter raise questions about nuclear war and the means used to prevent it.

"War is cruel and you cannot refine it," General Sherman told the citizens of Atlanta who protested against the brutality of his invasion of their city. Many other military and political leaders as well as moral philosophers have agreed with Sherman. If your cause is just in a war, you should use any means necessary to win it. To place moral constraints on the fighting of a war, the argument goes, would simply prolong it and could increase the chances of war in the future by making war more morally respectable.

In most wars most nations nevertheless have accepted some moral constraints on their conduct (such as not torturing prisoners) and the philosophical writing on just war has long distinguished the justice of a war from the justice of the means used to fight it. The former does not necessarily determine the latter. Even in the war against the Nazis, we should condemn some methods—for example, the practice of the Free French forces who enlisted Moroccan mercenaries by promising them that they could, with impunity, rape Italian women. And we want to distinguish moral from immoral actions of men fighting on the side of the aggressor nation: we praise General Rommel for ignoring Hitler's order to shoot all prisoners captured behind the lines.

The basic principle underlying most rules of war is that it is morally wrong to attack noncombatants. Noncombatants are defined as those who are not fighting or not supplying the means of fighting the war. Farmers and nurses are noncombatants, while munitions workers and soldiers are combatants. Different moral traditions give different reasons for this prohibition, but all regard it as important.

At the same time most philosophers of just wars recognize that noncombatants will inevitably be killed in modern warfare—sometimes justifiably so. The major problem then becomes either (1) to formulate the prohibition so as to justify some deaths of noncombatants or (2) to specify the conditions under which the prohibition may be suspended. The most prominent example of the first alternative is the doctrine of double-effect, which holds that the deaths of noncombatants is permissible if it is an unintended (though foreseen) side effect of a morally legitimate end. The doctrine, for example, would permit an air strike

3

against an enemy missile site even if civilians lived nearby. The other alternative would allow civilians to be killed directly only if necessary to stop the imminent destruction of a nation. In this view, British bombing of German cities may have been justified until 1942 but not thereafter.

Nuclear weapons, some have argued, make obsolete all these fine distinctions and the rules of war that depend on them. With the possible exception of tactical weapons, nuclear forces strike directly at civilian populations. The destruction of Hiroshima and Nagasaki could hardly be described as an unintended side effect; nor was the bombing necessary to prevent the defeat of the United States. But the new technology may increase the need to take the old rules of war seriously. Even some of those who favored the bombing of Hiroshima and Nagasaki recognized that it called for moral justification and believed they could provide it. Writing only a few months before President Harry S. Truman accepted his advice to use the bomb against Japan, Secretary of State Henry Stimson insisted that the "rule of sparing the civilian population should be applied as far as possible to the use of any new weapon." Stimson's own defense of the use of that weapon, reprinted as the first selection in this chapter, shows how he came to terms with that moral rule.

Nuclear deterrence also creates problems for the rules of war—or perhaps we should say the rules create problems for deterrence. The essence of deterrence, some say, is an immoral threat: if the enemy launches a nuclear attack against us, we will retaliate by destroying the enemy's population. Deterrence, others in turn argue, is morally justified because to threaten evil consequences is the best way, or the only way, to prevent them from occurring. But critics of deterrence object that the threat itself (if it is credible as it must be) increases the likelihood of nuclear war. In any case, the critics say, the threat remains immoral, and we should not accept indefinitely any system of defense based on such a threat.

The Decision to Use the Atomic Bomb
Henry L. Stimson

In recent months there has been much comment about the decision to use atomic bombs in attacks on the Japanese cities of Hiroshima and Nagasaki. This decision was one of the gravest made by our gov-

"The Decision to Use the Atomic Bomb" as it appeared in *Harper's Magazine*, later incorporated in chapter "The Atomic Bomb and the Surrender of Japan" in *On Active Service in Peace and War*, by Henry L. Stimson and McGeorge Bundy. Copyright 1947 by Henry L. Stimson. Reprinted by permission of Harper & Row, Publishers, Inc.

ernment in recent years, and it is entirely proper that it should be widely discussed. I have therefore decided to record for all who may be interested my understanding of the events which led up to the attack on Hiroshima on August 6, 1945, on Nagasaki on August 9, and the Japanese decision to surrender on August 10. No single individual can hope to know exactly what took place in the minds of all of those who had a share in these events, but what follows is an exact description of our thoughts and actions as I find them in the records and in my clearest recollection.

It was in the fall of 1941 that the question of atomic energy was first brought directly to my attention. At that time President Roosevelt appointed a committee consisting of Vice President Wallace, General Marshall, Dr. Vannevar Bush, Dr. James B. Conant, and myself. The function of this committee was to advise the President on questions of policy relating to the study of nuclear fission which was then proceeding both in this country and in Great Britain. For nearly four years thereafter I was directly connected with all major decisions of policy on the development and use of atomic energy, and from May 1, 1943, until my resignation as Secretary of War on September 21, 1945, I was directly responsible to the President for the administration of the entire undertaking; my chief advisers in this period were General Marshall, Dr. Bush, Dr. Conant, and Major General Leslie R. Groves, the officer in charge of the project. At the same time I was the President's senior adviser on the military employment of atomic energy.

The policy adopted and steadily pursued by President Roosevelt and his advisers was a simple one. It was to spare no effort in securing the earliest possible successful development of an atomic weapon. The reasons for this policy were equally simple. The original experimental achievement of atomic fission had occurred in Germany in 1938, and it was known that the Germans had continued their experiments. In 1941 and 1942 they were believed to be ahead of us, and it was vital that they should not be the first to bring atomic weapons into the field of battle. Furthermore, if we should be the first to develop the weapon, we should have a great new instrument for shortening the war and minimizing destruction. At no time from 1941 to 1945 did I ever hear it suggested by the President, or by any other responsible member of the government, that atomic energy should not be used in the war. All of us of course understood the terrible responsibility involved in our attempt to unlock the doors to such a devastating weapon; President Roosevelt particularly spoke to me many times of his own awareness of the catastrophic potentialities of our work. But we were at war, and the work must be done. I therefore emphasize that it was our common objective throughout the war to be the first to produce an atomic weapon and use it. The possible atomic weapon was considered to be a new and tremendously powerful explosive, as legitimate as any other of the deadly explosive weapons of modern war. The entire purpose was the production of a military weapon; on no other ground could the wartime expenditure of so much time and money have been justified. The exact circumstances in which that weapon might be used were unknown to any of us until the middle of 1945, and when that time came, as we shall presently see, the military use of atomic energy was connected with larger questions of national policy.

The extraordinary story of the successful development of the atomic bomb has been well told elsewhere. As time went on it became clear that the weapon would not be available in time for use in the European theater, and the war against Germany was successfully ended by the use of what are now called conventional means. But in the spring of 1945 it became evident that the climax of our prolonged atomic effort was at hand. By the nature of atomic chain reactions, it was impossible to state with certainty that we had succeeded until a bomb had actually exploded in a full-scale experiment; nevertheless it was considered exceedingly probable that we should by midsummer have successfully detonated the first atomic bomb. This was to be done at the Alamogordo Reservation in New Mexico. It was thus time for detailed consideration of our future plans. What had begun as a well-founded hope was now developing into a reality.

On March 15, 1945, I had my last talk with President Roosevelt. My diary record of this conversation gives a fairly clear picture of the state of our thinking at that time. I have removed the name of the distinguished public servant who was fearful lest the Manhattan (atomic) project be "a lemon"; it was an opinion common among those not fully informed.

"The President... had suggested that I come over to lunch today... First I took up with him a memorandum which he sent to me from _____, who had been alarmed at the rumors of extravagance in the Manhattan project. _____ suggested that it might become disastrous and he suggested that we get a body of 'outside' scientists to pass upon the project because rumors are going around that Vannevar Bush and Jim Conant have sold the President a lemon on the subject and ought to be checked up on. It was rather a jittery and nervous memorandum and rather silly, and I was prepared for it and I gave the President a list of the scientists who were actually engaged on it to show the very high standing of them and it comprised four Nobel Prize men, and also how practically every physicist of standing was engaged with us in the project. Then I outlined to him the future of it and when it was likely to come off and told him how important it was to get ready. I went over with him the two schools of thought that exist in respect to the future control after the war of this project, in case it is successful, one of them being the secret close-in attempted control of the project by those who control it now, and the other being the international control based upon freedom both of science and of access. I told him that those things must be settled before the first projectile is used and that he must be ready with a statement to come out to the people on it just as soon as that is done. He agreed to that...."

This conversation covered the three aspects of the question which were then uppermost in our minds. First, it was always necessary to suppress a lingering doubt that any such titanic undertaking could be successful. Second, we must consider the implications of success in terms of its long-range postwar effect. Third, we must face the problem that would be presented at the time of our first use of the weapon, for with that first use there must be some public statement.

I did not see Franklin Roosevelt again. The next time I went to the White House to discuss atomic energy was April 25, 1945, and I went to explain the nature of the problem to a man whose only previous knowledge of our activities was that of a Senator who had loyally accepted our assurance that the matter must be kept a secret from him. Now he was President and Commander-in-Chief, and the final responsibility in this as in so many other matters must be his. President Truman accepted this responsibility with the same fine spirit that Senator Truman had shown before in accepting our refusal to inform him.

I discussed with him the whole history of the project. We had with us General Groves, who explained in detail the progress which had been made and the probable future course of the work. I also discussed with President Truman the broader aspects of the subject, and the memorandum which I used in this discussion is again a fair sample of the state of our thinking at the time.

Memorandum discussed with President Truman April 25, 1945:

"1. Within four months we shall in all probability have completed the most terrible weapon ever known in human history, one bomb of which could destroy a whole city.

"2. Although we have shared its development with the U.K., physically the U.S. is at present in the position of controlling the resources with which to construct and use it and no other nation could reach this position for some years.

"3. Nevertheless it is practically certain that we could not remain in this position indefinitely.

"a. Various segments of its discovery and production are widely known among many scientists in many countries, although few scientists are now acquainted with the whole process which we have developed.

"b. Although its construction under present methods requires great scientific and industrial effort and raw materials, which are temporarily mainly within the possession and knowledge of U.S. and U.K., it is extremely probable that much easier and cheaper methods of production will be discovered by scientists in the future, together with the use of materials of much wider distribution. As a result, it is extremely probable that the future will make it possible for atomic bombs to be constructed by smaller nations or even groups, or at least by a larger nation in a much shorter time.

"4. As a result, it is indicated that the future may see a time when such a weapon may be constructed in secret and used suddenly and effectively with devastating power by a willful nation or group against an unsuspecting nation or group of much greater size and material power. With its aid even a very powerful unsuspecting nation might be conquered within a very few days by a very much smaller one. [A brief reference to the estimated capabilities of other nations is here omitted; it in no way affects the course of the argument.]

"5. The world in its present state of moral advancement compared with its technical development would be eventually at the mercy of such a weapon. In other words, modern civilization might be completely destroyed.

"6. To approach any world peace organization of any pattern now likely to be considered, without an appreciation by the leaders of our country of the power of

this new weapon, would seem to be unrealistic. No system of control heretofore considered would be adequate to control this menace. Both inside any particular country and between the nations of the world, the control of this weapon will undoubtedly be a matter of the greatest difficulty and would involve such thoroughgoing rights of inspection and internal controls as we have never heretofore contemplated.

"7. Furthermore, in the light of our present position with reference to this weapon, the question of sharing it with other nations and, if so shared, upon what terms, becomes a primary question of our foreign relations. Also our leadership in the war and in the development of this weapon has placed a certain moral responsibility upon us which we cannot shirk without very serious responsibility for any disaster to civilization which it would further.

"8. On the other hand, if the problem of the proper use of this weapon can be solved, we would have the opportunity to bring the world into a pattern in which the peace of the world and our civilization can be saved.

"9. As stated in General Groves' report, steps are under way looking towards the establishment of a select committee of particular qualifications for recommending action to the executive and legislative branches of our government when secrecy is no longer in full effect. The committee would also recommend the actions to be taken by the War Department prior to that time in anticipation of the postwar problems. All recommendations would of course be first submitted to the President."

The next step in our preparations was the appointment of the committee referred to in paragraph 9 above. This committee, which was known as the Interim Committee, was charged with the function of advising the President on the various questions raised by our apparently imminent success in developing the atomic weapon. I was its chairman, but the principal labor of guiding its extended deliberations fell to George L. Harrison, who acted as chairman in my absence. It will be useful to consider the work of the committee in some detail. Its members were the following, in addition to Mr. Harrison and myself:

James F. Byrnes (then a private citizen) as personal representative of the President.

Ralph A. Bard, Under Secretary of the Navy.

William L. Clayton, Assistant Secretary of State.

Dr. Vannevar Bush, Director, Office of Scientific Research and Development, and president of the Carnegie Institution of Washington.

Dr. Karl Compton, Chief of the Office of Field Service in the Office of Scientific Research and Development, and president of the Massachusetts Institute of Technology.

Dr. James B. Conant, Chairman of the National Defense Research Committee, and president of Harvard University.

The discussions of the committee ranged over the whole field of atomic energy, in its political, military, and scientific aspects. That part of its work which particularly concerns us here relates to its recommendations for the use of atomic energy against Japan, but it should be borne in mind that these recommendations were not made in a vacuum. The committee's work included the drafting of the statements which were published immediately after the first bombs were dropped, the drafting of a bill for the domestic control of atomic energy, and recommendations looking toward the international control of atomic energy. The Interim Committee was assisted in its work by a Scientific Panel whose members were the following: Dr. A. H. Compton, Dr. Enrico Fermi, Dr. E. O.

Lawrence, and Dr. J. R. Oppenheimer. All four were nuclear physicists of the first rank; all four had held positions of great importance in the atomic project from its inception. At a meeting with the Interim Committee and the Scientific Panel on May 31, 1945 I urged all those present to feel free to express themselves on any phase of the subject, scientific or political. Both General Marshall and I at this meeting expressed the view that atomic energy could not be considered simply in terms of military weapons but must also be considered in terms of a new relationship of man to the universe.

On June 1, after its discussions with the Scientific Panel, the Interim Committee unanimously adopted the following recommendations:

1. The bomb should be used against Japan as soon as possible.

2. It should be used on a dual target — that is, a military installation or war plant surrounded by or adjacent to houses and other buildings most susceptible to damage, and

3. It should be used without prior warning [of the nature of the weapon]. (One member of the committee, Mr. Bard, later changed his view and dissented from the third recommendation.)

In reaching these conclusions the Interim Committee carefully considered such alternatives as a detailed advance warning or a demonstration in some uninhabited area. Both of these suggestions were discarded as impractical. They were not regarded as likely to be effective in compelling a surrender of Japan and both of them involved serious risks. Even the New Mexico test would not give final proof that any given bomb was certain to explode when dropped from an airplane. Quite apart from the generally unfamiliar nature of atomic explosives, there was the whole problem of exploding a bomb at a predetermined height in the air by a complicated mechanism which could not be tested in the static test of New Mexico. Nothing would have been more damaging to our effort to obtain surrender than a warning or a demonstration followed by a dud—and this was a real possibility. Furthermore, we had no bombs to waste. It was vital that a sufficient effect be quickly obtained with the few we had.

The Interim Committee and the Scientific Panel also served as a channel through which suggestions from other scientists working on the atomic project were forwarded to me and to the President. Among the suggestions thus forwarded was one memorandum which questioned using the bomb at all against the enemy. On June 16, 1945, after consideration of that memorandum, the Scientific Panel made a report, from which I quote the following paragraphs:

"The opinions of our scientific colleagues on the initial use of these weapons are not unanimous: they range from the proposal of a purely technical demonstration to that of the military application best designed to induce surrender. Those who advocate a purely technical demonstration would wish to outlaw the use of atomic weapons, and have feared that if we use the weapons now our position in future negotiations will be prejudiced. Others emphasize the opportunity of saving American lives by immediate military use, and believe that such use will improve the international prospects, in that they are more concerned with the prevention of war than with the elimination of this special weapon. We find ourselves closer to these latter views: *we can propose no technical demonstration likely to bring an end to the war; we see no acceptable alternative to direct military use.* [Italics mine.]

"With regard to these general aspects of the use of atomic energy, it is clear that we, as scientific men, have no proprietary rights. It is true that we are among the few citizens who have had occasion to give

thoughtful consideration to these problems during the past few years. We have, however, no claim to special competence in solving the political, social, and military problems which are presented by the advent of atomic power."

The foregoing discussion presents the reasoning of the Interim Committee and its advisers. I have discussed the work of these gentlemen at length in order to make it clear that we sought the best advice that we could find. The committee's function was, of course, entirely advisory. The ultimate responsibility for the recommendation to the President rested upon me, and I have no desire to veil it. The conclusions of the committee were similar to my own, although I reached mine independently. I felt that to extract a genuine surrender from the Emperor and his military advisers, they must be administered a tremendous shock which would carry convincing proof of our power to destroy the Empire. Such an effective shock would save many times the number of lives, both American and Japanese, that it would cost.

The facts upon which my reasoning was based and steps taken to carry it out now follow.

The principal political, social, and military objective of the United States in the summer of 1945 was the prompt and complete surrender of Japan. Only the complete destruction of her military power could open the way to lasting peace.

Japan, in July 1945, had been seriously weakened by our increasingly violent attacks. It was known to us that she had gone so far as to make tentative proposals to the Soviet government, hoping to use the Russians as mediators in a negotiated peace. These vague proposals contemplated the retention by Japan of important conquered areas and were therefore not considered seriously. There was as yet no indication of any weakening in the Japanese determination to fight rather than accept unconditional surrender. If she should persist in her fight to the end, she had still a great military force.

In the middle of July 1945, the intelligence section of the War Department General Staff estimated Japanese military strength as follows: in the home islands, slightly under two million; in Korea, Manchuria, China proper, and Formosa, slightly over two million; in French Indo-China, Thailand, and Burma, over 200,000; in the East Indies area, including the Philippines, over 500,000; in the bypassed Pacific islands, over 100,000. The total strength of the Japanese Army was estimated at about five million men. These estimates later proved to be in very close agreement with official Japanese figures.

The Japanese Army was in much better condition than the Japanese Navy and Air Force. The Navy had practically ceased to exist except as a harrying force against an invasion fleet. The Air Force had been reduced mainly to reliance upon Kamikaze, or suicide, attacks. These latter, however, had already inflicted serious damage on our seagoing forces, and their possible effectiveness in a last ditch fight was a matter of real concern to our naval leaders.

As we understood it in July, there was a very strong possibility that the Japanese government might determine upon resistance to the end, in all the areas of the Far East under its control. In such an event the Allies would be faced with the enormous task of destroying an armed force of five million men and five thousand suicide aircraft, belonging to a race which had already amply demonstrated its ability to fight literally to the death.

The strategic plans of our armed forces for the defeat of Japan as they stood in July had been prepared without reliance upon the atomic bomb, which had not yet been tested in New Mexico. We were planning an intensified sea and air blockade and greatly intensified strategic air bombing through the summer and early fall, to

be followed on November 1 by an invasion of the southern island of Kyushu. This would be followed in turn by an invasion of the main island of Honshu in the spring of 1946. The total U.S. military and naval force involved in this grand design was of the order of five million men; if all those indirectly concerned are included, it was larger still.

We estimated that if we should be forced to carry this plan to its conclusion, the major fighting would not end until the latter part of 1946, at the earliest. I was informed that such operations might be expected to cost over a million casualties, to American forces alone. Additional large losses might be expected among our allies, and, of course, if our campaign were successful and if we could judge by previous experience, enemy casualties would be much larger than our own.

It was already clear in July that even before the invasion, we should be able to inflict enormously severe damage on the Japanese homeland by the combined application of "conventional" sea and air power. The critical question was whether this kind of action would induce surrender. It therefore became necessary to consider very carefully the probable state of mind of the enemy, and to assess with accuracy the line of conduct which might end his will to resist.

With these considerations in mind, I wrote a memorandum for the President, on July 2, which I believe fairly represents the thinking of the American government as it finally took shape in action. This memorandum was prepared after discussion and general agreement with Joseph C. Grew, Acting Secretary of State, and Secretary of the Navy Forrestal, and when I discussed it with the President, he expressed his general approval.

Memorandum for the President, July 2, 1945, on proposed program for Japan:

"1. The plans of operation up to and including the first landing have been authorized and the preparations for the operation are now actually going on. This situation was accepted by all members of your conference on Monday, June 18.

"2. There is reason to believe that the operation for the occupation of Japan following the landing may be a very long, costly, and arduous struggle on our part. The terrain, much of which I have visited several times, has left the impression on my memory of being one which would be susceptible to a last ditch defense such as has been made on Iwo Jima and Okinawa and which of course is very much larger than either of those two areas. According to my recollection it will be much more unfavorable with regard to tank maneuvering than either the Philippines or Germany.

"3. If we once land on one of the main islands and begin a forceful occupation of Japan, we shall probably have cast the die of last ditch resistance. The Japanese are highly patriotic and certainly susceptible to calls for fanatical resistance to repel an invasion. Once started in actual invasion, we shall in my opinion have to go through with an even more bitter finish fight than in Germany. We shall incur the losses incident to such a war and we shall have to leave the Japanese islands even more thoroughly destroyed than was the case with Germany. This would be due both to the difference in the Japanese and German personal character and the differences in the size and character of the terrain through which the operations will take place.

"4. A question then comes: Is there any alternative to such a forceful occupation of Japan which will secure for us the equivalent of an unconditional surrender of her forces and a permanent destruction of her power again to strike an aggressive blow at the 'peace of the Pacific'? I am inclined to think that there is enough such chance to make it well worthwhile our giving them a warning of what is to come and a definite opportunity to capitulate. As above suggested, it should be tried before the actual forceful occupation of the homeland islands is begun and furthermore the warning should be given in ample time to permit a national reaction to set in.

"We have the following enormously favorable factors on our side—factors much weightier than those we had against Germany:

"Japan has no allies.

"Her navy is nearly destroyed and she is vulnerable to a surface and underwater blockade which can deprive her of sufficient food and supplies for her population.

"She is terribly vulnerable to our concentrated air attack upon her crowded cities, industrial and food resources.

"She has against her not only the Anglo-American forces but the rising forces of China and the ominous threat of Russia.

"We have inexhaustible and untouched industrial resources to bring to bear against her diminishing potential.

"We have great moral superiority through being the victim of her first sneak attack.

"The problem is to translate these advantages into prompt and economical achievement of our objectives. I believe Japan is susceptible to reason in such a crisis to a much greater extent than is indicated by our current press and other current comment. Japan is not a nation composed wholly of mad fanatics of an entirely different mentality from ours. On the contrary, she has within the past century shown herself to possess extremely intelligent people, capable in an unprecedentedly short time of adopting not only the complicated technique of Occidental civilization but to a substantial extent their culture and their political and social ideas. Her advance in all these respects during the short period of sixty or seventy years has been one of the most astounding feats of national progress in history—a leap from the isolated feudalism of centuries into the position of one of the six or seven great powers of the world. She has not only built up powerful armies and navies. She has maintained an honest and effective national finance and respected position in many of the sciences in which we pride ourselves. Prior to the forcible seizure of power over her government by the fanatical military group in 1931, she had for ten years lived a reasonably responsible and respectable international life.

"My own opinion is in her favor on the two points involved in this question:

"a. I think the Japanese nation has the mental intelligence and versatile capacity in such a crisis to recognize the folly of a fight to the finish and to accept the proffer of what will amount to an unconditional surrender; and

"b. I think she has within her population enough liberal leaders (although now submerged by the terrorists) to be depended upon for her reconstruction as a responsible member of the family of nations. I think she is better in this respect than Germany was. Her liberals yielded only at the point of the pistol and, so far as I am aware, their liberal attitude has not been personally subverted in the way which was so general in Germany.

"On the other hand, I think that the attempt to exterminate her armies and her population by gunfire or other means will tend to produce a fusion of race solidity and antipathy which has no analogy in the case of Germany. We have a national interest in creating, if possible, a condition wherein the Japanese nation may live as a peaceful and useful member of the future Pacific community.

"5. It is therefore my conclusion that a carefully timed warning be given to Japan by the chief representatives of the United States, Great Britain, China, and, if then a belligerent, Russia by calling upon Japan to surrender and permit the occupation of her country in order to insure its

complete demilitarization for the sake of the future peace.

"This warning should contain the following elements:

"The varied and overwhelming character of the force we are about to bring to bear on the islands.

"The inevitability and completeness of the destruction which the full application of this force will entail.

"The determination of the Allies to destroy permanently all authority and influence of those who have deceived and misled the country into embarking on world conquest.

"The determination of the Allies to limit Japanese sovereignty to her main islands and to render them powerless to mount and support another war.

"The disavowal of any attempt to extirpate the Japanese as a race or to destroy them as a nation.

"A statement of our readiness, once her economy is purged of its militaristic influence, to permit the Japanese to maintain such industries, particularly of a light consumer character, as offer no threat of aggression against their neighbors, but which can produce a sustaining economy, and provide a reasonable standard of living. The statement should indicate our willingness, for this purpose, to give Japan trade access to external raw materials, but no longer any control over the sources of supply outside her main islands. It should also indicate our willingness, in accordance with our now established foreign trade policy, in due course to enter into mutually advantageous trade relations with her.

"The withdrawal from their country as soon as the above objectives of the Allies are accomplished, and as soon as there has been established a peacefully inclined government, of a character representative of the masses of the Japanese people. I personally think that if in saying this we should add that we do not exclude a constitutional monarchy under her present dynasty, it would substantially add to the chances of acceptance.

"6. Success of course will depend on the potency of the warning which we give her. She has an extremely sensitive national pride and, as we are now seeing every day, when actually locked with the enemy will fight to the very death. For that reason the warning must be tendered before the actual invasion has occurred and while the impending destruction, though clear beyond peradventure, has not yet reduced her to fanatical despair. If Russia is a part of the threat, the Russian attack, if actual, must not have progressed too far. Our own bombing should be confined to military objectives as far as possible."

It is important to emphasize the double character of the suggested warning. It was designed to promise destruction if Japan resisted, and hope, if she surrendered.

It will be noted that the atomic bomb is not mentioned in this memorandum. On grounds of secrecy the bomb was never mentioned except when absolutely necessary, and furthermore, it had not yet been tested. It was of course well forward in our minds as the memorandum was written and discussed that the bomb would be the best possible sanction if our warning were rejected.

The adoption of the policy outlined in the memorandum of July 2 was a decision of high politics; once it was accepted by the President, the position of the atomic bomb in our planning became quite clear. I find that I stated in my diary, as early as June 19, that "the last chance warning... must be given before an actual landing of the ground forces in Japan, and fortunately the plans provide for enough time to bring in the sanctions to our warning in the shape of heavy ordinary bombing attack and an attack of S-1." S-1 was a code name for the atomic bomb.

There was much discussion in Washington about the timing of the warning to Japan. The controlling factor in the end was the date already set for the Potsdam meeting of the Big Three. It was President Truman's decision that such a warning should be solemnly issued by the U.S. and the U.K. from this meeting, with the concurrence of the head of the Chinese government, so that it would be plain that *all* of Japan's principal enemies were in entire unity. This was done in the Potsdam ultimatum of July 26, which very closely followed the above memorandum of July 2 with the exception that it made no mention of the Japanese Emperor.

On July 28 the Premier of Japan, Suzuki, rejected the Potsdam ultimatum by announcing that it was "unworthy of public notice." In the face of this rejection we could only proceed to demonstrate that the ultimatum had meant exactly what it said when it stated that if the Japanese continued the war, "the full application of our military power, backed by our resolve, will mean the inevitable and complete destruction of the Japanese armed forces and just as inevitably the utter devastation of the Japanese homeland."

For such a purpose the atomic bomb was an eminently suitable weapon. The New Mexico test occurred while we were at Potsdam, on July 16. It was immediately clear that the power of the bomb measured up to our highest estimates. We had developed a weapon of such a revolutionary character that its use against the enemy might well be expected to produce exactly the kind of shock on the Japanese ruling oligarchy which we desired, strengthening the position of those who wished peace, and weakening that of the military party.

Because of the importance of the atomic mission against Japan, the detailed plans were brought to me by the military staff for approval. With President Truman's warm support I struck off the list of suggested targets the city of Kyoto. Although it was a target of considerable military importance, it had been the ancient capital of Japan and was a shrine of Japanese art and culture. We determined that it should be spared. I approved four other targets including the cities of Hiroshima and Nagasaki.

Hiroshima was bombed on August 6, and Nagasaki on August 9. These two cities were active working parts of the Japanese war effort. One was an army center; the other was naval and industrial. Hiroshima was the headquarters of the Japanese Army defending southern Japan and was a major military storage and assembly point. Nagasaki was a major seaport and it contained several large industrial plants of great wartime importance. We believed that our attacks had struck cities which must certainly be important to the Japanese military leaders, both Army and Navy, and we waited for a result. We waited one day.

Many accounts have been written about the Japanese surrender. After a prolonged Japanese cabinet session in which the deadlock was broken by the Emperor himself, the offer to surrender was made on August 10. It was based on the Potsdam terms, with a reservation concerning the sovereignty of the Emperor. While the Allied reply made no promises other than those already given, it implicitly recognized the Emperor's position by prescribing that his power must be subject to the orders of the Allied Supreme Commander. These terms were accepted on August 14 by the Japanese, and the instrument of surrender was formally signed on September 2, in Tokyo Bay. Our great objective was thus achieved, and all the evidence I have seen indicates that the controlling factor in the final Japanese decision to accept our terms of surrender was the atomic bomb.

The two atomic bombs which we had dropped were the only ones we had ready, and our rate of production at the time was very small. Had the war continued until the projected invasion on November 1, additional fire raids of B-29s would have been more destructive of life and property than the very limited number of atomic raids which we could have executed in the same period. But the atomic bomb was more than a weapon of terrible destruction; it was a psychological weapon. In March 1945, our Air Force had launched its first great incendiary raid on the Tokyo area. In this raid more damage was done and more casualties were inflicted than was the case at Hiroshima. Hundreds of bombers took part and hundreds of tons of incendiaries were dropped. Similar successive raids burned out a great part of the urban area of Japan, but the Japanese fought on. On August 6 one B-29 dropped a single atomic weapon on Hiroshima. Three days later a second bomb was dropped on Nagasaki and the war was over. So far as the Japanese could know, our ability to execute atomic attacks, if necessary by many planes at a time, was unlimited. As Dr. Karl Compton has said, "it was not one atomic bomb, or two, which brought surrender; it was the experience of what an atomic bomb will actually do to a community, *plus the dread of many more*, that was effective."

The bomb thus served exactly the purpose we intended. The peace party was able to take the path of surrender, and the whole weight of the Emperor's prestige was exerted in favor of peace. When the Emperor ordered surrender, and the small but dangerous group of fanatics who opposed him were brought under control, the Japanese became so subdued that the great undertaking of occupation and disarmament was completed with unprecedented ease.

In the foregoing pages I have tried to give an accurate account of my own personal observations of the circumstances which led up to the use of the atomic bomb and the reasons which underlay our use of it. To me they have always seemed compelling and clear, and I cannot see how any person vested with such responsibilities as mine could have taken any other course or given any other advice to his chiefs.

The Bomb, the War, and the Russians
Martin J. Sherwin

"THE BOTTOM FACTS"

Many of the questions that have plagued later commentators on the atomic bombings of Hiroshima and Nagasaki simply do not seem to have occurred at the time to the policymakers responsible for those decisions. Nowhere in Stimson's meticulous diary, for example, is there any suggestion of doubt or questioning of the assumption that the bomb should be used against Germany or Japan if the weapon was ready before the end of the war. From the time of the first organizational meeting for the atomic energy project held at the White House on October 9, 1941, members of the Top Policy Group conceived of the development of the weapon as an essential part of the total war effort. They asked whether it would be ready in time, not whether it should be used if it was; what were the diplomatic consequences of its development, not the moral implications of its military use.

This was not simply due to an absence of reflection. Stimson, for one, began to ponder seriously the revolutionary aspects of the atomic bomb during the winter of 1944–45. By March he was convinced that its development raised issues that "went right down to the bottom facts of human nature, morals and government." And yet this awareness of its profound implications apparently did not lead him to raise the sort of questions that might naturally seem to follow from such awareness. He never suggested to Roosevelt or Truman that its military use might incur a moral liability (an issue the Secretary did raise with regard to the manner in which conventional weapons were used), or that chances of securing Soviet postwar cooperation might be diminished if Stalin did not receive a commitment to international control prior to an atomic attack on Japan. The question naturally arises, why were these alternative policy choices not considered? Perhaps what Frankfurter once referred to as Stimson's habit of setting his mind "at one thing like the needle of an old victrola caught in a single groove" may help to explain how he overlooked exactly what he sought to avoid — an atomic energy policy that contributed to the destruction of the Grand Alliance. Yet it must be pointed out that Bush and Conant never seriously questioned the assumption of the bomb's use either. Like Niels Bohr, they made a clear distinction between, on the one hand, its military application, which they took to be a wartime strategic decision, and, on the other, its moral and diplomatic implications, which bore on the longer-

From *A World Destroyed: The Atomic Bomb and the Grand Alliance,* by Martin J. Sherwin. Copyright © 1973, 1975 by Martin J. Sherwin. Reprinted by permission of Alfred A. Knopf, Inc.

range issues of world peace and security and relations among nations. "What role it [the bomb] may play in the present war," Bohr had written to Roosevelt in July 1944, was a question "quite apart" from the overriding concern: the need to avoid an atomic arms race.

The preoccupation with winning the war obviously helped to foster this dichotomy in the minds of these men. But a closer look at how Bohr and Stimson respectively defined the nature of the diplomatic problem created by the bomb suggests that for the Secretary of War and his advisers (and ultimately for the President they advised) the dichotomy was, after all, more apparent than real. As a scientist, Bohr apprehended the significance of the new weapon even before it was developed, and he had no doubt that scientists in the Soviet Union would also understand its profound implications for the postwar world. He also was certain that they would convey the meaning of the development to Stalin, just as scientists in the United States and Great Britain had explained it to Roosevelt and Churchill. Thus the diplomatic problem, as Bohr analyzed it, was not the need to convince Stalin that the atomic bomb was an unprecedented weapon that threatened the life of the world, but the need to assure the Soviet leader that he had nothing to fear from the circumstances of its development. It was by informing Stalin during the war that the United States intended to cooperate with him in neutralizing the bomb through international control, Bohr reasoned, that it then became possible to consider its wartime use apart from its postwar role.

Stimson approached the issue differently. Without Bohr's training and without his faith in science and in scientists, atomic energy in its *un*developed state had a different meaning for him. Memoranda and interviews could not instill in a non-scientist with policymaking

responsibilities the intuitive understanding of a nuclear physicist whose work had led directly to the Manhattan Project. The very aspect of the atomic bomb upon which Bohr placed so much hope for achieving a new departure in international affairs—its uniqueness—made it unlikely that non-scientists would grasp its full implications and therefore act upon his proposals. In this sense Bohr was correct when he said that he did not speak the same language as Churchill, or as any other statesman, for that matter.

It was only after Bohr's proposal was rejected at the Hyde Park meeting in September 1944 that events forced Stimson to think deeply about the weapon under his charge. Beginning with the fixed assumption that the bomb would be used in the war, he developed a view of the relationship between it and American diplomacy that reinforced that assumption, or at least gave him no cause to question it. For he could not consider an untried weapon an effective diplomatic bargaining counter; on the contrary, its diplomatic value was related to, if not primarily dependent upon, its demonstrated worth as a military force. Only when its "actual certainty [was] fixed," Stimson believed, could it carry weight in dealings with the Soviet Union.

The need for assurance that the bomb would work raises the central question: Did Stimson's understanding that the bomb would play an important diplomatic role after the war actually prevent him from questioning the assumption that the bomb ought to be used during the war? It must be stressed, in considering this question, that Stimson harbored no crude hatred or racial antagonism for the Japanese people. Nor was he blind to moral considerations that might affect world public opinion. On May 16 he reported to Truman that he was anxious to hold the Air Force to "precision bombing" in Japan because "the reputation of the United States for fair play and humanitarianism is the world's biggest asset for peace in the coming decades." But his concern here, it is evident, was not with the use as such of weapons of mass destruction, but simply with the manner in which they were used. "The same rule of sparing the civilian population should be applied as far as possible to the use of any new weapon," he wrote in reference to the bomb. The possibility that its extraordinary and indiscriminate destructiveness represented a profound qualitative difference, and so cried out for its governance by a higher morality than guided the use of conventional weapons, simply did not occur to him. On the contrary, the problem of the bomb as he perceived it was how to effectively subsume its management under the existing canons of international behavior. His diary suggests why:

May 13, 1945: Having copied into his diary Grew's memorandum raising questions about the role of the Soviet Union in the Far East during and after the war, Stimson noted: "These are very vital questions.... [They] cut very deep and in my opinion are powerfully connected *with our success with S-1.*"

May 15, 1945: Recounting the meeting between the Secretaries of State, War, and the Navy, he described "a pretty red hot session first over the questions which Grew had propounded to use in relation to the Yalta Conference and our relations with Russia." He then remarked: "Over any such tangled wave of problems the S-1 secret would be dominant and yet we will not know until after that time [the beginning of July] probably, until after that meeting [the Potsdam Conference] whether this is a weapon in our hands or not. We think it will be shortly afterwards, but it seems a terrible thing to gamble with such big stakes in diplomacy without having your *master card* in your hand."

Stimson's diary reveals further that following that May 15 meeting, he discussed the war against Japan with Marshall. He noted that while the Navy did not favor an invasion, Marshall "has got the straightforward view and I think he is right and he feels that we must go ahead," adding, "Fortunately the actual invasion will not take place until after my secret is out. The Japanese campaign involves therefore two great uncertainties; first whether Russia will come in though we think that will be all right; and second, when and how S-1 will resolve itself."

May 16, 1945: Summarizing the discussion with Truman about precision bombing and new weapons noted above, he wrote: "We must find some way of persuading Russia to play ball."

Was the conveying of an implicit warning to Moscow, then, the *principal* reason—as some historians have argued—for deciding to use the atomic bomb against Japan? The weight of the evidence available suggests not. Stimson's own account of his decision seems more accurate: "My *chief purpose,*" he wrote in 1947, in defense of the bombings of Hiroshima and Nagasaki, "was to end the war in victory with the least possible cost in the lives of the men in the armies which I had helped to raise." But if the conclusion of the war was Stimson's *chief* purpose, what other purposes were there? And did they prevent him from questioning the assumption that the bomb ought to be used?

The problem raised by these latter questions—the influence of secondary considerations reinforcing the decision—defies an unequivocal answer. What can be said, however, is that, along with Truman and Byrnes and several others involved, Stimson consciously considered two diplomatic effects of a combat demonstration of the atomic bomb: first, the impact of the attack on Japan's leaders, who might be persuaded thereby to end the war; and second, the impact of that attack on the Soviet Union's leaders, who might then prove to be more cooperative. It is likely that the contemplation together of the anticipated effects upon both Japanese and Soviet leaders was what turned aside any inclination to question the use of the bomb.

In addition, however, to the diplomatic advantages policymakers anticipated, there were domestic political reactions they feared, and these, too, discouraged any policy other than the most devastating and rapid use of the bomb. Everyone involved in administering the atomic energy program lived with the thought that a congressional inquiry was the penalty he might pay for his labors. It was in preparation for just such an eventuality that the Briggs Committee, even before the Project was underway, had excluded émigré and even recently naturalized scientists from its meetings. At the time the Army assumed responsibility for the development of the bomb, and on several occasions thereafter, Under Secretary of War Robert P. Patterson informed Groves that the "greatest care should be taken in keeping thorough records, with detailed entries of decisions made, of conferences with persons concerned in the Project, of all progress made and of all financial transactions and expenditures... [for] the most exact accounting would be demanded by Congress at sometime in the future." Even Bohr's association with the Manhattan Project was a product of this concern. He was invited to join the Project, Richard Tolman wrote to Conant in October 1943, because Groves "would like to be able to say that everything possible had been done to get the best men." That these anxieties were not the result of mere bureaucratic paranoia is made clear by the wartime correspondence between the Secretary of War and the chairman of the Senate Special Committee Investigat-

ing the National Defense Program. "The responsibility therefore [sic] and for any waste or improper action which might otherwise be avoided rests squarely upon the War Department," Senator Harry Truman warned Stimson in March 1944. Then there was the warning to Roosevelt a year later from the director of the Office of War Mobilization, James Byrnes: "If the project proves a failure, it will then be subjected to relentless investigation and criticism." It is all the more necessary to remember the possible influence of these warnings by Truman and Byrnes in the ironic aftermath of events.

Beyond reasons directly related to the war, to postwar diplomacy, or to domestic policies, there was another, more subtle consideration moving some advisers to favor a combat demonstration of the bomb. "President Conant has written me," Stimson informed news commentator Raymond Swing in February 1947, "that one of the principal reasons he had for advising me that the bomb *must be used* was that that was the only way to awaken the world to the necessity of abolishing war altogether. No technological demonstration, even if it had been possible under the conditions of war — which it was not — could take the place of the actual use with its horrible results.... I think he was right and I think that was one of the main things which differentiated the eminent scientists who concurred with President Conant from the less realistic ones who didn't."

Among the most prominent of the "less realistic" scientists Stimson was referring to here was, of course, Leo Szilard, a premature realist on atomic energy matters since the thirties. On May 28, 1945, Szilard and two associates (Walter Bartky, Associate Dean of the Physical Sciences at the University of Chicago, and Harold Urey, head of the Manhattan Project's Gaseous Diffusion Laboratory at Columbia) traveled to Spartanburg, South Carolina, to discuss atomic energy matters with Byrnes. They were directed there by Matt Connelly, the President's appointments secretary, after an unsuccessful attempt to speak personally with Truman.

Since March 1945, Szilard had been applying his analytical energies to the problem of predicting the impact of the new weapon on American security, and on devising a workable plan for the international control of atomic energy. In a remarkably perceptive memorandum written in March he had discussed a number of central problems: the transition of nuclear weapons technology from atomic to hydrogen bombs, the greater vulnerability of an urbanized nation to nuclear attack, systems of control that ought to be considered, including control of raw materials and on-site inspection, and several other issues basic to any international control program. Having concluded that there was "no point" in trying to discuss his ideas with Groves, Conant, or Bush, he contacted Einstein. He needed a letter of introduction to the President, Szilard told his colleague, for there was "trouble ahead." A request for an interview with Roosevelt was then sent to Mrs. Roosevelt, who had intervened earlier in the war to bring the criticisms of the Chicago scientists to her husband's attention. "Perhaps the greatest immediate danger which faces us is the probability that our 'demonstration' of atomic bombs will precipitate a race in the production of these devices between the United States and Russia," Szilard warned in a memorandum prepared for a conference with Roosevelt scheduled for May 8. The United States government was about to arrive at decisions, he warned, that would control the course of events after the war. Those decisions ought to be based on careful estimates of future possibilities,

not simply "on the present evidence relating to atomic bombs." Always conscious of power considerations, and well aware of the potential diplomatic weight of the bomb, Szilard concluded a series of questions with the query: "Should... our 'demonstration' of atomic bombs and their use against Japan be delayed until a certain further stage in the political and technical development has been reached so that the United States shall be in a more favorable position in negotiations aimed at setting up a system of control?"

Szilard's reasoning here was not very different from Stimson's. They both looked to the bomb's power to persuade the Soviets to accept an American blueprint for world peace. But whereas the Secretary of War expected the early demonstration of that power to suffice to produce the desired effect, Szilard reasoned that the American lead in development would have to be overwhelming and unapproachable before such a demonstration had even a chance of having the desired effect.

At the Spartanburg interview the hopelessness of having such a calculated policy adopted became clear to Szilard. Byrnes seemed grossly ignorant about the implications of atomic energy and its diplomatic value. In response to the Secretary of State-designate's view that "our possessing and demonstrating the bomb would make Russia more manageable in Europe," Szilard argued that the "interests of peace might best be served and an arms race avoided by not using the bomb against Japan, keeping it secret, and letting the Russians think that our work on it had not succeeded." Byrnes responded that the nation had spent $2-billion on its development and Congress would want to know the results. "How would you get Congress to appropriate money for atomic energy research if you do not show results for the money which has been spent already?" he asked the astonished scientists.* They returned to Chicago convinced that Byrnes was inclined toward a policy that would make a postwar atomic arms race inevitable. As a direct result of the Spartanburg interview, Szilard initiated a movement among scientists at the University of Chicago to prevent the use of the atomic bomb against Japan. In the meantime, however, decisions were being taken that would outdistance any attempt to block the military use of the bomb.

"LOOKING AT THIS LIKE STATESMEN"

On May 31, 1945, three days after Truman set the date for the Potsdam Conference, the Interim Committee submitted a formal recommendation that the atomic bomb be used without warning against Japan. The Committee had met officially on three previous occasions— May 9, 14, and 18. Its members had reviewed the history of the Manhattan Project; received background briefings from Groves, Bush, Conant, and others; discussed the Quebec Agreement and the Combined Development Trust; appointed a Scientific Panel; considered the appointment of industrial and military panels; and designated William L. Laurence, science editor of *The New York Times*, to prepare statements to be issued *after* the atomic attacks. Yet the question of whether the bomb should be used at all had never actually been discussed. The minutes of the Interim Committee suggest why. The committee members had come together as advocates, the responsible ad-

visers of a new force in world affairs, convinced of the weapon's diplomatic and military potential, aware of its fantastic cost, and awed by their responsibilities. They were also constrained in their choices by several shared but unstated assumptions reinforced for scientists and policymakers alike by the entire history of the Manhattan Project: First, that the bomb was a legitimate weapon that would have been used against the Allies if Germany had won the race to develop it. Second, that its use would have a profound impact upon Japan's leaders as they debated whether or not to surrender. Third, that the American public would want it used under the circumstances. And fourth (an assumption from which one member of the Committee subsequently dissented), that its use ultimately would have a salutary effect on relations with the Soviet Union. These assumptions suggested, at least obliquely, that there were neither military, diplomatic, nor domestic reasons to oppose the use of the weapon. On the contrary, four years of war and the pressures to end it, four years of secrecy and the prospect of more; $2-billion and the question "For what?"; Japan's tenacious resistance and America's commitment to unconditional surrender; Soviet behavior and the need for international control—all these factors served to bolster the accepted point of view. And the structure of the Committee itself made the introduction of alternatives extremely difficult: its tight organization and its crowded agenda; its wide-ranging responsibilities for atomic energy policy and its limited knowledge of the military situation; its clear mandate to recommend postwar programs and the ambiguity, at best, of its responsibility for wartime decisions.

Stimson organized, chaired, and drew up agendas for the Committee's meetings. Although he did seek to create an at-

---

*Byrnes was not the only person associated with the Manhattan Project to express this attitude. Irving Stewart, a special assistant to Bush, suggested: "if the military importance [of the atomic bomb] is demonstrated, it may provide the necessary Constitutional [sic] support [to create a Commission on Atomic Energy]." Stewart to Bush, Aug. 25, 1944, AEC doc. no. 299.

mosphere in which everyone felt free to discuss any problem related to atomic energy, the minutes of the meetings indicate that discussions closely adhered to the questions Stimson presented. The task before the Committee was enormous, and time was short. There was little inclination to pursue unscheduled issues.

Stimson had prepared very carefully for the meeting of May 31, to which Arthur Compton, Enrico Fermi, Ernest Lawrence, and Robert Oppenheimer, the membership of the Scientific Panel, had been invited. He was anxious to impress upon them "that we were looking at this like statesmen and not like merely soldiers anxious to win the war at any cost." He had worked with Harrison, Bundy, and Groves throughout the previous day preparing the agenda, which included a statement summarizing the Committee's purpose in general—"to study and report on the whole problem of temporary controls and publicity during the war and to survey and make recommendations on post-war research, development and controls, both national and international"—and a second statement explaining a major purpose of this meeting in particular—"to give the Committee a chance to get acquainted with the [invited] scientists and vice versa." The memorandum also contained a list of questions that might arise. These included future military prospects, international competition, future research, future controls, the possibility that "they might be used to extend democratic rights and the dignity of man," and future non-military uses. There is no suggestion in the memorandum, or in the questions the Secretary placed before the assembled group, that his memory was serving him well when he wrote in his autobiography: "The first and greatest problem [for the Interim Committee] was the decision on the use of the bomb—should it be used against the Japanese, and if so, in what

manner?" The fact is that a discussion of this question was placed on the agenda only after it was raised casually in the course of conversation during lunch.

At 10:00 A.M. the members of the Interim Committee, the Scientific Panel, and invited guests Marshall, Groves, Bundy, and Arthur W. Page (a friend and assistant to Stimson) assembled in the Secretary of War's office. For the benefit of the Scientific Panel, Stimson opened the meeting with a general explanation of his own and Marshall's responsibility for recommendations on military matters to the President; he went on to assure them that the Committee did not regard the bomb "as a new weapon merely but as a revolutionary change in the relations of man to the universe" and that he wanted to take advantage of this; it might be "a Frankenstein which would eat us up" or it might be a project "by which the peace of the world would be helped in becoming secure." The implications of the bomb, he understood, "went far beyond the *needs* of the present war."

After these introductory remarks the members of the Scientific Panel expressed their views on questions related to postwar planning. Their orientation was toward expansion. Arthur Compton sketched the future of military weapons by outlining three stages of development. The bombs currently under production would soon be surpassed by a second generation of more powerful weapons. "While bombs produced from the products of the second stage had not yet been proven in actual operation," the minutes report, "such bombs were considered a *scientific certainty*." And a "third stage" for which nuclear fission would serve merely as a detonator, though far more difficult to achieve, might—Oppenheimer reported—reach production within a minimum of three years. There is no hint in the minutes that the eventual development of even the hydrogen bomb lay in doubt: the question was merely how soon it could be developed.

Oppenheimer's review of the explosive force for each stage must have strained the imaginations of the non-scientists present. A single bomb produced in the first stage was expected to have an explosive force of 2,000–20,000 tons of TNT. The second generation of weapons would yield the equivalent of 50,000–100,000 tons of TNT. It was possible that a bomb developed in the third stage might produce an explosive force equal to 10,000,000–100,000,000 tons of TNT.

No one, then, sitting at that table in the Pentagon on May 31 could have entertained serious doubts that atomic weapons would be available within months. Of this, the scientists were absolutely certain. Even a year earlier, Ernest Lawrence had confidently written: "The primary fact now is that the element of gamble in the overall picture no longer exists." The uncertainty that remained in May 1945 was merely as to how efficiently the initial bombs would work. Under these circumstances the sort of atomic energy programs the United States chose to pursue after the war was a pressing issue. Lawrence, as always, urged development on every front, and in the discussion that ensued, his opinion found support. Within a short time Stimson was able to conclude that there was a general agreement that after the war the industrial facilities of the atomic energy program should remain intact, that a sizable stockpile of material for military, industrial, and technical use should be acquired, and that the door to industrial development should be opened.

During the remainder of the morning, as the Committee moved from a general discussion of control and inspection to the problem of how to obtain international control, the "question of paramount concern was the attitude of Russia." Adopt-

ing the line of reasoning that Bohr had advocated during his visits to Los Alamos, Oppenheimer suggested that the United States approach the Russians about international control without giving them details of the progress achieved. He firmly believed that the Russian attitude in this matter should not be prejudged; they had always been friendly to science.

Marshall supported this general point of view by drawing on his own experience. The history of charges and counter-charges that were typical of American-Soviet relations, he related, were based on allegations that had generally proved to be unfounded. The seemingly uncooperative attitude of Russia in military matters resulted from their felt necessity to maintain security. He had accepted this and had acted accordingly. As to the postwar situation, and in matters other than purely military, he was in no position to express a view. He was inclined, however, to favor the buildup of a coalition of like-minded powers that could compel Russia to fall in line. He was confident that the United States need not fear that the Russians, if they were informed about the Manhattan Project, would disclose this information to the Japanese. Finally, he raised the question whether it might be desirable to invite two prominent Russian scientists to witness the first atomic bomb test scheduled for July at Alamogordo, New Mexico.

Byrnes, who heretofore had said little, strenuously objected. If information were given to the Russians, even in general terms, he feared that Stalin would ask to be brought into the partnership. This likelihood, he felt, was increased in view of American commitments and pledges of cooperation with the British, though he did not explain how the Soviets would know about them. Although Bush noted that not even the British had any blueprints of our plants, Byrnes could not be dissuaded. He did not explain his position further, yet subsequent events suggest that he believed the bomb's diplomatic value would be diluted if Stalin were informed of the weapon prior to its use. The most desirable program for him was to maintain superiority by pushing ahead as fast as possible in production and research, while at the same time making every effort to better our political relations with Russia. In any case, the issue appears to have been settled by his forthright stand. The morning session ended shortly afterwards, at approximately 1:15 P.M., after Arthur Compton summarized as the Committee's consensus that the United States had to assure itself a dominant position while working toward political agreements. No one saw any conflict between these two objectives. "Throughout the morning's discussion," Arthur Compton has written, "it seemed to be a foregone conclusion that the bomb would be used. It was regarding only the details of strategy and tactics that differing views were expressed."

There are two extant accounts of how the luncheon conversation turned to the question of using the bomb against Japan: a letter of August 17, 1945, from Lawrence to a friend, and a description published by Compton in 1956. Lawrence claims that Byrnes asked him to elaborate on a brief proposal he had made for a nonmilitary demonstration during the morning session; Compton recalls that he asked Stimson whether it might not be possible to arrange something less than a surprise atomic attack that would so impress the Japanese that they would see the uselessness of continuing the war. Whatever the case, the issue was discussed by those at the table, including at least Byrnes, Stimson, Compton, Lawrence, Oppenheimer, and Groves. Various possibilities were brought forward, but were discarded one after the other. Inured to the brutality of war by conventional means, someone countered that the

"number of people that would be killed by the bomb would not be greater in general magnitude than the number already killed in fire raids [on Tokyo]."* Another problem was that Oppenheimer could not think of a sufficiently spectacular demonstration. Groves and others at the table were convinced that a real target of built-up structures would be the most effective demonstration.

There were other considerations as well, Compton reports. If the Japanese received a warning that such a weapon would be exploded somewhere over Japan, their aircraft might create problems that could lead to the failure of the mission. If the test were conducted on neutral ground, it was hard to believe that the "determined and fanatical military men of Japan would be impressed." No one could think of any way to employ the new weapon that offered the same attractive combination of low risk and high gain as a surprise attack; and no one was willing to argue that a higher risk should be accepted.

When the Committee members returned to Stimson's office at 2:15 P.M., the Secretary altered the agenda. The first topic he now wanted considered was the effect of the atomic bomb on the Japanese and their will to fight. The initial discussion revolved around the explosive force of the weapon. One atomic bomb, it was pointed out, would not be very different from current Air Force strikes. But Oppenheimer suggested that the visual effect of an atomic bomb would be tremendous. It would be accompanied by "a brilliant luminescence which would rise to 10,000 or 20,000 feet," and the neutron

---

*On March 9–10 a quarter of that city had been destroyed by incendiary bombs; 83,000 persons were killed and 40,000 were injured in the most destructive conventional air raid in history. A. Russell Buchanan, *The United States and World War II*, 2 (New York), 1964, 577–78.

effect would be lethal for a radius of nearly a mile.

There was also a discussion of attempting several simultaneous attacks. Oppenheimer considered such a plan feasible, but Groves objected on the grounds that the advantage of gaining additional knowledge by successive bombings would be lost, and that such a program would require too much of those assembling the bomb.

After considerable discussion of types of targets and the desired effect, Stimson expressed the conclusion, on which there was general agreement, that the Japanese would not be given any warning; and that the bombing would not concentrate on a civilian area, but that an attempt would be made to make a profound psychological impression on as many Japanese as possible. Stimson accepted Conant's suggestion that the most desirable target would be a vital war plant employing a large number of workers and closely surrounded by workers' homes. No member of the Committee spoke to the contradiction between this conclusion and their earlier decision not to concentrate on a civilian area.

This critical discussion on the use of the bomb was over. It had not only confirmed the assumption that the new weapon was to be used, but that the *two* bombs that would be available early in August should be used. The destruction of both Hiroshima and Nagasaki was the result of a *single* decision. On the following day Brynes suggested, and the members of the Interim Committee agreed, that the Secretary of War should be advised that, "while

recognizing that the final selection of the target was essentially a military decision, the present view of the Committee was that the bomb should be used against Japan as soon as possible; that it be used on a war plant surrounded by workers' homes; and that it be used without prior warning."* On June 6 Stimson informed Truman of the Committee's decision.

---

*Why was Japan rather than Germany selected as the target for the atomic bomb? The minutes of the Military Policy Committee meeting of May 5, 1943 (declassified in March 1976), offer the most direct answer to this question: "The point of use of the first bomb was discussed and the general view appeared to be that its best point of use would be on a Japanese fleet concentration in the Harbor of Truk. General Styer suggested Tokio [sic], but it was pointed out that the bomb should be used where, if it failed to go off, it would land in water of sufficient depth to prevent easy salvage. The Japanese were selected as they would not be so apt to secure knowledge from it as would the Germans." MED-TS, folder 23A. Other reasons that may have contributed to the decision, settled on in the spring of 1944, are: (1) the war in Europe was expected to end first; (2) it was safer to assemble the bomb on a Pacific island than in England; (3) delivery against a target in a U.S. theater of war by a U.S. aircraft (B-29) emphasized "American" primacy in this Anglo-American development.

Bush makes an ambiguous reference to the use of the bomb on June 24, 1943: "We [he and FDR] then spoke briefly of the possible use against Japan, or the Japanese fleet, and I brought out, or I tried to, because at this point I do not think I was really successful in getting the idea across, that our point of view or our emphasis on the program would shift if we had in mind use against Japan as compared with use against Germany." "Memorandum of Conference with the President," AEC doc. no. 133. However, on April 23, 1945, Groves informed Stimson that "the target is and was always expected to be Japan." MED-TS folder 25, tab M. See also Hewlett and Anderson, *The New World*, 252–53.

Comment

The damage and the loss of lives that the atomic bomb caused in Hiroshima and Nagasaki were no greater than the destruction caused by some conventional attacks such as the firebombing of Tokyo or Dresden. What (if any) features of nuclear weapons make their use more morally questionable than the use of conventional weapons?

Compare Stimson's argument for the bombing with this defense given by Truman:

> We have used [the bomb] against those who attacked us without warning at Pearl Harbor, against those who have starved and beaten and executed American prisoners of war, against those who have abandoned all pretense of obeying international laws of warfare. We have used it in order to shorten the agony of the war.

Assume that dropping the bombs actually saved more American and Allied lives than any other option open to Truman. Would that justify his decision? What if the decision reduced the total number of lives lost (including Japanese lives)? Although Truman did not say so publicly, one reason he may have decided to use the bomb was to end the war quickly before Russia could enter and gain control over territory in the region. Would this have been a morally acceptable motive?

Evaluate the alternative courses of action that Truman considered or could have considered: (1) bombing only one city, (2) bombing an exclusively military target, (3) detonating one or two bombs over the ocean as a "demonstration," (4) intensifying the naval and air blockade, or (5) abandoning the demand for unconditional surrender.

James Conant, then president of Harvard and an influential science adviser to President Truman, argued that the bomb "must be used." It was "the only way to awaken the world to the necessity of abolishing war altogether." How would you at that time have assessed the effect of the bombing on postwar efforts to prevent nuclear war? Should such effects have been a morally relevant factor in Truman's decision?

The Role of Nuclear Weapons in Strategy

Caspar W. Weinberger

1. A Viable Deterrence Policy: Lessening Dependence on Nuclear Weapons

In the wake of World War II, the United States and the Western democracies developed a policy intended to prevent any recurrence of the tremendous carnage and devastation which the war had caused. To that end, the United States

From Secretary of Defense Caspar Weinberger's *Annual Report to Congress,* fiscal year 1984.

made clear that it would use its atomic weapons not for conquest or coercion, but for discouraging—for *deterring*—aggression and attack against ourselves and our allies.

Today, deterrence remains—as it has for the past 37 years—the cornerstone of our strategic nuclear policy. To deter successfully, we must be able—and must be seen to be able—to respond to any potential aggression in such a manner that the costs we will exact will substantially exceed any gains the aggressor might hope to achieve. We, for our part, are under no illusions about the dangers of a nuclear war between the major powers; we believe that neither side could win such a war. But this recognition on *our* part is not sufficient to prevent the outbreak of nuclear war; it is essential that the Soviet leadership understand this as well. We must make sure that the Soviet leadership, in calculating the risks of aggression, recognizes that because of our retaliatory capability, there can be no circumstance in which it could benefit by beginning a nuclear war at any level or of any duration. If the Soviets recognize that our forces can and will deny them their objectives at whatever level of nuclear conflict they contemplate and, in addition, that such a conflict could lead to the destruction of those political, military, and economic assets that they value most highly, then deterrence is effective and the risk of war diminished. It is this outcome we seek to achieve.

2. THE EVOLUTION OF U.S. NUCLEAR POLICY

During the late 1940s and early 1950s, America's virtual monopoly of intercontinental nuclear systems meant that our requirements for conventional war were relatively small. The Soviet Union understood that, under our policy of "massive retaliation," we might respond to a Soviet conventional attack on the U.S. or our allies with an atomic attack on the USSR. As the 1950s ended, however, the Soviets began developing and acquiring long-range nuclear capabilities. As their capacity for nuclear and conventional attack continued to grow, the U.S. threat to respond to a conventional, or even a limited nuclear, attack with massive nuclear retaliation became less and less credible; hence, it was not a stable deterrent. Accordingly, in the 1960s the U.S. and the NATO allies adopted the concept of "flexible response." This con-

cept had two goals: first, U.S. nuclear planning was modified in order to provide the President with the option of using nuclear forces selectively (rather than massively), thereby restoring credibility and stability to our nuclear deterrent. Additionally, the United States and the allies hoped that by improving conventional forces, they would reduce reliance on nuclear weapons to deter or cope with non-nuclear attack. Unfortunately, neither we nor our allies ever fully met this key goal. Thus, with our present effort to increase our conventional strength, the Reagan Administration is essentially trying to secure a long-established but elusive goal of American policy.

By the early 1960s, the U.S. had over 7,000 strategic nuclear weapons, most of which were carried by B-47s and the then-new B-52s. The Soviet Union had fewer than 500 strategic warheads. Throughout the 1960s, our nuclear posture presented the Soviet Union with a compelling deterrent if it considered launching a nuclear strike against the United States: because of the relatively small number of weapons the Soviet Union possessed and their ineffectiveness against any U.S. strategic forces, such an attack was impossible to executive successfully. If the Soviet planner targeted our missile silos and alert bomber bases with the systems he then possessed, he found that he would deplete his nuclear arsenal while not significantly reducing U.S. retaliatory forces. In other words, his ability to limit the certain, massive retaliatory destruction of his own forces and assets was rather small. If, on the other hand, the Soviet planner targeted U.S. cities, he would have to expect a U.S. retaliatory strike against his own cities, a strike by a U.S. arsenal considerably larger and much more capable than his own, by any measure. Again, he was deterred.

During the course of the 1970s the Soviet arsenal grew both in quantity and in quality (although the U.S. qualitative edge remained). The Soviets expanded their land-based missile force and hardened their protective silos, and continued the improvement of their defenses against air attack. At the same time, the United States made a choice to restrict its improvements to the yield and accuracy of its own missile forces so as not to threaten the Soviet Union with a sudden, disarming first strike. The net result of this was to allow the Soviet Union a "sanctuary" for its ICBM force, since U.S. forces by now could not attack them effectively. The Soviets, however, did not follow our self-imposed restraint. They developed a new generation of ICBMs specifically designed to destroy U.S. missile silos, which were hardened far less than Soviet silos, and the B-52 bases. By the late 1970s, this combination of vulnerable U.S. missiles and a Soviet missile "sanctuary" had reduced the effectiveness of our earlier deterrent and eased the problems of the Soviet war planners. Now, the Soviets could envision a potential nuclear confrontation in which they would threaten to destroy a very large part of our force in a first strike, while retaining overwhelming nuclear force to deter any retaliation we could carry out.

We cannot overemphasize the importance of a multiplicity of survivable strategic forces. Over the last 20 years, we have maintained a Triad of land-based ICBMs, manned bombers, and submarine-launched ballistic missiles as an effective means of preserving a stable deterrent. The unique characteristics of the independent and separate strategic components that make up the Triad bolster deterrence by acting in concert to complicate severely Soviet attack planning, making it more difficult, on the one hand, for them to plan and execute a successful attack, on all these components and, on the other hand, to defend against their combined and complementary retaliatory effects. The Triad also acts as a hedge against a possible technological

breakthrough that the Soviets might develop or obtain that could threaten the viability of any single strategic system. The importance of the Triad to deterrence is no more apparent than today, when each leg is in need of modernization.

3. NUCLEAR WEAPONS ISSUES

What has been said so far illustrates the complexity of the continuing task of maintaining an American nuclear force capable of surviving a Soviet attack that is aimed at destroying it. However, the maintenance of a persuasive capability to deter a Soviet nuclear attack directed solely at an ally is even more demanding. It should be most obvious in this connection that we need to be able to use force responsibly and discriminately, in a manner appropriate to the nature of a nuclear attack.

Yet, some believe that we must threaten explicitly, even solely, the mass destruction of civilians on the adversary side, thus inviting a corresponding destruction of civilian populations on our side, and that such a posture will achieve stability in deterrence. This is incorrect. Such a threat is neither moral nor prudent. The Reagan Administration's policy is that under no circumstances may such weapons be used deliberately for the purpose of destroying populations.

For this reason, we disagree with those who hold that deterrence should be based on nuclear weapons designed to destroy cities rather than military targets. Deliberately designing weapons aimed at populations is neither necessary nor sufficient for deterrence. If we are forced to retaliate and can only respond by destroying population centers, we invite the destruction of our own population. Such a deterrent strategy is hardly likely to carry conviction as a deterrent, particularly as a deterrent to nuclear — let alone conventional — attack on an ally.

To maintain a sound deterrent, we must make clear to our adversary that we would decisively and effectively answer his attack. To talk of actions that the U.S. Government could not, in good conscience, and in prudence, undertake tends to defeat the goal of deterrence.

Some of the same ambiguities cloud recent proposals that we abandon long-standing Alliance policy and pledge "No First Use" of nuclear weapons in response to Soviet conventional attacks in Europe. Indeed, if the Soviets thought that we would be so constrained, they might mass forces more heavily for offensive actions and gain a unilateral conventional advantage. To reduce further the prospects of nuclear war, we must strengthen NATO's conventional forces—not exchange unenforceable and unverifiable pledges. The danger of a "No First Use" pledge remains that it could increase the chances of war and thus increase the chances of nuclear conflict.

A PRUDENT APPROACH
TO NUCLEAR WEAPONS

If we are to maintain a responsible nuclear deterrent against nuclear attacks on our allies, as well as against nuclear attacks on the United States, we will need to continue to exploit our comparative advantage in technology. The movement for a nuclear freeze has been inspired in part by the mistaken belief that the United States has been steadily piling up more and more nuclear weapons. In fact, the United States has not been accumulating more weapons. The number in our stockpile was one-third higher in 1967 than in 1980. Nor have we been accumulating more destructive weapons. The average number of kilotons per weapon has declined since the late 1950s, and the total number of megatons in our stockpile was four times as high in 1960 than in 1980. With the retirement of the Titans, this total will decline even further. Moreover, the United States has had an intensive and consistent program to improve the safety

of the nuclear weapons in its stockpile against accidental detonation and its consequences, as well as to improve the security of these weapons against seizure and use by terrorists or other unauthorized persons. The weapons in our stockpile today have an average age of about 13 years. It is essential that we continue to replace them with new, safer, more secure, and less vulnerable weapons.

The various proposals for a nuclear freeze would prevent us from carrying out these programs and thus improving the safety and the security of our weapons, reducing the vulnerability of our delivery systems in the face of increasing threats, and replacing systems as they reach the end of their service life due simply to their age. Such proposals, hence, would reduce the stability of our deterrent against both "accidents" and deliberate destruction.

NUCLEAR ARMS CONTROL

It is the objective of the United States to maintain the lowest level of armaments compatible with the preservation of our, and our allies', security. While President Reagan is forced by the Soviet threat to pursue a force augmentation and modernization program, he has also undertaken a serious effort designed to reduce armaments through negotiation. In the nuclear area, the Reagan Administration took two important new arms control initiatives, on intermediate-range and strategic nuclear forces.

We can never, much as we would desire it, return to the kind of world that existed before the secrets of the atom were unlocked. But we can work to ensure that nuclear weapons are never used, by maintaining the forces necessary to convince any adversary that the cost of aggression would be far higher than any possible benefit. The United States has pursued this strategy of deterrence since the dawn of the nuclear age; and since that time deterrence has preserved the peace.

The primacy of deterrence has not changed, but the conditions for ensuring it have. The Reagan Administration's strategic modernization program is designed to preserve deterrence, in the face of an evolving threat, by increasing the survivability, accuracy, and credibility of our nuclear forces, and to offer the Soviet Union an incentive for genuine arms reduction, by demonstrating our commitment to maintaining a strategic balance.

Deterrence in Principle and Practice
National Conference of Catholic Bishops

The evolution of deterrence strategy has passed through several stages of declaratory policy. Using the U.S. case as an example, there is a significant difference between "massive retaliation" and "flexible response," and between "mutual assured destruction" and "countervailing strategy." It is also possible to distinguish between "counterforce" and "countervalue" targeting policies; and to contrast a posture of "minimum deterrence" with "extended deterrence." These terms are well known in the technical debate on nuclear policy; they are less well known and sometimes loosely used in the wider public debate. It is important to recognize that there has been substantial continuity in U.S. action policy in spite of real changes in declaratory policy. . . .

The moral and political paradox posed by deterrence was concisely stated by Vatican II:

"Undoubtedly, armaments are not amassed merely for use in wartime. Since the defensive strength of any nation is thought to depend on its capacity for immediate retaliation, the stockpiling of arms which grows from year to year serves, in a way hitherto unthought of, as a deterrent to potential attackers. Many people look upon this as the most effective way known at the present time for

From *The Challenge of Peace—The Pastoral Letter on War and Peace,* May 3, 1983. Copyright ©1983 by the United States Catholic Conference, Washington, D.C. All rights reserved.

maintaining some sort of peace among nations. Whatever one may think of this form of deterrent, people are convinced that the arms race, which quite a few countries have entered, is no infallible way of maintaining real peace and that the resulting so-called balance of power is no sure genuine path to achieving it. Rather than eliminate the causes of war, the arms race serves only to aggravate the position. . . ."

Without making a specific moral judgment on deterrence, the council clearly designated the elements of the arms race: the tension between "peace of a sort" preserved by deterrence and "genuine peace" required for a stable international life; the contradiction between what is spent for destructive capacity and what is needed for constructive development.

In the post-conciliar assessment of war and peace and specifically of deterrence, different parties to the political-moral debate within the church and in civil society have focused on one or another aspect of the problem. For some, the fact that nuclear weapons have not been used since 1945 means that deterrence has worked, and this fact satisfies the demands of both the political and the moral order. Others contest this assessment by highlighting the risk of failure involved in continued reliance on deterrence and pointing out how politically and morally catastrophic even a single failure would be. Still others note that the absence of nuclear war is not necessarily proof that the policy of deterrence has prevented it. Indeed, some would find in the policy of deterrence the driving force in the superpower arms race. Still other observers, many of them Catholic moralists, have stressed that deterrence may not morally include the intention of deliberately attacking civilian populations or noncombatants. . . .

Pope John Paul II makes this statement about the morality of deterrence:

"In current conditions 'deterrence' based on balance, certainly not as an end in itself but as a step on the way toward a progressive disarmament, may still be judged morally acceptable. Nonetheless in order to ensure peace, it is indispensable not to be satisfied with this minimum, which is always susceptible to the real danger of explosion."

In Pope John Paul II's assessment we perceive two dimensions of the contemporary dilemma of deterrence. One dimension is the danger of nuclear war with its human and moral costs. The possession of nuclear weapons, the continuing quantitative growth of the arms race and the danger of nuclear proliferation all point to the grave danger of basing "peace of a sort" on deterrence. The other dimension is the independence and freedom of nations and entire peoples, including the need to protect smaller nations from threats to their independence and integrity. Deterrence reflects the radical distrust which marks international politics. . . .

MORAL PRINCIPLES
AND POLICY CHOICES

Targeting doctrine raises significant moral questions because it is a significant determinant of what would occur if nuclear weapons were ever to be used. Although we acknowledge the need for deterrent, not all forms of deterrence are morally acceptable. There are moral

limits to deterrence policy as well as to policy regarding use. Specifically, it is not morally acceptable to intend to kill the innocent as part of a strategy of deterring nuclear war. The question of whether U.S. policy involves an intention to strike civilian centers (directly targeting civilian populations) has been one of our factual concerns.

This complex question has always produced a variety of responses, official and unofficial in character. The NCCB committee has received a series of statements of clarification of policy from U.S. government officials.* Essentially these statements declare that it is not U.S. strategic policy to target the Soviet civilian population as such or to use nuclear weapons deliberately for the purpose of destroying population centers.

These statements respond, in principle at least, to one moral criterion for assessing deterrence policy: the immunity of noncombatants from direct attack either by conventional or nuclear weapons.

These statements do not address or resolve another very troublesome moral problem, namely, that an attack on military targets or militarily significant industrial targets could involve "indirect" (i.e., unintended) but massive civilian casualties. We are advised, for example, that the U.S. strategic nuclear targeting

---

*Particularly helpful was the letter of Jan. 15, 1983, of William Clark, national security adviser, to Cardinal Bernardin. Clark stated: "For moral, political and military reasons, the United States does not target the Soviet civilian population as such. There is no deliberately opaque meaning conveyed in the last two words. We do not threaten the existence of Soviet civilization by threatening Soviet cities. Rather, we hold at risk the warmaking capability of the Soviet Union—its armed forces, and the industrial capacity to sustain war. It would be irresponsible for us to issue policy statements which might suggest to the Soviets that it would be to their advantage to establish privileged sanctuaries within heavily populated areas, thus inducing them to locate much of their war-fighting capability within those urban sanctuaries."

plan (SIOP—Single Integrated Operational Plan) has identified 60 "military" targets within the city of Moscow alone, and that 40,000 "military" targets for nuclear weapons have been identified in the whole of the Soviet Union. It is important to recognize that Soviet policy is subject to the same moral judgment; attacks on several "industrial targets" or politically significant targets in the United States could produce massive civilian casualties. The number of civilians who would necessarily be killed by such strikes is horrendous. This problem is unavoidable because of the way modern military facilities and production centers are so thoroughly interspersed with civilian living and working areas. It is aggravated if one side deliberately positions military targets in the midst of a civilian population.

In our consultations, administration officials readily admitted that while they hoped any nuclear exchange could be kept limited, they were prepared to retaliate in a massive way if necessary. They also agreed that once any substantial numbers of weapons were used, the civilian casualty levels would quickly become truly catastrophic and that even with attacks limited to "military" targets the number of deaths in a substantial exchange would be almost indistinguishable from what might occur if civilian centers had been deliberately and directly struck. These possibilities pose a different moral question and are to be judged by a different moral criterion: the principle of proportionality.

While any judgment of proportionality is always open to differing evaluations, there are actions which can be decisively judged to be disproportionate. A narrow adherence exclusively to the principle of non-combatant immunity as a criterion for policy is an inadequate moral posture for it ignores some evil and unacceptable consequences. Hence, we cannot be satis-

fied that the assertion of an intention not to strike civilians directly or even the most honest effort to implement that intention by itself constitutes a "moral policy" for the use of nuclear weapons.

The location of industrial or militarily significant economic targets within heavily populated areas or in those areas affected by radioactive fallout could well involve such massive civilian casualties that in our judgment such a strike would be deemed morally disproportionate, even though not intentionally indiscriminate.

The problem is not simply one of producing highly accurate weapons that might minimize civilian casualties in any single explosion, but one of increasing the likelihood of escalation at a level where many, even "discriminating," weapons would cumulatively kill very large numbers of civilians. Those civilian deaths would occur both immediately and from the long-term effects of social and economic devastation.

A second issue of concern to us is the relationship of deterrence doctrine to war-fighting strategies. We are aware of the argument that war-fighting capabilities enhance the credibility of the deterrent, particularly the strategy of extended deterrence. But the development of such capabilities raises other strategic and moral questions. The relationship of war-fighting capabilities and targeting doctrine exemplifies the difficult choices in this area of policy. Targeting civilian populations would violate the principle of discrimination—one of the central moral principles of a Christian ethic of war. But "counterforce targeting," while preferable from the perspective of protecting civilians, is often joined with a declaratory policy which conveys the notion that nuclear war is subject to precise rational and moral limits. We have already expressed our severe doubts about such a concept. Furthermore, a purely counterforce strategy may seem to threaten the viability of other nations' retaliatory forces, making deterrence unstable in a crisis and war more likely.

While we welcome any effort to protect civilian populations, we do not want to legitimize or encourage moves which extend deterrence beyond the specific objective of preventing the use of nuclear weapons or other actions which would lead directly to a nuclear exchange.

These considerations of concrete elements of nuclear deterrence policy, made in light of John Paul II's evaluation, but applying it through our own prudential judgments, lead us to a strictly conditioned moral acceptance of nuclear deterrence. We cannot consider it adequate as a long-term basis for peace.

This strictly conditioned judgment yields *criteria* for morally assessing the elements of deterrence strategy. Clearly, these criteria demonstrate that we cannot approve of every weapons system, strategic doctrine or policy initiative advanced in the name of strengthening deterrence. On the contrary, these criteria require continual public scrutiny of what our government proposes to do with the deterrent.

On the basis of these criteria we wish now to make some specific evaluations:

1. If nuclear deterrence exists only to prevent the *use* of nuclear weapons by others, then proposals to go beyond this to planning for prolonged periods of repeated nuclear strikes and counter-strikes, or "prevailing" in nuclear war, are not acceptable. They encourage notions that nuclear war can be engaged in with tolerable human and moral consequences. Rather, we must continually say no to the idea of nuclear war.

2. If nuclear deterrence is our goal, "sufficiency" to deter is an adequate strategy; the quest for nuclear superiority must be rejected.

3. Nuclear deterrence should be used as a step on the way toward progressive disarmament. Each proposed addition to our strategic system or change in strategic doctrine must be assessed precisely in light of whether it will render steps toward "progressive disarmament" more or less likely.

Moreover, these criteria provide us with the means to make some judgments and recommendations about the present direction of U.S. strategic policy. Progress toward a world freed of dependence on nuclear deterrence must be carefully carried out. But it must not be delayed. There is an urgent moral and political responsibility to use the "peace of a sort" we have as a framework to move toward authentic peace through nuclear arms control, reductions and disarmament. Of primary importance in this process is the need to prevent the development and deployment of destabilizing weapons systems on either side; a second requirement is to ensure that the more sophisticated command and control systems do not become mere hair triggers for automatic launch on warning; a third is the need to prevent the proliferation of nuclear weapons in the international system.

In light of these general judgments *we oppose* some specific proposals in respect to our present deterrence posture:

1. The addition of weapons which are likely to be vulnerable to attack, yet also possess a "prompt hard-target kill" capability that threatens to make the other side's retaliatory forces vulnerable. Such weapons may seem to be useful primarily in a first strike; we resist such weapons for this reason and we oppose Soviet deployment of such weapons which generate fear of a first strike against U.S. forces.

2. The willingness to foster strategic planning which seeks a nuclear war-fighting capability that goes beyond the

limited function of deterrence outlined in this letter.

3. Proposals which have the effect of lowering the nuclear threshold and blurring the difference between nuclear and conventional weapons.

In support of the concept of "sufficiency" as an adequate deterrent and in light of the present size and composition of both the U.S. and Soviet strategic arsenals, *we recommend:*

1. Support for immediate, bilateral, verifiable agreements to halt the testing, production and deployment of new nuclear weapons systems.

2. Support for negotiated bilateral deep cuts in the arsenals of both superpowers, particularly those weapons systems which have destabilizing characteristics; U.S. proposals like those for START (Strategic Arms Reduction Talks) and INF (Intermediate-Range Nuclear Forces) negotiations in Geneva are said to be designed to achieve deep cuts; our hope is that they will be pursued in a manner which will realize these goals.

3. Support for early and successful conclusion of negotiations of a comprehensive test ban treaty.

4. Removal by all parties of short-range nuclear weapons which multiply dangers disproportionate to their deterrent value.

5. Removal by all parties of nuclear weapons from areas where they are likely to be overrun in the early stages of war, thus forcing rapid and uncontrollable decisions on their use.

6. Strengthening of command and control over nuclear weapons to prevent inadvertent and unauthorized use.

These judgments are meant to exemplify how a lack of unequivocal condemnation of deterrence is meant only to be an attempt to acknowledge the role attributed to deterrence, but not to support its extension beyond the limited purpose discussed above. Some have urged us to condemn all aspects of nuclear deterrence.

This urging has been based on a variety of reasons, but has emphasized particularly the high and terrible risks that either deliberate use or accidental detonation of nuclear weapons could quickly escalate to something utterly disproportionate to any acceptable moral purpose. That determination requires highly technical judgments about hypothetical events. Although reasons exist which move some to condemn reliance on nuclear weapons for deterrence, we have not reached this conclusion for the reasons outlined in this letter.

Nevertheless, there must be no misunderstanding of our profound skepticism about the moral acceptability of any use of nuclear weapons. It is obvious that the use of any weapons which violate the principle of discrimination merits unequivocal condemnation. We are told that some weapons are designed for purely "counterforce" use against military forces and targets. The moral issue, however, is not resolved by the design of weapons or the planned intention for use; there are also consequences which must be assessed. It would be a perverted political policy or moral casuistry which tried to justify using a weapon which "indirectly" or "unintentionally" killed a million innocent people because they happened to live near a "militarily significant target."

Even the "indirect effects" of initiating nuclear war are sufficient to make it an unjustifiable moral risk in any form. It is not sufficient, for example, to contend that "our" side has plans for "limited" or "discriminate" use. Modern warfare is not readily contained by good intentions or technological designs. The psychological climate of the world is such that mention of the term "nuclear" generates uneasiness. Many contend that the use of one tactical nuclear weapon could produce panic, with completely unpredictable consequences. It is precisely this mix of political, psychological and technological uncertainty which has moved us in this letter to reinforce with moral prohibitions and prescriptions the prevailing political barrier against resort to nuclear weapons. Our support for enhanced command and control facilities, for major reductions in strategic and tactical nuclear forces, and for a "no first use" policy (as set forth in this letter) is meant to be seen as a complement to our desire to draw a moral line against nuclear war....

Arms control and disarmament must be a process of verifiable agreements especially between two superpowers. While we do not advocate a policy of unilateral disarmament, we believe the urgent need for control of the arms race requires a willingness for each side to take some first steps. The United States has already taken a number of important independent initiatives to reduce some of the gravest dangers and to encourage a constructive Soviet response; additional initiatives are encouraged. By independent initiatives we mean carefully chosen limited steps which the United States could take for a defined period of time, seeking to elicit a comparable step from the Soviet Union. If an appropriate response is not forthcoming, the United States would no longer be bound by steps taken.

Comment

Identify any positions in the documents that might be regarded as political compromises, and indicate whether you think the compromises are morally justified. Consider, for example, Weinberger's advocacy of both (1) a "force augmentation and modernization program" and (2) reduction of armaments through negotiation. The bishops resisted those "who urged us to condemn all aspects of nuclear deterrence"; is their more moderate position consistent with their own moral principles? With yours?

Weinberger writes that deterrence based on a threat against cities is "neither moral nor prudent." Does actual U.S. targeting doctrine differ in morally significant ways from the kind of deterrence that Weinberger rejects? Is a threat against military targets located near cities morally justifiable?

To some extent the disagreements about the acceptability of deterrence turn on differences in appraisals of the intentions of the Soviet Union. Should Soviet intentions be a decisive factor in our judgments about nuclear deterrence? To oppose nuclear deterrence, must one believe that full-scale nuclear war is worse than Soviet defeat of the United States? Worse in what sense?

Even if you conclude that the current system of deterrence is immoral, you need not be committed to the view that the United States should immediately dismantle its nuclear weapons. Such a move could destabilize the nuclear balance and increase the risk of nuclear war. What policy implications do follow from the conclusion that deterrence (or some form of it) is immoral? Evaluate these proposals: (1) increase in capacity to fight limited nuclear wars; (2) bilateral arms control negotiations and agreements; (3) declaration of "no first use"; (4) nuclear freeze; (5) unilateral reduction of nuclear weapons; and (6) unilateral disarmament.

Recommended Reading

The best contemporary discussion of the morality of war is Michael Walzer, *Just and Unjust Wars* (New York: Basic Books, 1977). The chapters most relevant to the question of the means of fighting war are 1 to 3, 8 to 13, 16, and 17. Two excellent collections that present a variety of views on the topic are: Marshall Cohen et al. (eds.), *War and Moral Responsibility* (Princeton, N.J.: Princeton University Press, 1974), especially the articles by Nagel and Brandt; and Richard Wasserstrom (ed.), *War and Morality* (Belmont, Calif.: Wadsworth, 1970), especially the articles by Ford, Narveson, and Wasserstrom. A good general survey of the problem from a utilitarian perspective is Jonathan Glover, *Causing Deaths and Saving Lives* (New York: Penguin, 1977), chapter 19 (see also the bibliography, pp. 318–24).

On the historical background to the decision to drop the bomb, see Martin Sherwin, *A World Destroyed* (New York: Random House, 1977), and Herbert Feis, *The Atomic Bomb and the End of World War II* (Princeton, N.J.: Princeton University Press, 1966). A philosopher's criticism of Truman is Elisabeth Anscombe, "Mr. Truman's Degree," in Anscombe, *Ethics, Religion and Politics* (Minneapolis: University of Minnesota Press, 1981), pp. 62–71.

A recent philosophical discussion of deterrence is Douglas Lackey, "Missiles and Morals: A Utilitarian Look at Deterrence," *Philosophy & Public Affairs*, 12 (Summer 1982), pp. 189–231. Critiques of this article and Lackey's reply are in *Philosophy & Public Affairs*, 12 (Summer 1983). Also see Douglas MacLean, ed., *The Security Gamble* (Totowa, N.J.: Rowman and Allanheld, 1984).

2 Deception

Introduction

The successful ruler, according to Machiavelli, must be "a great liar and hypocrite." Politicians have to appear to be moral even though they are not, because politics requires methods that citizens would find morally objectionable if they knew about them. We do not know how many politicians follow Machiavelli's advice today (those who do so most successfully may seem to be the least machiavellian). We do know that many public officials have tried to justify deception, and so have some political commentators and political theorists.

Deception involves intentionally causing (or attempting to cause) someone to believe something that you know (or should know) to be false. Political deception is not always easy to recognize, since it seldom comes in the form of an outright lie. More often, officials give us half-truths, which they hope we will not see are half-lies; or they offer us silence, which they hope will cause us to ignore inconvenient truths. Sometimes officials provide so much information that the truth is deliberately obscured, lost in a plethora of facts and figures. Thus the first task in analyzing a case of alleged deception is to decide whether deception actually occurred and precisely in what ways.

Those who want to justify political deception usually grant what ordinary morality maintains — that lying is generally wrong. But they go on to argue that no one (except perhaps Kant) believes that deception is always wrong. The general presumption against it can therefore be rebutted in certain circumstances, such as those that typically characterize politics. Politics is supposed to make deception more justifiable for several reasons: (1) political issues are complex and difficult to understand, especially when they must be presented in the mass media or in a short time; (2) the harmful effects of some political truths can be severe and irreversible; (3) the political effects result as much from what people believe as from what is actually true; and (4) organizing coalitions and other kinds of political action requires leaders to emphasize some parts of the truth to some people and different parts to others — telling the whole truth and nothing but the truth would make compromise almost impossible.

But, at least in a democracy, these reasons cannot give political leaders a general license to deceive whenever and wherever they think it necessary. Unless we can find out what officials have actually done — not just what they appear to have done — we cannot hold them accountable. At most, the special features of politics may justify exceptions to a general presumption against deception in a democracy.

If we conclude that deception may sometimes be necessary, our task should be to define carefully the conditions under which citizens should permit public officials to engage in deception. The main factors we should consider are: (1) the importance of the goal of the deception; (2) the availability of alternative means for achieving the goal; (3) the identity of the victims of the deception (other officials, other governments, all citizens); (4) the accountability of the deceivers (the possibility of approving the deception in advance or discovering it later); and (5) the containment of the deception (its effects on other actions by officials).

The cases in this section offer the chance to identify various kinds of deception and to discover what, if any, conditions would justify deception. The first selection is a group of minicases. They are simplified versions of actual episodes in recent American politics, and they provide an indication of the variety of the kinds of deception and circumstances in which politicians have tried to justify it.

In actual political life, moral difficulties do not come so neatly packaged with labels announcing "This is a dilemma of deception." In a more fully described and complex case, "The New York City Fiscal Crisis," many of the ethical issues lie buried in the intricate and sometimes tedious details of accounting routines. It is important to work through these details while keeping in mind the larger issues that they imply—such as the conflict between the obligation to keep the public informed and the obligation to protect the public welfare.

Lying in Office

Graham T. Allison and Lance M. Liebman

1. JFK, THE "DEAL," AND THE DENIAL

On Saturday, October 27, 1962, at the height of the Cuban Missile Crisis, President John F. Kennedy receives a letter from the Soviet government proposing to strike a deal. The Soviet Union, the letter offers, will dismantle and remove its missiles from Cuba if the United States agrees to a similar withdrawal of its nuclear-armed missiles stationed in Turkey. In fact, Kennedy twice ordered the removal of these obsolescent and vulnerable missiles in the months prior to

the October crisis. But each time the Turkish government had objected, and so the missiles remained—an easy target for Soviet retaliation should the United States be forced to take military action against the missiles in Cuba.

Kennedy believes, along with virtually all of his advisers, that the Soviet offer is unacceptable. To back down under fire, he reasons, would be to demonstrate that the United States was willing to trade off European security for its own. It would undermine the credibility of America's pledge to defend Europe against Soviet attack, and would invite the Soviets to stage another missile crisis elsewhere— only this time in a situation where the

Reprinted by permission of the authors. Copyright ©1980 by the President and Fellows of Harvard College.

military deck was not so heavily stacked in America's favor. But he also knows that tens of millions of Russians and Americans might soon be dead if he cannot find some other way to resolve the crisis.

Kennedy decides to ignore the Soviet proposal and to respond favorably to an earlier, private letter from Premier Khrushchev to himself, in which the Soviet leader had offered to withdraw the missiles in Cuba in return only for an American pledge not to invade the island. But to sweeten the deal, guessing that Khrushchev's colleagues may have subsequently raised the price of Soviet withdrawal, Kennedy has his brother Robert inform Soviet Ambassador Anatoly Dobrynin privately that, while there can be no Cuba-for-Turkey exchange made under pressure, the President had already ordered the removal of the American missiles in Turkey and would make sure the order was carried out speedily.

At a press conference on November 20, after the crisis had passed and after the congressional elections that were on Kennedy's mind during October 1962, the following exchange occurred:

> Q. Mr. President, in the various exchanges of the past three weeks, either between yourself and Chairman Khrushchev or at the United Nations, have any issues been touched on besides that of Cuba, and could you say how the events of these past three weeks might affect such an issue as Berlin or disarmament or nuclear testing?
> THE PRESIDENT: No. I instructed the negotiators to confine themselves to the matter of Cuba completely, and therefore no other matters were discussed. Disarmament, any matters affecting Western Europe, relations between the Warsaw pact countries and NATO, all the rest — none of these matters was to be in any way referred to or negotiated about until we had made

progress and come to some sort of a solution on Cuba. So that has been all we have done diplomatically with the Soviet Union the last month.

> Now if we're successful in Cuba, as I said, we would be hopeful that some of the other areas of tension could be relaxed. Obviously when you make progress in any area, then you have hopes that you can continue it. But up till now we have confined ourselves to Cuba, and we'll continue to do so until we feel the situation has reached a satisfactory state.

2. THE ELECTION DEBATE

It is November 1969. John Lindsay is running for reelection as mayor of New York. His principal opponent is Mario Procaccino, a conservative Democrat. In a TV debate the Sunday before election day, Procaccino charges that Lindsay has "made a deal with the landlords." More specifically, he claims that (1) Lindsay has a secret report on housing in New York City, (2) the report states that rent control is at the heart of the city's housing problem, and recommends revisions of the rent control law which will result in massive rent increases, and (3) the report is being suppressed until after the election.

In fact, Lindsay knows that two city consultants (RAND and McKinsey) have done such a study for the Housing and Development Administration. He has not seen their report, but has seen a preliminary summary of their findings, which do find that rent control is aggravating the city's housing shortage, and do recommend substantial revision of the rent control law in such a way that many rents will be significantly increased. At the recommendation of the Housing and Development Administrator, the reports have been labeled "highly confidential" and publication is being withheld until after the election. On the basis of the report's findings and the recommendations of other analysts in the city government, Lindsay believes that the report's analyses are essentially correct, and plans to seek substantial changes in rent control — after the election.

Lindsay knows that to announce his intention prior to the election would cost many votes. He suspects that to acknowledge the existence of the report will raise serious doubts in many voters' minds about his support for rent control. He believes that Procaccino would be a disastrous mayor for New York City. He replies:

> I haven't seen this so-called report; there could well be such a report. The mayor sees thousands of reports from various persons, and it's the mayor's decision that counts in this whole matter of governing New York City, and my decisions have been constant, not only to be firm on rent control, which I am. I believe in it. I think we must have it.

Two hours after the debate, Lindsay and his staff are at campaign headquarters. A young aide says, "The Mayor's answer to the rent control question was ambiguous. We'd better put out a firmer denial. How about this?" He then proposes the following press release:

> Mayor Lindsay today branded as ridiculous the charge that he is soft on rent control. He said the city is not studying the watering down of controls, and if any recommendation for higher rents is made, he will reject it out of hand.

3. MILLER AND FURLOUGHS

It is early 1970. Jerome Miller has just taken office as head of Massachusetts' Department of Youth Services, the agency responsible for managing the state's programs for juvenile offenders. After fifteen years of child-treatment experience, Miller — like many other progressives in his field — has come to believe that institutionalization is a disastrous policy, and that almost any environment outside the

large state detention centers is better for the child and cheaper for the state. He believes the old, prison-like "reform schools" are brutal, oppressive institutions that teach little more than the finer points of crime; his ultimate goal is to shut them down entirely and replace them with a network of smaller scale, community-based halfway houses. But first he must prove to the legislature and the communities in which the houses will be located that the kids can be trusted.

Miller's first step toward deinstitutionalization is a program of weekend furloughs for confined teenage offenders. One hundred boys and girls go home on Friday afternoon, and ninety-one come back Monday morning. Miller is not alarmed, since this result conforms to his expectations, based on similar programs elsewhere, in which virtually all of the wanderers have returned within a week. But the press wants to know what the "count" was immediately, and Miller fears that published reports of a 9% AWOL rate will kill any chances for deinstitutionalization. He tells the press on Monday afternoon that all the furlough children were back on time. By Friday, the nine missing offenders have all returned.

4. FIDDLING THE RULES COMMITTEE CHAIRMAN

Elizabeth Jackson is a private citizen, head of an ad hoc lobbying group formed to support the Equal Rights Amendment in her state. It is December 1975. Her state has not yet ratified the ERA, but ratification is closer than it has ever been in the three years since Congress sent the amendment to the states.

(Background note: The ERA was passed by both houses of Congress in 1972. The Congressional resolution provided that the amendment would become effective if ratified by the required three-fourths of the states, thirty-eight, within seven years. By the end of 1973, thirty-four states had ratified the ERA. After a flurry of ratifications in the first two years, the battle for the ERA has come down to a grinding effort to win the few more states needed. Time seems to be on the side of the opponents. The women's movement no longer enjoys the media attention which helped win the initial passage of the ERA by projecting the image of a potent new political force. The ERA opponents seem to be getting stronger, and are able to use delaying tactics to their advantage as the 1979 deadline approaches.)

In Jackson's state, the ERA forces have had little success until this year. Although most legislators are unwilling to be recorded against the ERA, its opponents have bottled it up in committee in both houses, preventing any floor votes. Last election, the key opponent in the House retired, perhaps because he was unwilling to face the vigorous campaign of an opponent whom Jackson helped recruit. With him gone, and with the help of the Majority Leader, Jackson's group forced the bill out of committee, and the full House approved it. Now the end of the session is a day away, and the ERA languishes in the Senate Rules Committee.

The chairman of the Rules Committee, Senator Henderson, is a progressive force in the generally conservative Senate. Although he is personally ambivalent about the ERA, he has indicated to Jackson that it will reach the Senate floor. His cordiality and cooperative attitude have encouraged Jackson to be optimistic, but the end of the session is near, and the ERA still sits in Rules. Jackson now suspects that Henderson is holding the bill as a favor to his colleagues who would rather not vote on it.

Jackson is desperate to get the ERA approved this year. She knows that the national campaign against the ERA, led by

Phyllis Schafly, is raising funds to support a more intensive lobbying effort next year. Moreover, her key supporter in the House, the Majority Leader, is leaving to run for Governor next year, and the Judiciary Committee chairman is running for Congress. Both of them helped to line up the necessary votes in the House, and without them next year, the prospects for the ERA look bleak. It looks to Jackson as if it's now or never.

She decides to change her tactics. She challenges Senator Henderson in his office. He's deliberately deceiving her, she charges, and she will make sure that he pays for it. He tells her that it is the Rules Committee members who are blocking the ERA, but she refuses to believe him. She tells him that her group is prepared to back Chris Carter, a young attorney active in local politics, who has agreed to run against Senator Henderson if he has sufficient funds and volunteers. She tells Senator Henderson that her group will contribute heavily to Carter unless ERA reaches the Senate floor.

In fact, she knows that her threat is pure fiction. While Carter has been rumored to be considering the race, she has not talked with him. The reason she has not is that she can see that her organization is running out of steam. They have no funds left, and fund-raising lately has been hardly worth the effort. Volunteers are tiring of the struggle, and will probably disappear if they are not successful this time. Furthermore, she herself would find it difficult to oppose Senator Henderson because of his critical role in the passage of a wide variety of progressive legislation.

5. HERMAN FIDDLES FINNEGAN

Suppose that the Acting Director of the Bureau of Consular and Security Affairs in the Department of State, Philip Herman, is trying to substitute a permanent visa for foreign visitors to the United States in place of the existing renewable visa. Only the United States, among its major allies and trading partners, maintains such a restrictive policy, a legacy of McCarthyist fear of Communist infiltration and subversion, and Herman is attempting to eliminate this imbalance. To do so, he needs Congressional approval. But the man he must convince is Representative Michael Finnegan, a fierce anti-Communist who heads the House Appropriations Subcommittee for the State Department. Finnegan is virulently opposed to any change in visa requirements that would make it possible for a single additional Communist to enter the country, no matter what benefits the United States might derive from increased foreign visitation. In fact, he has blocked such efforts before. Without Finnegan's approval, there can be no change in the visa. Thus, Herman falsely tells Finnegan that the State Department is under heavy foreign pressure to abolish visas entirely, that unless the U.S. liberalizes its visa regulations, other countries might retaliate by making it increasingly difficult for Americans to travel abroad, and that the best way to beat this pressure would be to adopt a permanent visa system, which would at least permit an initial check on suspect foreigners. Finnegan buys the story.

6. COVERT ACTION IN CHILE

It is early 1973. CIA Director Richard Helms has just been nominated by President Richard Nixon to be U.S. Ambassador to Iran, but before he can take the post, he must be approved by the Senate. During his confirmation hearings before the Foreign Relations Committee, he is asked questions about alleged CIA covert activity in Chile.

In 1970, the CIA had spent over $8 million to prevent the election of Dr. Salvador Allende Gossens, a Marxist, as Chile's President. Despite the CIA money, Allende won the election by a small plurality. But since no candidate won a majority of the vote, the Chilean Congress was required to choose between the top two vote-getters in the general election. In the past, the Congress had always selected the leading candidate, and 1970 appeared to be no exception.

Shortly after the election, President Nixon informed Director Helms that an Allende regime would not be acceptable to the United States and instructed him to organize a military coup d'etat in Chile to prevent Allende's accession to the presidency. The CIA was to take this highly sensitive action without coordination with the Departments of State or Defense and without informing the U.S. Ambassador to Chile. Instead, the Agency was to report, both for informational and approval purposes, only to the President's Assistant for National Security Affairs, Dr. Henry Kissinger, or his deputy.

Despite Helms' belief, expressed later, that the Agency was "being asked to almost do the impossible," he attempted to carry out the President's order. In a flurry of activity immediately prior to the scheduled meeting of the Chilean Congress, the CIA made twenty-one contacts with key military and police officials in Chile. Those Chileans who were inclined to stage a coup were given assurances of strong support at the highest levels of the U.S. government, both before and after a coup. Yet the coup never took place, and Dr. Allende took office. After the death in an abortive kidnap attempt of Chilean Army Commander-in-Chief General Rene Schneider, who opposed the coup, the plot was uncovered. CIA support for the conspirators was rumored, but the allegations were unconfirmed.

Now, in early 1973, with Allende still in power but facing increasing domestic opposition, Helms is asked about the CIA's alleged role in the 1970 coup attempt:

SENATOR SYMINGTON: Did you try in the Central Intelligence Agency to overthrow the government in Chile?

MR. HELMS: No, sir.

SENATOR SYMINGTON: Did you have any money passed to the opponents of Allende?

MR. HELMS: No, sir.

SENATOR SYMINGTON: So the stories you were involved in that war are wrong?

MR. HELMS: Yes, sir. I said to Senator Fulbright many months ago that if the Agency had really gotten in behind the other candidates and spent a lot of money and so forth the election might have come out differently.

Comment

Denial is often the first response of public officials accused of deception. Richard Helms (Case 6) claimed that he literally told the truth: the CIA did not try to overthrow the government of Chile, only to dissuade the Chilean Congress from confirming Allende's electoral victory; and the CIA did not give any money directly to the candidates, but only to groups that supported or opposed candidates. On what grounds should we decide that technically true statements count as deception? When should failure to disclose be considered deceptive?

In most of the cases, justifications for the deception typically mention the beneficial consequences of the deception. But we should distinguish: appeals to one's own reelection (Lindsay in Case 2), the success of a public cause (the ERA in Case 4), and the avoidance of nuclear war (Kennedy in Case 1). On what basis should we make such distinctions? Another kind of justification refers to features of the act of deception itself — such as the relations of the deceiver to the deceived. Perhaps enemies do not deserve the truth (but if so, does this include political enemies as in Case 5?). Politicians, like poker players, may know that the rules of the game allow some bluffing as in Case 4, but if so are citizens playing the game too?

In each case, consider whether there were any reasonable alternatives to the deception. Perhaps Kennedy could not have given a more accurate answer or could not even have declined to comment without undermining the "deal" that resolved the crisis. Can the same be said about Lindsay, Miller, and Helms? No doubt these officials felt themselves in a bind: to reply "no comment" would bring about the same result as if they fully disclosed what they wished to conceal. We should also look at the context in which such dilemmas arise. Could the officials have taken steps earlier that would have prevented the dilemma from ever arising? If so, how does that affect our evaluation of their later deception?

The New York City Fiscal Crisis

Jeremy Paul

New York City's budget is the third largest in the nation, exceeded only by the State of California's and the Federal Government's. In the best of times the management of this budget is an awesome responsibility, requiring a clear delineation of priorities and a firm understanding of ethical constraints. It was not the best times in January, 1974, when Abraham Beame was inaugurated as New York's mayor. The changing social and economic conditions that had plagued New York for at least a decade and the 1973–74 national recession combined to turn budget management from a responsibility into a nightmare. The long-term history of New York City fiscal abuses leading up to this nightmare by itself illustrates government's sometimes unwise tendency to pay for the present by borrowing against the future. Yet a close look at the time period immediately preceding the spring of 1975 collapse of the public market for New York City securities reveals some ethical problems that faced top city officials when suddenly future debts became present ones. These problems concerned the question of deception and full disclosure in government.

Immediately upon taking office, Mayor Beame pointed out that he had inherited a budget deficit for the fiscal year 1973–74 of 500 million dollars and a cumulative deficit of approximately 1.5 billion dollars. The most important problem for City officials and their supporters in the banks was to find some way to keep

Copyright © 1979, 1982 by the Woodrow Wilson School, Princeton University. Reprinted by permission.

the City solvent. "The primary responsibility of the Mayor," Mayor Beame said, "is to see that the people of New York get adequate police and fire protection, health care and education."[1] As the City's deficit grew and its case needs increased, these basic services were placed in jeopardy.

Throughout late 1974 and early 1975 the City had also become increasingly dependent for funds upon the public market for short term notes. To maintain the same level of social services, the City needed to continue borrowing money. To meet this need, Beame, Comptroller Goldin, and other city officials worked directly with the major underwriters in an effort to maintain investor confidence. Beame explained his efforts to keep the market open: "No business or government in the world can exist without the ability to borrow."[2]

The Securities and Exchange Commission, in its report on "Transactions in Securities of the City of New York," accuses the City and the banks of not only ethical but also legal violations during the efforts to market City notes. These alleged violations raised the issue of proper disclosure of financial information to investors in New York City securities. The legal issue assumed great importance in 1975 when the City declared a moratorium on short-term City notes. But behind this legal issue lay a broader question of moral and political responsibility: what must public officials disclose about the financial condition of a government at a particular time? In this period, full disclosure, in the view of officials, posed a grave risk of bankruptcy and therefore a threat to the services and jobs of millions of city residents.

The legal requirements concerning proper disclosure of information are described in Rule 10-b-5, a regulation issued by the Securities and Exchange Commission in accord with the Securities and Exchange Act of 1934. Unlike corporate bonds, municipal securities are not subject to the stringent requirements of registration and formal prospectus. The City often made this point in its own defense. Nevertheless, all issuers of securities are subject to the Rule, which states in part, "It shall be unlawful for any person, directly or indirectly...to make any untrue statement of a material fact or *to omit to state a material fact* in order to make the statements made, in the light of the circumstances under which they were made, not misleading...in connection with the purchase or sale of any security" [emphasis added]. In connection with the sale of New York City securities, the legal question then becomes: What were the material facts concerning the City's finances, and to what extent were they disclosed? To understand the ethical aspects of the problem, these questions must also be addressed but in the context of the broader political circumstances of the fiscal crisis.

The financial circumstances of the New York City fiscal crisis have three separate but related aspects. The first and most important is that for many years prior to Beame's inauguration, New York's growth in expenditures had been outpacing its growth in revenues resulting in an increasing and unwieldy budget deficit. Second, in order to show a balanced budget in the books, as required by the Local Finance Law of the State of New York, the City had for years been resorting to seemingly questionable accounting practices. These practices are the central focus of the disclosure question. Finally, the City relied heavily for its cash needs on the issuance of short-term notes.[3] Whether the City should have issued this debt without a more complete description of its finances, whether the banks should have underwritten these securities, and whether there were really any other workable alternatives were questions that observers raised.

The causes of fiscal strain on municipal treasuries were well known. White emmigration from the suburbs, black and Puerto Rican immigration into the cities, and the loss of urban jobs particularly in manufacturing, left New York and other northeastern cities with ever-increasing costs of public assistance and a corresponding diminishing tax base. In the case of New York, the figures are staggering; one study reveals that New York City's expenditures on public assistance payments and purchases of social and medical services grew by almost 800 percent from 1960–61 to 1972–73.[4] At the same time, employment in manufacturing in New York declined by 180,000, a drop of about 18 percent.[5] In addition, since 1970 employment in New York increased only in the public sector placing a further drain on City funds. As these pressures mounted, the City's own report agrees, that it was the "repeatedly publicized judgments of Governors, State Legislators, Mayors, and City Councilmen to resort to borrowing instead of fiscal restraint as a means of meeting needs."[6] Thus, as Mayor Beame began his term in office, New York was a city in debt and in trouble.

The exact size of the cumulative budget deficit at fiscal year end 1975 was a subject of much contention. Mayor Beame repeatedly said he had inherited a cumulative deficit of a billion and a half dollars at the end of the fiscal year 1973-74. Although Beame says he began work on reducing the deficit, his efforts were out-weighed by the effects of the recession, and the deficit continued to grow. Later, revised figures published on August 29, 1975, by the municipal assistance corporation (a state agency created in June, 1975, to convert three billion dollars of city notes into long-term securities) placed the deficit as of June 30, 1975, at 2.6 billion dollars.[7] Still later revised figures issued by the City Comptroller in October, 1976, which included estimates for accrued pension liabilities, placed the cumulative deficit figure at over 5 billion dollars.[8] The size of any one of these figures is enough to indicate that New York was plagued with severe fiscal problems.

Knowledge of New York City's large cumulative deficit was certainly not withheld from the public since Mayor Beame's statements about it were publicized continually by all of the major media from the time he took office. It is not for concealing this deficit that the Mayor and City officials were accused of inadequate disclosure. Yet there is a discrepancy between the Mayor's figure, repeatedly publicized at the time, and the later figures released by MAC and the City Comptroller. Without trying to resolve these discrepancies, we need to understand how they were an outgrowth of the City's continued use of questionable accounting practices. These legally sanctioned fiscal "gimmicks," which had been used to create the impression of a balanced budget in the years prior to 1974–75, were maintained by the Beame administration. It was chiefly because of these gimmicks that the SEC accused the City of withholding relevant information from the public.

Probably no technique of budget-balancing was more publicized or more heavily criticized than the transfer of funds from the capital budget to the expense budget. Pursuant to the City Charter, the City operates under two budgets, which are prepared for different purposes and are funded from different sources. The expense budget is designed to handle costs of operations such as police, fire, health, and educational services and is financed by Federal and State aid and tax revenues. Significantly, the expense budget is also charged with debt service. The capital budget is designed to pay for construction of capital projects such as schools, parks, bridges, and tunnels. Except for specific grants from the Federal and State governments, this budget is funded by the issuing of long-term debt.[9]

Over the years, the distinction between the two budgets became increasingly blurred. Beginning in 1965, the City embarked upon a steadily increasing and dangerous schedule of issuing debt for the capital budget and using these funds to meet operating expenses. Ironically, this practice had no greater critic than the then Comptroller Beame, whose comments were extensively reported by the press. Yet by the time he had become Mayor, the capitalization of expenses had become an integral part of the City's finances.

This capitalization of expenses moved the City closer and closer toward fiscal disaster as the high interest costs became part of the City's expense obligations, and the capital fund became too depleted to finance needed construction projects. By 1975, Beame's first budget, the expenses funded by the capital budget totalled 722 million dollars up from 195 million just five years earlier.[10]

The practice of capitalization of expenses was the most publicized of the City's book-balancing methods. A clear example of such publicity can be found in the *New York Times* editorial of November 4, 1974: "No one knows better than the Mayor the folly of continuing a course in which debt service takes an ever bigger share of the tax dollar while schools, subway lines, parks and other needed municipal facilities go unbuilt because *half of the capital budget is diverted to paying for salaries, pensions, and other day-to-day costs*"[11] [emphasis added]. The practice of using the capital budget to fund operating expenses was also criticized by the Citizens Budget Commission, a public interest group founded in 1932 as a watchdog for City finances. Finally, Comptroller Goldin himself pointed out and criticized the practice in a press release of June 3, 1974.[12] Mayor Beame could not have been expected single-handedly to end the practice although he says he wanted to do so. By the time he became Mayor, the City probably did not have the money for such constructive reforms.

The second kind of fiscal "gimmick" arose from the City's books themselves. Although no statute required municipalities to conform to generally accepted accounting principles, the SEC criticized the shoddy state of New York's accounts. In the words of one observer, the City "not only used every gimmick that had ever been invented but they came up with every gimmick that will ever be invented."[13]

Most important among these accounting practices was the following: the City kept its receivables as a whole on an accrual basis while it charged liabilities only as cash was actually dispensed. In other words, the city would credit a given fiscal year with revenues received in that year as well as all revenues which were estimated to be earned in that year but collectible in later years; at the same time the city charged the fiscal year only with money actually spent in that year. This practice was an effective way of hiding a portion of the City's true cumulative deficit. Examples of accrual basis receivables were the water and sewer charges, and the yearly estimate of accrued sales taxes known as the June accrual. On the liability side, the largest postponed charge was a two-

year lag in the City's pension fund contributions; the City recorded its contributions two years later than the liabilities were actually incurred. A final example of this pay-as-you-go accounting strategy was the reliance on one-shot sources of funds as if they were recurring revenues. This last practice, like the capitalization of expenses, was well publicized and highly criticized.[14]

None of these practices explicitly violated any state or Federal law. In fact, the state laws allowing these practices to occur are in many ways responsible for their existence. Over the years, as New York City came to the state asking for aid to help balance the budget, the state would agree to allow fiscal sleight of hand rather than choose to supply additional cash. Beyond legal issues, City officials evidently did not believe they were obliged to adopt accounting methods that would have revealed the underlying deficit. With respect to non-recurring revenues, Mayor Beame in his testimony before the SEC said that if (in accordance with conservative accounting) he had reserved such revenues instead of using them, he would have been forced to discontinue some needed city service.

The questionable practices evolved as an integral part of city finances over the years, and only a long-term plan of accounting revisions combined with fiscal austerity could have completely solved the problem. The Beame administration could have chosen to begin such a program, but it would have been politically unpopular and the sacrifices might have been great.

Although the poor state of the City's books with regard to the accrual method and the one-shot revenues was certainly not a secret, it contributed to the SEC's charges of a lack of disclosure. The SEC cites the Annual Reports of the Comptroller for 1974 and 1975 which "failed to disclose the City's unusual basis for recording water charges and sewer rent revenues."[15] More importantly, the SEC claims that the Annual Reports for fiscal years 1973 and 1974 "failed to explicitly set forth that the City recognized revenues on an accrual basis and expenditures on a cash basis."[16] Yet the SEC acknowledges that this method of revenue recognition was alluded to in the Annual Reports.

It is generally agreed that the SEC showed that the City's books were chaotic. Even the most trained observer trying to understand these books would have found them confusing. Such obfuscation was allowed to continue partly because independent audits of the City's accounts were not required. Comptroller Goldin tried to institute such audits of his books upon first taking office. In the meantime, his justification for their lack of clarity is summed up in a May 4, 1976, statement: "There was a strong feeling, I believe, that even though the City's accounting and budgeting had been revealed as a kind of Rube Goldberg conception — a system which defied understanding or control — it was better to leave it alone as long as it churned out enough money to meet the bills and pay the debts."[17]

The alleged overstatement of receivables was the most controversial of the practices. To make its case for inadequate disclosure, the SEC depends heavily upon its charges that City officials intentionally withheld information concerning receivables. The Commission states "there was no disclosure of the fact that the City carried disputed receivables on its books, did not reserve against the possibility of non-collection, and borrowed against these receivables by issuing RAN's [Revenue Anticipation Notes]."[18] Likewise, other critics claimed that no one outside the City Government was aware, until after the collapse of the market, that possibly uncollectible receivables were being kept on the books. According to Dr. Herbert

Ranschburg, the research director of the Citizens Budget Commission, "the one thing we didn't know and I don't think anybody (outside the City government) knew was that the City was 'kiting' its receivables."[19] Similarly, Jac Friedgut of Citibank, defending his bank's policy of underwriting the March 13 offer of City RAN's, states that he was unaware that the City's Report on Essential Facts (an additional disclosure document) contained "revenue which proved to be phony."[20]

The City's overestimation of receivables has two aspects. First, the City's figures concerning the amount of Federal and State aid it would receive proved to be inflated. Second, the City overestimated its eventual collection of real estate taxes. In 1976 the Office of the City Comptroller attributed 678 million dollars of the City's cumulative deficit to a re-evaluation of aid receivables.[21] And in the summer of 1975 the State Comptroller estimated 408 million dollars or 80 percent of the 502 million dollars of the City's real estate taxes had been overstated.[22] These overstatements were discovered well after the public market for City securities was already closed. They were not highlighted in City documents before this, nor were they emphasized by the Mayor, the Comptroller, or the press during late 1974 or early 1975 when the City was attempting to sell notes. Comptroller Goldin nevertheless stated, "I disclosed everything that I knew.[23]

Overstatements concerning Federal and State aid receivables came about in two ways. First, estimates made by low level City officials of anticipated funds from various Federal and State agencies were placed directly on the books as receivables. This definition of a receivable is explicitly permitted in Section 25 of the State Local Finance Law. These estimates in many cases proved to be too high and thus gave a false and more favorable picture of City finances. Mayor Beame said that he did not check such estimates but merely assumed them to be accurate, and, in his testimony before the SEC, he denied any deliberate overstatement of these receivables.[24] As for Goldin, his office was not responsible for preparing these estimates and was unable to audit them.

More important for the City's overall fiscal position was the continuing practice of leaving disputed receivables on the books. For example, the Federal government would announce a spending program for some social service such as day care centers. The City would then borrow money against expected revenue, using the loan to begin the service. If the Federal Government then changed its mind and cut back funds, the City would protest, arguing that such a reversal was a violation of an agreement. In the meantime, the City would maintain the expected revenue on the books as a receivable, ignoring the fact that it was disputed. This type of dispute could take years to resolve, and although City officials often received the funds, City books did not indicate the tenuous nature of such receivables.

Deputy Mayor Cavanaugh sought to justify the practice of keeping disputed receivables on the books by arguing that, if they were removed, they would become truly uncollectible. Mayor Beame said he was aware that some receivables on the City books were in dispute, and his actions seem to indicate that he concurred with Cavanaugh's assessment. Comptroller Goldin was made aware of the whole receivables question, and particularly the problems with overstated medicaid claims, in repeated memos from his adviser Steven Clifford. Goldin maintained, however, that he was unable to check the problem through an audit, and thus could

not verify that there were any specific overstatements.

Disclosure of the importance of full collection of all receivables to balance the City's books can be found in the foreward of the Comptroller's Annual Report of 1973-74. Although these receivables are acknowledged to be *unaudited,*[25] the SEC argued that a clear reference to the disputed nature of Federal and State aid receivables should have been made. Critics scored the City's failure to call attention to disputed receivables in its fiscal documents. Some saw Beame's constant reassurance to the financial community that "we are borrowing against firm receivables,"[26] as part of a strategy to emphasize the positive side of City finances in order to keep the public market open, and, not incidentally, to keep the Beame administration politically popular.

The second kind of receivable overstated by the City was the level of expected real estate taxes. This overstatement came about in two ways. First, despite the inevitability that some real estate taxes would prove uncollectible, the City failed to make an allowance for uncollectibles. The City issued TANs (Tax Anticipation Notes) against the full amount of real estate taxes receivable and according to law could roll these notes over for a period of five years before recognizing taxes as definitely uncollectible and writing them off. It was Beame's experience that after the five year period such write-offs had proven to be very small.[27] Yet during the recession, as more and more buildings were abandoned, permanently uncollectible real estate taxes reached higher levels. The SEC states that "there was no disclosure of the fact that a significant portion of the City's real estate tax receivables were uncollectible."[28] Both Beame and Goldin publicly complained about the increase in real estate tax delinquency. Apparently, what the

SEC means is that neither Beame nor Goldin admitted publicly in a disclosure document that these taxes would remain uncollectible. Beame, in keeping with his desire to emphasize the positive, preferred to assume that such taxes might be collected.

The other kind of overstatement of the real estate taxes is more difficult to explain. Completely undisclosed was the fact that some 126 million dollars of the City's uncollectible real estate taxes were on *City-owned* property.[29] Beame said that he did not know this taxing was taking place. The recession in New York had caused many landlords to default on real estate taxes so long that the City would foreclose on their property. This property (known as "in rem") became city-owned; yet it took some time for the City to recognize this and stop assessing taxes. The City's position was that this breakdown in communication was responsible for the self-taxation. Nevertheless, Steven Clifford, former special deputy Comptroller and a consultant to Goldin during this period, maintains that any effort made towards removing such City property from the tax rolls would not have been looked upon kindly by those in City Hall.[30]

Another important historical force confronting Beame was the city's increasing dependence upon short-term debt. "The City had dramatically increased its short-term debt six-fold from $747 million to $4.5 billion in the six years from 1969 to June 30, 1975."[31] During the six months from October 1974 to April 1975, the City sold through its underwriters about 4 billion dollars in short-term debt, an extraordinarily high figure in historical terms.[32] In fact, the heavy volume of borrowing alone was a major cause of the eventual collapse of the public market. The financial community simply could not find buyers for the vast quantity of City notes being issued so frequently.

In December 1974, members of the financial community met with top City officials to express their concern about the market for city bonds. In response to this meeting, Comptroller Goldin established a reduced borrowing schedule for the following six months. This schedule, however, still consisted of an average of 550 million dollars in short-term notes each month, the issuance of which was essential to continued operation of the City.

Whatever can be said, then, about the City's complete or incomplete disclosure concerning the different specific facts of New York's finances, there is no uncertainty regarding the City's overall strategy. The City continued to issue short-term notes through late 1974 and early 1975, and the top officials worked diligently to make these notes appear attractive. Both Beame and Goldin took the position in numerous public statements that investment in City securities was completely secure. Moreover, the City took direct action to expand the public market to a broader class of investors by reducing the minimum size of New York City's short-term notes from 25,000 to 10,000 dollars in November 1974.[33] Given the large budget deficit and the extremely precarious state of the City's finances, how could City officials justify this strategy? Publicly, the justification came in the form of the repeated distinction between problems in closing the budget gap and problems in paying off securities.

The public position of both Beame and Goldin concerning the sale of notes during this period was clear. While almost daily admitting to very serious budgetary problems, both Beame and Goldin constantly reassured investors of the soundness of City securities. Such reassurances were based primarily on the principle of "first lien." This principle, enunciated in the New York State Constitution, requires that the City use all revenues from taxes and federal and state aid to pay bonds and notes before making any other expenditures. Technically, the principle requires that bond and note holders be paid before police officers and firefighters. City officials maintained that there would always be enough revenue to cover bonds and notes, since the City each year took in many times the amount of its maturing debt. Therefore, no matter how bad things became, Beame and Goldin said City notes were safe (see Appendix).

The SEC questioned whether the principle of "first lien" applied to the principal amounts of City short-term debt. Although the Commission's argument may throw the "first lien" principle into doubt, it does not substantiate the claim that Beame and Goldin were intentionally misleading the public on this count. Both Beame and Goldin testified that they firmly believed in the constitutional guarantee of "first lien." Goldin argued that, as Comptroller, he was responsible for dispensing New York's money: "As far as I was concerned I was going to pay the bond and note holders first. It was as simple as that."[34] Strong confirmation of the constitutional position of Beame and Goldin came in the November 1976 ruling of the New York State Court of Appeals (New York's highest court), which declared the November 1975 Moratorium on City notes to be unconstitutional.[35] This moratorium was enacted by the state legislature over the objection of City officials. Despite the fact that the principle of "first lien" was upheld by the courts, the security of investing in City notes that may be refundable only if police officers and firefighers are not paid is not "as simple as that."

City officials repeatedly attempted to separate the issue of the City's financial problems from its ability to pay back its debt. Yet these two aspects of the crisis were essentially related. As problems with the budget became more severe, the City depended more and more upon borrowing. This dependence put a greater and greater strain on the City's ability to pay back its debt. If the sources of borrowing were cut off (as they eventually were), the City would be forced immediately to choose between maintaining its essential services and paying off noteholders. In this case, despite the most explicit and emphatic legal requirements to pay the debts first, officials would have been hard pressed to dispense cash to investors while watching the City collapse around them. Yet if they used funds to meet payroll expenses, the ensuing default on City securities would have had disastrous consequences for the entire national money market. To avoid this painful dilemma, city officials believed they had to continue borrowing. Thus, they did not mention the connection between the budget gap and the City's ability to pay its debt. Officials did not publicly question the principle of "first lien" despite the likelihood it would come under pressure. Although the legality of "first lien" was confirmed, short-term City note holders in November 1975 were forced to wait for their money while an unconstitutional moratorium was enforced. This moratorium gave State and Federal officials time to establish a scheme for fiscal recovery.

In addition to stressing the principle of "first lien," Beame made strenuous efforts to present City securities in a positive light. He fought publicly with the financial community about the "outrageous" interest rates being charged for underwriting bids. He was partially correct in publicly attributing these rates to national tight money policy and the weakened credit market caused by the default of the Urban Development Corporation, but these high rates were also attributable to the market's growing perception of the risk inherent in City notes. The Mayor also stressed the rapid repayment schedule for sizable portions of New York City debt while ignoring the fact that the money to meet this schedule would be raised by still further borrowing.[36] Beame and Goldin also stressed, in a letter to the *New York Times*, the large amount of real estate owned by the City although the ability of the City to convert such property into liquid assets was dubious.[37] Although the press was constantly reporting the serious fiscal problems of the City, the Mayor in his public statements spoke as a booster of City notes, ignoring the impact of the various bookkeeping methods on City accounts, and relying on the members of the financial community to "keep the market open." In his words, "I believe the financial community has a selling job to do to make the investing public see the financial strengths of [New York's] obligations."[38]

The financial community, chiefly the major New York banks—Chemical Bank, Manufacturers Hanover Trust Co., The Chase Manhattan Bank, Morgan Guaranty Trust Co., Bankers Trust Co., and Citibank—played a quasi-public role during the crisis. These banks, responsible for the underwriting and sale of City securities during this time, had access to City books and records. Because of their experience in the field of finance, these banks were knowledgeable participants in the City's efforts to market notes. According to Beame, after the formation of the Financial Community Liason Group (a group designed to help the City work out its fiscal problems and maintain market access) in January 1975, the bankers were privy to all relevant information.[39] Yet until March of 1975, the last month of successful City note sales, the banks made no more effort than City officials to disclose the City's plight.

The ethical position of the bankers was in some ways even more complex than that of City officials. All of the banks had huge capital investments in New York and stood to lose greatly if the City defaulted.

Furthermore, they were making a profit on their underwriting activity. Thus, on one hand, the banks had a large interest in keeping the market for City notes open. On the other hand, they had an obligation to their investors to check the security of the notes they were underwriting. In addition, Section 10-b-5 applied directly to these offerings, and the banks' lawyers warned them of possible questions about "due diligence" arising from an accurate presentation of the City's financial condition. In this respect, the dilemma for the bankers resembled that which faced City officials.

Nevertheless, the bankers were operating in a once-removed position. They could know nothing for sure. Concerning figures on the City's books such as estimates of receivables, the banks had little choice but to accept them as accurate. Furthermore, as Jac Friedgut, a Vice President of Citibank, pointed out, "there was a very thin line between opinion and fact concerning our assessment of the City's financial strength." Friedgut explained, "anything I said concerning the plight of the City might be accepted as fact, and even though it might be expert opinion, it was still only my opinion, and I had to be very careful because anything negative I said could prove to help lead to the close of the market."[40] The truth of this assessment was vividly confirmed after Friedgut's March 18, 1975, testimony before the New York Congressional delegation where he said that unless something gives, the City fiscal situation is not viable; City paper will be suspect regardless of interest rate.[41] Following this statement, Beame telephoned Citibank to complain that they were "bad mouthing" the City.

Other banks said less and thus received less criticism. Yet it is hard to determine exactly what any of them were supposed to say or do. A declaration by any one of the major banks that City notes were unsafe probably would have resulted in an immediate collapse of the public market. A withdrawal by any of the major banks from the underwriting syndicate would have brought about the same result. Furthermore, many of the banks did not have an internal structure that could have helped the officers understand enough about the City to take such drastic steps. The connection between the research (rating) division and the underwriting division in most of the banks was not close.

Besides an inadequate understanding of the City's financial position, the banks also lacked control over the spending choices made by the City. Unlike the Mayor, the banks could not decide to cut services in order to increase the security of City notes. The bankers were presented with City notes (take them or leave them), and for a long time, the banks chose to take them. The banks, then, did not break with the Mayor's policy by becoming a principal source of disclosure. The banks did, however, make an attempt to check on the City's accounting in February 1975 by requesting information concerning taxes receivable. When the Comptroller refused to comply with this "unprecedented request," the banks aborted a planned TAN offering. It was later shown that the City had insufficient taxes to make this offering, since the taxes supposedly receivable had been collected in January, 1975. Comptroller Goldin subsequently denied knowing that satisfying the banks' request would have revealed such damaging news.[42]

In addition, the banks were responsible for the March 13, 1975 issuance of "The Report of Essential Facts," a disclosure document that they felt would help keep the market open. This document, prepared with the aid of the City, ignored the major budget "gimmicks" and presented this particular issuance of RANs as being against firm receivables (which it was).

The document contained no outright false statements; yet it did not highlight the issue of receivables under dispute. When, despite the release of this document, Citibank ("which felt comfortable with the offering: unaware of the phony receivable issue"[43]) could not sell the notes, it was clear that the market for City notes was rapidly closing.

The SEC charged that the banks were "dumping" City securities. The SEC claimed that, because of the information known to the financial community concerning the plight of the City, the banks were selling off their investments in New York while at the same time they were underwriting City notes for the general public. If this charge were sustained, it would place the actions of the bankers in a very different light. It is one thing to continue to underwrite securities that are later shown to be suspect but quite another to underwrite securities that are deemed by a bank safe enough for the public but not safe enough for the bank.

There were important differences among the banks. Chemical, Citibank, and Morgan could most plausibly defend themselves against the charge of "dumping." Chemical's holdings in City securities actually increased during the period September 30, 1974 to April 30, 1975. The same is true of Morgan, although the SEC attributes this to Morgan's holding securities issued in March 1975 when the public market was closing. Citibank had no City securities in its investment account either at the beginning or at the end of the period. Manufacturers's total ownership of City securities declined from 180 million on September 30, 1974 to 163 million dollars on April 30, 1975 — apparently not a significant drop, but the SEC again attributes 40 million of the latter holdings to notes that Manufacturers could not market in March of 1975.[44]

The charges against Bankers and Chase are more difficult to answer. Bankers had a total initial position excluding syndicate and manager accounts of 118,670,000 dollars and as of April 30, 1975, its position amounted to approximately 58 million dollars. Of the latter amount, 40 million represented a position in the March BAN and RAN offerings, which apparently reflected an inability to dispose of the notes in the market place. Concerning Chase, the SEC states, "Chase's total September 30 position in City notes was approximately $165 million, and its position as of April 30, 1975 was approximately $59 million. Of this latter amount, approximately $43 million represents holdings in its trading account, apparently as a result of the inability to distribute the March BAN and RAN offerings. An analysis of Chase's investment account reflects the same pattern. As of September 30, its investment account held approximately $74 million in City notes, and as of April 30, its investment account held no City notes."[45]

None of these figures, however, establishes the motives of the different banks. Some of the declines in total holdings were caused by a large amount of maturation taking place during this period rather than a policy of deliberate sales. Likewise, sales of municipal securities can be made for tax reasons and other financial reasons, not only because the securities are deemed a substantial risk.

One aspect of the crisis with which the financial community was more familiar than City officials was the state of the market for City securities. As the market began to close, it was the financial community who became aware of it first. The reaction of the bankers was swift. In December, 1974, they informed City officials of the problem and, as we saw, this resulted in a reduced borrowing schedule. Likewise, the Financial Community Liason Group worked constantly with the Mayor to try to keep the market open. The SEC heard testimony regarding various meetings between Beame and members of the financial community, and confirmed that the bankers had expressed their concern. In fact, the danger to the credit market was a topic of constant debate between Beame and the bankers. Beame felt the underwriters should take more City notes into their own portfolios and that they should be able to market City notes at lower interest rates. Although Beame may have sincerely believed that the credit market would remain open, there was no doubt that the market was in danger throughout the period in question.

The threat posed by the national recession to New York's ability to sell securities was apparent to all, and indeed was highlighted by Beame and Goldin in public statements. Likewise, the glut caused by the large volume of city borrowings was also a matter of public record. Yet the real possibility that the credit market would close came about only because of a combination of these factors with the poor state of the City's finances. Furthermore, the possible collapse of the credit market was an extremely important fact to investors in City notes. For the City's finances were in such a state that if the City could no longer borrow, it would no longer have enough money to both provide services and pay off maturing debt. The SEC thus concludes that the state of the market was a material fact, and that the City officials had the obligation to make it public.

Although neither Beame nor Goldin ever publicly stated that the market would close, and although they did everything possible to keep it open and to persuade investors that it would remain open, the danger to the market and the risk inherent in City securities should have been apparent to any intelligent investor from simply looking at the interest rate. City tax-free notes paid rates of interest over twice those of similar issues and higher than many taxable notes. Were Beame and Goldin to have actually said that the market for city securities was on the verge of collapse, this could have been a self-fulfilling prophecy. Furthermore, the collapse of the market would (and indeed eventually did) necessitate drastic cuts in City services and a general decline in New York's quality of life. For a mayor whose toughest decision while in office was "the decision to lay off workers,"[46] to accept the collapse of the market without a fight was an untenable solution. Beame saw his primary duty as keeping the market open, not providing full disclosure. He later said that, "anybody who didn't know what was going on was either asleep or had his head in the sand."[47] If any deception actually took place (which Beame never conceded), some observers thought it justified to save the services and jobs for millions of city residents. As the *New York Times* later headlined, "'Deception' May Have Kept the City Solvent."[48]

EPILOGUE

It took the City four years to regain some control over its finances and re-establish its credibility in the securities market. During this time, the City suffered many of the consequences that Beame had feared, and had tried to avoid by his strategy of keeping the market open at all costs. The city was forced to lay off workers. Firefighters staged a work slow-down. Police warned that the streets were not safe. Sanitation workers and the teachers struck. Services were cut, the subway fare increased, and City University had to charge tuition.

To end the crisis, the City had to surrender some political authority to state officials and non-elected businessmen and lawyers. After months of difficult negotiations, the City, the state, the banks, and the unions agreed to establish a semi-permanent control board, which would have authority over the City's finances until the City paid off all its loans from the Municipal Assistance Corporation (MAC) and the federal government, and balanced its budget for three consecutive years. The board insisted that the "gimmicks" in the City budget be eliminated, and that fiscal austerity have priority over politically more popular policies.

The City made substantial progress toward recovery under Beame, though he lost his bid for relection in 1977, defeated by Ed Koch who had Governor Carey's support. In 1977-78, the city had no short-term debt at all, and entered the market on its own for the first time since 1975. The accounting practices later changed so that actual expenditures could be followed in detail. Aid receipts were not recorded until actually received, and reserve accounts were created to protect against the contingency of uncollectible aid and taxes. The definition of capital projects also was made stricter. Finally, a consortium of outside accountants was established to audit the City's books on a regular basis.

Some observers suggested that subsequent events showed that Beame gained little by his strategy of trying to present the city's finances in the best possible light to the public. The problems had to be confronted eventually anyhow, and he should have publicly faced up to them sooner than he did. Other observers believed, however, that if Beame had been able to continue to work quietly behind the scenes with state and federal officials, instead of in the glare of publicity and in an atmosphere of constant crisis, he could have brought the city out of its financial quagmire sooner and with less harm to the welfare of city workers and city residents. He could, moreover, have brought about a settlement that kept political authority in the hands of elected city officials rather than outside persons who were not primarily accountable to the citizens of New York. On this view, Beame's actions during 1974-75 at least gave city officials more time to strengthen their position vis-a-vis the state and federal government, and therefore put them in a better position to work out a settlement more favorable to the workers and residents of the City.

Whatever one's interpretation of subsequent events, Beame and his colleagues had to make choices in 1974-75 on the basis of the limited information and options available to them then. But they could have decided differently than they did. An appraisal of the ethics of their actions and their inactions is therefore possible.

APPENDIX:
PUBLIC STATEMENTS OF MAYOR BEAME
AND COMPTROLLER GOLDIN

NEWS RELEASE, OFFICE OF THE MAYOR,
OCTOBER 2, 1974:

The Mayor emphasized that the City's credit position was "solid and strong," even though the national economy is under the stresses of both inflation and recession, and even though these inflationary-recessionary trends are "creating some budget balancing problems for the City."

The Mayor said, "There is absolutely no question about the City's ability to repay all of its debts on time, and that this ability has improved over the last fifteen years."

LETTER OF MAYOR AND COMPTROLLER,
PUBLISHED IN THE NEW YORK TIMES,
NOVEMBER 11, 1974:

Bankruptcy means that liabilities exceed assets or that credit obligations cannot be met — a situation in which the City of New York, even in the darkest days of

From SEC Report, Washington, D.C.: Govt. Print. Off., 1977.

the Great Depression, never has found itself, nor will it. . . .

It should be clear, in connection with our municipal budget, that the Constitution of the State of New York makes our New York City bonds and notes a first lien on all revenues which include the real estate tax, all other City taxes, fees and permits, all state aid and all Federal aid.

Over and above the constitutional, legal and moral guarantees afforded to investors in New York City notes and bonds is the fact that they are investing in the world's wealthiest and soundest city as far as these obligations are concerned. . . .

This picture should be very reassuring to all city investors.

A recitation of these facts should by no means be construed as complacency in the face of the city's budget difficulties. While we have not always agreed on ways and means to place the budget in balance, we do agree that tough fiscal decisions and reforms, including substantial capital budget reductions, will have to be made in order to cope with runaway inflation, unemployment, business recession and the carryover effects of past fiscal practices. . . .

We will do what needs to be done in the general interest of taxpayers, for the preservation and strengthening of the city's economy and to insure the continuing soundness of the city's obligations as an investment medium.

NEWS RELEASE,
OFFICE OF THE COMPTROLLER,
DECEMBER 1, 1974:

. . . the budget deficit "should not impair confidence in the essential soundness and safety of the City's obligations."

SPEECH BY THE COMPTROLLER,
DECEMBER 20, 1974
(AT THE CITY CLUB OF NEW YORK):

New York's budget problems should be of only marginal interest to investors, who are protected by the State Constitutional guarantee making New York City bonds and notes a first lien on all revenues.

JOINT STATEMENT OF MAYOR
AND COMPTROLLER, JANUARY 11, 1975:

This City is not bankrupt, near bankrupt nor will it ever be bankrupt. This City has always repaid all of its obligations on time and it always will.

NEWS RELEASE, OFFICE OF COMPTROLLER,
MARCH 4, 1975:

For the truth is that from the time of the Revolutionary War, through the dark days of the Great Depression, and in every era of national economic uncertainty—New York City has compiled an unblemished record of full payment of bond principal and interest without a single default.

Investors in New York City securities are, therefore, absolutely protected.

NEWS RELEASE,
OFFICE OF THE COMPTROLLER,
MARCH 13, 1975:

We have experienced an insistent drumbeat of publicity on our budget problems, and this publicity has sometimes unfortunately failed to distinguish between balancing a budget, which *is* a problem; and meeting obligations to our creditors, which the City has never failed to do and which, it is my conviction, it never *will* fail to do, barring a complete collapse of our economic system and capital markets....

So the impact on New York of national and international inflation and recession which has affected all cities, is a separate issue, which should be of only marginal interest to investors.

NOTES

1. Interview with Mayor Beame—July 11, 1978.
2. Ibid.
3. SEC Report, "Transactions in the Securities of the City of New York," Subcommittee on Economic Stabilization of the Committee on Banking, Finance, and Urban Affairs—House of Representatives, 95th Congress, First Session, August 1977. U.S. Government Printing Office, Washington: 1977, chapter 3, p. 2.
4. City Report to the SEC, Nov. 23, 1976, ch. 2, p. 18.
5. City Report, ch. 2, p. 23.
6. City Report, ch. 2, p. 83.
7. SEC Report, ch. 3, p. 23.
8. Ibid.
9. SEC Report, ch. 2, p. 66.
10. Ibid.
11. *New York Times*, Nov. 4, 1974.
12. Response of the City of New York to the Report of the Staff of the SEC on Transactions in Securities of the City of New York, p. 14.
13. Interview with Dr. Herbert Rauschburg—June 28, 1978.
14. SEC Report, ch. 2, sec. 1, part B, pp. 8 ff.
15. SEC Report, ch. 2, p. 102.
16. SEC Report, ch. 2, p. 104.
17. SEC Report, ch. 3, p. 28.
18. SEC Report, ch. 3, p. 26.
19. Rauschburg Interview—June 28, 1978.
20. Interview with Jac Friedgut—June 15, 1978.
21. SEC Report, ch. 3, p. 23.
22. Ibid.
23. Interview with Harrison Goldin—July 18, 1978.
24. SEC Report, ch. 3, p. 38.
25. Response to the SEC, p. 68.
26. SEC Report, ch. 3, p. 39.
27. Beame Interview—July 11, 1978.
28. SEC Report, ch. 3, p. 27.
29. SEC Report, ch. 3, p. 26.
30. Interview with Steven Clifford—July 31, 1978.
31. SEC Report, Introduction, p. 3.
32. Ibid.
33. SEC Report, Chronology, p. 27.
34. Goldin Interview—July 18, 1978.
35. SEC Report, Chronology, p. 260.
36. SEC Report, ch. 3, p. 123.
37. Ibid., p. 122.
38. SEC Report, Chronology, p. 84.
39. Beame Interview—July 11, 1978.
40. Friedgut Interview—June 15, 1978.
41. Ibid.
42. Goldin Interview—July 18, 1978.

43. Friedgut Interview—June 15, 1978.
44. SEC Report, ch. 4, pp. 32 ff.
45. Ibid.

46. Beame Interview—July 11, 1978.
47. Ibid.
48. *New York Times,* Aug. 27, 1977, p. 1.

Comment

Mayor Beame and other officials denied that they made any false statements and also denied that they should have disclosed more than they did. As Beame said, "Anybody who didn't know what was going on was either asleep or had his head in the sand." Which (if any) officials' statements were so misleading as to constitute deception? Could there have been deceptive practices even if no one intended to deceive the public?

Beame and other officials gave, or could have given, two kinds of arguments to defend deception in this case. The first is, strictly speaking, a justification, and it appeals to the harmful consequences that full disclosure would have had for the city. In the face of such a claim, we should ask: (1) Who would have been harmed by the truth and to what degree? (2) What was the likelihood that disclosure would have actually produced these harmful consequences? If you think you need further information to answer these questions in this case, state precisely what it is and show how it would affect your conclusion about the justifiability of the deception.

The second kind of argument that city officials could give is better understood as an excuse than as a justification, since it concedes that unjustified deception occurred and seeks to eliminate or mitigate the blame that would otherwise fall on the officials. Beame and Goldin claimed that they did not know, or at least did not fully appreciate, the fact that the city counted as expected income real estate taxes on property that the city itself owned. Their claim is plausible, since it usually took a long time for the change of ownership of such property to show up on the books. Moreover, we would normally blame lower-level officials in such cases. But did Beame's actions or omissions discourage lower-level officials from questioning the estimate? And, if so, should Beame (or any other higher-level official) at least share responsibility for the misleading records?

Some commentators have argued that the issue of deception in this case is only part of the larger question of the political power exercised by the ruling economic elite in the city. They suggest that the collapse of the market was planned by bankers, corporate leaders, and government officials in order to force cuts in services that benefited the poor (for example, the low transit fare, daycare centers, hospitals, and free tuition at city university). What evidence would you need and what theoretical assumptions would you have to make in order to assess this argument?

Recommended Reading

The best survey of the problem of deception is Sissela Bok, *Lying: Moral Choice in Public and Private Life* (New York: Random House, 1979), especially chapters 1, 2, 4, 6 to 8, and 12. The appendix provides substantial excerpts from works by Augustine, Aquinas, Bacon, Grotius, Kant, Sidgwick, Harrod, Bonhoeffer, and Warnock. Also, see Bok's more recent book on a topic that is directly relevant to the problem of deception: *Secrets: On the Ethics of Concealment and Revelation* (New York: Pantheon, 1982), especially chapters 8, 12, 14, 17, and 18. Also, see Hannah Arendt, "Truth and Politics," in P. Laslett and W. G. Runciman (eds.), *Philosophy, Politics and Society*, third series (Oxford: Blackwell, 1967), pp. 104–33, and Charles Fried, *Right and Wrong* (Cambridge, Mass.: Harvard University Press, 1978), chapter 3.

On the fiscal crisis, see Charles Morris, *The Cost of Good Intentions: New York City and the Liberal Experiment* (New York: Norton, 1980), especially pp. 215–40; and Dennis Thompson, "Moral Responsibility and the New York City Fiscal Crisis," in J. Fleishman et al. (eds.), *Public Duties* (Cambridge, Mass.: Harvard University Press, 1981), pp. 266–85.

3 Using Citizens as Means and Breaking Promises

Introduction

"Treat man always as an end, never merely as a means." For Kant this was one version of the fundamental principle of morality, a principle that would prohibit absolutely all kinds of immoral actions. But even moral philosophers who are less absolutist recognize the principle as an important one. It expresses respect for the freedom of persons, telling us that we should not use other people only to serve our own purposes.

Notice that the principle does not say people may never be used as means, only that they should not be used *merely* as means. If you agree to let yourself be used for someone else's purposes, you are not being used merely as a means; your consent protects your freedom as an independent moral agent.

The trouble is, however, that some people may agree to be used without being fully aware of what they are agreeing to or without feeling fully free from pressure to agree to it. This is most likely when the agreement is between unequal parties — as when the government deals with individual citizens or small groups of citizens. In such encounters, governmental officials not only have more information and power than private citizens, but also can often claim to be pursuing nobler aims. Because officials serve the whole society (or imagine that they do), they may sometimes be justified and other times tempted to use some citizens as means of furthering projects that benefit other citizens.

Nowhere do these justifications and temptations seem stronger than in social experimentation, in which the government undertakes large-scale studies of proposed programs to see what their effects would be if they were enacted. Such experiments have been much more numerous and extensive than most people realize. With staffs and subjects numbering in the thousands and budgets in the millions, government-sponsored experiments in recent years have studied housing allowances, educational vouchers, educational performance contracts, health insurance plans, and guaranteed income programs. The Denver Income Maintenance Experiment (DIME) was part of the largest of these experiments, and it vividly illustrates most of their ethical problems.

The case is especially instructive because the officials themselves were aware of some of the ethical issues and even wrote memos about them. At the time, the experiment seemed to most to be benign and fully justifiable. But a closer look at it suggests a more complex judgment. Arguably, the subjects were induced to take part in a project that changed their lives in ways they were not told about and in ways some of them did not like. Insofar as the experiment benefited the subjects, citizens who were not given the opportunity to take part might complain, as some did, that the experimenters had been unfair to them. The case forces us to develop criteria for deciding when citizens may be used as means in governmental projects and when citizens may be said to consent to participation in them.

The DIME did not turn out the way officials had planned, and it had to be ended early. Because of the termination, the case raises a second set of issues: when do governments have moral commitments to citizens and under what conditions, if any, may those commitments be overridden? Few moral philosophers claim that commitments or promises may never be broken, but most have insisted that they may be broken only under special conditions. A promise may be overridden, for example, if circumstances have changed in ways that neither party could have foreseen when the promise was made. In politics, circumstances are always changing in unexpected ways, and many well-intentioned projects go awry. We therefore need to be quite careful about invoking "changed circumstances" to justify setting aside a promise the government makes. An assessment of what the government did with families in the DIME at the end of the experiment requires developing criteria for governments to follow when they have to pick up the pieces of projects that turn out badly.

The Denver Income Maintenance Experiment

Dennis Thompson

The Denver Income Maintenance Experiment (DIME) was the last in a series of four government-sponsored studies designed to discover to what extent (if any) recipients of a guaranteed income would change their behavior—chiefly whether they would work less. Policymakers hoped to use the results of the research to assess various income maintenance programs the government might

Copyright © 1980 by the Woodrow Wilson School, Princeton University. Reprinted by permission.

adopt (such as a negative income tax). The experiments constituted the largest, most sophisticated social research on public policy that the government had yet undertaken. Several leading social scientists wrote in 1978 that "the research represents a peak in the present state of the art and will become an important exemplar for future studies."

Some 4,800 families took part in the Seattle-Denver experiment, more than 70 percent in programs that lasted only three years and 25 percent in five-year programs. The rest comprised the DIME twenty-year group, whose characteristics in other respects matched the larger groups. In the twenty-year sample none of the families earned more than $5,000 a year before the experiment and most less than $3,000.

All of the experiments attempted to isolate the effects of income maintenance from the various other factors that might affect the work behavior of families who received the guaranteed income. A predetermined number of families who met the requirements for enrollment for each experiment were randomly selected and assigned to experimental or control groups. The experimental groups received income payments under one of several plans. These plans differed in the amount of income guaranteed to the families (the "basic benefit," which ranged from 50 percent to 135 percent of the poverty line), and in the proportion by which the guaranteed income would be reduced for each dollar of other income the family earned (the "benefit reduction rate," which ranged from 30 percent to 80 percent). Families in the experimental groups reported their income and household composition every month, and were interviewed several times a year. Families in the control groups received no benefit payments from the experiment but remained eligible for any welfare and Food Stamp assistance to which they were entitled. They received a small payment for the information they supplied to interviewers several times a year.

Although the Office of Economic Opportunity initiated the early research, the Department of Health, Education and Welfare administered the later experiments including DIME. Funding for DIME came from the Office of the Assistant Secretary for Planning and Evaluation, under a provision of the Social Security Act that authorized policy research. The Assistant Secretary (or his Deputy) formulated general policy on the experiments and supervised the work of contractors. The primary contractor was the Colorado Department of Social Services, which subcontracted with the Stanford Research Institute (SRI) to design the program and conduct data analysis, and with Mathematica Policy Research (MPR) to collect the data and administer the payments to the families. MPR maintained the only list of the names and addresses of the families enrolled in the program. The President of MPR had earlier demonstrated that he would go to jail rather than relinquish this list. No one at HEW ever knew the identities of the families in DIME (except for one man who sued the government, alleging that his wife had left him because of the independent income the experiment gave her).

THE DECISION TO INITIATE THE TWENTY-YEAR EXPERIMENT

Critics of the earlier experiments, as well as some of the researchers conducting them, had suspected that the short duration (three or even five years) could bias the conclusions. If subjects know that the experiment will end in a few years, they may be less likely to quit their jobs, or make other drastic changes in their habits of work, than they would if they expected the income guaranteed to continue indefinitely. Also, in a temporary experiment, especially when increased earnings reduced the benefits, some subjects such as women who worked part-time might try to reduce the amount of time they worked during the experiment, postponing until the experiment ended employment they might otherwise have accepted.

To answer these objections, SRI in 1973 proposed the formation of a new experimental group that would continue for twenty years. They suggested that this twenty-year subsample, when compared with the five-year group, would give a better indication of "the true long-run responses" of families in actual government programs, which (it was assumed) citizens perceive to be relatively permanent. HEW's project director for DIME, Joseph Corbett, tentatively approved the proposal in July 1973 and told SRI to submit for Departmental review a precise description of the procedures they would follow. MPR prepared the description, and SRI forwarded it to Corbett in August, 1973. During the next six months, HEW modified its contract with SRI to include the new research, and HEW officials began reviewing the proposal.

On March 4, 1974, the Assistant Secretary for Planning and Evaluation, William Morrill, wrote to the Undersecretary of HEW, recommending approval of a twenty-year subsample in DIME. He explained the need for such a sample (more or less as the SRI proposal had done) and then he added:

> While we plan to tell the families that the program will continue for 20 years, it is not necessary to run this experiment for the full 20 years to obtain the required information we desire. The true long run response of these families, who will expect the program to last for 20 years, can be observed by comparing their responses over a 5-year period with the responses of families participating in the shorter term experiments, who will expect their guarantee to last only 3–5 years.
>
> Hence, unless we find other compelling research reasons for continuing the families on the program for the full time period, we tentatively plan to terminate this new treatment group at the end of 5 years, giving the families a lump sum payment at that time to compensate them for the early termination of the program.
>
> In order to eliminate any ethical issues relating to the early termination of the 20-year sample, families would be given a choice at that time as to whether to accept the lum sum payment or to continue receiving their regular benefits. A plan for ad-

ministering the continued benefits would be developed during the course of the experiment.

The Assistant Secretary circulated this memo within the Department and encouraged extensive discussion. Other officials raised three major objections. First, the Undersecretary questioned the assumption that citizens perceive regular welfare programs to be more permanent than income maintenance experiments. To answer this question, the subcontractors conducted a survey in Seattle and Denver, and found that lower-income families have "a very high expectation for long run continuity of government cash transfer programs," whereas they expect experiments to last only a few years. Officials interpreted the survey as confirming the need for the twenty-year experiment, which would create expectations closer to those of citizens in a permanent program of income maintenance.

The Commissioner of Welfare, Robert Carleson, while not objecting to the general plan for a twenty-year experiment, criticized the specific proposal that "the subsample be terminated at five years and that lump sum payments be made." He argued that some of the families would almost certainly find out that the experiment would end in the fifth year, and would therefore adjust their behavior so that they would remain eligible for the monthly payment in that year and thus for the lump-sum payment. Even if officials managed to keep the plan secret, to give a lump-sum payment to those who happened to remain eligible in the fifth year would be arbitrary.

The Administrator for Social and Rehabilitation Service, James Dwight, raised a third objection, more explicitly ethical. On March 20, he wrote to Morrill:

> I continue to have serious reservations about the value of this experiment when contrasted with the ethical issues regarding public policy. The survey which was taken

reflects the perception that public programs will exist for 5 to 20 years at least. This leaves unanswered the question of to what extent this perception influences personal behavior. In answering this, as proposed, the involved families may: (1) take on long-range debt commitments; (2) decide to have more children than they otherwise would; (3) decide on early retirement; or (4) decide to forego savings or life insurance. In some cases the 5-year lump-sum terminations may have traumatic effects and may involve adverse publicity and lawsuits. If, on the other hand, it was emphasized that the transfer payments might be stopped at *any time,* the effect of the experiment would be negated. This issue of how to design this experiment must be viewed in the context of the serious questions raised about the ethics of using people as guinea pigs in research experiments without fully disclosing possible consequences.

After further discussions within the Department, the Assistant Secretary, Morrill sent an "action memorandum" to the Undersecretary on April 18, again recommending establishing a twenty-year group but this time without a "termination option":

> Under our proposed plan about 100 of the 5,000 families participating in the Seattle/Denver Experiment would be reassigned from a control group status to a new 20-year financial treatment. Because for research purposes we only need to maintain the new subsample for 5 years, we had earlier considered terminating the program at the end of 5 years and giving the families a lump-sum payment at that time to compensate them for the early ending of the program. The early termination with compensation option was proposed since it was thought that it would both satisfy our research needs and lessen our administrative burden and costs. However, in order to eliminate any possible ethical issues that might arise from the early termination option, we have revised our proposal to eliminate the option. Thus, we now propose to continue the program for the full twenty years.

> I would also like to respond to the points raised by Bob Carleson and Jim Dwight... Bob had no objection to the proposal except that he recommended that we continue the program for the full twenty years. Jim similarly expressed practical and ethical concerns about the early termination option. Our revision of the proposal to eliminate this option should satisfy their concerns. I hope this revision will also satisfy your concerns about the ethical issues involved in this proposal.

The Undersecretary approved the proposal, subject to some further consultation within the Department, and enrollment of the twenty-year group began in July 1974.

Initially, the experiment included about 110 families. The sample was kept small because of the high cost per family in a twenty-year study, and because SRI believed that even this small sample would reveal any large differences in behavior between the twenty-year group and the three- and five-year groups. However, for two different reasons, the sample soon had to be expanded. First, it turned out that many families in the original sample earned too much to benefit from the income maintenance payments, and that therefore the number of families actually receiving DIME payments would be too small to yield significant experimental results. Consequently, researchers added more families to the sample (evidently about 60). These families had been members of the three-year experimental group (unlike the original sample of 110 who came from the three-year control groups). HEW officials made sure that no family suffered financially as result of the transfer.

A second reason for the increase in the sample arose out of criticisms Mexican-American activists directed against DIME. The Mexican-American Legal Defense and Education Fund (MALDEF) complained that no Spanish-surnamed families had been invited to participate in the DIME, and charged that this exclusion represented discrimination against Mexican-Americans. Jacob Shockley, DIME project Director for the Colorado Department of Social Services, reported this charge to Corbett in Washington and warned that MALDEF might file a suit or make a complaint to HEW's Office of Civil Rights. Shockley noted that already the Regional Office of HEW had cited his own department for violations of regulations on affirmative action. Robert Williams, project director of DIME for MPR in Denver, wrote to SRI expressing similar worries. R. G. Spiegelman, SRI's project manager, then recommended to Corbett that twenty-five to thirty Mexican-American families be added to the twenty-year sample. Spiegelman's memorandum at one point referred to the "political implications of omitting such a sample," but mostly stressed the research value of including the Mexican-Americans. SRI had originally declined to add a sample of Mexican-Americans because of the additional cost and because the staff believed they could, from the other populations, extrapolate conclusions about Mexican-Americans. Now Spiegelman decided that the extrapolation would be too experimentally "risky" and thought "it would be preferable" to avoid it. Corbett and other HEW officials accepted the recommendation to add the Mexican-Americans to the DIME. By January 1975, the researchers had completed the expansion of the sample, which now totaled 195 families, including both those subjects added from the previous experimental groups and the new Mexican-Americans.

The MPR staff in Denver, supervised by Williams, enrolled the families in the experiment. Nearly all of the staff had experience in administering the earlier experiments, and now received additional training and detailed instructions. The

"enrollers" made personal contact with each family, presenting a package of materials, which included a letter inviting the family to join the experiment, and an agreement stipulating the terms of their participation. Shockley had written the letter, at the request of Spiegelman, who believed that the signature of a representative of the State government would enhance the credibility of the invitation and especially of the twenty-year guarantee. That the families believe this guarantee, Spiegelman wrote, is "of crucial importance to the success of the experiment." About the guarantee, Shockley's letter said:

> It is the intent of the Federal government to continue your family's income guarantee for a period of twenty years. Should it be necessary for the government to terminate this program before twenty years have elapsed, the government's plan is to make a cash settlement with your family to help cover the unused portion of your income guarantee period. [For full text, see Appendix I]

The staff member gave each family a copy of the letter, and explained the experiment and its rules. Enrollers were instructed to:

> ...explain that it is the intent of the government to run the program for 20 years. In response to questions, enrollers would be able to tell families that the government could cancel the program at any time, as it could do with any program, but that if the program were cancelled, it is the government's intention to compensate them. The amount of such compensation would depend on the size of the grant they are receiving at the time the program is terminated, the length of time the guarantee period has to run, and the availability of government funds.

There is no record of how many (if any) families asked questions about possible termination, nor is there any information about what enrollers actually told the families. The enrollment agreement, which the enrollers asked each head of household to sign, included this provision:

> Finally, I understand that my participation in the program is governed by the provisions of the *Rules of Operation* (a copy of the summary of which had been provided to me) and that while it is the intention of the Government to continue the program for twenty years, both the operation of the program and the duration of the payments are subject to modification as determined by the Secretary of Health, Education and Welfare, or his designee. [For full text, see Appendix II].

THE DECISION TO TERMINATE THE EXPERIMENT

In November 1978, staff from HEW, SRI, the state governments of Washington and Colorado and MPR's Denver office met in Menlo Park, California, to discuss the conclusion of SRI's "Analysis of the Labor Supply Response of the Twenty Year Families in the DIME." The first conclusion seemed innocuous: the study found no statistically significant "labor supply response" by the twenty-year group during the first year of the experiment. More ominous were two other conclusions—both raising the old worry about the size of the sample. The study found that the enlarged sample had not adequately met the problem. The sample was still too small to yield statistically significant comparisons and estimates. But the fatal blow came from the study's conclusion that "the nonrandom assignment of families to the twenty-year program...makes it extremely difficult to interpret any responses estimated for this group." Apparently no one had noticed that, among other things, the subjects in the experimental group had worked significantly less in the year before the experiment than had subjects in the control group. Various attempts to correct for

this difference proved unsatisfactory. Everyone at the Menlo Park meeting reluctantly but unequivocally agreed that the experiment had no research value.* The participants at the meeting concluded that families should be disenrolled as soon as suitable arrangements could be made, but they left unresolved the question of what compensation should be provided to the families. HEW initiated several further meetings and conversations with nearly all officials and groups involved in the experiment (though not with any of the families or their representatives).

In late January, 1979, Thomas Harper (of MPR's subsidiary, the Council for Grants to Families) in a letter to the families announced some changes in the rules of the program. No longer would interviewers collect data from the families, and no longer would benefits increase when the cost of living rose. New family members could not now join the program as easily as before. The letter also said:

> Although the interviews are ending, the payment program continues under revised Rules of Operation.... The DIME has been a successful study which has supplied significant information to the government. This information has already helped the government respond to the welfare needs of families throughout the country. The changes being made in the DIME program will not diminish that success.

---

*The participants relied chiefly on a paper by Philip K. Robins and Gary L. Stieger, "The Labor Supply Response of Twenty-Year Families in the Denver Income Maintenance Experiment," Menlo Park, Calif.: SRI International, 1978. A more recent review confirms the seriousness of the error in the expansion of the sample, but nevertheless draws some conclusions about the effect of income maintenance and suggests that continuing the experiment might have yielded some useful data about single female heads of families. See Robins and Stieger, "An Analysis of the Labor Supply Response of Twenty-Year Families in the D.I.M.E." Menlo Park, Calif.: SRI International, April 1980 (draft).

Now HEW officials turned to the question of what to do with the families in the DIME. A memorandum from Spiegelman at SRI outlined some of the issues that they considered. Any decision would have to recognize HEW's "obligations to the public": taxpayers could reasonably object to continuation of a program that yielded absolutely no research value. Spiegelman mentioned two kinds of "obligations to the families"—legal and moral. On legal obligations, SRI's attorney wrote: "The use of the words 'intent' and 'plan' in the agreement and the statements to the families indicate the 'good intentions' of the government rather than a legal commitment. Nevertheless, this is a difficult legal question." HEW's legal counsel later concluded that the government had no legal obligation at all to continue the income payments or even to offer any significant lump sum settlement, though some officials in HEW thought that some of the families, encouraged by welfare rights lawyers, might decide to sue.

The discussion of the moral obligations to the families seemed to take for granted that early termination was justified, and concentrated on the moral criteria that the procedures for termination should satisfy. First, safeguards should be provided to protect the families from exploitation in any negotiations with the government about the amount of a settlement. Later, other officials mentioned this point in arguing against any negotiations at all with the families. They wanted to avoid any direct discussions with the families or their representatives. Now that the government itself had financed and encouraged the growth of welfare rights organizations and legal aid offices, HEW officials felt they had to treat almost any contact with clients as a potential subject of litigation or formal complaint. As one HEW official remarked, "it may be on balance a good thing that citizens can now easily threaten bureaucrats like me with legal action, but it sure does change the way I can deal with the people in our programs. It's much more impersonal and distant."

The second moral criterion in the Spiegelman memo held that any termination settlement should recognize the fact that families may have made choices on the expectation that the program would continue, and would suffer serious losses when the income payments ceased. What recognizing this fact meant became clearer in Spiegelman's analysis of the "multiplier" that would determine the termination payments:

It is generally agreed that the program has a moral, if not legal, obligation to assure the families that they will be no worse off as a result of DIME participation than if they had not participated at all. The program must, therefore, underwrite the consequences of choices made that place them in jeopardy should the program be cancelled. They may have quit their job, had children, bought a home, moved to some preferred location, etc. Whatever their actions we owe them the time and resources to recover and return to a normal situation. The multiplier is viewed as an expression of the number of months the program is willing to support the family while it adjusts to a non-DIME environment of work and public support.

For some families, who are not dependent on DIME at all, a multiplier of zero months would be adequate to ensure their transition. Other families may never eliminate their dependency on DIME or some other form of public support. For these dependent families, a multiplier of 192 months, reflecting the entire period remaining in the agreement, might seem justified. But the fact of the availability of other public support is a convincing argument against it. Further, the discounted value of such a cash stream, using present bank interest rates indicates that a multiplier of 95 would purchase an equivalent annuity. And, assuming that the families would be eligible for other public support a multipler of less than 50 would provide an annuity that in combination would give the family the equivalent of the DIME program stipend. If it is argued that the program is really only morally obligated to help the family return to its former status a multiplier as high as 50 cannot be justified. The participants in our first seminar felt, intuitively, that a more appropriate period would be represented by a multiplier in the range of 24–30 months.

By the fall of 1979, Ben W. Heineman, Jr., who was now the Assistant Secretary, had decided against continuing payments to the families for the next fifteen years; he favored providing benefits at most for three years, making each monthly check somewhat smaller than the previous one (as a way of ensuring that families realized the payments would end). Before he could implement the decision, he resigned, and John Palmer, his principal deputy, became Acting Assistant Secretary in November, 1979. Palmer was inclined to agree with his predecessor's decision and prepared a draft memorandum justifying the decision and explaining how it would be implemented. Palmer's argument against continuing the program or offering a larger settlement was that "there is an implicit *quid pro quo* involved in participation in such an experiment and that since there is no longer any benefit to taxpayers and the Federal government in continuing the experiment, there is no reason for taxpayers to continue funding benefit payments that exceed AFDC plus Food Stamps and the added administrative costs."

Palmer also feared that to request from Congress the large appropriation necessary to continue the program or to provide large lump sum payments would create adverse public reaction, and jeopardize possibilities for policy research in the future. Already Senator William Armstrong of Colorado had publicly condemned the experiment as a waste of public funds. Officials in HEW's Legislative Liaison Office talked informally to members of the staff of some of the other Colorado delegations, who usually could be counted on to support HEW's liberal programs, but found little enthusiasm for the additional appropriations that would be necessary to give the DIME families a large settlement. Generally, the mood in Congress, effectively expressed in several unusual budget-cutting resolutions, threatened many of HEW's most important programs. At this point, however, the Liaison Office did not recommend against any settlement that would require Congressional approval. They did not want to seem to be in the position of ruling out the right course of action simply because it was not politically expedient; they presumably hoped that Palmer and his staff would reach the conclusion that a smaller settlement was justifiable on the merits.

The President of MPR and some of his staff had argued vigorously with HEW officials, insisting that the government had a moral commitment to continue the program for twenty years, or at least to provide a cash settlement that would be equivalent to what families would have received if the program had continued for twenty years. Like Spiegelman, they pointed out that the families may have relied on the government's promise, perhaps making irreversible decisions such as having another child or retiring early, that they would not have otherwise made. Since it would be impossible to prove that people had not made such decisions on this basis, the government should assume that people had done so, and provide a settlement compatible with this assumption. In his draft memorandum in January, Palmer rejected this line of argument, maintaining that the families were probably made better off by participation in the experiment than they would have been if they had stayed in the regular welfare system. With a reasonable period of notice, they should be able to adjust to pre-experimental life quite easily, at least no worse off than before.

Nevertheless, Palmer still had some doubts. He was not absolutely sure that the government did not have an "inviolable commitment" to these families. He was also troubled by the fact that he himself had been officially, if not actually, responsible for initiating the twenty-year sample in 1974. While serving as Director of Income Security Policy then, he had not paid much attention to the experiment because higher officials, especially Morrill, had taken a personal interest in it and usually dealt directly with officials in Palmer's Office of Research. But now Palmer thought that because of his own previous responsibility (however nominal), he personally might have some special obligation to the families, and that the government's commitment therefore might be stronger than it would have otherwise been. In early 1980, Michael Barth, Palmer's Deputy Assistant Secretary for Income Security Policy, while preparing the materials to implement the decision expressed in Palmer's draft memo, came to the conclusion that the decision was wrong. He persuaded Palmer at least to delay implementing it until Barth could conduct another review of the "options for termination."

Barth was well placed to help Palmer reach an objective decision. Barth had not held office when the DIME began; nor had he participated in major decisions about the experiment. Moreover, he intended for personal reasons to leave government shortly after Palmer made his decision, and could not be suspected of recommending a course of action mainly because it seemed easier to implement. He also believed that the Department on its own should determine the right course of action, and not pass the buck to Congress. Department officials should neither

ask Congress for a larger settlement than they themselves believed justified, nor should they refrain from proposing a larger settlement simply because they thought Congress might reject it. Barth began discussions with other officials in the Department, the contractors' offices and Congress, and then prepared a "background paper" drawing on these discussions and on earlier memoranda in the HEW files on the experiment.

Reviewing the current status of the program, Barth found that income maintenance payments for the families cost $500,000 in 1979. Administrative expenses added $200,000. To continue the program for the next fifteen years, as originally intended, would cost $9.2 million. The number of families had grown from 195 to 237 (adult family members who left their original families, and young adult family members who set up households of their own, had been permitted to remain in the experiment). At the end of 1979, 18 families were receiving $601–900 a month; 52 families, $301–600 a month; 31 families, $21–300 a month; and 125 families the minimum payment of $20 a month.

In his background paper Barth outlined the major "alternate courses of action" that had been discussed within HEW. Those still under serious consideration were:

A. Continue the experiment for the full fifteen years.

1. *Income conditioned payments.* Continue to base payments on reports of income. This would require maintaining a payment apparatus for the families left on DIME. Expected cost: $9.17 million.*

---

*This figure, as well as those under the options that follow, does not take into account the cost of AFDC and Food Stamps for which some families would be eligible if DIME ended. Therefore, the true cost to the taxpayer of any of these options would be somewhat less than the figures given (though by how much it would be difficult to determine).

(Present discounted value, using an interest rate of 10%: $5.31 million.)

Pros

—Fulfills original stated intent of the Government.
—Fulfills probable expectations of an otherwise disadvantaged and therefore possibly specially vulnerable population.

Cons

—Can be argued to be irresponsible use of public funds appropriated for research purposes, since no further research value is gained.
—Ability to implement is questionable, since either annual appropriations for fourteen years *or* one or more large appropriations for this purpose would have to be sought.
—Requires maintenance of expensive administrative mechanism to process income reports for small number of families for fifteen years.
—May generate substantial adverse publicity, since sample would have little or no research value, and ethical justification would not be widely accepted.
—Adjustment problems for families when payments end may be substantially worse than under early termination.

2. *Non-income conditioned payments.* Drop income-conditioning and pay fixed monthly payments equal to average in base period until end of enrollment period. Administration by private carrier possible. Cost (as of January 1980): $8.27 million. (Present discounted value: $4.70 million.)

Pros

—Fulfills original stated intent of the Government if non-income-tested payments are accepted as a continuation of the program.
—Fulfills probable expectations of an otherwise disadvantaged and therefore possibly specially vulnerable population.

Cons

—Same as previous option except that administrative mechanism would be much simpler.
—Families would lose "insurance value" of income conditioned payments.
—As families' economic circumstances change over time, some high-income families might receive very large payments, generating adverse publicity and raising questions of responsible use of public funds.

B. Terminate with lump sum payments.
1. *Early termination with compensation for fifteen years of payments.* Terminate program in 1980 and provide lump-sum payments (possibly in quarterly installments) equal to present discounted value of fifteen-year stream of expected payments. Cost: 10% discount rate—$5.38 million; 15% discount rate—$4.48 million; 20% discount rate—$3.86 million.

Pros

—Fully discharges ethical obligation on families if lump-sum payment is viewed as acceptable substitute for monthly income-conditioned payments.

Cons

—Can be argued to be irresponsible use of public funds appropriated for research purposes because, in comparison with lower-cost options, this option gives no additional benefit.
—Ability to implement is questionable, since additional appropriation of $3–4 million in FY 80-81 would be required.
—Lump-sum payments averaging $14,000 to $20,000, and as high as $86,000 to a single family, would generate serious adverse publicity.
—Calculation of expected future payments and selection of discount rate is arbitrary; may be hard to justify and defend in individual cases.

2. *Early termination with two-years' non-income-conditioned payments made in quarterly installments.* Terminate program in 1980, and make four fixed quar-

terly payments totalling twice the family's payments in the base year, subject to minimum of $500 and maximum of $12,000. Cost: $1.23 million.

Pros

—Clearly provides compensation for early termination.

—Provides fifteen-months lead time for families to adjust to cessation of payments; families know with certainty payments for last twelve months.

—Can be funded with available funds; no risk to families that plan won't be implemented for lack of funds.

Cons

—Does not discharge twenty-year commitment.

—Single payments of up to $3,000 may generate adverse publicity, and create budgeting problems for the families.

—Doubling the family's payments during the transition year may make adjustment problems worse, rather than better.

C. Terminate with non-income-conditioned transition payments.

1. *Three-year declining payment options.* Terminate payments in 1980, and provide three years of non-income-conditioned monthly transition payments equal initially to the family's average payment in a recent twelve-month base period. Payments decline 1.25% per month so that the final payment is 65% of the initial transition payment. Optional accelerated payments of up to $500 per month available. Assist families through counseling and other means to move into post-experimental life. Cost: $1.47 million.

Pros

—Fulfills obligation to families as defined in enrollment documents if transition payments are interpreted as compensation for early cessation of NIT payments.

—Provides at least thirty-six months lead time for families to adjust to end of payments.

—Payments are easy to calculate, explain, and administer.

—Can be funded with available funds; no risk to families that plan won't be implemented for lack of funds.

—Monthly payments probably less disruptive to family budgeting than lump sums or quarterly payments.

Cons

—May appear to be termination without compensation, in violation of Enrollment Agreement.

—Decline in transition payments renders recipients less well-off without providing enough stimulus to seek alternative means of support.

2. *Six-month option.* Using the unemployment compensation system as a guide, advise families that the government intends to terminate the program and that benefits will be phased out over a six-month period. Initial month's benefit would be the same as that in the previous option (i.e., the family's average payment in the prior twelve months). The phase-out might or might not involve a declining payment. Cost: with constant payment— $300,000; with phase-out of 10% per month—$185,000.

Pros

—Gives DIME twenty-year participants the same benefit period as unemployed persons.

Cons

—Does not discharge twenty-year commitment.

—Does not provide families with enough time to consider options and change plans.

Barth presented these options to three outside consultants whom he asked to recommend "the soundest course of action," specifically taking into account "moral/ethical" factors. On May 7, 1980, the consultants presented their recommendations, which ranged from a modified version of C.2 to versions of B.1.

Barth reported that officials in Colorado's Department of Social Services and HEW's Regional Office in Denver with whom he had talked favored some version of C.1. So apparently did some staff members of key Congressional delegations. The staff of Senator Gary Hart, who might have been expected to support a more generous settlement for the families, never responded to Barth's inquiries. From Senator Armstrong's previous public statements, HEW officials had inferred that he would disapprove of continuing the payments for more than a few months.

In June 1980, Palmer decided in favor of C.1. In addition, Palmer instituted a program of counseling and support to help the families during the period of transition. On July 11, he sent Secretary Patricia Harris a memorandum informing her of his decision. In September 1980, the department, now the Department of Health and Human Services (HHS), announced the end of the DIME. The families received their first transition payments in October.

Appendix I

State of Colorado
DEPARTMENT OF SOCIAL SERVICES

Dear Family:

You have been asked by a member of the staff of the Council for Grants to Families (a subsidiary of Mathematica, Inc.) to enroll in an experimental national income maintenance program funded by the United States Government through the state of Colorado. Under this program, you will be offered an annual income guarantee. The purpose of the experimental program is to help the government design an income maintenance program that will be best for the country. The experimental program contributes to this purpose by showing how various programs affect families. It is the intent of the Federal government to continue your family's income guarantee for a period of twenty years. Should it be necessary for the government to terminate this program before twenty years have elapsed, the government's plan is to make a cash settlement with your family to help cover the unused portion of your income guarantee period.

Each family asked to join the program has been selected at random from among similar families in Denver and is representative of many other families living in the area. I would like personally to urge you to join the program, as your participation is essential to its success.

If you have any questions concerning the program or your participation in it, please do not hesitate to call me. My number is 892-2556.

Sincerely,

COLORADO DEPARTMENT OF SOCIAL SERVICES

JACOB SHOCKLEY, PROJECT DIRECTOR
DENVER INCOME MAINTENANCE EXPERIMENT

Appendix II

COUNCIL FOR GRANTS TO FAMILIES

ENROLLMENT AGREEMENT

I agree to participate in the Denver Income Maintenance Experiment until _____ , 1994. A representative of the Council for Grants to Families has explained the program to me.

I agree to report to the Council every month all the income from all sources received by me and by all members of my family who are included in the program and to report promptly to the Council any change in address or in the number of people living with my family.

I also agree to take periodic interviews as requested by Urban Opinion Surveys, a division of Mathematica, Inc., or its successor, and to provide such other full and truthful information as may be required to conduct the experiment. I understand that any information given by me to Urban Opinion Surveys or the Council for Grants to Families will be used only to evaluate the program, will be held in strict confidence, and will never be released to any person without my written permission except if required by law.

I am aware that my family will not be eligible to receive payments from the Council above the minimum ($20 per month) for any period in which any member of my family is receiving Aid to Families with Dependent Children (AFDC).

I understand that my family will be eligible for a grant payment from the Council each month calculated according to the rules of the program. I also understand that the grant payments paid to my family are ours to use in any way we wish and that, unless we give incorrect information about our income, family size, or residential address, or receive payments in excess of those provided under the rules of the program, we will never be required to return any part of this money.

I understand further that the Council may add to my monthly payments reimbursement for some or all of my federal and state income tax payments (including social security payments), but that the Council may require repayment if it reimburses more than provided under the rules of the program during any calendar year.

Finally, I understand that my participation in the program is governed by the provisions of the Rules of Operation (a copy of the summary of which has been provided to me) and that while it is the intention of the Government to continue the program for twenty years, both the operation of the program and the duration of the payments are subject to modification as determined by the Secretary of Health, Education and Welfare or his designee.

Signed _____   Date _____
         Male Head of Household

      _____   Date _____
         Female Head of Household

Approved _____   Date _____
         Project Manager

Comment

It is a good idea to separate your analysis of the two parts of this case—the initiation and the termination of the experiment. Otherwise, knowing the experiment turned out badly, you may conclude too quickly that it should never have begun and fail to appreciate the strength of the case in favor of the experiment as officials saw it in 1974. Similarly, if you dwell on the possibility that the problems in terminating the experiment in 1980 could have been avoided if the experiment had been better planned and executed, you may find it more difficult to focus specifically on what Palmer should have done with the families. Palmer faced a dilemma that is common in modern government: what should officials do when others have not done what they should have done?

The first part of this case calls for an analysis of the criteria that officials used in deciding to initiate the DIME. One type of criterion, stipulated in the government's own regulations, is utilitarian: the risks of harm to the participants must be outweighed by the sum of the benefits to the participants and the social importance of the knowledge to be gained from the experiment. What exactly were the risks and benefits to the subjects? What were the benefits to society? Did officials appraise the risks and benefits adequately?

Critics of the utilitarian criterion point out that it leaves participants quite vulnerable, justifying a lot of inconvenience and even harm to them when the social value of the experiment is great or can plausibly be described as such (e.g., "eliminating poverty in our time"). Defenders of the criterion argue that the short-term harms to the subjects, which are likely to be more certain than the speculative long-term benefits, will usually have more weight in any proper utilitarian calculation. Also, consider this modification of the utilitarian criterion (proposed by David Kershaw): the experiment must "restore the *status quo ante*—to assure that...subjects are left after the experiment as if it had never existed."

A second kind of criterion pays more attention to the rights of the participants: people may not be used in experiments without their informed consent. In many experiments, participants cannot be told everything without undermining the purpose of the experiment. Could the participants in DIME have been told more than officials told them without destroying the experiment? To justify using people in experiments, what must officials do to make sure participants understand what they are told?

The standard for consent is not only adequate information but also the absence of undue pressure. Did the payments to the DIME families amount to "undue enticement" and vitiate their free choice? It is generally assumed that the standards for consent in social and medical experiments must be stricter than for ordinary governmental programs even if the risks are no greater. Why or why not is this assumption correct?

The second part of the case concerns the government's commitment to the families. Did the government make a morally binding commitment or promise? Consider (1) the families' expectations—whether they had good reason to rely on the government's commitment, and (2) the harm the families might experience—whether they would actually suffer harm by having relied on the government's apparent promise. If, for practical or moral reasons, the government could not reliably determine what harm the families might suffer (as evidently was true), how does this affect the commitment?

Even if the government had a binding commitment, we still have to ask, Must the government fulfill it? Promises may sometimes be legitimately set aside. Since the experiment no longer served its original purpose, could one rightly claim that the government no longer owed the families anything (Palmer's *quid pro quo* argument)? Could one argue that the government owed the greater duty to all citizens, including taxpayers and citizens on welfare who are less well off than the families in the DIME?

The government should not be viewed as a monolithic moral agent in this case. Part of the problem here is whether administrators should on their own authority settle with families or turn the matter over to Congress (whose support was necessary for any larger settlement than the one Palmer chose). Is the belief that going to Congress would jeopardize other important programs in HEW a legitimate moral reason not to attempt any larger settlement? What if, by going to Congress, officials risked getting less for the families than the settlement HEW could provide out of its own budget?

Recommended Reading

Kant explains and defends his principle of treating persons as ends in the second section of the *Metaphysical Foundations of Morals* (Indianapolis: Bobbs-Merrill, 1959). An excellent exposition of Kant's moral theory as applied to politics is Jeffrie Murphy, *Kant: The Philosophy of Right* (London: Macmillan, 1970). On the utilitarian criterion, see the Recommended Reading in the Introduction.

Two useful collections on the ethics of social experimentation are: Alice Rivlin and P. Michael Timpane (eds.), *Ethical and Legal Issues of Social Experimentation* (Washington, D.C.: Brookings, 1975); and Gordon Bermant et al. (eds.), *The Ethics of Social Intervention* (Washington, D.C.: Hemisphere Pub., 1978). On the DIME, see Dennis Thompson, "The Ethics of Social Experimentation: The Case of the DIME," *Public Policy*, 29 (Summer 1981), pp. 369–98.

The criterion of informed consent may be illuminated by consulting some theoretical writings on political consent: see Hanna Pitkin, "Obligation and Consent—II," *American Political Science Review,* 60 (March 1966), pp. 39–52; Michael Walzer, *Obligations* (New York: Simon and Schuster, 1971); and A. John Simmons, *Moral Principles and Political Obligations* (Princeton, N.J.: Princeton University Press, 1979).

For recent philosophical discussions of promises, see Charles Fried, *Contract as Promise* (Cambridge, Mass.: Harvard University Press, 1981); H. A. Prichard, "The Obligation to Keep a Promise," in *Moral Obligation* (Oxford: Clarendon Press, 1949), pp. 169–79; John Rawls, *A Theory of Justice* (Cambridge, Mass.: Harvard University Press, 1971), pp. 344–48; and Henry Sidgwick, *Methods of Ethics* (London: Macmillan, 1962), pp. 303–11.

4 Official Disobedience

Introduction

What should public officials do when they disagree with governmental policy? For nonelected officials this question poses a particularly difficult dilemma. They are bound to carry out the orders of others, yet they should not act contrary to their own moral convictions. Their duty to carry out policy rests in part on the requirements of the democratic process. We do not want officials whom we cannot hold accountable to impose their own views on us, overriding the policies determined by the democratic process. We may assume, furthermore, that officials consent to the terms of office. They know in advance what is expected of them, and they should not hold office if they cannot accept a policy once it is formulated. On this view, the moral responsibilities of the nonelected public official are completely captured by the injunction, "obey or resign."

Critics of this view argue, first, that it underestimates the discretion that administrators exercise in modern governments. Neither the law nor their superiors can determine all their decisions, and they must use their own judgment in many matters. Second, if all public officials followed this injunction, public offices would soon be populated only by people who never had any inclination to disagree with anything the government decided to do. Men and women of strong moral conviction would always resign. Third, officials have broader obligations to the public—not merely obligations to their own conscience or to their superiors. "Obey or resign" presents too limited a menu of moral options. Officials may be warranted in staying in office and expressing their opposition in various ways—for example, by internal opposition, public protest, refusal to carry out the policy personally, supporting outside opponents of the policy, or direct obstruction.

The methods that seem the most difficult to accept are those that are illegal or violate governmental procedures and lawful orders of superiors. The justification for such tactics resembles in part the rationale for civil disobedience by citizens. A democratic society benefits from permitting moral dissent. Extreme measures are sometimes necessary to force democratic majorities and governments to recognize that they have made a serious mistake, and sometimes officials are the only people in a position to bring such a mistake to public attention.

79

But since it is an extreme measure, civil disobedience is generally thought to be justified only under certain conditions. Those who disobey must: (1) act publicly; (2) act nonviolently; (3) appeal to principles shared by other citizens; (4) direct their challenge against a substantial injustice; and (5) exhaust all normal channels of protest.

The cases in this chapter present three instances of official disobedience that can help you understand whether official disobedience is justified and if so under what conditions. The first case—a protest by attorneys in the Justice Department against their superiors' decision to delay school desegregation—seems the easiest to justify under the traditional criteria of civil disobedience, but some critics of the attorneys believed that their protest went too far and others suggested that it did not go far enough. The case also raises the question of the moral responsibility not only of lawyers but of all professionals who hold public office—for example, doctors, engineers, journalists, and teachers.

The other selections in this chapter invite a comparison of two instances of unauthorized disclosure (otherwise known as leaks). Otto Otepka, a State Department official, passed classified information to a congressional staff member in an effort to undermine the department's policy on security clearance, which he believed endangered national security. Daniel Ellsberg gave the classified Pentagon Papers to the *New York Times* to encourage opposition to the Vietnam War. Unlike the attorneys in "Revolt at Justice," Otepka and Ellsberg acted alone and in secret.

Revolt at Justice

Gary J. Greenberg

When a lawyer is admitted to the bar, he takes an oath to support the Constitution of the United States. When a lawyer joins the Department of Justice, he takes another oath—the same one that is taken by the Attorney General and, in fact, by all federal employees.

That oath reads:

I solemnly swear (or affirm) that I will support and defend the Constitution of the United States against all enemies, foreign and domestic, that I will bear true faith and

From *Inside the System,* edited by Charles Peters and Timothy J. Adams. Copyright ©1970 by The Washington Monthly Corp. Reprinted by permission of Holt, Rinehart and Winston, CBS College Publ.

allegiance to the same; that I take this obligation freely, and without any mental reservation or purpose of evasion; and that I will well and faithfully discharge the duties of the office on which I am about to enter. So help me God.

It was largely because of this oath—and the pressures we were under to violate it—that a majority of the attorneys from the Civil Rights Division of the Department of Justice gathered in a Washington apartment in August of 1969. We wanted to ascertain whether, under the Constitution, there was any legal argument that might conceivably support the Nixon Administration's request in a Mississippi courtroom, for a delay in implementing desegregation in thirty-three of that state's school districts. The assembled lawyers concluded that there was not. Thus was born the reluctant movement that the press was to call "the revolt" in the Civil Rights Division.

August 19, 1969, was a historic date in the field of civil rights. It was on that day that Robert H. Finch, the Secretary of Health, Education, and Welfare, in letters to the U.S. District Judges for the Southern District of Mississippi and to the Chief Judge of the U.S. Fifth Circuit Court of Appeals, sought to withdraw school desegregation plans that his department had filed in the district court a week earlier. It marked the first time — since the Supreme Court's 1954 decision in *Brown* v. *Board of Education* — that the United States had broken faith with the black children of Mississippi and aligned itself with the forces of delay on the issue of school desegregation.

Less than a week later — on August 25 — Attorney General John N. Mitchell placed the Department of Justice imprimatur on Finch's actions when Jerris Leonard, the Assistant Attorney General in charge of the Civil Rights Division, joined local officials in a Mississippi district court to argue for a delay.

The same day, in Washington, some of my colleagues in the Civil Rights Division and I prepared and distributed a memorandum inviting the Division's attorneys to a meeting the next evening to discuss these and other recent events that had, in the words of the memo, cast ominous shadows over "the future course of law enforcement in civil rights." The meeting's purpose was "to determine whether we have a common position and what action, if any, would be appropriate to take."

The forty who attended the meeting that next night first heard detailed factual accounts from those lawyers with first-hand knowledge of the government's ac-

tions in school desegregation cases in Mississippi, Louisiana, and South Carolina. We discussed the legal principles at length. We could find, as lawyers, no grounds for these actions that did not run cross-grain to the Constitution. We concluded that the request for delay in Mississippi was not only politically motivated but unsupportable under the law we were sworn to uphold. I then asked whether the attorneys in the Civil Rights Division should protest the actions of Messrs. Mitchell, Finch, and Leonard. Much to my astonishment, the answer was an unhesitating, unequivocal, and unanimous call for action.

But how? The group's immediate, though probably unattainable, goal was a reversal of the Justice Department's actions in Mississippi. Beyond that, however, we wanted to ensure that future Mississippi-type decisions would not be made; we wanted guarantees that the Administration would, in the future, take the actions that were required by law, without reference to the political exigencies. We hoped that the protest could serve as a deterrent to future political accommodation. We agreed to write a dignified and reasonable statement of protest that would make our views known and demonstrate our unity and resolve. We chose a committee of six to draft the document.

Two evenings later, on August 28, we held another meeting to review the draft submitted by the committee. The fifty attorneys in attendance discussed the draft, modified it somewhat, and then adopted it unanimously. (It was later signed by sixty-five of the seventy-four nonsupervisory attorneys in the Civil Rights Division, some of whom had missed one or both of the meetings because they were out of town.)

The four-paragraph, 400-word document expressed, in painstaking language, the continuing concerns, motivations, and goals of the signatories. The last two paragraphs said:

It is our fear that a policy which dictates that clear legal mandates are to be sacrificed to other considerations will seriously impair the ability of the Civil Rights Division, and ultimately the Judiciary, to attend to the faithful execution of the federal civil-rights statutes. Such an impairment, by eroding public faith in our Constitutional institutions, is likely to damage the capacity of those institutions to accommodate conflicting interests and ensure the full enjoyment of fundamental rights for all.

We recognize that, as members of the Department of Justice, we have an obligation to follow the directives of our departmental superiors. However, we are compelled, in conscience, to urge that henceforth the enforcement policies of this Division be predicated solely upon relevant legal principles. We further request that this Department vigorously enforce those laws protecting human dignity and equal rights for all persons and by its actions promptly assure concerned citizens that the objectives of those laws will be pursued.

Why did the consciences of sixty-five federal employees compel them to protest a government law-enforcement decision? Why did sixty-five members of a profession that generally attracts the conservative and circumspect to its ranks — and reinforces these characteristics in three years of academic training — launch the first "revolt" within the federal bureaucracy?

Part of the answer lies in the fact that the new Administration was elected largely by voters who expected — and, from the rhetoric of the campaign, had every reason to expect — a slowdown in federal civil rights enforcement efforts. Those political debts ran counter to the devotion and commitment of the attorneys in the Civil Rights Division. They had labored long and hard in civil rights law enforcement, and had come to realize by experience that only unremitting pressure could bring about compliance with the civil rights statutes and the Fourteenth Amendment. Yet this conflict of commitments did not of itself lead to the revolt. There was no inevitability in the situation.

Certain other irritants played a part in creating an attitude among the attorneys which made "revolt" possible. There was Leonard himself, a politician from Wisconsin with no background in civil rights and, indeed, very little as a lawyer. He was insensitive to the problems of black citizens and other minority-group victims of discrimination. Almost from the beginning, he distrusted the attorneys he found in the Division. He demonstrated that distrust by isolating himself from the line attorneys. Still another element was the shock of his ineptitude as a lawyer. In marked contrast to the distinguished lawyers who had preceded him in his job, Leonard lacked the intellectual equipment to deal with the legal problems that came across his desk.

His handling of the Mississippi case enlarged this mood of irritation and frustration. Secretary Finch's letter — drafted in part, and approved in full, by Leonard — said that the HEW plans were certain to produce "a catastrophic educational setback" for the school children involved. Yet the Office of Education personnel who prepared the plans and Dr. Gregory Anrig, who supervised their work, and the Civil Rights Division attorneys, who were preparing to defend them in court, had found no major flaws. Indeed, Dr. Anrig, in transmitting the plans to the district court on August 11, wrote that in his judgment "each of the enclosed plans is educationally and administratively sound, both in terms of substance and in terms of timing." It was not until the afternoon of August 20, only hours before the attorneys were to defend the plans in court, that Leonard called them in Mississippi to inform them of the Administration's decision. Finally, in justifying the government's actions to his own supervisory attorneys—and in arranging that they, and not he, would inform the line attorneys of the reasons for the requested delay—Leonard could be no more candid than to say that the chief educator in the country had made an educational decision and that the Department of Justice had to back him up.

But, again, these superficial signs of malaise were not what led to the lawyers' widespread revolt. Discontent only created the atmosphere for it.

The revolt occurred for one paramount reason: the sixty-five attorneys had obligations to their profession and to the public interest. As lawyers, we are bound by the Canons of Professional Ethics and by our oaths upon admission to the bar; as officers of the United States, we were bound by our oaths of office.

Membership in the bar entails much more than a license to practice law. One becomes an officer of the courts, duty-bound to support the judiciary and to aid in every way in the administration of justice. The scope of this duty was nicely summarized by U.S. District Judge George M. Bourquin in the case of *In re Kelly* in 1917, when he wrote:

> Counsel must remember that they, too, are officers of the courts, administrators of justice, oath-bound servants of society; that their first duty is not to their clients, as many suppose, but is to the administration of justice; that to this their clients' success is wholly subordinate; that their conduct ought to and must be scrupulously observant of law and ethics; and to the extent that they fail therein, they injure themselves, wrong their brothers at the bar, bring reproach upon an honorable profession, betray the courts, and defeat justice.

The Canons of Ethics command that an attorney "obey his own conscience" (Canon 15) and strive to improve the administration of justice (Canon 29). The

Canons go on to echo Judge Bourquin's words:

> No...cause, civil or political, however important, is entitled to receive, nor should any lawyer render, any service or advice involving disloyalty to the law whose ministers we are, or disrespect of the judicial office, which we are bound to uphold.... When rendering any such improper service...the lawyer invites and merits stern and just condemnation.... Above all a lawyer will find his highest honor in a deserved reputation for fidelity to...public duty, as an honest man and as a patriotic and loyal citizen. [Canon 32]

Bearing these obligations in mind, examine for a moment the situation confronting the attorneys as a result of the decision to seek delay in Mississippi.

In May, 1954, the Supreme Court declared that "in the field of public education the doctrine of 'separate but equal' has no place. Separate educational facilities are inherently unequal." One year later, the Court decreed that school officials would be required to make a "prompt and reasonable start" toward achieving the Constitutional goal with "all deliberate speed." Tragically, a decade went by and little was accomplished; that was the era of "massive resistance." In 1964, the Supreme Court ruled that "the time for mere 'deliberate speed' has run out." In 1968, the Court held that school officials were under a Constitutional obligation to come forward with desegregation plans that worked, and to do so "*now*." The Fifth Circuit Court of Appeals interpreted that edict, in the summer of 1968, to mean that the dual school system, with its racially identifiable schools, had to be eliminated in all of the states within its jurisdiction by September, 1969. (Mississippi is one of those states.)

Secretary Finch's letter, besides suggesting the possibility of a catastrophic educational setback if desegregation were effected at once, spoke of the certainty of chaos and confusion in the school districts if delay were not allowed. That allegation was based upon the uncontestable existence of hostility to desegregation within the local communities. While there was a danger of chaos and confusion in the desegregation of public schools in Mississippi, the Supreme Court had ruled again and again that neither opposition to Constitutional rights nor the likelihood of a confrontation with those opposed to the Constitutional imperative may legally stand as a bar to the immediate vindication of those rights.*

Thus, while pledged by our oaths to support and defend the Constitution and bound by duty to follow our consciences and adhere to the law, we faced a situation in which the Administration had proposed to act in violation of the law. We knew that we could not remain silent, for silence, particularly in this Administration, is interpreted as support or acquiescence. Only through some form of protest could we live up to our obligations as lawyers and as officers of the United States. The form that this protest should take emerged so clearly that it then became a matter of inevitability, rather than a choice made from among several alternatives.

For the duty to serve the law, to promote the administration of justice, to support and defend the Constitution is more than a negative command; it is more than a "thou shalt not." It is an affirmative duty to act in a manner that would best serve and promote those interests. Thus, at the first group meeting, we immediately and unanimously rejected the notion of

---

*On October 29, of course, the Supreme Court unanimously rejected the Administration's efforts at delay by enunciating the rule that the Constitution requires desegregation "at once." That ruling is not a part of this narrative except as it demonstrated anew that the position we had taken on the law was unassailable.

mass resignation because it would have served no positive purpose. It would only have removed us from association with the supporters of delay; it would not have fulfilled our obligation to act affirmatively to ensure that Constitutional rights would be protected and that the civil rights laws would be vigorously enforced.

Many of the attorneys thought that our obligation could not be met by merely drafting, signing, and delivering a protest statement. If delay for the purpose of mollifying a hostile community did not comport with the Constitution—thus impelling us to raise our voices in protest—then we were likewise duty-bound not to support the Mitchell-Finch-Leonard position through any of our official actions. The bureaucratic concept of "loyalty" notwithstanding, some of us concluded that we could not, for example, defend the government's position in court.

The question arises as to whether the action taken by the group met the burden imposed upon us by our obligations to the law and to the public interest. Did our fidelity to these obligations demand more than the soft and lofty importunings of the protest statement? Should all of the attorneys have explicitly refused to defend in court the action taken in the Mississippi case? Should the attorneys have embarked on a more direct course of action to block the government's efforts to win a year's delay for school desegregation in Mississippi?

To begin with, we were hard pressed to come up with some appropriate alternative to the protest statement as a vehicle to make the views of sixty-five people known. But beyond that, it was vitally important to preserve the appearance of dignity and professionalism if our protest were not to be dismissed as the puerile rantings of a group of unresurrected idealists who, except for their attire, bore a close resemblance to the "Weathermen" and the "Crazies." To generate the public support we thought vital to the success of the protest, we had to act in a responsible and statesmanlike manner. Furthermore, it seemed to us that the presentation of any statement signed by nearly all of the attorneys in the Division would be a remarkable feat and that a demonstration of commitment was more important than the words actually used. In our view, the soft language implied everything that a blunter statement might have said. It also had the virtue of not putting the Administration up against a wall, which might have forced it to respond with a hard-line position of its own.

Though duty and conscience compelled a protest, reason dictated the nature of that protest. We did not merely seek an opportunity for catharsis; we sought to devise a course of action that had a chance to reap a harvest of practical results. This being the overriding consideration, the attorneys chose the course of a mildly worded group statement. Other overt manifestations of disagreement were left open for individuals to pursue as they saw fit.

The group action we took—that is, the drafting and signing of the statement—was a "protest," if by that we mean a dissent from the actions of one's administrative superiors. The language of the statement did not move into the area of "revolt," if by that we mean an explicit refusal to obey the orders of one's superiors—although the statement was intended to imply that "revolt" was in the air.

Compelled by what they felt to be their obligations to the law, individual attorneys took a number of actions on their own, most of them in that murky area where there is a confluence of protest and revolt.

Even before the first group meeting, the Division lawyers assigned to Mississippi expressed their disinclination to present the government's case for delay in the district court. As a consequence, Leonard made his first appearance in a federal district court as Assistant Attorney General and argued the motion for delay himself. In mid-September, two Division attorneys (the author being one) appeared in federal courts in other school desegregation cases. When pressed by those courts to reconcile the government's "desegregate-now" position in those cases with Leonard's position in Mississippi, both attorneys said they could not defend the government's action in Mississippi.* Some of the Division's attorneys went a step further: they passed information along to lawyers for the NAACP Legal Defense Fund in order to aid their Mississippi court battle against the delay requested by the Administration. Others spoke with the press to ensure that the public was fully aware of the role political pressures had played in the decision to seek delay.

These actions, while neither authorized nor approved by the group as a whole, were individual responses to the same crisis of conscience that had led to the

---

*In my situation, I was in St. Louis before the Eighth Circuit Court of Appeals, sitting *en banc* (i.e., the full seven judges of the court were present), arguing that a delay granted by the district court to an Arkansas school district for the desegregation of its high schools should be reversed. One of the judges asked whether I could assure the court that the Attorney General would not "come along and pull the rug out from under" them if they ordered instant integration. I was pressed to reconcile my request for immediate integration in Arkansas with the position taken in the Mississippi case. After the court listened to my attempts to distinguish between the two cases, one judge said it appeared to the court that the practical effect of the government's posture was that Mississippi was being given special treatment. At this point, a number of judges called upon me to state my personal views on the contradictory positions taken by the government. I responded by saying I assumed that the court knew from the press accounts of the "revolt" what the feelings were in the Division. I indicated that, as a signatory of the protest statement, I could not be expected to defend the government's action in Mississippi.

protest statement itself. One may have reservations as to the propriety of some or all of these acts of defiance. (Indeed, I have doubts as to whether it was proper for a Division attorney to furnish information to the NAACP after the government's action transformed the NAACP into an opposing party.) But it is important to recognize that the demands of conscience compelled more than just the signing of a piece of paper, and, in this sense, the protest was, realistically, a "revolt."

When the storm clouds first began to gather within the Civil Rights Division, the hierarchy of the Department of Justice, including the Attorney General and Leonard, reacted with a professed sense of surprise and even shock. Despite this, however, the Administration's actions were, at the outset, nothing short of accommodating.

The supervisory attorneys in the Division took the position that we had a perfect right, under the First Amendment, to meet and discuss matters of mutual concern. Prior to our second meeting, Leonard Garment, President Nixon's special consultant for youth and minority problems, let it be known through an intermediary that the Administration was likely to respond favorably to a reasonable and responsible protest. Indeed, Garment and the Deputy Attorney General, Richard G. Kleindienst, facilitated the protest by allowing us to hold our second meeting behind closed doors in the Department of Justice.

But later, when the Administration came to a fuller appreciation of the depth and unanimity of the protest, this attitude began to change.

On September 18, Leonard responded to the attorneys' statement for the Administration. We were informed that his reply was a final articulation of policy; in other words, if we did not like what we read, we should resign. The reply was curiously unresponsive. Whereas the attorneys' statement was carefully limited to questions concerning the intrusion of political influences into areas of law enforcement where only considerations of law belong, Leonard's reply outlined how the Administration would go about desegregating public schools. To this extent, the reply completely missed, or avoided, the point of the protest. We had never challenged the discretionary authority of the Attorney General and the President to determine the method by which the Constitutional imperative would be achieved. In matters where discretion is vested in the Attorney General to choose among policy alternatives, the attorneys have no business challenging his right to make the choice. But in the matter of enforcing Constitutionally required school desegregation in Mississippi, the Attorney General had no discretion. He was bound to uphold the dictates of the law, an obligation that could not be squared with the decision to seek delay.

Aside from its nonresponsiveness to the questions we had raised, Leonard's reply was disturbing on two other counts. First, it conceded, with delayed candor, that political pressures had played a role in the Mississippi decision. Second, it announced a new touchstone for civil rights law-enforcement policies: future actions would be taken on the basis of "soundness," rather than on the basis of the law. Thus, when defense appropriations are thrown into the balance, a decision to seek delay of school desegregation in Mississippi in return for the continued support of Senator John Stennis (D-Miss.) on the ABM can presumably be certified as "sound," notwithstanding its inconsistency with clear legal mandates.

The attorneys decided that we would neither accept the response nor resign. But the situation demanded further action, and we chose to reiterate our commitment to the law. On September 25, we delivered a new statement to the Attorney General and Leonard. It expressed our view that Leonard's reply "indicates an intention to continue with the policy of civil rights law enforcement toward which our August 29 statement was directed, a policy which, in our view, is inconsistent with clearly defined legal mandates."

The Attorney General's patience was wearing thin. The next day he told the press that "policy is going to be made by the Justice Department, not by a group of lawyers in the Civil Rights Division." At a news conference three days later, Leonard said that he thought the position taken by the attorneys was wrong. He warned that the revolt would have to end as of that date.

On October 1, Leonard called me to his office. He told me that he considered it to be the obligation of all of his attorneys to defend the government's Mississippi action in court. He asked whether I would be able to do so in the future. I said that I could not and would not. Our obligation was to represent the Attorney General, he said, and John Mitchell had decided that delay was the appropriate course to follow in Mississippi. I countered by explaining that I was obliged to represent the public interest in court and that my responsibility was to enforce the law. Leonard then made his attitude on the meaning of law enforcement very clear. "Around here the Attorney General is the law," he said. The difference of opinion was irreconcilable, and I was told to resign or be fired. I said I would forthwith submit a letter of resignation, and did — effective immediately. Leonard concluded the meeting by heaping effusive praise upon my abilities as a lawyer and offering to write a glowing letter of recommendation if I requested one. I did not.

Later that day, Leonard issued a memorandum that banned any "further unauthorized statement...regarding our work and our policies." He directed the attorneys to keep all "decisions of our work and policies within this Department."

Thus, the Administration's official attitude boiled down to an absolute ban on any further protest activity. The public was to be kept in the dark as a matter of policy. Law-enforcement decisions were to be made by John Mitchell, and the test for those decisions was to be soundness, including the relevant political considerations. The attorney's job was to articulate and defend the Attorney General's decisions in court, and this duty would apply without reference to one's individual oath of office and the dictates of conscience.

As attorneys, I and my former colleagues who still remain in the Civil Rights Division cannot accept this point of view. The Justice Department lawyer's primary obligation must be to the Constitution. That should hold true whether the attorney is John Mitchell, Jerris Leonard, or Gary Greenberg. In his role as an officer of the United States, the Justice Department lawyer represents the public interest. While Jerris Leonard equates that obligation with obedience to the President and the Attorney General, I and my former colleagues could not. The Justice Department lawyer is not hired to represent John Mitchell in court. He is hired to represent the United States.

The ban on future protest by attorneys was unreal. Indeed, it would have been self-deception for John Mitchell or Jerris Leonard to assume that the "massive resistance" in the Civil Rights Division was over. The revolt may have been driven underground, but the attorneys remain within the system. They retain their voice and their ability to influence policy from within. They continue to adhere to their view of the law, and they see their obligation to the public, and to their oath of office, as paramount. The attorneys remain a potent and organized deterrent, ready to act should there be another Mississippi.

Whether or not the revolt achieved its long-range objectives, one cannot yet judge. There are indications that in the area of civil rights, as in other matters, the Attorney General is either unaware or contemptuous of the forces that conflict with the politics of the Southern Strategy. The attorneys in the Civil Rights Division continue to take a hard line in individual cases. They assume this posture every day in the pleadings and briefs they present to the Attorney General and Leonard for approval. So long as the Administration is kept in the position of having to say no — an attitude adopted so far only in those few cases in which the political pressures

were intense — it is not likely that it can effect the wholesale retreat on enforcement of the civil rights laws which it seems ready to trade for public support. But while it is vital that the revolutionaries remain within the Division, and while their presence within the system may deter future Mississippi-type decisions, there is some question whether their determination will sustain them for the balance of this Administration. If not, the prospects for even the grudging enforcement of civil rights laws are bleak indeed.

A NOTE ON THE LITIGATION*

On July 3, 1969, the Fifth Circuit Court of Appeals ordered desegregation plans submitted and put into effect by that fall in thirty-three Mississippi school districts. The Justice Department and the Mississippi Attorney General asked for a delay, arguing that the time was too short and administrative problems too difficult to accomplish an orderly implementation of the plans before September. Both the District Court and the Court of Appeals accepted this argument, and on August 28, the Court of Appeals suspended its July 3 order and postponed the date for submission of new plans until December 1. Plaintiffs in fourteen of these districts appealed to the U.S. Supreme Court. On September 5, Justice Black, as Circuit Justice, denied their request for an immediate suspension of the postponement even though he personally believed the postponement was unjustified. [*Alexander et al.* v. *Holmes County Board of Education,* 396 US 19 (1969)]. Black wrote in part:

> ...when an individual justice is asked to grant special relief, such as a stay, he must consider in light of past decisions and other

*Prepared with the assistance of Mike Comiskey.

factors what action the entire Court might possibly take.... Although Green [*Green* v. *County School Board of New Kent* 391 US 430 (1968)] reiterated that the time for all deliberate speed had passed, there is language in that opinion which might be interpreted as approving a "transition period" during which federal courts would continue to supervise the passage of the Southern schools from dual to unitary systems. Although I feel there is a strong possibility that the full Court would agree with my views, I cannot say definitely that they would, and therefore I am compelled to consider the factors relied upon in the courts below for postponing the effective date of the original desegregation order.... The District Court found as a matter of fact that the time was too short, and the Court of Appeals held that these findings were supported by the evidence. I am unable to say that these findings are not supported. Therefore, deplorable as it is to me, I must uphold the court's order which both sides indicate could have the effect of delaying total desegregation of these schools for as long as a year.

When the full court heard the case on October 23, Assistant Attorney General Leonard and the Solicitor General argued again for delay. Although they insisted that the government was fully dedicated to ending segregated schools, they maintained that the best means of achieving this goal was to follow the Court of Appeals' order so that the school boards would have time to develop reasonable plans for desegregation. They argued that the views of the lower courts should be respected because of their "close familiarity with these cases and distinguished experience in the field." In a *per curiam* opinion decided on October 29, the Supreme Court rejected these arguments and vacated the Court of Appeals' suspension order. A unanimous Supreme Court held that all motions for additional time should have been denied. Continued operation of segregated schools under a standard of allowing "all deliberate speed" was no longer constitutionally permissible, and every school district was obligated to terminate dual school systems at once and to operate only unitary schools.

Comment

Although the initial protest was seen as an exercise of free speech, further opposition became disobedience once Leonard ordered the attorneys to cease their public protest or resign. Was Greenberg right to resign at this point? The attorneys who remained in office (carrying out their duties but still publicly opposing the policy) engaged in a kind of civil disobedience in office. Does their action meet the traditional test of justifiable civil disobedience? In what respects (if any) should that test be revised to deal with disobedience by officials?

Evaluate the actions of the attorneys whose protest went beyond signing the petition by (1) expressing opposition to the government's case in Mississippi while representing the government in another desegregation case in another district; (2) refusing to present the government's case for delay in any district; (3) giving the press inside information that might fuel public opposition to the Attorney General's policy; and (4) passing information to lawyers for the opponents of the government's case. Would any other means of protest have been better?

To what extent does the justifiability of disobedience depend on assuming that the Attorney General's position was against the law? Suppose (contrary to Greenberg) that the Attorney General was acting within his lawful discretion but against the moral rights of some Mississippi citizens. On what basis could you defend the protest or other forms of opposition?

If you accept some part of the "revolt," ask yourself to what extent your acceptance depends on your agreement with the policy the attorneys favored. Reverse some of the facts in the case and see if your conclusions change. Consider, for example, whether (and why or why not) your judgment would change if the protest had been organized by lawyers who opposed an attorney general's effort to speed up school desegregation beyond what was required by law.

The Odd Couple

Taylor Branch

The public reaction to two whistle-blowers, Otto F. Otepka and Daniel Ellsberg, clearly illustrates the disorienting spells cast upon fervent observers by the spectacle and drama of disclosures that involve national security. Otepka violated our national security by slipping classified documents to veteran Red-hunter Julien G. Sourwine, counsel to the Senate Internal Security Subcommittee. He was fired for his transgressions in 1963, lost his position as chief of the State Department's security-evaluation division, became a martyr of the right wing, and is considered by some to be the first whistle-blower in the modern period. Ellsberg violated our national security by slipping classified documents, later to be called the Pentagon Papers, to numerous senators and newspapers. He was indicted for his transgressions in 1971, lost his security clearance at the RAND Corporation, became a martyr of the left wing, and is often considered the capstone whistle-blower of recent years.

While these two men are ideological opposites, there are unmistakable similarities between their respective exploits, viewed on a suitably high plane of reflection after all the human juices and interesting particulars have been drained away to leave the arid generalities in which lawyers earn their keep. Like colliding planets, Ellsberg and Otepka still operate by the same laws of motion in some ways, following their higher instincts regarding the public interest as

Reprinted with permission from *The Washington Monthly* (Oct. 1971). Copyright 1971 by The Washington Monthly Co., 2712 Ontario Rd., N.W., Washington, D.C. 20009.

they see it, exposing treachery in places of power regarding questions of life and death. These similarities suggest that anyone who wants to fight institutional rigor mortis by encouraging people to speak out from within government is obliged by honesty and consistency to take his Otepkas with his Ellsbergs, and vice versa—to take a man like Otepka, who thought his bosses were ruining the country by being too sweet to communists everywhere, with one like Ellsberg, who thought his former colleagues were ruining the country by killing numerous people and lying about the whole affair. Regardless of who is right on the lofty world-view questions, the comments on the two men by prestigious newspapers and politicians suggest a strange kinship that bears some examination.

Otepka had been in the government for twenty-seven years and in the Office of Security for ten years when he was fired on November 5, 1963, on charges of "conduct unbecoming an officer of the Department of State." President Kennedy, setting a precedent for dealing with criticism from the right, assuaged a Calley-like tide by announcing that "I will examine the matter myself when it comes time," but he was killed before the review process got underway. It seems that Otepka, described by *Reader's Digest* as a "tall, quiet, darkly handsome man," by *Newsweek* as "a sad-eyed, introverted man," and by *The New York Times* only as "stocky," (descriptions indicative of the impact of political position on the eye), had been running afoul of important people in the Kennedy Administration for some time.

In 1955, for example, he had refused to dispense with the formalities of the security clearance procedure for Walt W. Rostow, when Secretary of State Dulles wanted Rostow on State's Committee on Operations. Subjecting Rostow to a full-dress examination of his character was considered an affront to his dignity. When President Kennedy wanted Rostow on the team in 1961, Otepka again refused to waive security proceedings, which, some say, is why Rostow ended up in the White House while Otepka was at State, rather than going through the State security mill. (Apparently Otepka was a bit troubled by the internationalist leanings of Rostow's writings on economic development, hesitant to be taken in by possible ruses like Rostow's "non-Communist Manifesto," *The Stages of Economic Growth.* Also, as a professor, Rostow's commitment against communism was suspect a priori. Although subsequent events and the Pentagon Papers were to show that Otepka was dead wrong in his doubts about Rostow, some beneficiaries of hindsight have wished that he had possessed more clout in his efforts to keep Rostow out of the government.)

In addition to the Rostow rebuke, Otepka had nettled the new administration by locating and firing the State Department employee who had leaked a secret survey of U.S. prestige abroad to the Kennedy campaign forces in 1960. The survey, showing a dip in America's international esteem, was used with telling effect by John Kennedy in the campaign to show that the Republicans were blowing things in foreign policy, partly by following what seemed to be a deliberate path toward national weakness. Otepka had also been critical of the lax security procedures for the Cuba desk officers at the State Department, one of whom, William Wieland, was considered by the Republican Party almost single-handedly responsible for delivering Cuba into the enemy camp. Otepka testified before a Senate committee that he had dissented from the decision to clear Wieland without further study of his inner proclivities, and so much stir was created over Wieland that President Kennedy was forced to defend him publicly in a press conference.

Finally, Otepka had refused to waive security investigations for six men of decorum whom Secretary Rusk wanted in 1962 for the Advisory Committee on Management Improvement to the Assistant Secretary of State for International Organization Affairs. The six, which included Harding Bancroft, Sol Linowitz, and Andrew Cordier, were chosen to that august and rather useless body to study whether or not American employees of international organizations should be required to pass U.S. security investigations. The issue itself was one of some controversy, spurred on by a letter to *The New York Times* on July 30, 1962, that attacked the security regulations as a dangerous legacy of the McCarthy era. The letter came from Leonard Boudin, who is now the chief attorney for Daniel Ellsberg. In any case, Otepka refused to waive security clearances for men who were going to study the need for security clearances, and that kind of zeal to check out the private leanings of prestigious people had long since aggrieved the Kennedy Administration.

John F. Reilly, Assistant Secretary of State for Security, was so intent upon getting rid of his anachronistic subordinate, the John Wayne rough rider on the New Frontier, that he bugged Otepka's telephone and set up an elaborate system of surveillance to catch him in an act of shame that would stand up as evidence for doing him in. Reilly's sleuths scoured Otepka's "burn bag," a receptacle used to mark for instant destruction items like doodle pads and carbon paper and other parts of the afterbirth of state secrets that might leave telltale signs, and finally scored one day when they found classification stamps which Otepka had clipped from classified documents. Thus declassified informally, the documents were being sent by Otto over to old J. G. Sourwine at the Senate Internal Security Subcommittee, where they were used to help surprise and embarrass Otto's bosses regarding how lightly they took the red menace right here at home. The burn bag also contained a used typewriter ribbon, an instant replay of which revealed that Otepka had worked up a primer of questions for Sourwine that he could use to catch State Department officials in factual errors regarding the communist question.

OTTO'S HIGHEST LOYALTY

When the State Department used the burn bag evidence to fire Otepka, the fireworks and orations began. *The Chicago Tribune* skipped over the classified document problem to define the issue as a test of the principle of patriotism: "There can be no doubt that this case reflects an intention by the Kennedy Administration to conduct a purge of patriots." The Charleston, South Carolina, *News & Courier* agreed: "To reprimand a U.S. citizen for doing his duty would be a shame and an outrage." *Reader's Digest* later published an article called "The Ordeal of Otto Otepka," subtitled, "Why have State Department employees been using tactics of a police state to oust a dedicated security officer whose only sin seems to be loyalty to his country?", which pretty well summed up the conservative presentation of the problem. The police state argument reflects the tactical guideline that it is easier to attack the process by which the opponent operates than the substance of what he says. However, it also bore some risk of the "corner problem," by which people paint themselves

into a corner through the hasty use of principles whose future application might haunt them. In this case, the *Digest's* forthright position against a police state was quite risky. It not only made it tougher to argue in subsequent tirades that the State Department was undisciplined and namby-pamby, but it also would require a redefinition of the issues when the wiretapping and surveillance of J. Edgar Hoover came to the fore. Most conservative journals ignored the classification question and the he-broke-a-rule point of view, except perhaps to note in passing that classification was nonsense in general and that Otepka's leakage of secret material did not hurt the national interest anyway, but rather struck another blow against the pinkos in the State Department.

Meanwhile, in the Senate, members surveyed the Otepka affair and concluded that the main issue at stake was, as is so often the case, the dignity of the U.S. Senate. Conservative Senator Williams of Delaware remarked that, "In this instance, all that Mr. Otepka was guilty of was cooperating with a congressional committee." Senator Dominick of Colorado thanked Senator Dodd for having "pointed out the very difficult position Senate committees would find themselves in if it continued to be held that the executive branch could prevent any of its employees from coming before Senate committees, either by threatening them with dismissal or by verbally preventing them from testifying under that threat." Dodd, a foreign policy buff, defined the question in terms of national survival: "If those forces bent on destroying Otepka and the no-nonsense security approach he represents are successful, who knows how many more Chinas or Cubas we may lose?" But Dodd, too, was anxious about the powers of himself and his colleagues, and he entered a long discourse with Senators Strom Thurmond and Frank

Lausche on November 5, the day Otepka's dismissal was consummated, which Thurmond climaxed by declaring that the Kennedy Administration's action would "nullify our system of government by tending to destroy the constitutional system of checks and balances." There was no commander-in-chief talk on that day, no talk about how the President's powers were essential to survive in a hostile international environment. The conservatives were safe from the corner problem, however, because the war in Vietnam had not yet begun. The doves in the Senate would not really discover the checks and balances principle until about 1968, leaving the conservatives ample time to switch over to the commander-in-chief line without undue embarrassment.

"Orderly Procedures Are Essential"

The liberals in the Senate were exceedingly mousy about Otepka as the supporters of the Kennedy Administration sought to ride out the storm in public silence. This does not necessarily mean that they were apathetic, for some Otepka supporters claim that there was great pressure to let the Otepka fervor die out like the groundswell for General MacArthur. Clark Mollenhoff, a straightforward, very conservative reporter for *The Des Moines Register,* made a speech about the obstacles to coverage of the case:

> I realize the broad range of direct and indirect pressures brought to discourage a defense of Otepka, for I met most of them at some stage from my friends in the Kennedy Administration. One put it crudely: "What are you lining up with Otepka and all those far-right nuts for? Do you want to destroy yourself?"
> There were also hints that I could be cut off from White House contacts and other high Administration contacts if I continued to push for the facts in the Otepka case.

Liberal newspapers made slightly more noise in the dispute than their compatriot senators, and their editorial writers swept aside all the chaff about higher loyalty and patriotism and the dignity of Congress to focus on the principles at stake, with a fixity that is born of discipline. *The Washington Post*, for example, zeroed in on the law and order question, following the rule that it is always best to attack on matters of procedure: "For all of Senator Dodd's sputtering, he must know that what Otto Otepka did was not only unlawful but unconscionable as well. Mr. Otepka certainly knew this himself — which is no doubt why he did it covertly instead of candidly. He gave classified information to someone not authorized to receive it." *The New York Times* took a similar line, with slightly greater emphasis on propriety: "The disturbing aspect of this case is that both Mr. Otepka and members of the Senate subcommittee have defended their actions on grounds of 'higher loyalty'.... Orderly procedures are essential if the vital division of powers between the legislative and executive branches is not to be undermined. The use of 'underground' methods to obtain classified documents from lower level officials is a dangerous departure from such orderly procedures."

The liberal press also used words like "controversial," "McCarthyism," "tattle," and "infidelity" as often as possible in connection with Otepka's name. This strategy, following from the rule that it is often useful to adopt your opponent's principles and turn them back on him in verbal counterinsurgency, amounted to McCarthyism turned on its head, as Marx did to Hegel, or guilt by association with McCarthy. Thus, when Otepka defended himself by citing the government employees' Code of Ethics (which charges employees to place loyalty to conscience, country, and the "highest moral principles" above "loyalty to persons, party or government department"), the *Washington Post* news story stated that "the last time that issue was raised with public prominence, it was raised by Senator McCarthy in sweeping form...." A *New York Times* story by Neil Sheehan in 1969 continued this theme of the beat-them-at-their-own-game campaign: "The enthusiastic pursuit of 'subversive elements' in the government loosed by the late Senator Joseph McCarthy slowed to a desultory walk in later years, but Mr. Otepka...did not change."

"HIS TRAINED JACKAL, JACK ANDERSON"

Otepka returned to the public light in 1969, when President Nixon made good on his campaign promise to review the case "with a view to seeing that justice is accorded this man who served his country so long and well." The Subversive Activities Control Board seemed like an appropriate resting spot for a seasoned personnel sniffer, who could spend the rest of his days perusing political groups for loyalty blemishes. Actually, the SACB was a secondary choice for Otepka, who really wanted to go back to the State Department but was frustrated in his desire by Secretary of State Rogers, who did not want him. Senator Dirksen, claiming Otepka as a constituent and an ideological brother, suggested the SACB spot and went to work with the other conservative senators to give the board and its $36,000-a-year members something to do. They knew that Otepka would be an additional burden in the annual battle with the liberals over the fact that the SACB members are so inert that they appear strikingly like welfare recipients, at ten times the poverty standard.

The task of selling Otepka himself was undertaken with the old principles of patriotism and higher loyalty. In the Senate, the four hoariest members of the Judiciary Committee — Eastland, Mc-Clellan, Dirksen, and Hruska — assembled for a confirmation hearing to pay homage to the SACB nominee. "You have been punished because you attempted to protect your country," said Chairman Eastland to Otto, and the four senators respectfully declined to ask the witness anything other than his name.

And Senator Dodd, now deceased, led the fight on the floor of the Senate and helped organize Otepka Day, on which patriots around the nation celebrated his resurrection. Every time Senator Dodd took the floor to wax eloquent about Otepka's higher mission against international communism, he represented the largest collection of loyalty contradictions ever assembled in one place — a veritable one-man intersection of passions on the morality of exposure. For since Dodd had first praised Otepka for exposing the State Department with pilfered documents and denounced the State Department for firing the higher patriotism of Otepka, Dodd himself had been exposed for pocketing campaign contributions and other financial misdealings. While Dodd praised the patriot who exposed corruption in the State Department, he fired the infidel who exposed corruption in himself — his administrative assistant of twelve years, James Boyd. Boyd's medium of exposure, the Drew Pearson/Jack Anderson column, decided to switch in the Otepka affair — exposing the exposer, Otepka, because of his leanings to the right. In this vortex of half-hero, it was not surprising that Dodd would resort to arguments tinged with the *ad hominem,* "The press campaign against Otto Otepka has been spearheaded by Drew Pearson, the lying character assassin and his trained jackal, Jack Anderson."

In the end, however, Dodd regained the lofty, joined by the honey tongue of Senator Dirksen — who read to the Senate a moving letter from Mrs. Otepka, describing the hardships the family had faced since Otto had been demoted in 1967, while his dismissal was still being appealed, to a $15,000-a-year job that was so "demeaning" that Otto protested by taking a leave without pay and forced her to go to work to support him. What is $36,000 for a patriot, asked Dirksen and Dodd of their fellow senators, and the two crusaders went to their graves knowing that the world would be better with Otepka on the SACB. Otepka, for his part, called the Senate confirmation "my vindication," and a well-deserved one to boot, because as he later wrote, "I have disagreed only with those who quarrel with the truth. I shall continue to disagree."

NAILING DOWN THE CASE

The vindication did not come easily, for during the period when Senate confirmation was pending, *The New York Times* practiced an enthusiastic brand of beat-them-at-their-own-gamism. Reporter Neil Sheehan was dispatched to check up on Otepka's acquaintances, and began his April 4, 1969, story as follows: "A fund with John Birch Society ties has paid about 80 percent of the $26,500 in legal costs incurred by Otto F. Otepka in his four-year fight to win reinstatement as the State Department's chief security evaluator." The story went on to pin down Otepka's "ties" to the Birchers by declaring that "last summer he attended the four-day annual God, Family, and Country rally in Boston, organized by Birch Society leaders." Sheehan also tracked down James M. Stewart, chief fund-raiser of the American Defense Fund, which channeled money to Otepka's lawyers. Stewart looked and acted like a Bircher, although Sheehan wrote triumphantly that he "would neither affirm nor deny whether he was a member of the Birch Society," saying, like Pete Seeger, "I am not answering that question because it is

irrelevant." Beyond such waffling on the affiliation question, Stewart further hanged himself with his reading material, because Sheehan found out, after a hard-nosed inquiry, that "he does subscribe to a number of Birch Society publications."

Having established that Otepka's legal defense was being solicited by a man who might as well have been a Bircher, if he were not in fact a bona fide one, and that Otepka himself was hanging around in right wing crowds, the editorial board of *The New York Times* concluded that Otto was ineligible for membership on the SACB. According to the April 8, 1969, editorial, "The disclosure that Otto Otepka received $22,000 from a fund with extreme right-wing associations should be enough to kill his nomination to the Subversive Activities Control Board. After this, senators of conscience cannot vote to confirm Mr. Otepka in a $36,000-a-year job, where his work, if any, will be to judge the loyalty of American citizens and organizations."

Rather than taking the political view that the whole SACB concept is unconstitutional and therefore should not be supported—or the resigned view that the SACB is a useless bit of welfare, doing nothing, but that it was a shame for the President to use his discretion to appoint, in the *Times'* view, a schmuck like Otto—the editorial rested its case on the assertion that Otto was too tainted to do the job right as a subversive-hunter, and that a neutral mainstreamer would be more efficient. The *Times* thus ventured onto the turf of subversive-hunting and declared Otepka ineligible by the very standards the SACB uses to ferret out dangerous organizations.

An average newspaper might have rested its case there, but fortunately the *Times* is not an average newspaper and therefore was possessed of a "wait a minute" person on the board—the long view of responsibility. Apparently, such a person noticed that the Otepka editorial might look like McCarthyism to some readers, and told his colleagues that such an impression, left uncorrected, would be detrimental to the *Times'* historical commitment against Joe McCarthy's methods. So the argument was sealed with the addition of the following mop-up paragraph:

> The far right doubtless will cry "guilt by association," the charge made long ago by civil libertarians against the likes of Mr. Otepka, but there is a crucial difference here. Mr. Otepka's link to Birchites is no youthful indiscretion of many years ago but an activity carried on as recently as last summer.

Thus, the editorial board took the precautionary measure of protecting its flank against charges of McCarthyism by recalling the best case against old Senator Joe — the telling point about the unfairness of using "youthful indiscretions" that the *Times* itself had once made — and beating it down. This done, the *Times* had at least as strong an indictment against Otepka as McCarthy would have had against his victims if he had not ruined it all by rummaging through their old college notebooks.

The fact that Otto's sins did not fall in the "youthful indiscretion" category probably did carry some weight with a liberal readership — with people who remembered going to the verbal barricades for Alger Hiss and others like him over whether their doings on the left were permanent blemishes of character or merely the wanderings of callow youth. Those people who (perhaps for tactical reasons) had said that what was really wrong with Joe McCarthy was his reliance on outdated evidence, his once-a-subversive-always-a-subversive line, would be relieved to learn that Otepka, unlike Hiss, was still at it. "As recently as last summer," concluded the

Times, in an apparent reference to the God, Family, and Country rally that Sheehan had uncovered. (Some sources suggest that the freshness of Otto's blight could have been established also by the subscription dates on James Stewart's magazines.) Anyone who bought all of McCarthyism except for the Senator's attacks on people for what they did in the past would be sympathetic to disqualifying Otto from the SACB for associations that persisted well into his maturity.

"HIS PECULIAR INFIDELITY"

After Sheehan wrote another story for the Sunday *Times* on April 20, emphasizing Otepka's right-wing associations and his likeness to a bureaucratic version of Joe McCarthy, Senator Strom Thurmond strode to Otto's battlements by declaring on the Senate floor that the *Times* had deliberately smeared Otepka. He charged that *Times* executive editor Harding Bancroft had commissioned the Sheehan investigation in order to get even with Otto for vexations caused back in 1962, when Bancroft was examined for loyalty before going on the Advisory Committee on Management Improvement to the Assistant Secretary of State for International Organization Affairs, or ACMIASSIOA. The *Times* had no comment on this counter-smear, holding to its position that its interest in Otepka sprang from the logical force of the youthful indiscretion editorial.

Whatever the motivation behind the Sheehan articles, their spirit caught on in the Senate, culminating in Senator Stephen Young's speech against the Otepka nomination on June 24, minutes before the vote. Senator Young avowed that James Stewart, who raised money to give to Otepka's lawyer to use in Otepka's defense, had, on June 16, 1969 "attended a fund-raising party at the home of Julius W. Butler...an admitted fund-raiser for the John Birch Society and active in several John Birch front organizations.... The guests at Mr. Butler's home last week included Robert Welch, founder and head of the John Birch Society, who spoke at length spewing forth the usual John Birch lunatic obsessions. Mr. and Mrs. James Stewart, I am told, were in charge of the refreshments that were served at the meeting and were introduced to the crowd and received with applause."

All this failed, and the Senate confirmed Otepka by a vote of 61 to 28. *The Washington Post* emphasized the fidelity question in its editorial lament: "Otto Otepka's long and unfaithful service to the State Department certainly entitled him to some reward from those on Capitol Hill who were the beneficiaries of his peculiar form of infidelity." *The New York Times*, as is its custom, focused on the who-are-you question to bewail Otto as a "living symbol of some of the worst days of the McCarthy-McCarran era."

THE ELLSBERG REVERSE

Two years after his investigation of Otepka, Neil Sheehan was ensconced in a New York hideaway as head of a *New York Times* writing team that prepared stories based on the top-secret Pentagon Papers — slipped to the *Times, The Washington Post*, and other parties by Daniel Ellsberg. Rather than investigating the left wing associations of Ellsberg (such demented pariahs as Noam Chomsky, SDS leaders, the staff of *The Harvard Crimson,* and the editors of *The Washington Monthly*), or noting the glazed-eyed, Martin Lutherish manner in which Ellsberg had been starting speeches by confessing himself as a war criminal, Sheehan stuck to the material at hand and exposed the deceptions perpetrated by Ellsberg's former bosses. It is possible that Sheehan's views on classified material had changed over the two years

since 1969, as had his views on the war in Vietnam. As late as 1967 Sheehan had described himself as only half way along the path from war support to war opposition in a *Times* magazine article entitled "No Longer a Hawk, But Not Yet a Dove." By 1971, he had progressed far enough to write a piece in the *Times* speculating on the possible criminality of people behind him on the path, and this progress helped both Sheehan and Ellsberg decide that the classified document issue paled in significance compared with the overriding injustice of the war.

Of course, the decisions regarding publication of the Pentagon Papers were not made by Sheehan, but by the management of the *Times* and the other papers involved. By 1971, the editors of the *Times* had decided that the real issue involved in the exposure of classified documents was not orderly procedures, but the people's right to know as embodied in the freedom of the press. A June 15 editorial in the *Times* stated that the paper felt it had an obligation to publish the Pentagon Papers "once these materials fell into our hands." The *Times*, almost as disposed to see conflicts in light of its own powers as the Senate is likely to see them turning on Senate dignity, defined its position so narrowly that it left Dan Ellsberg out in the cold. Rather than presenting the Pentagon Papers as a joint venture between Ellsberg and the newspaper, the *Times* argued that retribution for "declassifying" the Pentagon Papers was a matter between Ellsberg and the government. The *Times* took responsibility for the papers only when they fell on its doorstep out of nowhere, after which their news value required publication. (There is considerable circumstantial evidence that the *Times* was not as passive in the matter as it implies.)

The *Times*' forthright exposition of press duties in matters hot enough to be classified must have convinced Otto Otepka that *he* could in the future slip classified documents to *The New York Times* and expect to see them published. He must have been heartened by the *Times'* objectivity—by the fact that the editors took no overt political or moral position regarding why the war papers should be read in spite of their classifications, and that there was no editorial at all on the war series until the government stupidly tried to suppress it and introduced the freedom of the press question. The editors then said that the people should have a chance to read the papers, that neither the government nor the press should stand in the way of such fireside enlightenment, and that no one but the people can really tell what they mean. Otto must have reasoned that the people could also decide what his documents meant—that they could supply the political judgment if the press would only give them the chance, as the *Times* said it should.

Of course, Otto is no fool at $36,000-a-year, and he might have concluded that the *Times'* opinion on the war really did have something to do with its willingness to publish the Pentagon Papers, despite appearances and circumstantial evidence to the contrary. He might have guessed that the *Times* would not have published material like the Pentagon Papers in 1961, 1968, or even in 1969 when he joined the SACB. Even so, the newspaper's changing views on the war would also help get Otto exposure. His previous efforts to sully the reputations and political judgment of war criminals like Walt Rostow and McGeorge Bundy had not been appreciated at all, but the *Times* seemed to have come around enough on the war that it would go for a batch of documents on such men now. Both the *Times'* increasing readiness to examine the doings of war

criminals and its agnosticism about the actual meaning of the Pentagon Papers should logically work in Otto's favor— and get his documents at least in the back pages. Nevertheless Otepka must fear lest the strictures about orderly procedures reappear, rising ever above the freedom of the press to leave him out in the cold again.

Despite apparent abandonment by *The New York Times*, the need for orderly procedures was identified as the central issue in the Pentagon Papers controversy by such newspapers as the Richmond *Times-Dispatch*. This journal, which had been all courage and patriotism and Paul Revere when Otto was riding, might well have dipped into *The Washington Post's* clipping file on Otepka for its editorial on Ellsberg: "If each clerk, administrative assistant, or under secretary could ignore departmental policy and decide for himself how information should be classified, nothing would be safe." Senator Gordon Allot, a supporter of Otto, chimed in with his attention similarly focused on the rules, as he felt they should apply to *The New York Times*: "The point is that the *Times* has neither the right nor the duty to decide which classified documents should be classified in which way."

The State Department has been one of the few bastions of consistency in the Otepka and Ellsberg matters, opposing both men on the procedural grounds of loyalty and classification rules. But while the State Department has seen both the Ellsberg and Otepka cases through a monocle, most of the rest of us have been so wall-eyed on the matter that we have seen no parallel between them at all. When columnist Carl Rowan suggested that Otepka was "a sort of Daniel Ellsberg in reverse," most of his readers were shocked at the connection proposed, even a reverse one.

One reader, Otto Otepka, scoffed at such a kinship in an interview with UPI reporter Marguerite Davis, who wrote that "Otepka said he gave no classified documents to newspapers but merely provided senators, at their request, with information to support his own sworn testimony." Thus, even Otto— convicted by *The New York Times* on a technicality—distinguishes himself from Dan Ellsberg on a technicality, and a misleading one at that since part of the "information" he gave the senators was a batch of classified documents.

FIDDLING OVER RULES

It is highly ironic that the cases of these two men, whose purposes are so far apart ideologically that it is dangerous to suggest a similarity at any level, have been argued on virtually interchangeable principles. None of them—the Senate's right to know, the people's right to know, freedom of the press, orderly procedures, or national security—went to the heart of the matter. Both men made an essentially moral choice, much like the civil rights sit-ins, to take a specifically illegal step in order to dramatize an injustice that they felt transcended the classification system. Otepka thought the classification system was important, but that the Administration's spinelessness in the Cold War was more important. Ellsberg thought the classification system was important (which is why his decision produced such personal anguish), but that the history of the Vietnam war was more important in its lessons about the past and the nature of the war. Both men made their decisions in the midst of ethical conflict, and any evaluation of them demands that you take a position on why that stand is or is not worthy of support. In other words, given that it is possible for something to be important enough to transcend the classification regulations, you have to make a

political judgment about the purposes of Otepka and Ellsberg.

It is well for those of us who support what Ellsberg did—because the Pentagon Papers changed some minds on the war—to keep the Otepka episode in mind. Thinking of his arguments and the furor around him should keep people from being opportunists in debate—from latching on to the arbitrary rules that pop up here and there, like prairie dogs, around any such controversy. These rules, and the sonorous platitudes that editorial writers and politicians trumpet in their names, provide ludicrously poor guidance in evaluating as serious and complex a matter as the Pentagon Papers. By themselves, the rules make an ungrounded compass, each one pointing east for Ellsberg and west for Otepka, in a spectacle that is nearly comic in the conviction people work up over principles like orderly procedures.

Arguing in support of Dan Ellsberg on the basis of the obvious weaknesses in the classification system is shaky because it runs headlong into opposite impulses regarding Otepka. But more importantly, such an argument misses the point. It is like speaking out for a sit-in because of improprieties in the disturbing-the-peace laws, when the real issue is race. Whatever positive force there is in what Ellsberg did comes from the nature of the war and what the Pentagon Papers say about the war—from political and moral issues that have no simple ground rules. When the debate strays from that central question, it loses both its passion and its logic, leaving a dusty bag of rules that Otto Otepka can use just as well. When the discussion centers on personalities and sideline skirmishes, it makes fewer converts for the antiwar message of the Pentagon Papers and Ellsberg, and thus detracts from what he is trying to accomplish.

Ellsberg and the Pentagon Papers

Fred G. Leebron

Daniel Ellsberg was a "defense intellectual," one of a number of well-educated men attracted to government in the early 1960s by the challenge of making defense policy more rational. After finishing his doctoral dissertation at Harvard in 1958, Ellsberg joined the RAND Corporation, a private non-profit research organization that produced studies for the government, especially for the Air Force. In 1964, Ellsberg moved into a high staff position in the Defense Department, served as a spokesman for the government's position on Vietnam in teach-ins at universities, and then volunteered to go to Vietnam himself, where among other assignments he worked on the pacification programs.

Ellsberg returned to the United States in 1967, and soon was back at RAND, working on the top secret study that would be known as the Pentagon Papers. Initiated by Secretary of Defense Robert MacNamara, the study was to chronicle, from the inside and with objectivity, American involvement in Vietnam. Morton Halperin, Deputy Assistant Secretary of Defense, and his assistant, Leslie Gelb, were in charge of the study. Ellsberg wrote a 350-page draft of one volume before illness caused him to take a less active role as a consultant for the study. This also gave him more time for reflection, and he began to reconsider his own views about America's role in Vietnam.

"Once I asked my father why his father had come to the United States from Russia," Daniel Ellsberg recalls. "'To be

Copyright ©1982 by the Woodrow Wilson School, Princeton University. Reprinted by permission.

free,' my father said. He didn't want to be drafted into the Imperial Army for seven years. 'We came to be free.'"[1] Many years later, Ellsberg was to make full use of that freedom—abusing it in the eyes of his critics, advancing it in the view of his defenders—when he leaked classified government documents to the *New York Times*.

THE EARLY YEARS

Ellsberg was born in Chicago in 1931, the son of middle-class parents. When he was fifteen, his family was involved in a car accident that left his mother and sister dead.[2] At fifteen, he was sent to Cranbrook, an "exclusive prep school" in the suburbs of Detroit. Ellsberg enjoyed his time there. "My heroes," he remembers, "were people like Walter Reuther, labor leaders...."[3] He was an excellent student, compiling a 95.5 grade average and scoring a perfect 800 on the verbal part of the SATs. When supporting Ellsberg's application to Harvard, Cranbrook's Senior Master told the admissions board that Ellsberg was "a brilliant, superior student...inclined at times to feel superior, but no recluse." His classmates also considered him favorably, voting Ellsberg "most likely to make a contribution to human progress." Harvard accepted him.[4]

At Harvard, Ellsberg tried just about everything, including creative writing, psychology and economics. He wrote a short story for the *Advocate*, entitled "The Long Wait," about "a Humphrey Bogart-type involved in marijuana deals." The hero knew himself well:

It wasn't so much that I didn't trust other guys' nerve or ability, as that I didn't trust their luck. So long as I didn't have to depend on anybody else I always had a feeling that I could get through anything that happened. Guys used to think I rode through on guts, but it was really just the way I felt.[5]

Ellsberg finally settled down at the *Crimson*. Preoccupied with his individuality, Ellsberg recalls, "I think—though there may have been one or two others—that I was the first *Advocate* person to be on the *Crimson* since John Reed, who wrote *Ten Days That Shook the World*. There must be something to that." Ellsberg was an enthusiastic contributor to the *Crimson*, and one night stayed up to write the entire editorial page. He wrote in a journal for occasional relief:

4 a.m. Boy, I want you to know, this is the last time D.E. signs up for two pieces in one night...8 a.m. D.E. is tired...9 a.m. D.E. is sick...11 a.m. The worst part of it is, when you stay up all night writing two pieces for the ed page, all you write is crap...12:00. Okay, friends, that's all.

Beneath Ellsberg's last entry, one editor wrote, "D.E. has a martyr complex."[6]

In 1951, his junior year, Ellsberg married a Radcliffe junior, Carol Cummings, the daughter of a Marine officer.[7] His senior thesis was entitled "Theories of Rational Choice Under Uncertainty: The Contribution of von Neumann and Morgenstern," concerning "the new economic theory of games." Both the field and the topic were new, and the thesis was graded *summa* by all three readers.[8] It received one criticism: "If there is one principal shortcoming in the work, it is an unfortunate tendency to be somewhat erratic in the pursuit of a single line of investigation, which leads to a lack of depth and completeness."[9]

After graduating from Harvard with a B.A. in economics, Ellsberg received a Woodrow Wilson fellowship to study economics at Cambridge. He met many Communists there, but they were unable to offer him any explanation of Stalin's terror. Ellsberg recalls, "They'd shut off my arguments by saying that everything I was reading in the papers was lies. But I knew there had to be at least some grain of truth to what I was reading. There really were bad things going on." Upon returning from England to complete his Master's at Harvard, Ellsberg, confronted with the escalating Cold War, became a "Truman Democrat": "I was a liberal on domestic matters and, on foreign policy, a tough guy." But the 1950's in the United States were also replete with labor corruption, and Ellsberg shifted his concentration from domestic matters to foreign policy. A friend explains:

The thing people forget is that whatever one thought of Joe McCarthy, Joseph Stalin really scared the daylights out of everyone, from the far right to the pretty far left. It wasn't so much an anti-Communist feeling as an anti-Russian one.... I knew people in the fifties who switched from the United World Federalists to the CIA.[10]

Upon receiving his Master's, Ellsberg joined the Marines. Ellsberg remarks, "It was not the normal thing to do. But I wanted to find out what the service was like. Except for one other guy, I think I was the only one of my old *Crimson* crowd to give up my deferment." Ellsberg "ranked first in his 1,100-man officers-candidate class,"[11] and notes, "I was, I think, the only first lieutenant in the Second Marine Division to have a rifle company."[12] He did not see combat, and was scheduled to return in 1956 to Harvard as a Junior Fellow, when his battalion was sent to the Suez Canal to cover the takeover there. Ellsberg recalls:

So I spent a day thinking about what I would feel like to be back to Harvard and read in the papers about my batallion in combat. I couldn't stand the thought, so I sent a telegram to the commandant of the Marine Corps asking to extend for one year so I could accompany the batallion.[13]

But Ellsberg also had to write a letter to the head of Society of Fellows at Harvard in order to gain an extension on the fellowship offer. In so doing, Ellsberg "described in detail plans to evacuate Americans from the Suez area." A carbon of the letter was found in his desk, and he was interrogated for twelve hours, because of the breach of security. Ellsberg assured the MP's that his motives were innocent.[14] After that, Ellsberg gained his first "top secret" clearance, because the command had to determine how to land at the Suez.[15]

Ellsberg, however, saw no real combat, and returned in 1957 to gain his doctorate at Harvard. Entitled, "Risk, Ambiguity and Decision," the opening sentence of his dissertation read:

> To act reasonably, one must judge actions by their consequences. But what if their consequences are uncertain? One must still, no doubt, act reasonably: the problem is to decide what this may mean.[16]

Ellsberg was still a Junior Fellow at Harvard, when he began his association with The Rand Corporation in 1958.[17] He became a full-time employee in 1959.

ELLSBERG AT RAND AND DEFENSE

In the late Fifties, even Rand did not have the sort of reputation that would attract a liberal. The "think tank" was founded in 1946 with Air Force patronage as a private, non-profit institution.[18] An Ellsberg friend recalled that in the 1950's "Rand had an Air Force sort of look to it. It was heavily Air Force money and it used all those social gimmicks."[19] When he decided to work for Rand, Ellsberg remembers that a tutor accused him of selling out to the organization. Ellsberg, though, says:

> I spent the summer of '58 at Rand in part because they were interested in my particular academic interest, which was "decision-making under uncertainty"; and I found them all hard at work on what came to seem to me the most urgent problem facing mankind. That was the missile gap.... I would have worked for Rand for nothing. It seemed the most important problem in the world.[20]

Rand became the foremost military policy think tank in America while Ellsberg was there. And its president during most of Ellsberg's tenure, Henry Rowen, became Ellsberg's closest friend. Among other things, Rand accepted Ellsberg on the basis of his academic prowess and a security clearance administered by federal authorities.[21] As *Newsweek* was to describe some time later, Rand "made its name on discretion as well as brainpower — on the premise that it could be trusted to keep a secret."[22]

In 1959, when Ellsberg joined Rand as an economist, he and his family moved to Los Angeles, and Ellsberg worked at the Santa Monica Rand headquarters. A friend recalls that Ellsberg concentrated completely on the missile gap issue:

> There was Russia, Stalin, nuclear weapons — all that was an essential part of Dan's life.... But Dan was on the liberal side; he was in favor of putting more covers on the buttons, so some mad colonel wouldn't set the whole thing off.[23]

Ellsberg himself recalls, "At Rand we believed the Russians were going full blast for a capability to destroy our retaliatory capability, and intelligence estimates pointed that way." Concerning Vietnam, however, Ellsberg felt differently. After a short fact-finding tour there, he wrote Kennedy that he "found the situation there unpromising." He says, "I felt the President had arbitrarily chosen Vietnam as a place to test himself."[24]

Ellsberg also worked closely with the Administration on the Cuban Missile Crisis. (Later, when Sorensen and Schlesinger had published their JFK memoirs, Ellsberg was to note the "questionable precedent" of their using "technically still-classified" material in the books.) Caught up as he was in missiles and foot soldiers, Ellsberg neglected his family. His wife sued for divorce in late 1964.[25]

In 1964, Ellsberg had joined the Defense Department as a Special Assistant in its Department of International Security Affairs (ISA).[26] It was in 1964 or 1965, while working at the Pentagon prior to heading for Vietnam, that Ellsberg first felt "while reading through documents late at night (of events leading up to and including the Tonkin Gulf incident) that I was looking at future exhibits (in war crime trials)."[27]

Prior to leaving for Vietnam in 1965, Ellsberg talked at college teach-ins as a Defense Department spokesman. Debating with Harvard Government Professor Stanley Hoffman, Ellsberg summed up his pre-tour attitude:

> The question is not whether the odds are against us or whether we have given up the goal of total victory. The primary issue is to improve conditions in the South...there might be a time when we have to ask how we can fail best.[28]

Recalls Hoffman, "I liked him. He was not a government mouthpiece or an intellectual adding machine, but a human being you could argue with. Not a Bundy."[29]

Ellsberg did not go to Vietnam by accident. Initially, he wished to re-enlist in the Marines, but found that he would not then have the desired authority (he wanted to command a platoon). So he volunteered to be a member of Major General Edward G. Lansdale's unit to work on counter-insurgency techniques. Ellsberg noted, "I was the only volunteer

that he ended up taking. I seemed to be the kind of nut he liked to have on his team." And Ellsberg again was concerned with the victims' lot: "I chose to educate myself on pacification, to learn the realities of what the war was like in the countryside."[30]

Arriving in Saigon in 1965, Ellsberg headed for Rand headquarters. There he met Anthony J. Russo, another Rand researcher, who was doing studies on the mistreatment of Vietcong prisoners. Ellsberg learned all he could from his disillusioned colleague, and then proceeded into "the field."[31] Ellsberg admitted he was gung-ho, "but not more so than a lot of other Americans, civilians and military."[32] His own rationale for going into the field concerned the nature of the advice he was expected to give:

> A lot of this advice had to do with the risks that they should be prepared to run. And I was one of those, and not the only one, who felt that you should not give advice on questions like that unless you were prepared to go out of your way to share those risks to some extent.[33]

A reporter in Vietnam at the time recalls:

> There was Ellsberg, dressed in fatigues and jungle boots, telling the infantrymen to get off their goddamned asses, to get on the offensive and stay on the offensive. He carried a submachine gun and was practically taking over the company.[34]

Another journalist, Frances Fitzgerald, had a different interpretation of Ellsberg's aggressive behavior:

> Like every American in the goddamned country, Dan had to get out in the field. Everyone had to pick up a gun.... It was the whole romance of danger and death.... You thought you were better than other people.... But the Hemingway approach finally soured. It was not World War I. All that machinery, that gigantic arsenal, was

being aimed at Asians running around in pajamas.[35]

Ellsberg was then advocating training fifty-seven-man teams of Vietnamese — Political Action Teams — that "were supposed to provide the South Vietnamese peasants with the same sort of political dedication that the communists provided in the North." A visiting reported noted with disdain the "assembly-line-like approach to political warfare," and the fact that the question of ideological motivation for the PAT's remained unanswered. Ellsberg, however, "sent back critical memos on the [pacification] program to Washington via a friend (technically a violation of government procedure) when he thought his criticism was not getting proper attention by American officials in Saigon."[36]

In December of the same year, Ellsberg was appointed Special Assistant to Deputy Ambassador William Porter, with the intention of increasing his own focus on the relationship between military and civil operations. The same month, he sent Washington a report entitled, "The Day Loc Tien Was Pacified," illustrating how no part of the combat zone was really being pacified — but rather only endangered.[37] Finally, Ellsberg recalls, "By mid-1967 I felt we were destroying the society and the war must be stopped."[38] Still, he intended to remain in Vietnam to see the war through.[39] Ellsberg recalls:

> My plan was to go into the field with every single unit we had in Vietnam. Starting at the DMZ and working all the way down to the Delta. Fortunately, I got hepatitis before I got killed.[40]

Ellsberg wrote from his sickbed in Bangkok:

> It has been, most of it, an intensely frustrating and sad year and a half, though with a good deal of excitement and moments of hope.... I have virtually decided to go home, and make my contribution to the Vietnam problem we all share from here.[41]

THE PENTAGON PAPERS AND ELLSBERG'S REVELATIONS

In the spring of 1967, while still abroad, Ellsberg urged a friend at Defense to propose that McNamara begin a study of "U.S. decision-making in Vietnam on the model of Dick Neustadt's study of the Skybolt crisis." Ellsberg offered himself as a participant. A few weeks later, Ellsberg recalls, "McNamara himself proposed his historical study, mentioning the Skybolt as a guideline."[42]

In July of 1967, Ellsberg returned to the U.S., as he recalls, in the midst of the Detroit riot and the Newark riot: "So [I] immediately became far more aware of the domestic costs of the war, and that forced [me] to look harder at the question of whether it was really essential for us to be there."[43] And by the fall of 1967, Ellsberg was working on the new top-secret study to become known as the Pentagon Papers: "once again employed by Rand.... I was at work."[44]

The Pentagon Papers project actually began in the summer of 1967, under the direction of Morton H. Halperin, Deputy Assistant Secretary of Defense for ISA. Halperin, in turn, appointed Leslie H. Gelb, his assistant at ISA, to head the specific task force in charge of the study. Both men were former Rand employees.[45]

The study utilized thirty-six scholars, representing Defense, Rand and several universities. It eventually produced 3,000 pages of analysis and history, and included 4,000 pages of classified documents.[46] Ellsberg initially completed "a 350-page draft of the Pentagon volume on the '61 Vietnam decisions," before the aftereffects of hepatitis reduced him to a passive consultant role in early 1968.[47] It was then that Ellsberg carefully reconsidered both his own and his country's involvement in Vietnam.

In April of 1968, Ellsberg attended a Princeton conference on "Revolution in a

Changing World," and met Janaki Tschannerl, an Indian woman. Ellsberg remembers:

> She gave me a vision, as a Gandhian, of a different way of living and resistance, of exercising power non-violently. And as I saw it at that time, Martin Luther King began to seem to me to be our last hope. And he was killed that weekend.[48]

The friend recalls the following conversation:

> What do you do?... I work.... What kind of work do you do?... I think.... What do you think about?... Viet Nam.... What do you think about Viet Nam?... How in God's name are we going to get out of there?[49]

About that time, Ellsberg began psychoanalysis with Dr. Lewis Fielding in Beverly Hills. Meeting four times a week, treatment continued for two and a half years.[50]

By the time the Pentagon study was completed in December 1968, the Johnson Administration was on its way out. Paul Warnke, now Assistant Secretary of Defense for ISA, and both Gelb and Halperin, were anxious to ensure the study's classified status. Wrote journalist Peter Schrag:

> Gelb, Warnke and Halperin, wishing to retain control of documents on which they had worked, pooled their copies of the Papers and, under a special agreement with Henry Rowen, the President of Rand, sent them to Rand for storage.

The agreement contained the provision that the documents "would only be accessible to those who had specific permission from two of the three 'owners'—Gelb, Warnke, Halperin."[51] Ellsberg later told *Look* magazine that the "owners" had agreed from the very beginning to give Ellsberg access to the full study:

> ...they were very anxious to get me. I was only willing to do it on the condition that I would be able to profit from it in-

tellectually by reading the whole study. That was the price I asked for participating as a researcher. So I was given the commitment that I would be able to read this thing ultimately. No other researcher got that commitment on the study. Rand was not given access. I was only given personal access on the basis of this prior agreement. The point then was that I was the only researcher in the country with authorized access to the entire study.[52]

Halperin, Gelb, and Warnke denied that such an arrangement existed. Rowen tried to get Ellsberg access to the document: "(there was, at the very least, an intimation that Warnke did not trust Ellsberg to keep the papers confidential)." The second time, however, Rowen told Halperin that the Pentagon study would be an important aid in Ellsberg's study on "lessons of Vietnam." Halperin obtained Gelb's permission and, without consulting Warnke, authorized Ellsberg's access to the study.[53]

Before Ellsberg had a chance to read the study, however, Henry Kissinger summoned him to New York on Christmas Day. Kissinger had initiated a study at Rand on Vietnam and wanted Ellsberg to help him finish the analysis in order to prepare Nixon on the topic. Ellsberg's analysis, National Security Study Memorandum No. 1 (NSSM-1), took the form of questions "which analyzed the major uncertainties, contradictions and controversies among the agencies dealing with Vietnam." Kissinger distributed it, and Ellsberg went to Washington to help out: "I spent February in the Executive Office Building reading and helping to summarize the answers to my questions... for the President." Ellsberg eventually leaked NSSM-1 (in June of 1971) to Senators Mike Gravel and Charles Mathias. He was evidently upset that Kissinger had deleted Ellsberg's option of withdrawal from the final list of policy alternatives sent to the National Security Council.[54]

Thereafter, employed by Rand, Ellsberg read the Pentagon Papers. He read the seven-thousand pages of analysis, history and documentation by the end of the summer of 1969. His reaction to the documents was nothing less than astonishment. Recalls an acquaintance:

> I had a sense of a man thoroughly disillusioned by what he had learned.... There isn't an ounce of cynicism in his body. When he found out about all the deceptions and lies, he did not react in the normal cynical way—"Well, it's the government, what do you expect?" Ellsberg was scandalized. He was scandalized to discover that *people are not good.*[55]

Ellsberg, himself, concentrated his analysis of the study on the aspect of presidential participation in Vietnam:

> And I was still in a state of mind (prior to the reading) that thought: This is terrible. The President isn't getting the truth. I had this impression "if only the Czar knew."... But reading 7,000 pages of the Pentagon Papers has shown me that the President of the United States is part of the problem.[56]

Ellsberg also pointed out that he was the only person in the country who had both read the entire study and been to Vietnam:

> ... At that point the experiences I had had in Vietnam came to bear very strongly on me. The village burned by both sides, the refugee camps. There would have been no war had there not been an American commitment of funds and troops to keep it going. The Vietnamese majority may have preferred various forms of local leadership other than the Vietcong, but the question became: Do they feel strongly enough to fight the VC without us leading them? The answer was no. So we were responsible for all aspects of the war, including the villages the VC had burned.[57]

Considering the documents of the Pentagon study "the best we have—a good starting point for a real understanding of the war, the U.S. equivalent of the Nuremburg war crime documents," Ellsberg decided both to convey his view of the war and to get other government officials to read the study.[58]

The decision to use the Pentagon Papers as a modus operandi for changing government policy grew from the final lesson that Ellsberg learned from reading the study:

> ... that domestic political considerations were so important to the President that mere discussion or argument within the Executive Branch would never affect the policy. The only way to affect it was to change the political calculations by the President, to change the political pressures. ... You could say that if the President wants to get out, the only way to make it possible for him is to assure him that he will not be subject to fatal attack and he will not be attacked by the other party if he does get out.
>
> So my first efforts were entirely along the lines of getting Congress and leading Democrats to urge the President, or even require him, to get out, so that the responsibility wouldn't fall entirely on his shoulders.[59]

To set about re-educating government officials required great effort. Ellsberg returned to his old friend Anthony Russo, since fired by Rand, and enlisted his help in copying the top secret documents.[60] With the help of an unsuspecting third party, the documents were successfully copied.

Then, in November of 1969, during a visit to Washington, Ellsberg met for the first time Senator J. W. Fulbright, Chairman of the Senate Foreign Relations Committee. Fulbright was publicly committed to the American withdrawal from Vietnam. In 1964, he had been a member of the Congress skillfully manipulated by President Johnson into passing the Gulf of Tonkin resolution—an act he considered to be the "functional equivalent" of a declaration of war on North Vietnam. Ellsberg "played on that anger," informing Fulbright of the existence of the top secret Pentagon Papers, and giving him a portion of the study dealing with the Tonkin Gulf incident. At that time, Ellsberg asked Fulbright to make public the Pentagon Papers, "perhaps through full congressional release of their contents."[61]

Fulbright hesitated:

> I didn't want to get Ellsberg in trouble. I considered what to do with the portions he gave me—having executive hearings or something of that nature. But I decided that the best way would be to get them officially. Anyway, it wasn't clear then of what use they actually were in stopping the war.

He put the documents in the safe at the Foreign Relations Committee office, and, just two days after meeting Ellsberg, wrote to Defense Secretary Melvin Laird, requesting a copy of the Pentagon study.[62]

After months of delay, Laird refused Fulbright's request. Although frustrated, Fulbright could not bring himself illegally to divulge the Pentagon Papers:

> I thought there would be a big to-do by the Administration on the question of classification, which might divert from the contents of the Papers. I thought that if we used them without release, the big attack would be on the procedure.... If I had done it, this would have brought a good deal of criticism on the Committee; certain Republican members would have raised hell.... I still thought they should be the subject of legitimate hearings.

Journalist Sanford Ungar explained that "any breach of security on [Fulbright's] part could be used as a basis for denying him such material in the future. Then he in turn might be answerable to his colleagues in the Senate for their inability to learn that little bit of the inside story...."[63]

In September of 1969, Ellsberg attended a conference of the War Resisters' League at Haverford College near Philadelphia. On the final night of the conference, Ellsberg recalls:

Randy [Kehler, a Harvard graduate] gave a talk about the peace movement. He talked of all the people in the movement who were going to jail. Then, out of the blue, he said, "and I'm very proud that I'm soon going to be joining them." He was resisting the draft and, sure enough, he was soon in prison.

Well, I remember thinking, you see—this is our best, our very best, and we're sending them to prison, more important, we're in a world where they feel they just had to go to prison.... All of a sudden, it set new standards for me of what one could be expected, or asked, to do, in the way of resistance to the war. I realized that these young men were very patriotic. And suddenly I realized that I too would have to enter a kind of resistance to the war even if I too had to go to prison.[64]

Ellsberg sent the top secret study to Senator George McGovern. McGovern refused to act on it. Ellsberg thought McGovern's refusal to accept the papers was grounded in cowardice. But McGovern explains the situation somewhat differently:

> I concluded after talking with him for a while that he was a hawk with a bad conscience. I've had a dozen professors and preachers and foreign service officers give me memoranda in the past that they said would end the war if disclosed.... I had no idea what he had, and I didn't know if his judgment was good or bad. I didn't even know whether he was rational.

John Holum, McGovern's legislative assistant, disliked the aggressive Ellsberg: "There are a lot of people you encounter who are recent converts on the war. They usually don't have much to offer."[65] But in retrospect, McGovern concludes "that if a member of Congress had been willing to act, the press and the people might have been able to obtain and digest the information in the Pentagon Papers much more easily."[66]

In the winter of 1969–70, Ellsberg was a consultant to Senator Charles Goodell of New York, helping the Senator draft a proposal for the immediate withdrawal of U.S. troops from Vietnam. Goodell remembers, "it was obvious the guy knew something. We had to round off the figures and fuzz the details so people wouldn't think we had access to some sort of classified data."[67] Even with Ellsberg's expertise, the proposal got nowhere.

In 1970, Ellsberg decided that he had to act more convincingly on his own. First, spurred on by the U.S.-supported arrest of his friend Tran Ngoc Chau, a member of South Vietnam's National Assembly, by President Thieu, Ellsberg resigned from Rand:

> ...In order to be able to speak freely, in a way that seemed impossible to do at Rand, and not because Rand officers forbade me, but because every time I criticized the war I caused great apprehension among my colleagues that they were about to lose their contract, and hence their jobs.[68]

Ellsberg gained a brief audience with Kissinger, saying, "Henry, I smell 1964 all over again." Ellsberg recalls:

> I asked him if he had a copy of the McNamara study in the White House. "Yes," he said. "Did you read it?" I asked. "No," Kissinger said. "Anybody on your staff work it over?" Again, Kissinger said, "No." I urged him to read at least the summaries — about 100 pages — and the chronologies. "But we make decisions very differently now," Henry said.[69]

Then came Jackson State, Kent State, and the bombing of Cambodia.[70]

By the time Nixon started on Laos, Ellsberg, according to one Senator's assistant, had been "all over Washington. He was seeing anybody who might help."[71]

Ellsberg had now begun to see his enlistment of government officials as a futile endeavor. He approached several lawyers, in the hopes that they would initiate "civil suits or injunctions claiming the unconstitutionality of the war," believing that such court action "would provide a channel whereby the Pentagon documents could enter public consciousness." The documents, he felt, would alter the public's perception of the war, then forming a general political consensus on ending the war, leading to the ultimate abandonment by Nixon of his war policy. But no lawyers "rose" to meet Ellsberg's challenge.[72]

All legal channels exhausted, Ellsberg perceived the extralegal alternative: release of the classified documents directly to the public. As a writer of both letters to the editor and book reviews, Ellsberg considered the nation's newspapers as the only possible channel for the direct release of the papers into the "public consciousness." But he was still unsure of which paper to turn to, or which specific person to approach.[73]

It was then that Ellsberg learned that *Times* reporter Neil Sheehan was preparing an article on thirty-three anti-war books for that paper's book review section. Ellsberg and Sheehan had known each other in Vietnam, where Sheehan had been a reporter. And now, in his article, "Should We Have War Crime Trials?" Sheehan wrote that government officials had "never read the laws governing the conduct of war...or if they did, they interpreted them rather loosely."

Within days, Ellsberg contacted Sheehan. And days later, in late March, Sheehan and his wife went up to Cambridge to pick up the documents. On a Sunday in late Spring, June 13, 1971, under the headline, "Vietnam Archive: Pentagon Study Traces 3 Decades of Growing U.S. Involvement," the Pentagon Papers appeared in the *Times*.[74]

The Pentagon Papers chronicled three decades of American military and diplomatic policy in Indochina. By reproducing the actual memoranda, cablegrams, and orders of government officials, and by including narrative analyses by the government historians, the Papers revealed what decisions were made, how and why they were made and who made them. They showed that four administrations had committed the U.S. to defending South Vietnam to a much greater extent than their statements to Congress or the public indicated. For example, in the spring of 1964, nearly a year before President Johnson revealed the depth of U.S. involvement in Vietnam, he had stepped up the covert warfare against North Vietnam and had begun planning overt war. Many of these decisions ran counter to the estimates of the government's own intelligence agencies, which indicated that the military pressure and bombing in this period had not achieved any significant effect. Although the Papers contained few conclusions that critics had not already reached about U.S. policy, they gave official support to many of those conclusions, and provided the detailed information that made the conclusions more striking.

In a speech he gave in Boston shortly before the *Times* published the papers, Ellsberg read poignantly from the memoirs of Nazi official Albert Speer, who had turned away so that he would not see the horrors of the Third Reich: "For *being in a position to know and nevertheless shunning knowledge creates direct responsibility for the consequences —from the very beginning.*" Nearing the end of his dramatic talk (during which he sometimes cried), Ellsberg spoke in his own words:

> It is, then, my own long *persistence in ignorance* of the history of the conflict [Vietnam] and of our involvement and of the full impact of the American way of war that I find most to blame in myself. As I look back over my role in the last eight years, it is with a heavy sense of guilt.[75]

Why did Ellsberg act at this moment? He recalls:

> As I found out these various people were unwilling to help, I began to feel that the FBI might already know something about it and might pick me up at any time, swoop in and take everything before I got it out. My main fear was that the whole thing would be aborted.[76]

Ellsberg suggested that he might directly be responsible for the new tactics of Nixon: "But as the invasions mounted up, I thought, if I'd gotten the Papers released earlier, maybe I could have prevented all that."[77]

Ellsberg also said that he hoped, by his example, that "a few other ex-officials would come clean."[78]

Ellsberg did not view America's involvement in Vietnam as historian Arthur Schlesinger did in 1964: a matter of stumbling "unknowingly into a 'quagmire' in Vietnam and simply never knowing how to get out." Instead, Ellsberg concluded that Vietnam was the logical result of America's "Asia first" policy stretching back to 1949. It was during that year that Congressman John Kennedy declared to his colleagues on the House floor that they must "assume the responsibility of preventing the onrushing tide of communism from engulfing all of Asia."[79] Ellsberg viewed the ensuing policy as a direct result of the "fear of McCarthyism":

> It was the motivation of the Democratic President not to add the fall of Indochina to the fall of China. The very fact the decision-making looked similar year by year from then on, supported the conjecture that no American President, Republican or Democrat, wanted to be the President who lost the war or who lost Saigon.

According to Ellsberg, every president felt compelled to weigh domestic anti-communism more heavily than any military or foreign policy objective. The only way, then, to change the course of foreign policy was to show the Executive Branch that the overwhelming consensus in America was to withdraw from Vietnam. The best (and perhaps only) way to shape this consensus was to show the public that Vietnam was against national interests. Publication of the Pentagon Papers, Ellsberg believed, would shape this new public perception, forcing the hand of the Executive Branch, who would then realize that domestic political pressures were reversed, and that involvement in the war should end.[80]

But Ellsberg knew that releasing the classified documents was an illegal act. He defined his illegal transgression as "non-violent civil disobedience," which was "a way of making a dramatic statement of conscience."[81]

Journalists and Ellsberg's friends offer different interpretations. Journalist Peter Schrag, for example, felt that "the act was also an effort to establish credibility with the people he was trying to reach."[82] Schrag quoted Ellsberg: "When I first started facing such audiences and the person introducing me felt compelled to go down the whole list of my past associations, my heart would sink with each sentence."[83] Indeed, in May of 1971, Ellsberg went to an anti-war rally in Washington, and by several accounts, took charge of the affair. He said afterward, "I tried to get arrested, but I guess I didn't look young enough."[84]

Friends of Ellsberg varied in their interpretations of his motives in divulging the documents. Said one:

> Ever since I've known him, he's had this almost evangelistic need to communicate to you the truth he's just discovered. I suspect, that's the way it was with the Pentagon Papers. He couldn't stand having the truths he's discovered in them hidden from the public view.[85]

Some friends even asserted it was a matter of ego that led Ellsberg to release the Pentagon Papers. Said one friend, "One morning Dan woke up, and saw he was forty years old and not famous yet. Turning forty does something to people

and Dan always thought he was bigger than other men."[86]

Another friend remarked:

> It was ego. Any act of conscience, if it has potentially vast consequences, becomes inevitably, in part, playing God. But that has to be weighed against the consequences of not playing God.... I don't think he can get away from guilt.... Dan was not acting so much out of personal guilt as out of national guilt, but the personal element was in there somewhere.[87]

POLITICAL AND ETHICAL REACTION

Within a week of the publication of the first installment of the Papers, the FBI discovered that Ellsberg had been the source of the leak. An indictment by a federal grand jury on June 28, 1971, charged Ellsberg with "unauthorized possession of...documents and writings related to the national defense," and the possession of these copies—all but one being classified—for "his own use." Maximum sentence for conviction of either offense was ten years imprisonment and a $10,000 fine.[88] The indictment also charged Ellsberg with a violation of the Espionage Act, which asserted that Ellsberg had "reason to believe" the information in the documents "could be used to the injury of the United States or to the advantage of any foreign nation."[89]

Ellsberg directly refuted the charge of violating the Espionage Act. There were several of the original forty-seven volumes of the Pentagon study that contained accounts of sensitive negotiations among Washington, Hanoi and Moscow. Ellsberg said:

> None of these studies were given to any newspapers. They were given to the Senate Foreign Relations Committee.... Obviously, I didn't think there was a single page... that would do grave damage to the national interest, or I wouldn't have released them.[90]

White House reaction to the publication of the documents was eventually aggressive (the initial low-keyed headline in the *Times* may have disarmed the staff momentarily). Nixon said that the publication of the Papers "created a situation in which the ability of the government to carry on foreign relations even in the best of circumstances could have been severely compromised."[91] Also, because one of the first *Times'* articles contained part of the Wheeler Report (a document on the Tet Offensive that Ellsberg also obtained and released), which was not part of the Pentagon study, "serious questions" were raised "about what and how much else might have been taken. There was every reason to believe that this was a security leak of unprecedented proportions."[92]

Ellsberg's release of the study had occurred at "a particularly sensitive time." After months of negotiating to establish a secret channel to Peking, Henry Kissinger's secret visit there was just "three and a half weeks away" when the leak occurred. Also, on May 31, Kissinger had made what was considered an important proposal to Hanoi during secret talks in Paris. Writes Kissinger: "For the first time in the war Hanoi had deigned to say that it would study an American proposal... If Hanoi concluded that our domestic support was eroding, for whatever reason, it was bound to hold fast to its position." Regarding Peking, Kissinger noted that because of "the massive hemorrhage of state secrets... Our nightmare at the moment was that Peking might conclude our government was too unsteady, too harassed, and too insecure to be a useful partner." But Kissinger concluded that the leak had no substantial effect on either the Peking visit or the Hanoi negotiations.[93]

In his memoirs, Nixon recalls that the "CIA was worried that past or current informants would be exposed... In fact, one secret contact dried up immediately." He also asserted that governments acting as "diplomatic go-betweens" registered "official protests" because, even though

Ellsberg did not release the "diplomacy" volumes, the participants regarded the leak as a breach of security.[94]

Journalist Anthony Lukas identified three White House fears at the time. The first was that Ellsberg and his "co-conspirators" had even more damaging secrets to release, or even to pass to the Soviet Union. The second fear was that Ellsberg's action would inspire others within the government to leak classified materials. Third was "a corollary concern —that conservatives might leak information about the as yet secret Nixon-Kissinger plans for rapprochement with Moscow and Peking in an effort to sabotage them." Although rumors circulated at the time, no concern was truly substantiated. However, the White House did tighten controls, enlisting a group of self-styled "plumbers" to fix the "leaks." These men planned the break-in at Ellsberg's psychiatrist, in an effort to gather more information concerning the former Rand researcher.[95]

Rand reaction was not favorable. One analyst said, "It's just monstrous, unbelievably disloyal to do what he did, an arrogant, egotistical act by a guy with a martyr complex." Another analyst commented upon the schism in Rand, and evaluated Ellsberg's act:

> ...What he [Ellsberg] did was simply not supposed to happen. Everyone with a top-security clearance gets a tough investigation and after that, it's up to a man's sense of loyalty and honor. You cannot maintain an atmosphere of loyalty and self-respect if you have guards looking into briefcases.[96]

Various procedural delays led Judge Matthew Byrne, Jr. to declare a mistrial on December 8, 1972. By then, twelve additional counts of theft, violation of the Espionage Act and conspiracy had been filed against Ellsberg and co-defendant Anthony Russo. Finally, on May 11, 1973, because of evidence reaching Byrne concerning the break-in at Ellsberg's psychiatrist's in August of 1971, he declared another mistrial and dismissed all charges against Ellsberg and Russo.[97]

Ellsberg continued demonstrating against the war in Vietnam, up to the Communist victory there in 1975. Then, he shifted his energies to protesting the nuclear arms build-up and advocating disarmament. "In October 1976, Ellsberg was arrested with forty others at a demonstration in front of the Pentagon. In March 1978, he organized and led a protest march on the nuclear weapons plant at Rock Flats, Nevada."[98]

Things at Rand were much worse. Henry Rowen, Ellsberg's best friend, was forced to give up his position as president of the organization.[99] Ellsberg defended himself against the charge that he had betrayed his friend: "After all, there were thousands of very real people—among them some of my friends—who would also be deeply affected—even killed—by a continuation of the war."[100]

Rand, itself, lost control to the Air Force of all its top secret documents. Its funding also slipped—but that was a development evident in the fall from grace that most military think tanks experienced since the Tet Offensive in 1968. Wrote Peter Schrag: "Ellsberg simply dramatized the demise and forced the keepers of the mystery of military science into self-serving denials and contradictions to save themselves."[101]

Watergate and all it enveloped—including the break-in by G. Gordon Liddy and Howard Hunt at Fielding's office—forced Nixon to resign in August of 1974. Both that and the final capitulation of South Vietnam to the Communists in 1975 served as the confirmation of all of Ellsberg's suspicions: an overpowering Executive Branch and a useless, immoral war.

At an awards dinner given by the Federal Employees for Peace in September of 1971, Daniel Ellsberg received its Employee of the Year Award. Part of the award was a large scroll. Inscribed on the scroll was the code of ethics of Government service: "Put loyalty to highest moral principle and to country above loyalty to persons, party or Government department."[102]

Many people not present that night, among them scholars, public officials, and fellow citizens also felt that Daniel Ellsberg had served that code well. Many others continued to believe that he had not.

NOTES

1. J. Anthony Lukas, "After the Pentagon Papers—A Month in the New Life of Daniel Ellsberg," *New York Times Magazine*, Dec. 12, 1971, p. 98.

2. For his reaction, see Joe McGinniss, "The Ordeal of Daniel Ellsberg," *Playboy*, 19, Oct. 1972, p. 197.

3. Frank Rich, "Q: Do the Claims of Conscience Outweigh the Duties of Citizenship, Testimony of The Witness, Daniel Ellsberg," *Esquire*, Dec. 1971, p. 286.

4. Ibid.

5. Ibid.

6. Ibid.

7. McGinniss, p. 197.

8. Rich, p. 286.

9. Ibid., p. 287.

10. Ibid.

11. McGinniss, p. 197.

12. J. Robert Moskin, "Ellsberg Talks," *Look*, 35, Oct. 5, 1971, p. 32.

13. Ibid., p. 33.

14. Rich, p. 288.

15. Moskin, p. 33.

16. McGinniss, p. 197.

17. Rich, p. 288.

18. "Plugging Leaks in a Think Tank," *Newsweek*, 78, July 12, 1971, p. 29.

19. Rich, p. 288.

20. Moskin, p. 32.

21. John Walsh, "Pentagon Papers: Repercussions for Rand and Other Think Tanks," *Science*, 173 (July 23, 1971), no. 3994: 311.

22. "Plugging Leaks," p. 28.

23. Rich, p. 290.

24. Ibid.

25. Ibid.

26. "The Suspect: A Hawk Who Turned Dove." *Newsweek*, 77, June 28, 1971, p. 16.

27. Todd Gitlin, "Ellsberg and the New Heroism," *Commonweal*, Sept. 3, 1971, p. 450.

28. Rich, p. 292.

29. Ibid.

30. Moskin, p. 33.

31. Studs Terkel, "Servants of the State," *Harpers*, 244, p. 52.

32. Moskin, p. 33.

33. Ibid.

34. "Ellsberg: The Battle Over the Right to Know," *Time*, 98, July 5, 1971, p. 9.

35. Rich, pp. 293–94.

36. John P. Roche, "Recollections of Ellsberg," *Washington Post*, July 24, 1971, Sec. A, p. 19.

37. Rich, p. 293.

38. Ibid.

39. Ibid.

40. McGinniss, p. 197.

41. Rich, p. 294.

42. Peter Schrag, *Test of Loyalty* (New York: Simon and Schuster, 1974), p. 35. Also see Schrag, "The Ellsberg Affair," *Saturday Review*, Nov. 13, 1971.

43. Moskin, p. 34.

44. Schrag, *Test*, p. 35.

45. Ibid.

46. Ibid.

47. Rich, p. 294.

48. Lukas, pp. 103–4.

49. Schrag, *Test*, pp. 437–38.

50. "Ellsberg: The Battle," p. 11.

51. Schrag, *Test*, p. 37.

52. Moskin, p. 34.

53. Schrag, *Test*, pp. 37–38.

54. Ibid. pp. 39–40.

55. Rich, p. 294.

56. Lukas, p. 98.

57. Rich, p. 294.

58. "The Suspect," p. 16.

59. Moskin, p. 39.

60. Schrag, *Test*, p. 45.

61. Sanford J. Ungar, *The Papers and the Papers* (New York: E. P. Dutton, 1972), pp. 67–68.

62. Ibid., p. 68.

63. Ibid., p. 72.

64. Lukas, p. 106.

65. Ungar, p. 82.

66. Ibid., p. 83.

67. Schrag, *Test*, p. 48.

68. Terkel, p. 56.

69. "The Suspect," p. 16.

70. Schrag, *Test*, p. 51.

71. Ibid., p. 49.

72. Moskin, p. 39.

73. Ibid.

74. Schrag, *Test*, pp. 54, 80.

75. McGinnis, pp. 197–98.

76. Rich, p. 300.

77. Ibid.

78. Schrag, "Ellsberg Affair," p. 36.

79. Ungar, p. 79.

80. Moskin, p. 39.

81. Ibid., p. 41.

82. Ibid., p. 36.

83. Ibid.

84. "Ellsberg: The Battle," p. 9.

85. Lukas, p. 104.

86. Rich, p. 302.

87. Ibid.

88. "The Man Who Started It All," *Newsweek*, 78, July 12, 1971, p. 20.

89. Ibid.

90. Ibid.

91. Schrag, *Test*, p. 82.

92. Ibid., p. 83.

93. Henry Kissinger, *White House Years* (Boston: Little, Brown, 1979), p. 730.

94. Richard Nixon, *The Memoirs of Richard Nixon* (New York: Grosset & Dunlap, 1978), p. 509.

95. J. Anthony Lukas, *Nightmare* (New York: Viking Press, 1976), p. 71.

96. "Plugging Leaks," p. 29.

97. Eleanora W. Schoenebaum, ed., *Profiles of an Era, The Nixon/Ford Years* (New York: Harcourt, Brace, Jovanovich, 1979), pp. 191–92.

98. Ibid., p. 192.

99. Schrag, *Test*, p. 257.

100. Lukas, p. 105.

101. Schrag, *Test*, p. 257.

102. Lukas, p. 98.

Comment

Do you agree that "anyone who wishes to justify civil disobedience by officials must take his Otepkas with his Ellsbergs"? Both Otepka and Ellsberg broke the law and acted alone in secret and in the service of what they believed to be an important public interest. The obvious way of distinguishing the two acts of disobedience is to say that one sought the right end and the other did not. But this evades the problem of what means are justifiable when society disagrees about the ends. Consider whether these differences in the means make any moral difference: (1) releasing information to the press/to a congressional staffer; (2) extensive efforts to appeal to other officials/few such efforts; (3) some/no likelihood that release of information could endanger national security; (4) status as a private citizen/public official at the time of the act.

The State Department's view about such disobedience would treat Otepka and Ellsberg alike: both were wrong. Evaluate the best argument you can construct for this view. An alternative position that also treats Otepka and Ellsberg alike would conclude that both were justified. One difficulty with this conclusion is that neither acted publicly, as the traditional theory of civil disobedience requires. Should official disobedience always have to be public to be legitimate? Does the comparison of Ellsberg and Otepka suggest any revisions in the traditional criteria of civil disobedience if they are applied to officials?

Recommended Reading

The best modern statement of the theory of civil disobedience is John Rawls, *A Theory of Justice* (Cambridge, Mass.: Harvard University Press, 1971), pp. 363–91. For a brief critique, see Brian Barry, *The Liberal Theory of Justice* (New York: Oxford University Press, 1973), pp. 151–53. A useful collection on the subject is Jeffrie Murphy (ed.), *Civil Disobedience and Violence* (Belmont, Calif.: Wadsworth, 1971).

General discussions of the concept of obligation that relate to civil disobedience are Michael Walzer, *Obligations* (New York: Simon and Schuster, 1971), chapter 1 and 2; A. John Simmons, *Moral Principles and Political Obligations* (Princeton, N.J.: Princeton University Press, 1979).

On dissident officials, see Sissela Bok, "Blowing the Whistle," in Joel Fleishman et al. (eds.), *Public Duties* (Cambridge, Mass.: Harvard University Press, 1982), pp. 204–20. The practical and theoretical aspects of resignation are discussed in Edward Weisband and Thomas Franck, *Resignation in Protest* (New York: Penguin, 1975), and Albert Hirschman, *Exit, Voice and Loyalty* (Cambridge, Mass.: Harvard University Press, 1970).

Part Two
The Ethics of Policy

5 Policy Analysis

Introduction

The question of means and ends—the focus of the first part of this book—speaks to only part of the moral world of politics. No less important is the question of the ends themselves: how should we choose among competing goals of policy? The most common framework for answering this question is some version of policy analysis, including cost-benefit, cost-effective, and risk-benefit analysis.

All of these approaches rest on the moral foundation of utilitarianism (insofar as they have any moral foundation at all). They assume (1) that all the ends or values of policies can be compared by a common measure of expected utility (also called happiness, satisfaction, or welfare) and (2) that the best policy or set of policies is that which maximizes the total expected utility. The great appeal of this approach is that it appears to resolve conflicts among competing ends and seems to do so in a neutral way by simply adding up all the preferences of all citizens. It also appears democratic since it purports to give the most people as much as possible of whatever they want.

Critics of policy analysis attack both of its assumptions. First, they point to problems of aggregation—the way the policy analyst adds up preferences to arrive at total utility. Among criticisms of this kind are charges: (1) that individual utilities cannot be compared (How can we say whether cheaper fuel for me is worth a slight risk of nuclear contamination to you?); (2) that ultimate values cannot be traded off against other goods (How can we put a price on life itself?); and (3) that individual preferences cannot be taken as given (How can we assume that participation in the political process will not change people's perception of risks?).

The second set of criticisms concern problems of distribution. Critics challenge the maximization principle because it ignores how utility is allocated among individuals. They object that for the sake of maximizing general utility, policy analysts will sacrifice the rights of (1) disadvantaged citizens in their own society; (2) the welfare of poorer nations; and (3) the welfare of future generations. Policy analysts try to take account of such groups, but the problem of distributive justice remains the most formidable obstacle to the acceptance of their method.

The issue of nuclear energy, like many technological questions, lends itself to the techniques of policy analysis. To choose the best energy policy, we have to compare many different values, each with different probabilities attached to it and each subject to technical interpretation. Of the many analyses of nuclear energy, the best known is the Reactor Safety Study (also called the Rasmussen Report), commissioned by the U.S. Atomic Energy Commission in 1975. The report used a special kind of policy analysis ("fault tree" analysis) to estimate the risks from accidents in nuclear power plants. Such an estimate, of course, is only part of the broader analysis that would be necessary to determine the role nuclear power should play in meeting the energy needs of society. But an examination of the report reveals some of the strengths and weaknesses of relying on technical analyses of issues that have wider ethical implications.

A systematic assessment of the risks of nuclear power—the first step in assigning utility to policy options—can help dispel some of the confusion and irrational fear that stand in the way of developing a rational energy policy in the public interest. Even the analysis of risk, however, is likely to be controversial. The critics cited in the Report of the House Subcommittee on Energy and the Environment challenge the Rasmussen Report seemingly on technical grounds. But, as in other scientific disputes, the technical disagreements reflect ethical differences about such questions as what risks people should accept and who should decide what are acceptable levels of risk. Beyond the problem of adding up the risks, the problem of distributing them—within a society and to future generations—receives little notice in either the Rasmussen Report or the subcommittee's report. Although neither report claims to deal with all the issues in the controversy over nuclear power, we must read them with as much attention to what they omit as to what they include.

The Reactor Safety Study
Norman C. Rasmussen et al.

SECTION 1. INTRODUCTION AND RESULTS

The Reactor Safety Study was sponsored by the U.S. Atomic Energy Commission to estimate the public risks that could be involved in potential accidents in commercial nuclear power plants of the type now in use. It was performed under the independent direction of Professor Norman C. Rasmussen of the Massachusetts Institute of Technology. The risks had to be estimated, rather than measured, because although there are about 50 such plants now operating, there have been no nuclear accidents to date resulting in significant releases of radioactivity in

Published by the U.S. Nuclear Regulatory Commission, October 1975.

U.S. commercial nuclear power plants. Many of the methods used to develop these estimates are based on those that were developed by the Department of Defense and the National Aeronautics and Space Administration in the last 10 years and are coming into increasing use in recent years.

The objective of the study was to make a realistic estimate of these risks and, to provide perspective, to compare them with non-nuclear risks to which our society and its individuals are already exposed. This information may be of help in determining the future reliance by society on nuclear power as a source of electricity.

The results from this study suggest that the risks to the public from potential accidents in nuclear power plants are comparatively small. This is based on the following considerations:

a. The possible consequences of potential reactor accidents are predicted to be no larger, and in many cases much smaller, than those of non-nuclear accidents. The consequences are predicted to be smaller than people have been led to believe by previous studies which deliberately maximized estimates of these consequences.

b. The likelihood of reactor accidents is much smaller than that of many non-nuclear accidents having similar consequences. All non-nuclear accidents examined in this study, including fires, explosions, toxic chemical releases, dam failures, airplane crashes, earthquakes, hurricanes and tornadoes, are much more likely to occur and can have consequences comparable to, or larger than, those of nuclear accidents.

Figures 1, 2, and 3 compare the nuclear reactor accident risks predicted for the 100 plants expected to be operating by about 1980 with risks from other man-caused and natural events to which society is generally already exposed. The following information is contained in the figures:

a. Figures 1 and 2 show the likelihood and number of fatalities from both nuclear and a variety of non-nuclear accidents. These figures indicate that non-nuclear events are about 10,000 times more likely to produce large numbers of fatalities than nuclear plants.*

---

*The fatalities shown in Figs. 1 and 2 for the 100 nuclear plants are those that would be predicted to occur within a short period of time after the potential reactor accident. This was done to provide a consistent comparison to the non-nuclear events which also cause fatalities in the same time frame. As in potential nuclear accidents, there also exist possibilities for injuries and longer term health effects from non-nuclear accidents. Data or predictions of this type are not available for non-nuclear events and so comparisons cannot easily be made.

b. Figure 3 shows the likelihood and dollar value of property damage associated with nuclear and non-nuclear accidents. Nuclear plants are about 1000 times less likely to cause comparable large dollar value accidents than other sources. Property damage is associated with three effects:

1. the cost of relocating people away from contaminated areas,

2. the decontamination of land to avoid overexposing people to radioactivity,

3. the cost of ensuring that people are not exposed to potential sources of radioactivity in food and water supplies.

In addition to the overall risk information in Figs. 1 through 3, it is useful to consider the risk to individuals of being fatally injured by various types of accidents. The bulk of the information shown in Table 1 is taken from the 1973 *Statistical Abstracts of the U.S.* and applies to the year 1969, the latest year for which these data were tabulated when this study was performed. The predicted nuclear accident risks are very small compared to other possible causes of fatal injuries.

In addition to fatalities and property damage, a number of other health effects could be caused by nuclear accidents. These include injuries and long-term health effects such as cancers, genetic effects, and thyroid gland illness. The early illness expected in potential accidents would be about 10 times as large as the fatalities shown in Figs. 1 and 2; for comparison there are 8 million injuries caused annually by other accidents. The number of cases of genetic effects and long-term cancer fatalities is predicted to be smaller than the normal incidence rate of these diseases. Even for a large accident, the small increases in these diseases would be difficult to detect from the normal incidence rate.

Thyroid illnesses that might result from a large accident are mainly the formation of nodules on the thyroid gland; these can

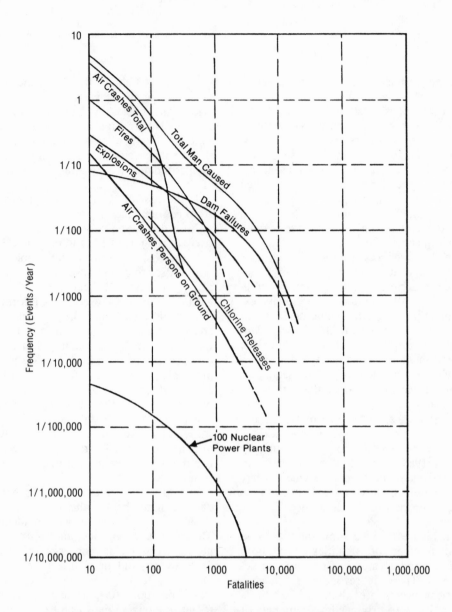

FIGURE 1. FREQUENCY OF FATALITIES DUE TO MAN-CAUSED EVENTS

Notes: 1. Fatalities due to auto accidents are not shown because data are not available. Auto accidents cause about 50,000 fatalities per year.

2. Approximate uncertainties for nuclear events are estimated to be represented by factors of 1/4 and 4 on consequence magnitudes and by factors of 1/5 and 5 on probabilities.

3. For natural and man caused occurrences the uncertainty in probability of largest recorded consequence magnitude is estimated to be represented by factors of 1/20 and 5. Smaller magnitudes have less uncertainty.

120

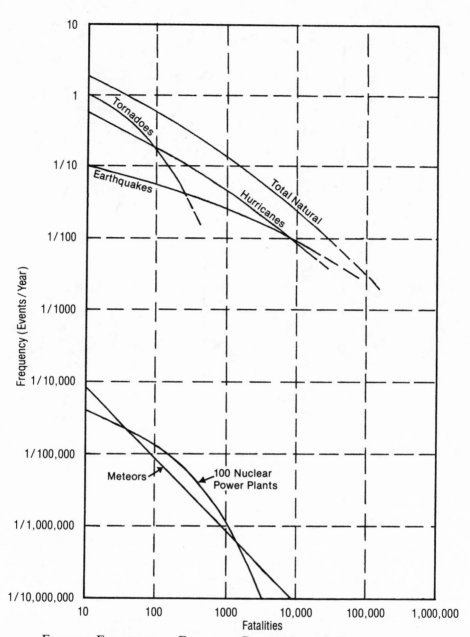

FIGURE 2. FREQUENCY OF FATALITIES DUE TO NATURAL EVENTS

Notes: 1. For natural and man caused occurrences the uncertainty in probability of largest recorded consequence magnitude is estimated to be represented by factors of 1/20 and 5. Smaller magnitudes have less uncertainty.

2. Approximate uncertainties for nuclear events are estimated to be represented by factors of 1/4 and 4 on consequence magnitudes and by factors of 1/5 and 5 on probabilities.

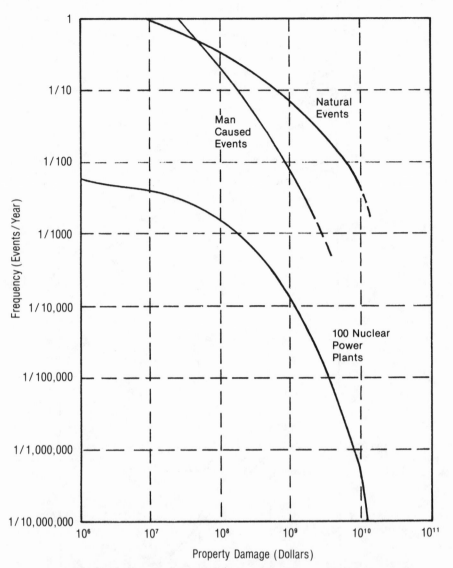

FIGURE 3. FREQUENCY OF PROPERTY DAMAGE DUE TO NATURAL AND
MAN-CAUSED EVENTS

Notes: 1. Property damage due to auto accidents is not included because data
are not available for low probability events. Auto accidents cause about
$15 billion damage each year.

2. Approximate uncertainties for nuclear events are estimated to be
represented by factors of 1/5 and 2 on consequence magnitudes and
by factors of 1/5 and 5 on probabilities.

3. For natural and man caused occurrences the uncertainty in probability of largest recorded consequence magnitude is estimated to be
represented by factors of 1/20 and 5. Smaller magnitudes have less
uncertainty.

TABLE 1. AVERAGE RISK OF FATALITY BY VARIOUS CAUSES

Accident Type	Total Number	Individual Chance per Year
Motor Vehicle	55,791	1 in 4,000
Falls	17,827	1 in 10,000
Fires and Hot Substances	7,451	1 in 25,000
Drowning	6,181	1 in 30,000
Firearms	2,309	1 in 100,000
Air Travel	1,778	1 in 100,000
Falling Objects	1,271	1 in 160,000
Electrocution	1,148	1 in 160,000
Lightning	160	1 in 2,000,000
Tornadoes	91	1 in 2,500,000
Hurricanes	93	1 in 2,500,000
All Accidents	111,992	1 in 1,600
Nuclear Reactor Accidents (100 plants)		1 in 5,000,000,000

be treated by medical procedures and rarely lead to serious consequences. For most accidents, the number of nodules caused would be small compared to their normal incidence rate. The number that might be produced in very unlikely accidents would be about equal to their normal occurrence in the exposed population. These would be observed during a period of 10 to 40 years following the accident.

While the study has presented the estimated risks from nuclear power plant accidents and compared them with other risks that exist in our society, it has made no judgment on the acceptability of nuclear risks. The judgment as to what level of risk is acceptable should be made by a broader segment of society than that involved in this study.

SECTION 2. QUESTIONS AND ANSWERS ABOUT THE STUDY

This section of the summary presents more information about the details of the study than was covered in the introduction. It is presented in question and answer format for ease of reference.

2.1 WHO DID THIS STUDY AND HOW MUCH EFFORT WAS INVOLVED?

The study was done principally at the Atomic Energy Commission headquarters by a group of scientists and engineers who had the skills needed to carry out the study's tasks. They came from a variety of organizations, including the AEC, the national laboratories, private laboratories, and universities. About 10 people were AEC employees. The Director of the study was Professor Norman C. Rasmussen of the Department of Nuclear Engineering of the Massachusetts Institute of Technology, who served as an AEC consultant during the course of the study. The Staff Director who had the day-to-day responsibility for the project was Mr. Saul Levine of the AEC. The study was started in the summer of 1972 and took three years to complete. A total of 60 people, various consultants, 70 man-years of effort, and about four million dollars were involved.

2.2 WHAT KIND OF NUCLEAR POWER PLANTS ARE COVERED BY THE STUDY?

The study considered large power reactors of the pressurized water and boiling water type being used in the U.S. today. Reactors of the present generation are all water cooled, and therefore the study limited itself to this type. Although high temperature gas cooled and liquid metal fast breeder reactor designs are now under development, reactors of this type are not expected to have any significant role in U.S. electric power production in this decade; thus they were not considered.

Nuclear power plants produce electricity by the fissioning (or splitting) of uranium atoms. The nuclear reactor fuel in which the uranium atoms fission is in a large steel vessel. The reactor fuel consists of about 100 tons of uranium. The uranium is inside metal rods about 1/2 inch in diameter and about 12 feet long. These rods are formed into fuel bundles of about 50–200 rods each. Each reactor contains several hundred bundles. The vessel is filled with water, which is needed both to cool the fuel and to maintain the fission chain reaction.

The heat released in the uranium by the fission process heats the water and forms steam; the steam turns a turbine to generate electricity. Similarly, coal and oil plants generate electricity using fossil fuel to boil water.

Today's nuclear power plants are very large. A typical plant has an electrical capacity of 1,000,000 kilowatts, or 1,000 megawatts. This is enough electricity for a city of about five hundred thousand people.

2.3 CAN A NUCLEAR POWER PLANT EXPLODE LIKE AN ATOM BOMB?

No. It is impossible for nuclear power plants to explode like a nuclear weapon. The laws of physics do not permit this because the fuel contains only a small fraction (3–5%) of the special type of uranium (called uranium-235) that must be used in weapons.

2.4 HOW IS RISK DEFINED?

The idea of risk involves both the likelihood and consequences of an event. Thus, to estimate the risk involved in driving an automobile, one would need to know the likelihood of an accident in which, for example, an individual could be 1) injured or 2) killed. Thus there are two different consequences, injury or fatality, each with its own likelihood. For injury, an individual's chance per year is about one in 130 and for fatality, it is about one in 4000. This type of data concerns the risk to individuals and can affect attitudes and habits that individuals have toward driving.

However, from an overall societal viewpoint, different types of data are of interest. Here, 1.5 million injuries per year and 55,000 fatalities per year due to automobile accidents represent the kind of information that might be of use in making decisions on highway and automobile safety.

The same type of logic applies to reactors. From the viewpoint of a person living in the general vicinity of a reactor, the likelihood of being killed in any one year in a reactor accident is one chance in 5 billion, and the likelihood of being injured in any one year in a reactor accident is one chance in 75,000,000.

2.5 WHAT CAUSES THE RISKS ASSOCIATED WITH NUCLEAR POWER PLANT ACCIDENTS?

The risks from nuclear power plants are due to the radioactivity formed by the fission process. In normal operation nuclear power plants release minute amounts of this radioactivity under controlled conditions. In the event of highly unlikely accidents, larger amounts of radioactivity could be released and could cause significant risks.

The fragments of the uranium atom that remain after it fissions are radioactive. These radioactive atoms are called fission products. They disintegrate further with the release of nuclear radiations. Many of them decay away quickly, in a matter of minutes or hours, to nonradioactive forms. Others decay away more slowly and require months, and in a few cases, many years to decay. The fission products accumulating in the fuel rods include both gases and solids. Included are iodine, gases like krypton and xenon, and solids like cesium and strontium.

2.6 HOW CAN RADIOACTIVITY BE RELEASED?

The only way that potentially large amounts of radioactivity could be released is by melting the fuel in the reactor core. The fuel that is removed from a reactor after use and stored at the plant site also contains considerable amounts of radioactivity. However, accidental releases from such used fuel were found to be quite unlikely and small compared to potential releases of radioactivity from the fuel in the reactor core.

The safety design of reactors includes a series of systems to prevent the overheating of fuel and to control potential releases of radioactivity from the fuel. Thus, for a potential accidental release of radioactivity to the environment to occur, there must be a series of sequential failures that would cause the fuel to overheat and release its radioactivity. There would also have to be failures in the systems designed to remove and contain the radioactivity.

The study has examined a very large number of potential paths by which potential radioactive releases might occur and has identified those that determine the risks. This involved defining the ways in which the fuel in the core could melt and the ways in which systems to control the release of radioactivity could fail.

2.7 HOW MIGHT A CORE MELT ACCIDENT OCCUR?

It is significant that in some 200 reactor-years of commercial operation of reactors of the type considered in the report there have been no fuel melting accidents. To melt the fuel requires a failure in the cooling system or the occurrence of a heat imbalance that would allow the fuel to heat up to its melting point, about 5,000°F.

To those unfamiliar with the characteristics of reactors, it might seem that all that is required to prevent fuel from overheating is a system to promptly stop, or shut down, the fission process at the first sign of trouble. Although reactors have such systems, they alone are not enough since the radioactive decay of fission fragments in the fuel continues to generate heat (called decay heat) that must be removed even after the fission process stops. Thus, redundant decay heat removal systems are also provided in reactors. In addition, emergency core cooling systems (ECCS) are provided to cope with a series of potential but unlikely accidents, caused by ruptures in, and loss of coolant from, the normal cooling system.

The Reactor Safety Study has defined two broad types of situations that might potentially lead to a melting of the reactor core: the loss-of-coolant accident (LOCA) and transients. In the event of a potential loss of coolant, the normal cooling water would be lost from the cooling systems and core melting would be prevented by the use of the emergency core cooling system (ECCS). However, melting could occur in a loss of coolant if the ECCS were to fail to operate.

The term "transient" refers to any one of a number of conditions which could occur in a plant and would require the reactor to be shut down. Following shutdown, the decay heat removal systems would operate to keep the core from overheating. Certain failures in either the shutdown or the decay heat removal systems also have the potential to cause melting of the core.

2.8 WHAT FEATURES ARE PROVIDED
IN REACTORS TO COPE WITH A
CORE MELT ACCIDENT?

Nuclear power plants have numerous systems designed to prevent core melting. Furthermore, there are inherent physical processes and additional features that come into play to remove and contain the radioactivity released from the molten fuel should core melting occur. Although there are features provided to keep the containment building from being damaged for some time after the core melts, the containment would ultimately fail, causing a release of radioactivity.

An essentially leaktight containment building is provided to prevent the initial dispersion of the airborne radioactivity into the environment. Although the containment would fail in time if the core were to melt, until that time, the radioactivity released from the fuel would be deposited by natural processes on the surfaces inside the containment. In addition, plants are provided with systems to contain and trap the radioactivity released within the containment building. These systems include such things as water sprays and pools to wash radioactivity out of the building atmosphere and filters to trap radioactive particles prior to their release. Since the containment building is made essentially leaktight, the radioactivity is contained as long as the building remains intact. Even if the building were to have sizable leaks, large amounts of the radioactivity would likely be removed by the systems provided for that purpose or would be deposited on interior surfaces of the building by natural processes.

Even though the containment building would be expected to remain intact for some time following a core melt, eventually the molten mass would be expected to eat its way through the concrete floor into the ground below. Following this, much of the radioactive material would be trapped in the soil; however, a small amount would escape to the surface and be released. Almost all of the non-gaseous radioactivity would be trapped in the soil.

It is possible to postulate core melt accidents in which the containment building would fail by overpressurization or by missiles created by the accident. Such accidents are less likely but could release a larger amount of airborne radioactivity and have more serious consequences. The consequences of these less likely accidents have been included in the study's results shown in Figs. 1 through 3.

2.9 HOW MIGHT THE LOSS-OF-COOLANT
ACCIDENT LEAD TO A CORE MELT?

Loss of coolant accidents are postulated to result from failures in the normal reactor cooling water system, and plants are designed to cope with such failures. The water in the reactor cooling systems is at a very high pressure (between 50 to 100 times the pressure in a car tire) and if a rupture were to occur in the pipes, pumps, valves, or vessels that contain it, then a "blowout" would happen. In this case some of the water would flash to steam and blow out of the hole. This could be serious since the fuel could melt if additional cooling were not supplied in a rather short time.

The loss of normal cooling in the event of a LOCA would stop the chain reaction, so that the amount of heat produced would drop very rapidly to a few percent of its operating level. However, after this sudden drop the amount of heat being produced would decrease much more slowly and would be controlled by the decay of the radioactivity in the fuel.

Although this decrease in heat generation is helpful, it would not be enough to prevent the fuel from melting unless additional cooling were supplied. To deal with this situation, reactors have emergency core cooling systems (ECCS) whose function is to provide cooling for just such events. These systems have pumps, pipes, valves, and water supplies which are capable of dealing with breaks of various sizes. They are also designed to be redundant so that if some components fail to operate, the core can still be cooled.

The study has examined a large number of potential sequences of events following LOCAs of various sizes. In almost all of the cases, the LOCA must be followed by failures in the emergency core cooling system for the core to melt. The principal exception to this is the massive failure of the large pressure vessel that contains the core. However, the accumulated experience with pressure vessels indicates that the chance of such a failure is small. In fact the study found that the likelihood of pressure vessel failure was so small that it did not contribute to the overall risk from reactor accidents.

2.10 HOW MIGHT A REACTOR TRANSIENT LEAD TO A CORE MELT?

The term "reactor transient" refers to a number of events that require the reactor to be shut down. These range from normal shutdown for such things as refueling to such unplanned but expected events as loss of power to the plant from the utility transmission lines. The reactor is designed to cope with unplanned transients by automatically shutting down. Following shutdown, cooling systems would be operated to remove the heat produced by the radioactivity in the fuel. There are several different cooling systems capable of removing this heat, but if they all should fail, the heat being produced would be sufficient to eventually boil away all the cooling water and melt the core.

In addition to the above pathway to core melt, it is also possible to postulate core melt resulting from the failure of the reactor shutdown systems following a transient event. In this case it would be possible for the amounts of heat generated to be such that the available cooling systems might not cope with it and core melt could result.

2.11 HOW LIKELY IS A CORE MELT ACCIDENT?

The Reactor Safety Study carefully examined the various paths leading to core melt. Using methods developed in recent years for estimating the likelihood of such accidents, a probability of occurrence was determined for each core melt accident identified. These probabilities were combined to obtain the total probability of melting the core. The value obtained was about one in 20,000 per reactor per year. With 100 reactors operating, as is anticipated for the U.S. by about 1980, this means that the chance for one such accident is one in 200 per year.

2.12 WHAT IS THE NATURE OF THE HEALTH EFFECTS THAT A CORE MELT ACCIDENT MIGHT PRODUCE?

It is possible for a potential core melt accident to release enough radioactivity so that some fatalities might occur within a short time (about one year) after the accident. Other people may be exposed to radiation levels which would produce observable effects which would require medical attention but from which they would recover. In addition, some people may receive even lower exposures, which would produce no noticeable effects but might increase the incidence of certain diseases over a period of many years. The observable effects which occur shortly after the accident are called early, or acute, effects.

The delayed, or latent, effects of radiation exposure could cause some increase in the incidence of diseases such as cancer, genetic effects, and thyroid gland illnesses in the exposed population. In general these effects would appear as an increase in these diseases over a 10 to 50 year period following the exposure. Such effects may be difficult to notice because the increase is expected to be small compared to the normal incidence rate of these diseases.

The study has estimated the increased incidence of potentially fatal cancers over the 50 years following an accident. The number of latent cancer fatalities are predicted to be relatively small compared to their normal incidence. Thyroid illness refers mainly to small lumps, or nodules, on the thyroid gland. The nodules are treated by medical procedures that sometimes involve simple surgery, and these are unlikely to lead to serious consequences. Medication may also be needed to supplement the gland function.

Radiation is recognized as one of the factors that can produce genetic effects which appear as defects in a subsequent generation. From the total population exposure caused by the accident, the expected increase in genetic effects in subsequent generations can be estimated. These effects are predicted to be small compared to their normal incidence rate.

2.13 WHAT ARE THE MOST LIKELY
CONSEQUENCES OF A CORE MELT ACCIDENT?

As stated, the probability of a core melt accident is on the average one in 20,000 per reactor per year. The most likely consequences of such an accident are given [in Table 2].

2.14 HOW DOES THE AVERAGE ANNUAL RISK
FROM NUCLEAR ACCIDENTS
COMPARE TO OTHER COMMON RISKS?

Considering the 15 million people who live within 25 miles of current or planned

TABLE 2. MOST LIKELY CONSEQUENCES OF A
CORE MELT ACCIDENT

	Consequences
Fatalities	<1
Injuries	<1
Latent Fatalities per year	<1
Thyroid Nodules per year	<1
Genetic Defects per year	<1
Property Damage[a]	<$1,000,000

(a) This does not include damage that might occur to the plant or costs for replacing the power generation lost by such damage.

U.S. reactor sites, and based on current accident rates in the U.S., the annual numbers of fatalities and injuries expected from various sources are shown in [Table 3].

2.15 WHAT IS THE NUMBER OF FATALITIES
AND INJURIES EXPECTED AS A RESULT
OF A CORE MELT ACCIDENT?

A core melt accident is similar to many other types of major accidents such as fires, explosions, dam failures, etc., in that a wide range of consequences is possible depending on the exact conditions under which the accident occurs. In the case of a core melt, the consequences would depend mainly on three factors: the amount of radioactivity released, the way it is dispersed by the prevailing weather conditions, and the number of people exposed to the radiation. With these three factors known, it is possible to make a reasonable estimate of the consequences.

TABLE 3. ANNUAL FATALITIES AND INJURIES
EXPECTED AMONG THE 15 MILLION PEOPLE
LIVING WITHIN 25 MILES OF U.S.
REACTOR SITES

Accident Type	Fatalities	Injuries
Automobile	4,200	375,000
Falls	1,500	75,000
Fire	560	22,000
Electrocution	90	—
Lightning	8	—
Reactors (100 plants)		

The study calculated the health effects and the probability of occurrence for 140,000 possible combinations of radioactive release magnitude, weather type, and population exposed. The probability of a given release was determined from careful examination of the probability of various reactor system failures. The probability of various weather conditions was obtained from weather data collected at many reactor sites. The probability of various numbers of people being exposed was obtained from U.S. census data for current and planned U.S. reactor sites. These thousands of computations were carried out with the aid of a large digital computer.

These results showed that the probability of an accident resulting in 10 or more fatalities is predicted to be about 1 in 3,000,000 per plant per year. The probability of 100 or more fatalities is predicted to be about 1 in 10,000,000 and for 1000 or more, 1 in 100,000,000. The largest value reported in the study was 3300 fatalities, with a probability of about one in a billion.

The above estimates are derived from a consequence model which includes statistical calculations to describe evacuations of people out of the path of airborne radioactivity. This evacuation model was developed from data describing evacuations that have been performed during non-nuclear events.

If a group of 100 similar plants are considered, then the chance of an accident causing 10 or more fatalities is 1 in 30,000 per year. For accidents involving 1000 or more fatalities the number is 1 in 1,000,000 per year. Interestingly, this value coincides with the probability that a meteor would strike a U.S. population center and cause 1000 fatalities.

[Table 4] can be used to compare the likelihood of a nuclear accident to non-nuclear accidents that could cause the same consequences.

These include man-caused as well as natural events. Many of these probabilities are obtained from historical records, but others are so small that no such event has ever been observed. In the latter cases the probability has been calculated using techniques similar to those used for the nuclear plant.

In regard to injuries from potential nuclear power plant accidents, the

TABLE 4. AVERAGE PROBABILITY OF MAJOR MAN-CAUSED AND NATURAL EVENTS

Type of Event	Probability of 100 or More Fatalities	Probability of 1000 or More Fatalities
Man-Caused		
Airplane Crash	1 in 2 years	1 in 2000 years
Fire	1 in 7 years	1 in 200 years
Explosion	1 in 16 years	1 in 120 years
Toxic Gas	1 in 100 years	1 in 1000 years
Natural		
Tornado	1 in 5 years	very small
Hurricane	1 in 5 years	1 in 25 years
Earthquake	1 in 20 years	1 in 50 years
Meteorite Impact	1 in 100,000 years	1 in 1,000,000 years
Reactors		
100 plants	1 in 100,000 years	1 in 1,000,000 years

number of injuries that would require medical attention shortly after an accident is about 10 times larger than the number of fatalities predicted.

2.16 WHAT IS THE MAGNITUDE OF THE LATENT, OR LONG-TERM, HEALTH EFFECTS?

As with the short-term effects, the incidence of latent cancers, treatable latent thyroid illness, and genetic effects would vary with the exact accident conditions. [Table 5] below illustrates the potential size of such events. The first column shows the consequences that would be produced by core melt accidents, the most likely of which has one chance in 20,000 per reactor per year of occurring. The second column shows the consequences for an accident that has a chance of 1 in a million of occurring. The third column shows the normal incidence rate.

In these accidents, only the induction of thyroid nodules would be observable, and this only in the case of larger, less likely accidents. These nodules are easily diagnosed and treatable by medical or surgical procedures. The incidence of other effects would be low and should not be discernible in view of the high normal incidence of these two diseases. [See Table 5.]

2.17 WHAT TYPE OF PROPERTY DAMAGE MIGHT A CORE MELT ACCIDENT PRODUCE?

A nuclear accident would cause no physical damage to property beyond the plant site but may contaminate it with radioactivity. At high levels of contamination, people would have to be relocated from their homes until decontamination procedures permitted their return. At levels lower than this, but involving a larger area, decontamination procedures would also be required, but people would be able to continue to live in the area. The area requiring decontamina-

TABLE 5. INCIDENCE PER YEAR
OF LATENT HEALTH EFFECTS
FOLLOWING A POTENTIAL REACTOR ACCIDENT

| Health Effect (per year) | Chance per Reactor per Year | | Normal[b] Incidence Rate in Exposed Population (per year) |
	One in 20,000[a]	One in 1,000,000[a]	
Latent Cancers	<1	170	17,000
Thyroid Illness	<1	1400	8000
Genetic Effects	<1	25	8000

(a) The rates due to reactor accidents are temporary and would decrease with time. The bulk of the cancers and thyroid modules would occur over a few decades and the genetic effects would be significantly reduced in five generations.

(b) This is the normal incidence that would be expected for a population of 10,000,000 people who might receive some exposure in a very large accident over the time period that the potential reactor accident effects might occur.

tion would involve a few hundred to a few thousand square miles. The principal concern in this larger area would be to monitor farm produce to keep the amount of radioactivity ingested through the food chain small. Farms in this area would have their produce monitored, and any produce above a safe level could not be used.

The core melt accident having a likelihood of one in 20,000 per plant per year would most likely result in little or no contamination. The probability of an accident that requires relocation of 20 square miles is one in 100,000 per reactor per year. Eighty per cent of all core melt accidents would be expected to be less severe than this. The largest accident might require relocation from 290 square miles. In an accident such as this, agricultural products, particularly milk, would have to be monitored for a month or two over an area about 50 times larger until the iodine decayed away. After that, the area requiring monitoring would be very much smaller.

2.18 WHAT WOULD BE THE COST OF THE
CONSEQUENCES OF A CORE MELT ACCIDENT?

As with the other consequences, the
cost would depend upon the exact circumstances of the accident. The cost
calculated by the Reactor Safety Study included the cost of moving and housing the
people that were relocated, the cost
caused by denial of land use and the cost
associated with the denial of use of
reproducible assets such as dwellings and
factories, and costs associated with the
cleanup of contaminated property. The
core melt accident having a likelihood of
one in 20,000 per reactor per year would
most likely cause property damage of less
than $1,000,000. The chance of an acci-
dent causing $150,000,000 damage would
be about one in 100,000 per reactor per
year. The probability would be about one
in 1,000,000 per plant per year of causing
damage of about one billion dollars. The
maximum value would be predicted to be
about 14 billion dollars, with a probability of about one in 1,000,000,000 per
plant per year.

This property damage risk from
nuclear accidents can be compared to
other risks in several ways. The largest
man-caused events that have occurred are
fires. In recent years there have been an
average of three fires with damage in excess of 10 million dollars every year.
About once every two years there is a fire
with damage in the 50 to 100 million
dollar range. There have been four hurricanes in the last 10 years which caused
damage in the range of 0.5 to 5 billion
dollars. Recent earthquake estimates suggest that a one billion dollar earthquake
can be expected in the U.S. about once
every 50 years.

A comparison of the preceding costs
shows that, although a severe reactor accident would be very costly, the costs would
be within the range of other serious accidents experienced by society and the
probability of such a nuclear accident is
estimated to be smaller than that of the
other events.

2.19 WHAT WILL BE THE CHANCE OF A
REACTOR MELTDOWN IN THE YEAR 2000
IF WE HAVE 1000 REACTORS OPERATING?

One might be tempted to take the per
plant probability of a particular reactor
accident and multiply it by 1000 to
estimate the chance of an accident in the
year 2000. This is not a valid calculation,
however, because it assumes that the reactors to be built during the next 25 years
will be the same as those being built today.
Experience with other technologies, such
as automobiles and aircraft for example,
generally shows that, as more units are
built and more experience is gained, the
overall safety record improves in terms of
fewer accidents occurring per unit. There
are changes in plants now being constructed that appear to be improved as
compared to the plants analyzed in the
study.

2.20 HOW DO WE KNOW THAT THE STUDY
HAS INCLUDED ALL ACCIDENTS
IN THE ANALYSIS?

The study devoted a large amount of its
effort to ensuring that it covered those
potential accidents of importance to
determining the public risk. It relied
heavily on over 20 years of experience
that exists in the identification and
analysis of potential reactor accidents. It
also went considerably beyond earlier
analyses that have been performed by
considering a large number of potential
failures that had never before been
analyzed. For example, the failure of
reactor systems that can lead to core melt
and the failure of systems that affect the
consequences of core melt have been
analyzed. The consequences of the failure
of the massive steel reactor vessel and of
the containment were considered for the

first time. The likelihood that various external forces such as earthquakes, floods, and tornadoes could cause accidents was also analyzed.

In addition there are further factors that give a high degree of confidence that the important and significant accidents affecting risk have been included. These are: (1) the identification of all significant sources of radioactivity located at nuclear power plants, (2) the fact that a large release of radioactivity can occur only if the reactor fuel were to melt, and (3) knowledge of the physical phenomena which can cause fuel to melt. This type of approach led to the screening of thousands of potential accident paths to identify those that would essentially determine the public risk.

While there is no way of proving that all possible accident sequences which contribute to public risk have been considered in the study, the systematic approach used in identifying possible accident sequences makes it unlikely that an accident was overlooked which would significantly change the overall risk.

2.21 WHAT TECHNIQUES WERE USED
IN PERFORMING THE STUDY?

Methodologies developed over the past 10 years by the Department of Defense and the National Aeronautics and Space Administration were used in the study. As used in this study, these techniques, called event trees and fault trees, helped to define potential accident paths and their likelihood of occurrence.

An event tree defines an initial failure within the plant. It then examines the course of events which follow as determined by the operation or failure of various systems that are provided to prevent the core from melting and to prevent the release of radioactivity to the environment. Event trees were used in this study to define thousands of potential accident paths which were examined to determine their likelihood of occurrence and the amount of radioactivity that they might release.

Fault trees were used to determine the likelihood of failure of the various systems identified in the event tree accident paths. A fault tree starts with the definition of an undesired event, such as the failure of a system to operate, and then determines, using engineering and mathematical logic, the ways in which the system can fail. Using data covering (1) the failure of components such as pumps, pipes and valves, (2) the likelihood of operator errors, and (3) the likelihood of maintenance errors, it is possible to estimate the likelihood of system failure, even where no data on total system failure exist.

The likelihood and the size of radioactive releases from potential accident paths were used in combination with the likelihood of various weather conditions and population distributions in the vicinity of the reactor to calculate the consequences of the various potential accidents.

Observations on the Reactor Safety Study

U.S. House, Subcommittee on Energy and the Environment

The subcommittee received a wide range of commentary, pro and con, concerning

Published by the U.S. Government Printing Office, Washington, D.C., January 1977.

the Reactor Safety Study. In addition to testimony presented at the hearing, the hearing record includes eleven responses to Chairman Udall's request for comments upon a series of issues around which discussion of the Study has centered.

Typical of generally favorable summary comments are the following:

> To my mind the most important finding of NUREG 75/014 (Reactor Safety Study) is that the probability of a meltdown in a PWR [Pressurized Water Reactor] reactor is about 1 in 20,000 per reactor per year, and that 9 out of 10 times in such an accident the aboveground containment would not be breached. (Letter from Dr. Alvin Weinberg, Oak Ridge Associated Universities, to Chairman Udall, June 21, 1976.)

> I conclude that the analysis was appropriate and adequate, probably within a factor of about 10. Beyond that, I cannot be specific. Nevertheless, that puts the likelihood of low-probability, high-consequence events into the class of very rare phenomena, and the actuarial damage to be expected from them is very low. (Letter from Dr. David Rose, Massachusetts Institute of Technology, to subcommittee Chairman Udall: June 18, 1976.)

> My opinion is that the Reactor Safety Study is highly relevant, satisfactory and a workmanlike job....
> On the whole, I believe that the Rasmussen Report leans to the conservative side and reactors are, in fact, even less likely to malfunction than as stated in WASH-1400 (NUREG 75/014) [Reactor Safety Study]. (Letter from Dr. Edward Teller, Lawrence Livermore Laboratory, to Chairman Udall, August 16, 1976.)

Major areas of critical comment concern: (A) the method of presentation of the Study's results and conclusions; (B) the Study's emphasis of short-term effects vis-a-vis those which will occur over the decades following the accident; (C) the treatment of uncertainty in discussion of the risk associated with low-probability, high-consequence events; (D) the failure to discuss the substantial accident consequence variability that might result from some reactors being located much closer than others to population centers; (E) an

obtuseness of presentation which made the report difficult to analyze; and (F) failure to compare risks of nuclear energy with those associated with other energy options.

A. PRESENTATION OF RESULTS AND CONCLUSIONS

The Study was presented in a manner which can readily give the impression that hazards associated with nuclear powers are "acceptably low." This impression is conveyed in spite of a disclaimer which appears as the final paragraph in Section I of the Study's Executive Summary:

> While the Study has presented the estimated risks from nuclear powerplant accidents and compared them with other risks that exist in our society, it has made no judgment on the acceptability of nuclear risks. The judgment as to what level of risk is acceptable should be made by a broader segment of society than that involved in this Study.

The misleading impression (namely that the risk is "acceptably low") results from the contents of Section I of the Study's Executive Summary which consists primarily of comparisons of various kinds of risks. According to the material presented in Section I the probability of a person dying as a result of a nuclear powerplant accident is exceedingly small in comparison to the probability of death from other accidental causes such as motor vehicle accidents, falls, or fires. The data presented indicates that the risk of death from a nuclear accident approximates the risk of death from a falling meteor.

However, Section I of the Executive Summary provides little indication that the significance of the results presented therein is subject to a wide ranging debate. The data in Section I are criticized (as the following discussion indicates) on grounds of gross understatement of uncertainty; incomplete fatality estimates; inadequate discussion of variability of consequences; and absence of the most relevant risk comparisons, namely, comparison of nuclear risks with those associated with other energy technologies.

Thus although the NRC says, on the one hand, that the Reactor Safety Study makes no judgment concerning the "acceptability" of nuclear risks, an NRC environmental impact statement prepared in relation to the Diablo Canyon nuclear generating stations, states:

> The risk of accidental radiation exposure has been addressed in depth in the Commission's Reactor Safety Study and found to be acceptably low.

Representative Bingham's view of the study's presentation of the data was:

> I myself, as a fairly careful lay student of these matters, was enormously impressed by these photographs [i.e., Executive Summary, Figures 1-1, 1-2, and 1-3]. If somebody had asked me a week afterward what was the main impact of the Rasmussen Study, I would have referred to these photographs. The print, even though it is there, simply doesn't catch up to the impact of the photographs.

In his testimony at the subcommittee's hearings, Dr. Frank von Hippel, who was the organizer and a member of the American Physical Society Study on Light Water Reactor Safety, noted the misleading nature of the presentation; he said:

> Indeed, it appears that even the Chairman of the Nuclear Regulatory Commission has been misled in this connection. Only last month, he told the Pacific Coast Electrical Association that the risks from potential nuclear accidents would be comparable to those from meteorites.

The risk comparisons, without qualifications, have, in fact, been widely quoted. One example appears on the first page of a Middle South Utilities brochure presenting arguments in favor of nuclear power.

B. LONG-TERM VERSUS SHORT-TERM EFFECTS OF NUCLEAR ACCIDENTS

A pervasive criticism of the Reactor Safety Study is its failure to emphasize that the greatest health hazard associated with nuclear powerplant accidents would be in the long-term effects.

Page 2 of the Executive Summary contains graphs which compare nuclear accident probabilities and consequences with those associated with other commercial activities and with natural events.

For example, Executive Summary, Figure 1-2 of the Reactor Safety Study indicates that with 100 nuclear powerplants in operation, there would be 1 chance in 10,000 per year of an accident at 1 of these reactors resulting in 10 or more fatalities. Figure 1-2 suggests as many people will be killed by meteor impact as by nuclear powerplant accidents. The caption associated with the figure does not indicate, however, that it refers to "early" fatalities and that over a thirty- or forty-year period there would be a much larger number of deaths due to latent cancers caused by radiation exposure resulting from the accident. Figure 5-12 which appears on page 97 of the Study's main report indicates that the 1 in 10,000 accident which caused ten "early" deaths also would cause approximately 200 latent deaths per year; the text on page 74 says that such deaths might be expected to occur over a period of ten to forty years following the accident. Therefore, the same accident which caused approximately ten "early" deaths would also cause approximately 6,000 "latent" but fatal cancers.

While the second section of the Study's Executive Summary does contain a table on page 10 indicating that the number of latent cancer deaths is far in excess of the "early" deaths, the data are difficult to compare with the figures showing "early" fatalities on page 2 of the Study's Executive Summary. Moreover, the caption does not make clear that the latent deaths will occur over a thirty-year period and that, therefore, the 170 deaths expected each year should be multiplied by 30 to obtain the total number.

Also of interest is that the table on page 10 presents data in terms of "probability per reactor year" rather than in terms of "probability per 100 reactor years" which is the basis for the figures on page 2. Therefore, the 1 in 1,000,000 probability indicated on page 10 corresponds to the 1 in 10,000 probability shown on page 2. The switch from presenting data on the basis of 100 reactor year probabilities to individual reactor year probabilities tends to further downplay the total accident risk.

Mr. Saul Levine, Deputy Director of the NRC's Office of Nuclear Regulatory Research, explained in the hearings that the data were presented in this fashion because there were insufficient data concerning latent deaths associated with other types of accidents. This explanation is not readily reconcilable with the fact that the above noted table on page 10 did contain a comparison of nuclear-accident related cancers with those that would occur normally. Dr. Rasmussen said the page 10 comparison was significant because "the large majority of the normally occurring incidence of cancer fatalities are related to man-caused environmental factors." The implication is that the number of cancers caused by nuclear accidents is small in comparison to that arising from other industrial activities.

Mr. Levine further justified the overall method of presentation by noting all the relevant data were included in the report. He implied that critics had not taken proper account of the difficulty in summarizing a 2,300-page report in ten or fifteen pages.

In addressing this matter, Dr. Wolfgang Panofsky (who was Chairman of the Committee that prepared the review of the American Physical Society Study on Light Water Reactor Safety) stated at the hearing:

> I am referring to the latent effect matter. I do take a slightly less benign view of that presentation. The reason is that in terms of total fatalities caused by a potential accident, the latent effects potentially can cause several hundred times or so more deaths than the prompt effects.
>
> Therefore, they do deserve a more prominent display in comparison to other events which are within the realm of human experience than is apparent from the summary.
>
> Now it is indeed true that latent effects from an accident are of a very different nature. They essentially increase the likelihood of disease and death in the affected population.
>
> There are no good data of a comparable nature for other incidents. However, there are some data. As Mr. Levine himself said, there are data of increased morbidity and risk to life of coal-fired plants.
>
> So there are bases of judgment where one could compare the latent deaths from potential reactor accidents with those of other manmade experiences, other experiences of man.
>
> I feel it is not constructive to avoid displaying explicitly that one consequence of nuclear accidents which predominates by substantial factor over the other causes.

C. TREATMENT OF UNCERTAINTY AND LOW PROBABILITY EVENTS

Several reviewers were critical of the Study's seeming confidence in its presentation of conclusions concerning the likelihood and effects of low-probability, high-consequence events. Dr. Henry Kendall, professor of physics at the Massachusetts Institute of Technology and founding member of the Union of Concerned Scientists, enumerated in his testimony at the June 11 hearing what he believed to be weaknesses in the Study's approach with regard to its ability to identify all important accident sequences, its ability to take account of equipment design inadequacies, its assumptions concerning human error as a contribution to accidents, and its assumptions concerning the interdependence of reactor components wherein one failure leads to another or wherein multiple failures occur as a consequence of the same external event (common mode failures). Dr. Kendall said:

1. I regard it as impossible that RSS [Reactor Safety Study] was able to identify all of the important accident sequences. There are far too many damaging examples of serious accident chains in complex technologies—including in the nuclear experience—to support the RSS view of success in this area.

2. The RSS methodology does not include the design adequacy of equipment. This can introduce serious errors. Fault tree methodology poorly treats design adequacy considerations.

3. Human error can make major contributions to accidents. It is the least tractable source of failure in a fault tree analysis and was not treated adequately in RSS.

4. Fault tree analysis can reflect the dependency of one component failure on another if the dependency is known. However, in the vast majority of cases studied in RSS, components are assumed to fail independently. Subtle but crucially important dependencies can arise from physical proximity, unexpected component response to the abnormal circumstance of an accident or design error. Experiences with reactor accidents show this to be an important consideration as such dependencies have badly aggravated otherwise innocuous events. RSS made unsubstantiated assumptions about this dependency.

5. RSS significantly understates the role of common mode failures. Common mode failures are relatively uncommon unscheduled events in which redundant and presumably independent systems are nevertheless simultaneously disabled through some common cause. Such events do occur. For example, multiple redundant reactor

shutdown mechanisms have been found to be wholly inoperative. This is a very critical issue and RSS has made an apparently sincere effort to assess it by adopting certain analytical assumptions, concluding that such failures do not contribute importantly to reactor risk. However, the same assumptions applied to combinations of common mode failures that have actually occurred assess them to be virtually impossible, indicating that this is a more important source of risk than recognized by RSS. I doubt that it is, in principle, possible to locate all such potential failures.

Dr. von Hippel was also critical of the failures to emphasize uncertainties inherent in the analysis:

Consider now the question of accident probabilities. No uncertainties are shown on the figure where the Rasmussen group displays their computed results—yet, when you examine the calculation by which these predictions were obtained, you find enormous uncertainties. Whole categories of accident-initiating events such as earthquakes and fires were dismissed with hand-waving arguments; sabotage was explicitly not considered; it was assumed without substantial analysis that the performance of emergency systems would not be degraded by accident conditions when the reactor building would be filled with superheated steam and water; the design of only two reactors was looked at in detail and the results would therefore be vitiated if there were a real "lemon" out there somewhere; and, when crucial numbers were not available, they were simply guessed—although different investigators might have guessed values 10 to 100 times larger or smaller. It was for such reasons that the American Physical Society Reactor Safety Study concluded that "based on our experience with problems of this nature involving very low probabilities, we do not now have confidence in the presently calculated absolute values of the probabilities."

Dr. Panofsky was asked by subcommittee member Representative John Seiberling to comment upon the question of understatement of risk:

My testimony mainly addressed itself to the fact that the uncertainty of the risk assessment in my view is a great deal larger than that given in the Rasmussen report.

The reason for that statement is that even though the fault tree analysis method presents a heroic effort to deal with an extraordinarily difficult situation, it cannot be any better than the information which you put into it, and this is particularly important in the case of common mode failures.

You are dealing with a situation where the range of probability estimates which you have to span as you go from what one calls "independent failures" and "dependent failures" is so large that when averaging over the two, you cannot help but obtain an estimate which will be very uncertain, because you do not have enough physical information.

The power of mathematics and probabilities are limited if you don't have sufficient physical information.

Therefore, you can have underestimates and you can have overestimates. Obviously underestimates of risks are the ones of greatest concern to everyone. However, I have no way to say whether I am criticizing the report on the basis of either underestimates or overestimates.

I am just criticizing it in reference to exaggerated statements of certainty.

In discussing EPA's assessment of the Study, Dr. William Rowe, EPA Deputy Assistant Administrator for Radiation Programs testified:

It is not possible to combine these uncertainties directly to obtain an overall corrective risk value because they address different aspects of probabilities and consequences and because the most likely values within these ranges cannot be derived from the information in the Reactor Safety Study report. However, we believe that the Study has understated the risk based on underestimated health effects, evacuation doses, and probabilities of releases. The range is believed to be between a value of one and a value of several hundred.

As a footnote, I should indicate that over the past several days we have been talking with the NRC staff and they have provided us with information which is not quite apparent from the Study, and it is most likely we are probably talking about the lower end of that range.

Related to the criticism that the Study understated uncertainty in its conclusions, are doubts concerning the Study's ability to develop estimates of the likelihood of improbable events. Thus there is the question of the impact of the Browns Ferry fire* and its consequences upon the credibility of the Study's conclusions.

Mr. Levine indicated in his testimony that, assuming occurrence of the control system damage created by the fire, there was still only a probability of approximately 0.5 percent that a core meltdown would result. The basis for this estimate is discussed at length in appendix XI of the Study; the assertion is that although several control systems were not operating as a consequence of control cables having been destroyed in the fire, there was a substantial probability that redundant safety systems were in working order, and that these could be used, as indeed they were, to prevent development of a situation in which there might be a core meltdown. The NRC's overall conclusion is:

...the potential for a core melt accident as a result of the Browns Ferry fire is about 20 percent of that obtained from all other causes analyzed by the Reactor Safety

---

*The fire occurred on Mar. 22, 1975 at TVA's Browns Ferry nuclear powerplant in Alabama. On that date, two of the plant's 1,067-megawatt boiling water reactors were operating and a third was under construction. The fire started when a candle flame, used to test for air leaks at a point where cables passed through a wall, ignited a polyurethane sealant. The resulting fire damaged approximately 1,600 cables, causing many electrical short circuits. Following the accident, the two reactors were shut down for approximately 18 months while repairs and modifications were made. Losses suffered by TVA, as a result of the plants not operating for this period, were in excess of $200 million.

Study and is within uncertainty bounds of the predictions.

Countering NRC's contention that the Browns Ferry fire gave no reason for significantly revising the Study's conclusions, are claims that it was fortuitous that the fire did not eliminate redundancy to the point where there would be a meltdown of the reactor core. For example, Dr. Kendall stated:

> It is my belief based on the study my colleagues and I have carried out so far and on private talks with engineers from TVA that the absence of core melting in the Browns Ferry fire was a matter of considerable good luck. We can all be grateful that in the actual event a melting accident was avoided. In my view the accident was *a close call*. It was not, as RSS and NRC assert, an accident at all times under adequate control, with safety reserves, and with negligible risk of uncontrolled development toward melting. This is simply not the case.

The NRC's Advisory Committee on Reactor Safeguards (ACRS) commented as follows on the adequacy of the Study's analysis to take account of multiple, correlated errors in procedures, design, judgment, and construction such as those leading to the Browns Ferry fire:

> The ACRS believes that the methodology of NUREG 75/014 [the Study] is useful in accounting for that portion of the risk resulting from identifiable potential common mode or dependent failures, and can be used to search out the possibility of multiple correlated errors. *However, the methodology cannot guarantee that all major contributors to risk will be identified, and a considerable element of subjective judgment is involved in assigning many of the quantitative input parameters.* Both for nuclear and nonnuclear applications, for complex systems, where multiple, correlated failures or common cause failures may be significant, the record shows that investigators working independently will frequently make estimates of system unreliability which differ from one another

by a large factor. *At this stage of its review, the ACRS believes that a substantial effort may be required to develop and apply dependable methods for quantitatively accounting for the very large number of multiple correlated or dependent failure paths and to obtain the necessary failure rate data bases.* [Emphasis added.]

> Whether multiple correlated errors will dominate the overall risk, however, is subject to question, particularly if simpler postulated accident sequences are generally the dominant contributors to the likelihood of system failure....

D. VARIABILITY IN ACCIDENT CONSEQUENCES

In a paper which appears in the spring 1976 issue of the *Bell Journal of Economics* and submitted for the hearing record, Dr. Joel Yellin (Associate Professor of Social Sciences at MIT) states that the Study's usefulness as an aid to policymakers is diminished by virtue of the analysis having averaged risks over 68 reactor sites, rather than indicating specifically the wide variation among individual sites. Dr. Yellin notes that risks associated with particular sites vary by a factor of 1,000; e.g., between the Maine Yankee plant located in Wiscasset, Maine and the Zion plant in Illinois. The Yellin analysis infers that the Study's conclusions concerning prompt fatalities are heavily dominated by accidents at plants located near large populations.

E. OBTUSE AND INCOMPLETE PRESENTATION

Several reviewers commented that the Study was organized in a manner such that it was difficult to determine the validity of the analysis.

Dr. Panofsky testified:

> It is almost impossible to make an overall thorough critical review of the report for a number of reasons: One is the sheer length of the report and the second is that the method of presentation of the report leaves much to be desired in terms of clarity and

exact statement as to origin of data and procedures actually used. Most people have read only the summary report, or the brief executive summary. However, these versions do not do justice to the main body of the report, and in some crucial instances seriously misrepresent the conclusions of the main report.

Dr. Rowe said the EPA reviewers had found the Study incomplete with regard to its discussion of accident consequences:

> Because the description of the formulation of the estimate was incomplete, EPA was not able to evaluate the assessment in terms of the range of uncertainties. We have found, however, that what we consider more reasonable assumptions in health effects, emergency actions, and estimates of probabilities of releases, would cause modifications of the overall risk analysis.

Dr. von Hippel was also critical of the presentation. He said:

> The report itself, in all its 2400 pages of detail, is virtually impenetrable to all but the professional reader. Indeed, I am not even sure about the professional reader.

F. NUCLEAR RISK VIS-A-VIS RISKS ASSOCIATED WITH OTHER ENERGY OPTIONS

The Study presented comparisons of nuclear risks with those associated with various natural phenomena and man-caused events. The Study did not compare nuclear risks with those arising from the use of other energy technologies. There are, for example, little data to indicate the health consequences arising from the use of coal for electric generation. Dr. Panofsky said the following in regard to this omission:

> The Rasmussen Report compares nuclear reactor risks with those associated with totally unrelated natural or manmade accidents. While such comparisons are of interest, it is more important from an energy policy point of view to compare the risk to

public health produced by a growing reactor industry with those hazards posed by competing means of generating electrical energy. The Rasmussen Report does not deal with this question, although it is crucial in judging "acceptability" of risk. There is little question that the matter of reactor safety has been subjected to considerably more searching inquiry than the public health dangers of competing technologies. The health and environmental hazards of the only feasible immediate alternative to a growing nuclear industry, namely, increased coal production, are receiving increased attention; without going into detail here I can say that such comparisons tend to lead to the conclusion that expanded coal production imposes a larger social burden in regard to occupational and public health and adverse environmental consequences than does nuclear energy. I do not have to remind members of this committee that the current direct financial burden on the Federal Government stemming from payments to coal mineworkers and their families to compensate for occupational respiratory disease has been above $1 billion per year.

G. APPLICABILITY OF STUDY RESULTS TO MANY REACTORS

The Study's conclusions are intended to apply to the first 100 large nuclear generating stations to be constructed in the United States. The analysis itself is based on the actual design of two operating reactors: the 788-megawatt Surry unit I, a pressurized water reactor; and the 1,065-megawatt Peach Bottom unit II, a boiling water reactor. Some comments on the Study concerned whether the analysis based on two reactors can be used to reach conclusions concerning ninety-eight other plants.

The Study itself addressed this question and concluded that the analysis when applied to other reactors will tend to overstate the risk.... The basis for this conclusion was, in effect, that reactor safety research and actual experience in design and operations will lead to a level of risk lower than that perceived today.

Some concern has been expressed that unique design features of particular reactors may lead to much more serious accidents than would be indicated by the analysis applied to Surry and Peach Bottom. In appearing before the Advisory Committee on Reactor Safeguards on January 4, 1977, Dr. Rowe said:

A point which deserves stress is that those performing further work in assessment of nuclear powerplant accident risks should not ignore any deficiency [indicated] in the Reactor Safety Study simply because it has been concluded that refinement in that specific case would not make a significant change in the overall results published in WASH-1400. With another nuclear powerplant design, having a different set of safety systems, the same deficiency may be important.

Comment

As these reports illustrate, policy analysis often seems inaccessible to citizens because of its technical vocabulary and quantitative techniques. Yet citizens should be able to evaluate such analyses in general terms by considering whether they address the right questions. Examine the Rasmussen Report in this spirit by asking: Are the basic assumptions plausible? Are any ethical issues treated as merely technical questions? What important ethical factors are ignored?

"Who...could have guessed," Robert Goodin asks, "that technicians would plug a leaky coolant pipe with a basketball or connect a radioactive waste storage tank to the plant's drinking water system or carry a lighted candle into electrical cable housing at Browns Ferry?" Can the "human factor" be adequately taken into account in risk analysis? If so, how? If not, does this render the analysis ethically and politically useless?

The authors of the Rasmussen Report say that they "made no judgment on the acceptability of nuclear risks." That judgment, they write, "should be made by a broader segment of society." Is the report completely neutral on the question of the acceptability of risks?

On what principles should we decide whether society should accept new risks? For example, is a risk acceptable if it is no greater than the ones we already live with? By what process should government decide whether risks are acceptable? Who should be included in the "broader segment of society" that decides the acceptability of risks—people living near a power plant or everyone who will benefit from the energy?

The waste from nuclear power plants exposes future generations to severe dangers from radioactivity. The assumptions of policy analysis tend to discount these dangers because they are so remote. People in the distant future, it is suggested, are likely to have ways of coping with such waste. In any case, they will be better off in many other ways than we are, because they will be enjoying the fruits of the investments made by earlier generations. To what extent and in what ways should we consider the welfare of distant future generations when we choose among energy policies?

The conventional decision-making rule in policy analysis says "choose the policy that maximizes the total expected utility." (The total expected utility is the sum of the benefits minus the harms, discounting for the uncertainty of each.) Some critics of conventional policy analysis suggest that because the risks of nuclear energy are so uncertain and potential harm so great we should adopt more cautious decision-making rules. Assess the moral implications of the following rules: (1) Keep the options open (reject irreversible policies). (2) Protect the vulnerable (give special weight to future generations). (3) Maximize minimum payoff (make sure the worst outcome is as good as possible). (4) Avoid harm (give more weight to causing harms than to failing to produce benefits of the same size). Under what circumstances would these rules lead us to prefer energy sources such as solar and fossil fuel over nuclear power? How would you justify each of the rules?

Recommended Reading

An excellent introduction to how advocates of policy analysis intend it to be used is Edith Stokey and Richard Zeckhauser, *A Primer for Policy Analysis* (New York: Norton, 1978). For a flavor of the ethical controversy over policy analysis, see Charles Wolf, Jr., "Ethics and Policy Analysis," in Joel Fleishman et al. (eds.), *Public Duties* (Cambridge, Mass.: Harvard University Press, 1981), pp. 131–41; Steven Kelman, "Cost-Benefit Analysis: An Ethical Critique," *Regulation* (Jan./Feb., 1981), pp. 33–40; Alasdair MacIntyre, "Utilitarianism and Cost/Benefit Analysis," in Tom Beauchamp and Norman Bowie (eds.), *Ethical Theory and Business* (Englewood Cliffs, N.J.: Prentice-Hall, 1979), pp. 266–76; and Tom Beauchamp, "A Reply to MacIntyre," in Beauchamp and Bowie, pp. 276–82. Also see Charles W. Anderson, "The Place of Principles in Policy Analysis," *American Political Science Review*, 73 (Sept., 1979), pp. 711–23. More generally on utilitarianism and its problems, see the Recommended Reading in the Introduction.

The best single theoretical review of studies of nuclear power is Robert Goodin, *Political Theory and Public Policy* (Chicago: University of Chicago Press, 1982), chapter 10.

On the question of the value of life in public policy, see Steven Rhoads (ed.) *Valuing Life: Public Policy Dilemmas* (Boulder, Colo.: Westview Press, 1980); and Charles Fried, *Anatomy of Values* (Cambridge, Mass.: Harvard University Press, 1970), chapter 12. For the problem of future generations, see Brian Barry, "Justice Between Generations," in P. M. S. Hacker and J. Raz (eds.), *Law, Morality and Society* (Oxford: Clarendon, 1977), pp. 268–84.

6 Distributive Justice

Introduction

On what principles should government control the distribution of goods to citizens? Utilitarians and their progeny (discussed in the previous chapter) do not believe that any special theory of justice is necessary. The right distribution is simply the one that maximizes the total welfare of most citizens. While utilitarianism is widely criticized for ignoring claims of individuals that even the welfare of the whole society should not override, the critics do not agree on what theory of justice to put in its place.

Libertarians argue that governments should secure only liberty, not distribute goods. Goods come into the world attached to specific people who have earned, inherited, or received them by free exchange, and for the state to redistribute their property without their consent is a violation of their fundamental right to liberty. Because "taxation is on a par with forced labor" (Robert Nozick), even a democratic government may not tax the rich to provide welfare for the poor. Nor may it protect the rich from competition by sheltering their industries or licensing their professions. Individual liberty, understood as noninterference, trumps social welfare and democracy.

Egalitarian critics argue that, just as utilitarianism can be faulted for submerging individuals beneath all social purposes, so libertarianism can be criticized for elevating them above all social responsibility. For egalitarians, our social interdependence creates certain duties of mutual aid.

Most egalitarian theories of distributive justice also give priority to basic liberty over social welfare. But their list of basic liberties differs from that of libertarians. It includes political liberty, freedom of religion, speech, and assembly, and the right to hold personal property. But it does not include an absolute right to commercial property or unqualified freedom of contract. According to egalitarians, although liberty has priority it is not the only good that governments should distribute. Other primary goods include income and wealth, the distributions of which are just (according to John Rawls' difference principle) only if they maximize the welfare of the least advantaged citizens.

Egalitarians are commonly criticized for subordinating individual liberty to equality. This criticism is compelling only if one accepts the libertarian understanding of liberty and its absolute value. A more general problem is that the maximization of some primary goods (such as health care) might require an egalitarian government to neglect other primary goods, since there is virtually no limit to the resources that can be spent on making people healthy.

Democratic theories of distributive justice build upon this criticism. The people, constituted by democratic majorities at various levels of government, should have the right to determine priorities among goods according to what they deem most important to their collective ways of life. Most democratic theorists recognize that majorities should have this right only when the procedures by which they make decisions are fair. But the requirements of this standard of procedural fairness are controversial. Some democrats argue that it requires governments only to secure certain basic liberties, such as freedom of speech, association, and the right to vote. Others claim that it also requires governments to guarantee the distribution of a higher level of welfare — education, food, housing, and health care — for all citizens. The first position has been criticized for permitting majority tyranny over disadvantaged minorities, the second, for smuggling egalitarian values into democratic theory and thereby encroaching on the rights of democratic majorities who may not favor so much equality.

The political controversy over the distribution of health care in the United States is an instructive problem in distributive justice. Good health care is necessary for pursuing most other things in life. Yet equal access to health care would require the government not only to redistribute resources from the rich and healthy to the poor and infirm, but also to restrict the freedom of doctors and other health care providers. Such redistributions and restrictions may be warranted, but on what principles and to what extent? Congress's decision in 1972 to fund dialysis for all victims of end-stage renal disease is part of this continuing controversy over whether government has a right or a responsibility to provide its citizens with the preconditions of a good life. By considering whether Congress made the correct decision and used the right process to make it, we can refine our understanding of the relative strengths and weaknesses of competing theories of distributive justice.

The Policy Debate on End-Stage Renal Disease

Richard A. Rettig

INTRODUCTION

It was Saturday morning, September 30, 1972, barely one month before the November presidential election. The

Reprinted by permission from *Law and Contemporary Problems,* Vol. 40 (Autumn 1976), pp. 196–204, 212–30. Copyright © 1976, Duke University School of Law.

Senate was in session, hardly a normal weekend event in Washington. It was rushing to complete action on H.R. 1, the Social Security Amendments of 1972. At 11:30 a.m., Senator Vance Hartke of Indiana secured the floor and proposed that the bill be amended to extend Medicare coverage to victims of end-stage renal disease. This coverage would preserve the lives of relatively few individuals, at a very substantial cost. During the brief debate — thirty minutes were allocated to the amendment — only Senator Wallace Bennett of Utah spoke against the provision. With nearly half the Senate members absent, the measure was adopted by a vote of fifty-two "Yeas" and three "Nays."

The remaining steps of the legislative process were traversed with comparable speed. The conference committee of the House Ways and Means Committee and the Senate Finance Committee met for only a single day to consider differences on the entire bill. The kidney disease amendment received no more than ten minutes' discussion and the Senate proposal was accepted in its essentials with a slight modification in one provision. Both House and Senate accepted the conference committee report on October 17, and President Nixon signed H.R. 1 into law as Public Law 92-603 on October 30, 1972. The kidney disease provision was included as section 2991. In this way, the nation resolved an extended policy debate over kidney disease that reached back more than a decade.

This paper is an analysis of that policy debate, one that deserves our attention for at least two reasons. First, it is thought by many that the kidney disease amendment is an instance of the unwillingness of public officials to withhold financial assistance to an identified set of individuals who would clearly die without such assistance. Zeckhauser, for example, has argued:

> When risks of lives are involved, an important valued belief is that society will not give up a life to save dollars, even a great many dollars. Rarely is this belief, widely held albeit mistaken, put to a clear test. When it is, it may be desirable for society to spend an inordinate amount on each of a few lives to preserve a comforting myth.

Such a myth-preserving action was taken when the federal government assumed the costs of renal dialysis.

The analysis of the policy debate preceding the enactment of Section 2991 provides evidence pertinent to evaluating this claim that society is unwilling to sacrifice lives for dollars. Though Zeckhauser's interpretation may be of some merit, it tends to exaggerate the importance of the "myth." It overlooks the length of the policy debate over federal responsibility for financing the treatment of individuals having end stage renal disease, a debate that began in the early 1960s and was not resolved until 1972, and it overlooks the strong resistance to patient care financing that was encountered at every juncture of the debate, even though the plight of victims of kidney failure continued to be dramatized by the news media. Finally, the "myth preserving" interpretation overlooks the alternative explanation that the 1972 legislation was the practically inevitable next step in a series of partial federal government responses to the existence of the life-saving therapies of hemodialysis and renal transplantation.

The second reason for analyzing the end-stage renal disease policy debate is to consider its implications for other diseases that might be candidates for catastrophic health insurance coverage. A panel of the Institute of Medicine, for instance, worried in 1973 that Section 2991 might become a precedent for extending such coverage to other clinical conditions on a categorical disease-by-disease basis. Hemophilia victims, for example, would appear to have as valid a claim to federal patient treatment financing as kidney failure victims. The policy debate on kidney disease, however, strongly suggests that more than the existence of life-saving therapy and an identified group of patients is needed before government action is forthcoming.

I. BACKGROUND

In the 1960s two therapies—hemodialysis and renal transplantation—emerged which had the capability of saving the lives of individuals with chronic (or end-stage) kidney failure. Hemodialysis is the process by which metabolic waste products normally cleared by the kidney through the urinary tract are "washed" from the blood stream by means of an artificial kidney. Renal transplantation is that surgical procedure by which a healthy kidney from one individual is implanted in an individual with end-stage renal disease; the transplanted kidney functions as the individual's own kidneys once did. Clinically, the artificial kidney machine is the first artificial substitute for a whole organ and kidney transplantation is the first surgical procedure for transplanting a whole natural organ from one individual to another. These therapies are non-elective procedures for those with end-stage renal disease; if they do not receive this treatment they die.

In Public Law 92-603, the Social Security Amendments of 1972, Medicare health insurance coverage for end-stage renal disease was effectively extended to more than 90 per cent of the population of the United States. The 1965 law which established Medicare provided health insurance coverage to the aged—those over sixty-five years of age—and this included coverage for renal failure. Restrictive patient selection criteria for hemodialysis and renal transplantation patients, and limited knowledge of this specific form of the general benefit, however, resulted in receipt by relatively few individuals of Medicare benefits for end-stage renal disease.

Public Law 92-603, enacted on October 30, 1972, provided Medicare coverage to the under-65 population and did so in two ways. First, those individuals under age sixty-five who qualified for cash benefits under social security or the railroad retirement system because of a disability so incapacitating that they were prevented from working became eligible, after a twenty-four month waiting period, for Medicare's hospital and supplementary medical insurance protection. This protection included coverage for end-stage renal disease.

Second, a substantial number of potential end-stage renal disease patients, approximately sixty per cent of the total, could not qualify for Medicare on either the basis of age or entitlement to cash disability benefits. Medicare coverage was extended to this larger group by section 2991 of the Act. Section 2991 provided that every individual not yet sixty-five years old, who was fully or currently insured or entitled to monthly insurance benefits under social security, or who was the spouse or dependent child of such an individual, and who was "medically determined to have chronic renal disease" and to require hemodialysis or renal transplantation, shall, in the language of the Act, "be deemed to be disabled for purposes of coverage under parts A and B of Medicare subject to the deductible, premium, and co-payment provisions of Title XVIII."

Both renal dialysis and transplantation are very expensive therapies, requiring resources normally well beyond the financial means of all but the most affluent. A General Accounting Office (GAO) study of the costs of dialysis, based upon 1972 data for ninety-six center dialysis programs in eleven states and two counties, and ten home dialysis programs in six states, indicated the following [data (see Table 1)].

The costs of transplantation are also significant. Charges for 1973 in twenty-four facilities analyzed by the GAO ranged from $5,500 to $20,500 and averaged about $12,800. The Department of Health, Education, and Welfare cited

TABLE 1. ANNUAL COST OF DIALYSIS

		Center Dialysis (96)		Home Dialysis (10)	
	Total (96)	Hospital (81)	Non-Hospital (15)	1st Year	2nd Year
Average Charge	$30,100	$30,500	$27,600	$14,900	$7,000
Range		11,500– 49,100	12,800– 46,800		

Source: Comptroller General of the U.S., Treatment of Chronic Kidney Failure: Dialysis, Transplant, Costs, and the Need for More Vigorous Efforts 40-41 (1975).
Note: Data are for 1972.

costs to the GAO of $14,000 for a transplant from a living related donor. Included in costs were hospital room, board, ancillary charges, and professional fees. The costs of therapy to a given individual can vary substantially according to the therapy or combination of therapies received and a number of other contingencies. All methods of therapy are expensive, a successful transplant being by far the least costly and most satisfactory mode of therapy.

Prior to passage of section 299I, the number of beneficiaries of end-stage renal disease treatment was relatively small. The number of reported dialysis patients alive in July 1970 was 2,874; in July 1971, it was 4,375; and a year later, 5,786. The total number of kidney transplants reported for 1967, 1968, 1969, 1970, and 1971 was 428, 635, 787, 996, and 1,172 respectively. Since passage of the Act, the number of beneficiaries has greatly increased, although the total number is still a small fraction of the population of the United States. The number of renal disease patients who had qualified for Medicare coverage as of March 31, 1975 was 25,066, of whom 20,764 were still living as of that date. Approximately 60 per cent of the total qualified on the basis of section 299I. It is estimated that the number of patients alive and receiving renal disease benefits will reach 50,000 to 70,000 by 1990. It is interesting to note, by contrast, the situation affecting hemophiliacs. Although legislation has been introduced in recent Congresses to extend financial assistance for treatment payment to hemophiliacs, Medicare coverage has not yet been made available. Hemophilia is a disease whose central symptom is serious bleeding. The estimated number of patients is 100,000, of whom approximately 25,000 are severely or moderately severely affected. These 25,000 patients require continuous replacement of fresh whole blood, plasma, or clotting concentrates. Replacement materials cost from $2,000 to $5,000 per patient per year. Costs of replacement therapy, and of reconstructive surgery for the most severely crippled, are rarely covered by third-party payments. Therapy capable of preventing bleeding episodes is far more expensive and can range from $20,000 to $40,000 per year.

The extended Medicare coverage for end-stage renal disease went into effect on July 1, 1973 [see Table 2]. The estimated incurred costs for the first year of the program were $150 million for section 299I beneficiaries and an additional $100 million for patients eligible under the aged and disabled provisions. The estimated incurred costs for the first, second, third, and fourth years for both section 299I and all Medicare renal patients are shown below. It is estimated that the annual costs for renal disease patients will exceed $1 billion by 1984.

II. THE BEGINNINGS OF THE POLICY DEBATE

In order to understand how society grappled with value-of-life decisions

TABLE 2. ESTIMATED MEDICARE INCURRED COSTS OF
END-STAGE RENAL DISEASE
(IN MILLIONS)

	Fiscal Year			
	1974	1975	1976	1977
Sec. 299I patients	$150	$225	$300	$360
All renal patients	250	350	500	600

Source: Ways and Means, Background Information 15.

posed by section 299I, it is important to recognize that the nature of the end-stage renal disease issue was clearly understood at least a decade before the matter was resolved. The federal government did not move in haste or in ignorance to the decision it made in 1972.

The use of the artificial kidney machine for providing long-term, intermittent hemodialysis for preserving lives of individuals with end-stage renal disease became possible in 1960. In that year, Dr. Belding H. Scribner, a physician at the University of Washington School of Medicine, and his colleagues invented a vascular access device known as a "cannulae" and "shunt." This device made it possible to connect patients to an artificial kidney machine for the purpose of cleansing their bloodstream of the products of metabolic waste and then to disconnect them at the end of ten to twelve hours of treatment.

Scribner inserted the cannulae and shunt in his first patient on March 9, 1960, and immediately began dialysis. Scribner was so enthusiastic about his technique that he took ten "how to do it" kits to Chicago the next month, where he demonstrated for his medical-scientific colleagues the process of patient cannulation. Clyde Shields, his first patient, also made the trip. Scribner's own account of that meeting indicates that there was general agreement that the cannulation technique was promising but that considerable pessimism existed regarding the biochemical aspects of dialysis. Questions dealing with the potential patient load

revealed substantial differences of opinion, but most thought the load would be considerable. Efforts to determine the size of that load were deferred to a later date. "The question of public release of information and fund raising was not discussed in detail," Scribner wrote, "because it is just too early to say much."

On May 19, 1960, Scribner wrote Dr. George M. Wheatley, a vice president of Metropolitan Life Insurance Company in New York City, to inquire about prospective patient load data: "It is becoming more and more clear that by this technique of continuous hemodialysis and the technique of cannulation of the blood vessels, we are going to considerably alter the course of terminal illness in patients with chronic uremia." Clearly, moving this new medical technique from clinical research to widespread medical use was of great importance to Scribner within weeks of his first patients being placed upon the machine.

Costs also came quickly into focus. July 1960 estimates by Scribner of costs for treating fifteen patients came to $99,000 – $16,000 for equipment, $40,000 for once-a-week dialysis, and $43,000 for medical personnel. Minus equipment, per patient costs were $5,533 per year. The recognition that thrice-weekly dialysis was medically more desirable later exposed these estimates as quite low. Even so, it was clear from the start that substantial costs were associated with this new procedure.

By 1962, cost considerations and the related scarcity of facilities permeated all discussions of dialysis. Writing in the *New York Times* about the Seattle experience, Harold Schmeck called the emergence of hemodialysis "[o]ne of the most dramatic stories of medical triumph and tragedy in recent history." The triumph lay in the fact that "[a] handful of men and women who should be dead, by normal medical criteria, are living and leading nearly normal lives." The tragedy lay in the fact that "because facilities for cure are limited, inevitable death of kidney disease [was in store] for thousands of others." Annual costs of treatment were estimated to be $10,000 per patient.

In early November 1962, a *Life* magazine article by Shana Alexander described the dilemma created by the existence of a life-saving therapy and the scarcity of facilities to provide it. Treatment costs were estimated to be $15,000 per patient per year. The article went on to describe the anonymous, seven-member lay committee in Seattle which was charged with deciding which individuals should have access to the limited number of machines after medical evaluation of prospective patients. Factors identified as important to the committee in their determinations included the patient's age and sex, marital status and number of dependents, income, net worth, emotional stability, educational background, occupation, past performance, future potential, and personal references. The value-of-life dilemma was thus conveyed in stark terms to an audience of millions.

At a joint conference in June 1963 between the American Medical Association and the National Kidney Disease Foundation, the Seattle presentation enumerated "adequate funding" and preparation as the first of several prerequisites for a successful hemodialysis treatment program. Costs, it was indicated, could reach "upwards of $20,000 per patient per year," and initial capitalization for a ten-bed center was estimated to be $300,000 to $500,000. The financial workshop report indicated that it "has asked more questions than it has been able to find answers for at this point." The workshop on socioeconomic and moral questions, however, headed by a Jesuit priest, put the problem in clearer perspective:

> At this moment there are only a certain number of people who are able to be helped through the technique of hemodialysis. In the immediate future, also, just a small number of people will be able to be treated. No matter what the decision of our conferences about the medical and financial factors, the implementation of a full-scale program will take a number of years. Therefore, we in this country will be faced with the moral problem of having at hand a method of saving life which is not available to all who need it.

Finally, the implications of hemodialysis for the federal government were also recognized early. In 1964, the Senate Appropriations Committee indicated that the Public Health Service had the statutory authority to provide demonstration and training funds for artificial kidney programs. That authority, however, did not extend to patient-care financing:

> The Federal Government has borne the cost of treatment for its legal beneficiaries and shared these treatment costs when it has been in connection with research investigation or demonstration. Traditionally, payment for treatment of illness has been the responsibility of the patient or the local community. If the Federal Government were to share the full cost of lifetime treatment for all who suffer from these chronic diseases and conditions, the financial burden would be excessive.

III. MAJOR FACTORS
AFFECTING THE POLICY DEBATE

Six factors played major roles in the lengthy policy debate on patient-care financing. These factors were:

1. The changing evaluation of the two life-saving medical procedures—dialysis

and transplantation — as they were clinically developed;

2. the changing distribution of power within the medical-scientific community;

3. the gradual extension of government involvement in renal disease;

4. the evolution of the federal role in health care in general;

5. the importance of identifying and publicizing the lives at stake; and

6. the "sotto voce" character of the policy debates.

Each of these elements deserves close analysis. [Rettig's analyses of factors 3–6 are reprinted here.]

3. THE GRADUAL EXTENSION OF GOVERNMENT INVOLVEMENT

In retrospect, one can observe a logical development of federal policy toward both dialysis and transplantation as each emerged from biomedical research and was introduced into patient care. That "logic" can be seen in the contribution of federal policy from research and development, to demonstration and training, and then to capacity-building within the Department of Health, Education, and Welfare.

a. Research and Development

The support of biomedical research has long been a widely sanctioned role for the federal government. In the mid-1960s, soon after dialysis and renal transplantation appeared, supporting research programs were established within the National Institutes of Health.

The possibility of using immuno-suppressive drugs to control the rejection by the host of a transplanted kidney was suggested to the scientific community in 1959 and was taken up quickly by medical scientists engaged in experiments with kidney transplantation. The first application to humans was in 1961. Within a short time, control of the immunological rejection phenomenon in kidney trans-plantation by immuno-suppressive drugs had displaced the earlier use of whole-body irradiation in clinical research. In 1964, as a result of this work, the Committee on Appropriations of the House of Representatives added two million dollars to the budget request of the National Institute of Allergy and Infectious Diseases "to start a real program in the study of immunological defense mechanisms as they relate to the rejection, by one person's body, of transplanted tissues from the body of another person." The Senate Appropriations Committee, in that same year, concurred. "This rejection phenomenon," it noted, "rather than surgical technique, is today the most serious obstacle to successful organ transplants." The Transplant Immunology Program, within the National Institute of Allergy and Infectious Diseases, was established in direct response to the implications of research results and in an effort to pursue those implications.

The establishment of the Artificial Kidney/Chronic Uremia Program within the National Institute of Arthritis and Metabolic Diseases occurred more slowly. Scribner testified in 1962 about the need for research funds to improve hemodialysis, and the Senate did add an additional one million dollars to the Institute's fiscal 1963 budget request "for expanded research in diseases of the kidney." It also recommended that "a considerable portion" be devoted to further research on the artificial kidney. Although the 1962 Senate Appropriations Committee report described hemodialysis as a "brilliant triumph of medical research," its 1963 report more modestly referred to it as "an excellent example of practical accomplishment." Neither the Senate nor House appropriations committee saw fit in either fiscal 1964 or 1965 to take additional action.

Substantial pressures were brought to bear upon the Congress, the National Institutes of Health, and the executive branch during these years to create a program of research on the artificial kidney. Finally, in connection with the fiscal 1966 appropriation, the House recommended two million dollars more than the budget request from the Arthritis and Metabolic Disease Institute, for "the development of a better artificial kidney than the machines which now exist." The Senate Appropriations Committee, impressed with the need for "simpler and less costly techniques," added an additional one million dollars to the House allowance to enable research and development work to proceed "with all possible speed." But the evidence indicates a program of research and development for a better dialysis machine was not established quickly.

b. Demonstration and Training

A thornier policy question arose in connection with funding dialysis centers through Public Health Service funds. Scribner and his colleagues in Seattle had established a community treatment center in 1962. Through a combination of support from private philanthropy and community fund-raising, an active dialysis center was in existence when the 1962 Life magazine article appeared. In 1963, a Public Health Service grant was made to this center to assist it in meeting its financial obligations.

The policy discussion generated by this grant dealt with several considerations, two of which were addressed by the Senate Appropriations Committee in its report on the fiscal 1965 appropriation. First, the committee pointed out, chronic illness and aging formula grant funds were available "for the States to use at their discretion for the support of community dialysis centers"; furthermore, the Public Health Service had the authority under the Community Health Services and Facilities Act of 1963 to use funds for community dialysis centers. Second, the

committee report made clear that such funds were legitimate for demonstration and training but not for payment for treatment of illness.

There was an underlying issue that troubled the Senate Appropriations Committee. The two grants that had been awarded before 1964, one to Seattle and the other to Downstate Medical Center in Brooklyn, were step-funded over a three-year period so federal funds would be phased out during that time. It was assumed by Public Health Service officials that community financial support would be established at the end of the three years. The Senate, especially Senator Lister Hill of Alabama, was skeptical that community support would be forthcoming. In 1964, the committee indicated that it had decided against an amendment proposed by Senator Henry M. Jackson of Washington to provide one million dollars for two additional centers.

In 1965, in connection with the fiscal 1966 appropriation, the House Appropriations Committee recommended an additional two million dollars beyond the budget request of $1.4 million for supporting hemodialysis centers. The committee's report noted that this amount fell short of the five million dollars recommended by the Public Health Service advisory groups. The Senate committee concurred with the House in providing a total of $3.4 million for the support of fourteen community dialysis centers.

The members of the House and Senate Appropriations Committees, where much control over federal government health policy resided in the 1960s, knew what they were doing. They were prompted to action in 1965, in part, by the knowledge that NBC Television was preparing, for release that fall, a documentary program which would contrast the millions of dollars being spent on the space program with the government's apparent unwillingness to spend money to save lives on earth. However, the Senate, in setting forth the legal authority for Public Health Service action, limiting the scope of that action to demonstration and training, and providing modest funds for fourteen community dialysis centers, showed a fundamental unwillingness to accept federal government responsibility for paying for the costs of treatment.

Indeed, the federal government moved to further limit its involvement in community dialysis centers in 1968 and 1969. The Health Service and Mental Health Administration, under whose authority the kidney centers program was then being administered, took action to terminate grant support. A May 1969 memorandum from the director of the Kidney Disease Control Program to the Administration indicated that support had terminated for four centers, one other center was soon to go off federal funding, fourth year funding extensions to the original three-year grants had been negotiated with seven centers on the condition that this support was to be terminal, and fourth year support was not anticipated for two other centers.

c. Capacity-building

The development of hemodialysis centers around the country led to a stream of legislative proposals for expanding federal government programs from 1965 onward. Senator Jackson was the foremost advocate of such legislation in the Senate; Representative Roybal, among others, in the House. But this flurry of proposed legislation literally went nowhere. No hearings were held on any legislation during the period from 1965 through 1969. All congressional action was effectively confined within the appropriations committees.

Reluctance to see an expanded role for the federal government in hemodialysis was not limited to the legislative branch. In early 1969, the director of the Regional

Medical Programs Service, in a memorandum to the deputy administrator of the Health Services and Mental Health Administration, wrote in response to a request for comments on proposed legislation to support treatment of end-stage kidney disease:

> I judge that the major question we should ask ourselves as we review the proposed legislation is this: "Can we and should we at this time make an all out effort to establish facilities for the treatment of all patients with end-stage kidney disease who can benefit from hemodialysis?" My answer is no.

After recommending a strategy directed at prevention, early detection, and early treatment of kidney disease, this official described the proposal to finance treatment of end-stage renal disease through Social Security as "quite unsound." He cogently summarized his views on the central issue:

> Our present system of health care controls costs in cases like this by setting up barriers to adequate care by making accessibility and financing difficult or impossible. The cost in dollars, facilities, and health manpower of a national kidney program which would remove these barriers to patients with end-stage kidney disease are so great that for the time being we may have to leave them erect.

Kidney disease legislation was finally enacted in 1970. The legislative authority for the Regional Medical Programs Service was amended to read, "The Heart Disease, Cancer, Stroke, and *Kidney Disease* Amendments of 1970." The HEW kidney disease program initiated in the chronic diseases division of the Public Health Service in 1965 was now legally lodged in the Regional Medical Programs Service, where it had been administratively lodged since 1969. This legislation established a means whereby community dialysis centers could receive financial support through the fifty-five regions of the Service. Policy control was centralized, but funds for centers were allocated on a decentralized basis through the regions. The net effect of this arrangement was to increase dialysis capacity at the local community level, even though there remained great reluctance at the highest levels of the federal government to adopt legislation that would provide directly for patient-care financing.

The apparent progression from research and development through demonstration and training to capacity-building is obviously a reconstruction of events. The "technical logic" of HEW policy development looks more rational in retrospect than it did at the time. It is true, however, that federal health policy within the statutory framework of the Public Health Service Act was primarily oriented toward medical research while concurrently engaged in a search for effective means to bring the results of research into medical practice. Within this framework, policy consistently stopped short of assuming a federal government role for payment of patient treatment costs. Policy toward end-stage renal disease was clearly constrained by these broader considerations.

d. The Veterans Administration

The United States Government did assume responsibility for financing treatment for veterans who were eligible for medical benefits from the Veterans Administration. In 1963, the VA announced the initiation of a program to establish dialysis units in thirty VA hospitals around the country. This was done over the next few years and by July 1, 1972, the VA was dialyzing 16 per cent of the total reported dialysis patients in the country.

The VA reached the decision to provide dialysis treatment largely within its own organization. It did request apportionment of construction funds for refurbishing hospitals to create dialysis units,

however, from the Bureau of the Budget in 1965, a request which prompted much discussion within the Bureau about its implications. Consultations between Budget officials and the Office of Science and Technology led to a decision, implemented in 1966, to establish a committee of experts to advise the Bureau on government-wide policy toward dialysis and transplantation. This group, known as the Gottschalk Committee, after its chairman, Dr. Carl W. Gottschalk, of the University of North Carolina, issued its report in September 1967. Among other things, the report provided the Bureau of the Budget with a basis to urge combined dialysis and transplantation units within VA hospitals and to promote home dialysis — a less costly mode of treatment — as an alternative to hospital-based dialysis. The legal basis of VA action in providing dialysis treatment was clear. To reverse the VA policy decision once it had been made would have been a momentous political task. Even so, the VA action was scrutinized by the Bureau of the Budget and stimulated that agency to explore more fully the policy implications of available treatment for end-stage renal disease.

4. THE EVOLUTION OF THE FEDERAL GOVERNMENT'S ROLE IN HEALTH

The policy debate on payment for treatment of end-stage renal disease paralleled the larger debate about the appropriate role of the federal government in the provision of health services generally. This larger debate, moreover, occurred not with respect to the Public Health Service or the Veterans Administration but with respect to the Social Security system. In 1965, Congress added titles XVIII and XIX to the Social Security Act, thus establishing Medicare and Medicaid programs and the principle that the aged and indigent deserved government-financed health insurance. This major initiative in federal health policy was necessary, but not sufficient, to provide a statutory basis for patient-care financing for end-stage renal disease.

In 1967, the Gottschalk Committee recommended financing patient care for end-stage kidney disease patients through an amendment to title XVIII (Medicare) of the Social Security Act. The Committee argued that the Johnson administration's recommendation that the disabled be aided should be the basis for payment for kidney disease patients, although the disability recommendation was not enacted in 1967. The disability recommendation did result, however, in the undertaking of a study within the Social Security Administration in 1968. This study laid the groundwork for providing Medicare health insurance benefits to the most severely disabled. The provision of such benefits did not actually occur, however, until the passage of the Social Security Amendments of 1972, the same legislation that included section 2991.

The language of section 2991 reflects the importance of this expansion of the federal health insurance role. After stipulating the conditions of eligibility — under sixty-five, fully or currently insured or entitled to monthly benefits, medically determined to have chronic renal disease — the provision said such individuals *shall be deemed to be disabled* for purposes of coverage under Medicare. It is unclear what formula would have been used for renal diseases if the expansion of Medicare benefits to the disabled had not been occurring simultaneously.

Senator Russell B. Long, chairman of the Senate Finance Committee, was then, as now, advocating health insurance for catastrophic illness. Kidney disease was seen as a catastrophic illness, severely depleting or exhausting the financial resources of nearly all of those who required therapy. Therefore, in addition to

being included under the general language of the disability provision, financing of treatment for end-stage renal disease was also seen as the first step toward providing catastrophic medical insurance through Medicare.

As long as kidney disease programs were authorized and funded under the authority of the Public Health Service Act, it was possible to confine the government's responsibility to activities that stopped short of patient-care financing. To bridge the gap, it was necessary to shift the context of the policy debate from that framework to that provided by Title XVIII of the Social Security Act, but even this was not sufficient to ensure the commitment made in section 2991. The ability of the Congress and its staff to relate end-stage renal disease to disability and prospectively to catastrophic health insurance was also necessary.

5. THE IMPORTANCE OF IDENTIFIED LIVES

The policy debate which preceded the enactment of section 2991 does not reveal an automatic reflexive response by the government to the victims of end-stage renal disease. Rather, it suggests a "tipping process" at work. It was necessary for the cumulative effect of an increasing number of government programs to be felt, as discussed above. Moreover, it appears that widespread publicity of lives lost for the lack of scarce medical resources was necessary, including specific dramatization of identified lives at stake. Finally, the number of patients being kept alive had to increase to the point where they simply could not be ignored.

During the 1960s and early 1970s a substantial stream of newspaper and television coverage publicized the plight of individuals with end-stage kidney disease. Two major, early examples are the 1962 magazine article and 1965 NBC documentary mentioned above. Scribner thought that the effects of this publicity would be immediate and would generate intense public demand for a strong federal government commitment to providing treatment for those with chronic kidney failure. The limited response in both cases came as a great surprise to him. The effect of such publicity was obviously cumulative, not immediate, in its influence on policy.

Publicity included dramatization of particular identified lives. In 1965, Dr. Theodore Tsaltas, the Philadelphia physician who was dialyzing himself, testified, with substantial emotional impact, before the House Committee on Appropriations, testimony later seen on the NBC TV documentary. In 1966, on a visit to Seattle, Representative John E. Fogarty, chairman of the House committee, observed a patient dialyzing himself in his home. A New York City resident testified and was dialyzed before the House Ways and Means Committee in November 1971, a demonstration which apparently contributed to the willingness of Representative Wilbur Mills to support a kidney disease amendment to Medicare. Without question, the publicity and dramatization of these identified lives affected the policy debate, although the extent of their influence with legislators at any given time is unclear.

The number of patients undergoing dialysis grew steadily prior to the 1972 legislation. The Gottschalk Committee had data on 247 individuals who had begun dialysis treatment in Public Health Service supported programs from 1960 to March 1967, of whom forty-two, or 17 per cent, had died. The committee estimated that this number amounted to one-fourth to one-third of all those who had begun treatment since 1960, indicating a total of 750 to 1,000 patients. Using the 17 per cent mortality rate, the estimate was that approximately 620 to 830 dialysis patients were alive in March 1967. Data from the National Dialysis Registry indicate that

the number of patients being kept alive on dialysis had increased to 2,874 by June 30, 1970 and to 5,786 two years later.

An interesting question for future research is: When and under what circumstances does the number of identified lives become so large that patient-care financing becomes an imperative? As noted earlier, the victims of some other deadly conditions including, most notably, hemophiliacs, have not been treated as generously by the government as the victims of end-stage renal disease.

6. THE "SOTTO VOCE" CHARACTER OF THE POLICY DEBATE

Though the plight of the victims of chronic kidney failure was kept before the public by both local and national newspapers, magazines, and broadcast media, the policy debate *per se* was not very public in character. The issues in the debate were clearly understood and vigorously discussed, as indicated above, but the debate itself had low public visibility and limited public participation. Let us summarize the above discussion in this regard.

All the policy issues were extensively discussed within the medical-scientific community. The settings for these discussions were controlled by the medical, scientific, and voluntary health organizations concerned with renal disease. These organizations were dominated by the research community in the early 1960s, but clinicians came to play an increasingly important role as time passed. Nevertheless, these discussions within the medical-scientific community were basically inaccessible to the public.

Congressional discussions of the issues posed by end-stage kidney disease were confined for many years to the appropriations committees of the House and Senate. Existing legislative authority was deemed adequate for the range of acceptable policy responses until 1970. No kidney disease legislation was enacted until that year, though numerous bills were proposed from 1965 onward. Nor was there any full discussion of the issues in congressional committee hearings on kidney disease during the policy debate. Not even the 1972 legislation, as we shall see in a moment, received thorough legislative attention.

Executive branch discussions of the policy issues were often focused on specific budgetary questions, matters of very low public visibility. The various legislative proposals introduced in the Congress generated important analyses within the executive branch, but the absence of legislative hearings meant that the positions developed were never publicly articulated. The effort to address the policy issues through the Gottschalk Committee, moreover, was deliberately kept at a very low profile and the release of its report to the public was done in an almost surreptitious manner. The executive branch displayed no enthusiasm at all for a public discussion of the issues.

The policy debate on patient-care financing for kidney disease was carried out mainly within the inner councils of the medical-scientific community and the political-governmental system. Two explanations are suggested for this "sotto voce" character of the debate. One hypothesis is that there existed a basic asymmetry in the relative power of the opponents and proponents of federal government financing of treatment costs with opponents controlling access to the formal decision-making agenda of government for an extended time and thus able to prevent the issue from being considered. Alternatively, it is possible to argue that both opponents and proponents were reluctant to have this issue fully considered in a public debate, fearing perhaps that it was too divisive for the polity to handle. The evidence supports both propositions to some extent, sug-

gesting that this particular "value of life" issue posed great difficulties for the normal functioning of policy formation processes.

IV. RESOLUTION OF THE DEBATE

This analysis has discussed a number of the factors which influenced the extended policy debate on patient-care financing for end-stage renal disease. The evidence reveals great reluctance by the government to assume the financial responsibility for paying patient treatment costs. In 1972 the policy debate was finally and suddenly resolved.

In early 1971, at the outset of the Ninety-second Congress, the Nixon Administration proposed a number of major amendments to the Social Security Act. The bill which was introduced in the House of Representatives as H.R. 1 dealt with consolidation of fifty-four federal-state programs for the needy aged, blind, and disabled; the establishment of more effective cost controls on Medicare and Medicaid; the provision of health care to Medicare and Medicaid recipients through health maintenance organizations; and various modifications of the Social Security benefit structure. But "by far the most significant and the most needed provisions of H.R. 1," in the words of Elliott Richardson, then Secretary of Health, Education, and Welfare, were "those which reform the family welfare system and replace it with a new national program."

The welfare reform debate was very protracted, especially in the Senate. In addition to the Nixon Administration's proposal Louisiana Senator Russell B. Long, chairman of the Finance Committee, was advocating a more conservative welfare reform bill and Senator Abraham Ribicoff of Connecticut was proposing a more liberal version. None of the three parties had the votes to prevail over the other two, nor were any two able to compromise differences. By midsummer 1972, it was clear that welfare reform legislation had effectively been killed.

The prolonged debate on welfare reform had consumed so much time that passage of any bill was threatened. Since H.R. 1 contained many important provisions apart from welfare reform, no one wished the Congress to fail in enacting legislation. This commitment to pass some kind of bill was reinforced by the desire to avoid the experience of 1970, when the House had refused to meet with the Senate in a joint conference committee late in the session because there was so little time to negotiate important differences prior to the November election. This time, both House and Senate were determined to have legislation on the President's desk before election day, November 7, 1972.

At no point in the extensive hearings on H.R. 1 did either the House or the Senate hear testimony on renal disease. It is true, however, that in November 1971 the House Ways and Means Committee, in connection with hearings on national health insurance, heard testimony which urged that end-stage renal disease be included in any such program. Moreover, in December, Representative Mills introduced a bill that would have amended the Social Security Act to provide patient-care financing for chronic renal disease patients, a bill more notable for signaling Mr. Mills's intentions than for the care with which it was drafted. But neither the Ways and Means Committee hearing nor Mills's legislative proposal was part of the legislative history of H.R. 1. Furthermore, there was no activity within the Senate Finance Committee during this time which remotely related end-stage renal disease to H.R. 1.

The end-stage renal disease amendment was not considered until the provisions of the entire H.R. 1 bill were being debated seriatim on the Senate floor. On September 30, as indicated at the beginning of this article, Senator Vance Hartke proposed an amendment on chronic renal disease. His proposal was accepted with little debate by the Senate and with a slight change in one provision by the House and Senate conference committee. After the Senate and House approved the conference committee report, President Nixon signed H.R. 1 on October 30, 1972.

A number of interesting arguments were raised in the Senate floor debate, most of them by Senator Hartke. He argued that the nation spent billions for transportation, outer space, defense, cosmetics, and appliances, "but when it comes to maintaining our health, we revert to the primitive values and attitudes of the distant past." A tragic irony of the 20th century was that people were dying because access to proper medical care was limited by cost. An extension of that irony was that medical research had produced "two proven lifesaving therapies for terminal patients," but that only a small percentage of the potential beneficiaries received them. The fundamental question was this: "How do we explain that the difference between life and death is a matter of dollars? How do we explain that those who are wealthy have a greater chance to enjoy a longer life than those who are not?" The Senator's recommendation was to "begin to set our national priorities straight by undertaking a national effort to bring kidney disease treatment within the reach of all those in need."

The central issue was reiterated by several other Senators. Senator Jackson, Democrat of Washington, thought it was —"a great tragedy, in a nation as affluent as ours, that we have to consciously make a decision all over America as to the people who will live and the people who will die." He recalled the Seattle experience in allocating scarce dialysis machines, and believed that the nation could do better.

Senator Chiles, Democrat of Florida, honorary chairman of the Florida Kidney Foundation, Inc. that year, reiterated the same point:

> ...in this country with so much affluence, to think that there are people who will die this year merely because we do not have enough of these machines and do not have enough dollars, so that we do have to make the choice of who will live and who will die, when we already know we have a good treatment that can succeed and keep these people alive, while we are working out other improvements in transplants, finding cures, and everything else necessary. This should not happen in this country.

The notable point was that the reluctance to sacrifice lives for dollars was articulated not as an absolute value, but as one that bore some relation to national wealth or affluence.

Still, proponents of the amendment were not indifferent to the costs of treatment. Senators Hartke, Jackson, and Magnuson, Democrat of Washington, all suggested that the costs of dialysis would continue to go down with new advances in the technology of the artificial kidney. Hartke also argued for kidney transplantation in glowing terms and looked forward to substantial cost reductions for this surgical procedure. Costs of dialysis, moreover, could be offset in Hartke's view by the prospect that 60 per cent could return to work with retraining while "most of the remaining 40 per cent need no retraining whatsoever." In short, there was reason to be optimistic in unit cost terms.

Aggregate costs to the nation, moreover, were seen as manageable. Preliminary estimates, Hartke indicated, were that first year costs would be about $75 million, and the fourth year cost about $250 million. He also suggested that the $90 to $110 million the amendment would cost annually "is a minor cost to maintain life." He did not reconcile these differing

numbers. "It is possible," he suggested, "that these costs could be covered by the slight actuarial surplus in the hospital insurance trust fund and the slight reduction in costs now estimated for the regular medicare program for the disabled." But if a medicare tax increase "of a small amount is necessary, it would be quite normal," he said.

Senator Wallace Bennett, Republican of Utah, was the only one who spoke in opposition to the amendment. He thought the Senate was about to vote $100 million to $250 million for dialysis and transplantation, but presented no more justification for his figures than did Hartke. He argued that the amendment, like various other amendments added the previous day, overloaded the bill, represented "Christmas in September," and was "an additional straw that will break the back of the social security system." Bennett also argued that the amendment was the "wrong vehicle." Kidney disease was being singled out for special treatment. "A more reasonable way to handle this amendment," the Utah Republican argued, "would have been to delay action until it can become part of a broader health insurance bill."

Senator Russell B. Long, Democrat of Louisiana and floor manager of H.R. 1 in his role as chairman of the Senate Finance Committee, responded to Bennett's last argument:

> The next Congress will tackle health insurance issues, and I am sure during that debate we will deal with health insurance problems in general, and I hope that specifically we will deal with the problem of insuring against catastrophic illness. I am cosponsoring this proposal at this time because these very unfortunate citizens with chronic renal failure cannot wait for Congress to debate these broader issues. They need help—it is critical—and that help must come now as many of them, without assistance, simply will not be alive for another two years.

The medical means to deal with end-stage renal disease were at hand. One should not, under such circumstances, pass up a legislative opportunity to act.

On January 11, 1973, Richard D. Lyons, a *New York Times* reporter, challenged the cost estimates that Hartke had used in the Senate debate. Based on information supplied by HEW officials, Lyons wrote:

> Original cost estimates ranged from $35 million to $75 million in the first fiscal year of operation. The debate record in both houses shows that the highest estimate was $250 million in the fourth year. Yet calculations made by Federal experts after passage set first year costs at $135 million, rising to $1 billion annually a decade from now.

Lyons quoted several prominent Senators and Representatives to the effect that they would not have supported the provision had they known the full magnitude of the anticipated costs.

This story was the basis for a Sunday editorial — "Medicarelessness" — on January 14, 1973, in which the *New York Times* criticized Congress for not knowing what it was doing and for not recognizing the implications of its decision.

> The point is not that victims of renal disease are unworthy of help, but that Government resources have to be allocated to meeting many needs. If a billion dollars has to go to prolonging the lives of thousands of kidney disease victims, that is a billion dollars that cannot go to eradicating slums, improving education or finding a cure for cancer.

The editorial concluded by stating that "society has a right to expect that the legislators will understand what they are doing and know the magnitude of the commitment they are making when they pass special interest legislation, whether for kidney disease sufferers or anybody else."

The implication that Congress was not fully informed in its action, though challenged by the National Kidney Foundation, has achieved some currency. A 1975 report by the Subcommittee on Health and the Subcommittee on Oversight of the House Ways and Means Committee developed the data cited above in Table [2] on incurred costs of the end-stage renal disease program, costs substantially greater than estimated by Senator Hartke. A more recent report by the Subcommittee on Oversight explicitly juxtaposed the estimates for section 2991 only, which were available to the conferees and those then available to the subcommittee for the third and fourth years of the program in the manner demonstrated by Table [3]. The costs of section 2991, it should be remembered, are estimated to be only 60 percent of all Medicare renal costs. The estimated incurred costs for all renal patients for fiscal years 1976 and 1977 were $500 million and $600 million respectively, a far cry from Senator Hartke's original estimates.

Did Congress know what it was doing when it passed section 2991 as part of H.R. 1? It is clear that the Congress was

TABLE 3. ESTIMATED INCURRED COSTS OF SECTION 2991
THIRD AND FOURTH YEARS

Fiscal Year	1972 Data available to conferees (cash disbursement)	1975 Revised latest estimate (incurred cost)
1976	$198,000,000	$300,000,000
1977	$252,000,000	$360,000,000

Source: House Comm. on Ways and Means, 94th Cong., 1st Sess., Reports on Administration by the Social Security Administration of the End-Stage Renal Disease Program Established by Public Law 92-603 (with Additional Views) and on Social Security Medicare Research Studies 2 (Comm. Print 1975).

wrong on the cost estimates of the end-stage renal disease provision. It is also the case that it did not inform itself on the immediate issues through the process of legislative hearings on the proposed amendment. But the lengthy policy debate on patient-care financing was one to which many members of Congress had contributed. And the Congress had received information on the need for financing patient-care costs for kidney disease from the National Kidney Foundation, especially since 1969 when Dr. George E. Schreiner became president of the N.K.F. and hired Mr. Charles Plante to represent its interests on Capitol Hill. Senator Long, moreover, had introduced catastrophic health insurance legislation in 1970 and had been persuaded that end-stage renal disease was a special case requiring catastrophic coverage well before September 1972. The Congress, though perhaps not fully informed, was hardly without knowledge of the central issues.

Are there circumstances under which the outcome might have been different? One can only speculate, but three situations deserve mention. First, if there had been a thorough set of legislative hearings on the inclusion of end-stage renal disease under Medicare coverage, a few votes on the provision itself might have been changed. Whether the vote might have gone in the other direction is impossible to say, but it is not likely that the provision would have been defeated. Thorough hearings, however, would have deprived the *Times* of much of the basis for its criticism. They also would have precluded the development of Congressional grumbling, like that of the House Ways and Means Committee, that a major, threshold crossing, precedent setting decision was made in a casual legislative manner. Second, if better information had been available on unit costs of therapy and aggregate costs to the Medicare program, more Senators and Representatives

would have paused before approving the amendment. It is easier to imagine that good cost information would have had a greater effect than thorough legislative hearings alone might have had, but again the impact on final outcome is speculative. Finally, had the debate taken place in 1974, rather than in 1972, when the country was in the midst of a severe recession, or in 1975, when concern for the short-term and long-term financial viability of the social security system was high, the concerns of Senator Bennett would have produced greater resonance among other legislators. Whether these three conditions, singly or in combination, might have resulted in a different outcome, however, is simply a matter of conjecture.

V. POLICY IMPLICATIONS

How does this analysis of the policy debate on financing treatment for victims of end-stage renal disease bear upon the proposition that society is unwilling to sacrifice identified lives for dollars? Zeckhauser has argued that the 1972 legislation establishing Medicare benefits for end-stage renal disease was an instance of this reluctance. His formulation, quoted at the outset, is worth quoting again:

> When risks of lives are involved, an important valued belief is that society will not give up a life to save dollars, even a great many dollars. Rarely is this belief, widely held albeit mistaken, put to a clear test. When it is, it may be desirable for society to spend an inordinate amount on each of a few lives to preserve a comforting myth. Such a myth-preserving action was taken when the federal government assumed the costs of renal dialysis.

In the policy debate preceding enactment of Section 2991, the argument was frequently made that life-saving therapy should not be denied because of lack of money—and without doubt this argument was a powerful one. Its power, however, should not be overestimated:

only after more than a decade of debate was a treatment payment program finally approved.

Over the entire length of the protracted debate there were always strong voices of opposition to a treatment payment program. These voices were found within the medical-scientific community, the executive branch, and the legislative branch. Their opposition is eloquent testimony to the fact that policy makers are not always prepared to save lives at any cost. This opposition often made its case in "sotto voce" fashion and argued against a treatment payment program in some indirect fashion, *e.g.,* renal dialysis was still an experimental procedure, dialysis treatment should be financed at the community level, dialysis treatment should be financed only as part of a broad health insurance bill. The basic issue of the cost of financing dialysis treatment was, however, always understood and sometimes explicitly stated, as in the *New York Times* editorial comment that "the point is not that victims of renal disease are unworthy of help, but that Government resources have to be allocated to meeting many needs."

The proponents of a treatment payment program were only able to achieve their goal as a result of a complex and gradual process. A sequence of federal government actions — involving financing of research and development, demonstration, and capacity-building within HEW, and patient-care financing of eligible veterans by the V.A. — set the stage for passage of section 2991. The deepening federal role was, in turn, the product of a number of other processes, including the development of an identified group of patients, the cumulative effect of publicity, and the evolution of the federal role in health in general. In short, although society is reluctant to sacrifice lives for dollars, this reluctance did not swiftly and by its strength alone win federal financing for the victims of end-stage renal disease.

What are the implications of the end-stage renal disease experience for federal policy making relative to other catastrophic diseases? In 1973, a panel of the Institute of Medicine expressed apprehension that the kidney disease provision pointed in the direction of disease-by-disease coverage of catastrophic illness. The panel expressed "unanimous agreement that coverage of discrete categories similar in kind to end-stage renal disease would be an inappropriate course to follow in the foreseeable future for providing expensive care to those who are unable to afford it." Though the panel was stating a legitimate concern, there was no disposition to move in the direction they feared at the time of their report and there has been no action in that direction in the four years since the passage of the 1972 social security amendments. Policy attention, instead, has been focused on including medical insurance for other forms of catastrophic disease in either catastrophic health insurance legislation or in an even broader program of national health insurance. The federal role in health would appear to be more controlling of policy determination than the existence of life-saving therapies to which people are denied access because of cost.

On the other hand, were the debate over the form of national health insurance — catastrophic or general — to remain unresolved over an extended time, it is conceivable that pressures could mount in an irresistible manner to do for hemophilia, for instance, what has been done for chronic kidney failure. The kidney experience, however, suggests that the probability of categorical disease-by-disease action being taken would be increased if a number of other factors were present. First, the treatment would have to meet the criterion of being an established therapy, not merely an experimental procedure. Then, the likelihood of patient-care financing would be increased if there had been a prior set of partial government responses to the problem, responses that stopped short of paying treatment costs. Third, the population of identified lives associated with the particular disease would have to grow to a point where the number was politically significant and the plight of such individuals was being continuously dramatized by print and broadcast media. Finally, the probability of government action would be increased if, in addition to the identified patients, there developed an identified set of institutions and group of physicians responsible for providing the particular therapy. If these factors were present, and the larger health insurance debate remained unresolved, disease-by-disease action might be the pathway the country chose to follow.

Finally, an observation about the political process is in order. The policy debate on end-stage renal disease, including the manner of its resolution, suggests that the responsible public officials and professional elites experienced a good deal of difficulty in discussing the question of "who shall live" in a deliberative and public manner. Is the political system capable of openly discussing its policy alternatives and making choices in such circumstances? Or are such choices simply too divisive to be handled well by the polity? If they are too divisive, we may expect vigorous debates on similar cases to be conducted in the inner councils of medical-science and policy making institutions but without extended public discussion. And perhaps we may also expect the resolution of future debates to occur in the almost surreptitious manner witnessed with respect to section 299I. But shielding important policy choices from full and open public discussion robs those decisions of an important measure of legitimacy in the eyes of the public. While financial costs of such decisions may be substantial, the more elusive costs to the polity of choices made without full public participation may be even greater. Perhaps the growing interest in and discussion of the ethical implications of biomedical research, and the meaning and value of life and death, foreshadows a societal capability and willingness to deal with value-of-life questions in a public manner.

Dialysis After Nearly a Decade

Gina Bari Kolata

On the Saturday morning of 30 September 1972 the Senate hurriedly passed an amendment to the Social Security bill, thereby extending Medicare coverage to patients with kidney failure. Thus began the End Stage Renal Disease (ESRD) program, an extraordinary experiment in health care delivery, the wisdom of which has been questioned but

Reprinted by permission from *Science*, Vol. 208 (May 2, 1980), pp. 473–76. Copyright © 1980 by the American Association for the Advancement of Science.

the continuation of which is a near certainty. The program is a study of national health insurance in a microcosm, and a number of physicians and close observers say they question the government's ability to administer even a program this comparatively small and self-contained.

The program now reaches about 50,000 patients and costs the government $1 billion a year in medical bills. Many patients who would have died of kidney failure are now alive, but all are not necessarily well. The "new" dialysis population includes patients with serious chronic illness such as cancer and heart disease and senile patients who are delivered to dialysis centers three times a week from their nursing homes. For some patients, the dialysis machine has become the equivalent of the respirator, sustaining life when hope of regaining health is gone. In light of the enormous costs of the program, some of the benefits are questionable.

The impetus for the ESRD program began in the 1960's, when it first became possible to save the lives of patients whose kidneys had failed. But dialysis was new, experimental, and costly, with limited facilities that could not possibly accommodate the numbers of individuals who could benefit. Although kidney transplants were sometimes done they were often unsuccessful; about 40 percent of the patients died within a year. The more common way to save these patients was to dialyze their blood with artificial kidney machines.

In the early 1960's dialysis was highly publicized as a heroic and dramatic procedure. Blood is circulated from a vein in the patient's arm through an artificial kidney machine, where it is cleansed of toxins before returning through a tube to the patient's arm. The cost of dialysis, however, was near $40,000 a year for each patient. As was pointed out in newspaper and magazine articles at the time, someone had to choose which patients should be offered dialysis and which allowed to die. In Seattle, an anonymous committee of seven community members made these decisions. In Boston, Constantine Hampers recalls, "We [the doctors] used to sit around and decide who would go on dialysis. I felt terrible about making those decisions and tended to blot them out of my mind." Today, Hampers is chairman of the board of National Medical Care, a company that provides dialysis services at outpatient centers.

In 1972, when the amendment to provide federal funds for dialysis or kidney transplants was being debated, the senators were all too aware of the ethical problems that arise when doctors or lay committees have to decide how to allocate scarce medical resources. The only thing standing in the way of more machines was money—not technology. Vance Hartke (D-Ind.), who sponsored the amendment, asked, "How do we explain that the difference between life and death in this country is a matter of dollars?" Senator Lawton Chiles (D-Fla.) said, "in this country, with so much affluence, to think that there are people who will die this year merely because we do not have enough of these machines and do not have enough money."

The decision to start the ESRD program was founded on humanitarian motives. But like other programs in which it was "only a question of money," it has come back to haunt the government with a set of perplexing problems, not the least of which is a tremendous growth in costs.

In 1979, 48,000 dialysis patients were treated at a cost to the government of about $1 billion, up from $250 million in 1972. (A few thousand patients receive kidney transplants each year, but most of them are given kidneys from cadavers, more than half of which are rejected within 1 year. So the ESRD program is essentially a dialysis program.) Although end stage renal disease patients constitute only 0.2 percent of the total Medicare population, they account for 5 percent of the Medicare funds. Yet, when inflation is taken into account, the costs of dialysis per patient, now about $28,000 a year, have decreased since the program began. The number of patients being kept alive after kidney failure, however, has increased more than eightfold since 1972 and is expected to continue rising to about 70,000 patients by 1990. High as it is, the $1 billion figure understates the true costs to the government. As Richard Rettig of the Rand Corporation points out, a substantial number—there are no good data available on just how many—of the patients also collect federal disability payments.

When the government began paying for dialysis, the patient population changed. The average age of patients in 1972 was between 37 and 43, and fewer than 20 percent were over the age of 50. Now the average age is more than 50. According to Christopher Blagg, director of the Northwest Kidney Center in Seattle, it used to be unheard of for elderly and very sick patients to be dialyzed.

John Sadler of the University of Maryland Medical School in Baltimore was one of the physicians who lobbied for the ESRD program. Looking back, he sees that he and his colleagues were naïve. "We had [in 1972] what was in many ways an idealized population. A large fraction of the patients were in a productive period of their lives. They were young and [apart from their kidney failure] had little else wrong with them." Sadler and others agreed that most such kidney patients could be rehabilitated to lead productive lives.

All too often now, rehabilitation has proved to be impossible or has been neglected. "We have patients who have never worked, patients who are retired, and patients for whom a low paying job can't compete with the disability payments available to them," says Sadler. In the days before the ESRD program, when resources were scarce, they were spent on patients who could benefit from them medically in the most complete sense—not only by having blood detoxified but by being made well to resume useful lives. Now, with payment for all, the program is getting a lot of people whose lives can't be rehabilitated by dialysis alone, and that may account for the "failure" to rehabilitate.

Rettig, who has closely followed the politics and economics of the ESRD program, says that whether there is any effort to rehabilitate patients who are capable of working depends largely on the dialysis unit and the physician in charge. For example, one patient from a central Ohio dialysis center spoke at a seminar Rettig conducted and revealed that he was the only one of the approximately 40 patients at the center who was working. "Moreover," Rettig recalls, "this patient said that the other patients found it amazing to think that it was possible to return to work." A patient from a Washington, D.C. center who works full time says that his center's directors discouraged patient rehabilitation when they moved back the starting time for the evening dialysis shift from 7:00 to 5:30 p.m. When he complained that he didn't even finish work until 5:30 and the center is more than 10 miles from his office, he says he was told that he was being unreasonable.

The picture that Sadler, Rettig, and others paint of dialysis patients hardly resembles that envisioned by the Senate when it debated the amendment that established the ESRD program. In 1972 Senator Hartke said, "Sixty percent of those on dialysis can return to work but require retraining and most of the remaining 40 percent need no retraining whatsoever. These are people who can be active and productive, but only if they have the life-saving treatment they need so badly."

According to doctors who treat them, dialysis patients are often deeply unhappy. Edmund Lowrie, director of the Kidney Center in Boston, says that when patients are tested with the Minnesota Multiphasic Personality Inventory, their scores show that many are depressed and have a tendency toward hypochondria. "They feel captured by the medical profession," Lowrie says.

Alan M. Goldstein, a clinical psychologist at the John Jay College of Criminal Justice in New York, says that dialysis patients have a suicide rate seven times higher than the national average. This is comparable to the rate for patients with other chronic diseases, he explains. Some kill themselves outright, but others do so indirectly by missing medical appointments and failing to follow the strict diet required of those on dialysis.

In the early days of dialysis, suicide was essentially nonexistent, according to Belding Scribner of the University of Washington in Seattle. But in 1964, Scribner predicted that as dialysis became less of an extraordinary treatment the number of suicides would increase. "Now dialysis is perceived as a burden rather than a way of saving lives," he points out. Before the ESRD program, patients with kidney failure expected to die and were so glad to be alive when they were given dialysis that suicide was virtually inconceivable. Also, of course, the early patients were carefully selected—they were young and had positive attitudes toward life, Scribner explains.

Now that dialysis is taken for granted, its burdensome aspects are brought into sharp focus. It is impossible for dialysis patients ever to forget that their kidneys have failed, for they must adhere to a rigid diet that is low in sodium, low in potassium, and low in fluids. Some patients, for example, are allowed only a pint of fluid each day. Sandra Madison, head nurse at the Kidney Center, explains that if patients break their diet regularly, they can develop life-threatening potassium or fluid imbalances. She has seen patients gain as much as 20 pounds in the 2 or 3 days between dialysis sessions because they ignored their fluid restrictions. Dialysis then can be extremely uncomfortable, causing severe cramps, weakness, and nausea. "The body does not easily adjust to extremes," Madison says.

Dialysis itself takes a toll on patients, whether or not they break their diets. The patients are not physiologically normal; they are anemic, prone to bone degeneration, and male patients often are impotent. Then there is the inconvenience of dialysis. It takes an average of 4 hours for a dialysis treatment and patients must be dialyzed three times a week. Although some patients are dialyzed at home with the help of a trained family member or friend, most go to dialysis centers such as the proprietary ones run by National Medical Care. But the staffs at the centers sometimes have strained relationships with the patients and the patients say they have inadequate avenues of complaint.

Lowrie explains that the close long-term relationships between patients and staffs at dialysis centers often lead to difficult situations. The patients develop close ties with the doctors, nurses, and technicians, but in some cases these ties are not helpful. Lowrie says, "There are rules of behavior. A professional cannot show aggression. The patient is unbridled and can be unkind, to say the least. It can be hard to maintain a professional distance."

The patients, on the other hand, often tell a different story. Some say they dislike and distrust their doctors but have no choices because they have nowhere else to go for dialysis. Dialysis facilities are centralized and to switch from one center to another often requires commuting a long distance, which can be especially difficult for sick patients. Some patients claim their doctors are insensitive to their complaints and tell them bluntly that if they are unhappy, they can leave. Others say that they are afraid of their doctors since their very lives depend on the doctors' good graces. Doctors such as Lowrie, Sadler, and Blagg say these complaints are familiar and hard to deal with, especially since emotionally upset patients sometimes selectively hear or misinterpret what their doctors say.

Since the ESRD program is federally sponsored, patients feel that Congress is a recourse. Yet they say that when they complain to their senators or representatives or to federal officials, they get only polite responses that, essentially, brush off their concerns. For example, a Washington, D.C. man has an entire file of letters he wrote to various officials about what he thinks is substandard medical care in the center where he is dialyzed. In no case did he get an adequate response, he says.

A government official, who wishes not to be named, agrees that patients have a hard time being heard. "It's not that the patients have not complained to the right person. There *is* no right person to complain to."

A number of physicians believe that the government is remiss in not keeping tabs on quality of care. There is no way to pick out centers with abnormally high mortality rates, for example, since even such minimal data are not available.

Sadler, who has long been politically involved in the design of the ESRD program, says the government "has a total disregard for quality of care." The government has data in its own computers that provide at least a gross estimate of the minimum quality of care, but that information is never retrieved, according to Sadler. He says that the government, in its bills for services, has data on such things as the number of times patients are hospitalized each year, the number of times they receive blood transfusions, and the number of times they are dialyzed outside their usual setting (in a hospital, for example, if they usually are dialyzed in an outpatient center). "We have told the government for the past 8 years how to measure quality of care," Sadler says. He can only conclude that the federal bureaucracy is not set up to deal with this matter.

Blagg, another of the political doctors, agrees with Sadler. "The government talks about quality of care but it hasn't done anything yet to measure it," he says. Blagg thinks that Sadler's suggested measures are reasonable.

In addition to their concerns about patient rehabilitation, patient complaints, and the lack of even the most minimal information on quality of care, physicians and other health care specialists say they are disturbed by the increasing number of terminally ill or incompetent patients who are dialyzed. In other countries, England, in particular, doctors do not refer such patients for dialysis. But in this country, where Congress intended that dialysis be available to all those who need it, it has become legally and morally difficult to refuse patients.

Blagg and Scribner, for example, tell of a woman patient of theirs who, at age 67 and after 12 years of dialysis, began having severe convulsions. She spent more than 3 months in a hospital at a cost of more than $50,000 while in a stupor from repeated seizures and high doses of anticonvulsant medications.

Her family wanted her dialysis to be discontinued but Scribner and Blagg were strongly advised by the state attorney general not to stop the dialysis treatments. The legal argument was that only the woman herself could request that her dialysis be terminated. She, of course, could not make that request because of her mental condition. This quandary was resolved, Blagg says, when the patient died.

Then there is the highly publicized case of Earle Spring, a nursing home patient in Springfield, Massachusetts. Spring is senile, although he has lucid periods, and his family has requested that his dialysis be terminated. But the Massachusetts courts have ruled that the decision on whether to terminate Spring's dialysis must be made on the basis of what he would want if he were capable of communicating. At present, the final decision has not been made and Spring continues to be dialyzed.

Spring and the patient of Scribner and Blagg are extreme cases, although, according to Scribner and others, incompetent patients are growing in number. But there is still another class of patients for whom the value of dialysis has been questioned. These are patients who, in addition to kidney failure, have underlying serious chronic diseases.

Sadler is quite candid in describing what he says to these patients, who, he explains, include patients with disseminated cancer, patients with debilitating heart disease, and others such as blind, depressed diabetics. "I sit down and say, 'Dialysis will correct your uremia but, because you have a progressive disease, the struggle to survive will be difficult and death also will be a struggle.'" Usually, Sadler says, the patients ask him some questions, then conclude that they do not want dialysis.

It is Sadler's opinion and that of others, including Hampers, that the current federal policy of offering dialysis to everyone is unwise and a waste of resources. Hampers suggests that, difficult as it may be, the government could appoint a committee to set up guidelines for deciding whom to treat. Scribner points out, however, that the setting up of such a committee would be impossible. It would have ramifications far beyond that of dialysis and the government would not want to get into the business of deciding whose lives are worth saving and at what cost.

A number of physicians and health care specialists say they are deeply disappointed in the way the government has run the ESRD program. Both physicians and patients tend to become frustrated when faced with bureaucratic entanglements that seem to be routine. Typical of the complaints that are voiced is Blagg's statement that: "There has been and still is no effective leadership for the program at the federal level." Scribner says, "The government has failed completely. No one is in charge." Says Rettig, "The data system is a shambles." And says Lowrie, "The government has been totally unable to manage the program."

Worse yet, say these specialists, there is no indication that the situation will change. Since its inception, the program has been plagued with bureaucratic reorganization, high personnel turnovers, and a lack of efficient organization.

Philip Jos, who was until very recently the director of the Office of ESRD in the Social Security Administration, responds by saying that these criticisms must be put into perspective, that so far over 100,000 individuals have benefited from the program. Moreover, according to Jos, the government has been responsive to the community's views and has not been reluctant to change its policies when necessary. "Notwithstanding the problems of the program, when one fairly views its accomplishments a judgment that it represents a complete failure of program management by the government is unsupportable," he says.

Comment

Did Congress make a moral mistake in funding dialysis? To answer this question, we need to consider the practical alternatives open to Congress: no funding at all, partial funding, full funding of dialysis, or funding of a more comprehensive policy of national health insurance. Distinguish between the choices available to individual senators and those available to the Senate as a whole. How should an individual senator view the alternative proposed by

Senator Bennett, to "delay action [on renal dialysis] until it can become part of a broader health insurance bill"?

Try to find the principles that underlie the arguments made on the Senate floor in favor of funding and then consider objections to them. What principle supports Senator Hartke's judgment that it is unjust to place defense spending above treatment of renal dialysis? On what grounds is health care properly considered a more important good than many others? Which others?

Senators Chiles and Jackson seem to agree that it is unfair "to consciously make a decision...as to the people who will live and the people who will die" among those who suffer from end-stage renal disease. Is it equally unfair to discriminate in favor of those who suffer from renal disease and against other fatal diseases for which life-saving treatments exist? Should the decision to fund dialysis rest, as Hartke implies, on estimates of the future productivity of renal patients or the declining cost of treatment?

Consider how each of these factual claims should, if true, affect a senator's decision: (1) funding renal dialysis would "break the back of the social security system"; (2) a decision not to fund dialysis would have no effect on Congress's future support of other important social programs; (3) fully funding renal dialysis would make it politically impossible to fund other expensive, life-maintaining medical therapies; (4) if dialysis were fully funded, the suicide rate among dialysis patients would be much higher and the quality of life significantly lower than for the average American; and (5) the total cost of dialysis quadrupled over the seven-year period 1972–79, but the cost per patient decreased by half. What relevant information could we reasonably expect senators to have obtained before making their decision?

Should the Senate be faulted for carrying on the debate over dialysis in a *sotto voce* fashion? How might the debate have differed had it been more public?

It is easy to criticize Congress retrospectively for funding dialysis if one does not consider the implications of no federal funding. Note Constantine Hampers' recollection of the time that he "used to sit around and decide who would go on dialysis." By 1979, he thought that the government should appoint a committee to make those same decisions about who should live and who should die. Who should be on such a committee (or committees)? What guidelines should they use in deciding who would receive dialysis? Consider how you would weigh the following standards for treatment: prospect of the treatment's success, research potential, benefit to individual, benefit to society, past contributions to society, compensation for past deprivations, membership in a community. Would an elected committee be preferable to an appointed one?

Recommended Reading

The most consistent statement of libertarian theory is Robert Nozick's *Anarchy, State and Utopia* (New York: Basic Books, 1974), especially pp. 149–231. For the libertarian case against government subsidies for medical care, see Robert Sade, "Medical Care as a Right: A Refutation," *New England Journal of Medicine*, 285 (1971), pp. 1288–92; and Loren E. Lomasky, "Medical Progress and National Health Care," *Philosophy and Public Affairs*, 10 (Winter 1981), pp. 65–88. See also "Letters to the Editor in Response to Sade," *New England Journal of Medicine*, 286 (1972), pp. 488–93.

John Rawls' *A Theory of Justice* (Cambridge, Mass.: Harvard University Press, 1971) is the most systematic statement of egalitarianism. See especially pp. 90–108 and 221–34. For a Rawlsian defense of distributing health care based on need, see Norman Daniels, "Health-Care Needs and Distributive Justice," in Ronald Bayer et al. (eds.) *In Search of Equity: Health Needs and the Health Care System* (New York: Plenum Press, 1983), pp. 1–42. For an assessment of the egalitarian case, see Amy Gutmann, "For and Against Equal Access to Health Care," in *In Search of Equity*, pp. 43–68. Peter Singer provides a sophisticated utilitarian case for a national health service in "Freedoms and Utilities in the Distribution of Health Care," in G. Dworkin et al. (eds.) *Markets and Morals* (Washington, D.C.: Hemisphere Pub., 1977), pp. 149–73.

7 Equal Opportunity

Introduction

Imagine a hundred yard dash in which one of the two runners has his legs shackled together. He has progressed 10 yards, while the unshackled runner has gone 50 yards. How do they rectify the situation? Do they merely remove the shackles and allow the race to proceed? Then they could say that "equal opportunity" now prevailed. But one of the runners would still be forty yards ahead of the other. Would it not be the better part of justice to allow the previously shackled runner to make up the forty-yard gap; or to start the race all over again? — Lyndon B. Johnson

Deciding what is the better part of justice in a footrace is easy. The social problem that President Johnson intended his analogy to address is difficult: What employment policies does justice require in a society with a history of discrimination? The problem is hard in part because the stakes are so high. Jobs are a means to income, power, prestige, and self-respect. Yet the race for employment cannot be started over again, and employers may not be obliged to help those who have been shackled by discrimination make up the distance in the ongoing race.

The most widely accepted principle governing the allocation of jobs in our society is nondiscrimination. The nondiscrimination principle has two parts. The first stipulates that the qualifications for a job be relevant to its social function. The second specifies that all qualified candidates be given equal consideration for the job.

This simple statement of the principle masks the complexity of its application in particular cases. What qualifications are relevant, for example, to the job of teaching mathematics in a public high school? Knowledge of mathematics clearly is relevant, but the job should not necessarily go to the candidate who knows the most mathematics. Just as relevant to the job but much harder to measure is teaching ability. Certain personality traits — ability to get along with other teachers or to win the respect of students — also predict success on the job. But it would be unfair to refuse to hire blacks or women because other teachers cannot get along with them or because some students have less respect for them.

171

We must therefore add a proviso to the principle of relevance: candidates should not be disqualified on grounds of prejudice.

Equal consideration certainly prohibits employers from refusing to look at a candidate just because the person is a woman or black. But it may also require employers actively to seek applications from women and blacks if they are not applying for jobs because of past discrimination. Equal consideration therefore may require different treatment for different categories of people: more active recruitment for blacks and women than for white males and more active recruitment for blacks than for women.

Proponents of preferential hiring — the selection of basically qualified persons of a disadvantaged group over more qualified persons of an advantaged group — reject the nondiscrimination standard. They correctly point out that the standard does not permit employers to choose less qualified candidates for a job because they are underrepresented in the workforce or have been discriminated against in the past. Although they concede that nondiscrimination would be the right procedure in a just society, they argue that only preferential treatment can satisfy the principle of fair equality of opportunity in a society burdened by a history of injustice.

There are two distinct interpretations of how preferential hiring remedies past discrimination. The first is that preferential hiring makes up the distance that women and minorities have lost in the race for employment by giving them the jobs they would have had if they had not been discriminated against. Critics argue that preferential hiring is at best an imperfect means of achieving this goal because the most qualified women and minorities often have suffered the least past discrimination. On the second interpretation, preferential hiring provides compensation or restitution for past injuries. Critics of this view question whether jobs are the most effective or fairest means of compensation. They suggest that the costs of preferential hiring are inequitably distributed and the benefits are rarely directed toward those who have suffered the most.

The cases in this section illustrate two types of problems in the justice of hiring — general policies involving many jobs and political decisions concerning one position. In judging the AT&T settlement, which affected the jobs of thousands of people, we must rely in part upon statistical summaries and generalizations concerning the past employment practices and future goals of the employer. Although we still are concerned with justice to individuals, we must attend to the general categories in which policy speaks. Only one job was at stake in "The Appointment of an Acting Commissioner of Education," and it is therefore possible to look closely at the qualifications of each candidate. But because the position was a high-level, politically sensitive office, it is harder to separate the goals of equal opportunity and affirmative action from other considerations, such as political objectives. Having determined the best qualified candidate for a public office, we must then consider whether these other considerations are more important than the qualifications of the individual.

The AT&T Case and Affirmative Action
Robert K. Fullinwider

I. INTRODUCTION

On January 18, 1973, American Telephone and Telegraph Company (AT&T) entered into an agreement with several agencies of the federal government to implement what was called by the judge who approved it the "largest and most impressive civil rights settlement in the history of this nation."[1] Over a six-year period AT&T spent millions of dollars and undertook extensive overhaul of its personnel policies to carry out the terms of the agreement.

Several pieces of litigation flowed directly from the agreement itself. Moreover, the government used its "victory" over AT&T as the springboard for further successes, gaining affirmative action agreements with Delta Airlines later in 1973 and with the Bank of America and several trucking companies in 1974. Also in the same year it won an agreement with nine steel companies, representing 73 percent of the steel industry, which resulted in a backpay settlement of $31,000,000 and extensive changes in the employment practices of the companies.[2]

The case began in late 1970 when AT&T applied to the Federal Communications Commission (FCC) for an increase in long distance rates. In December of 1970, the Equal Employment Opportunity Commission (EEOC) asked to intervene in the proceedings. The EEOC had been created by Title VII of the Civil Rights Act of 1964 to enforce

Copyright © 1981 by Robert K. Fullinwider. Reprinted by permission.

the Title's prohibition of employment discrimination. At the time EEOC sought to intervene in the FCC hearings it had received more than 2,000 individual charges of illegal discrimination against AT&T.[3] Because the FCC's own rules prohibited discrimination in the industries it regulated, the EEOC decided to take advantage of the pending rate hearing to press a case against AT&T on many grounds, accusing it of violating equal pay and anti-discrimination legislation as well as FCC rules.

In January 1971, the FCC decided to establish a separate set of hearings on the employment practices of AT&T and to allow the intervention of EEOC. The hearings were to determine if AT&T's practices violated equal employment opportunity policies and to "determine... what order, or requirements, if any, should be adopted by the Commission."[4] During sixty days of hearings, involving 150 witnesses and hundreds of exhibits, a voluminous record of AT&T employment practices was created.[5]

EEOC charged that AT&T engaged in widespread sex segregation of jobs. Males were consistently channeled away from "female" jobs and females away from "male" jobs; transfers and promotion policies maintained the segregation; most of the lowest paying jobs were "female" jobs; and women were paid less than men when they did comparable work.

Of AT&T's 800,000 employees in 1970 (encompassing those employed by AT&T and its Bell System companies but excluding Western Electric and Bell Labs), more than half were women. Yet women comprised only 1 percent of career management personnel. Those women who held career management positions were generally limited to staff positions, without supervisory functions. Upper management personnel were drawn from two sources. On one hand, they were recruited into management training courses from colleges and universities. Company policy limited or excluded women from these courses. Secondly, management personnel were also recruited from within the Bell companies, primarily from craft positions. These were "male" occupations.[6]

At the nonmanagement level, operator, clerical, and inside sales jobs were considered "female" jobs; craft and outside sales jobs were considered "male." Men and women applicants were given different tests and channeled into different divisions.

> Since women were not allowed to take the tests, they could not qualify for craft jobs in the Plant Department. When openings arose in the Plant Department, women employees with seniority were not permitted to bid on them.[7]

Of the more than 400,000 women employed by AT&T in 1971, 80 percent of them were in three job categories: operator, clerical, and administrative (secretarial). Each of these were overwhelmingly "female" jobs. Sex-segregation of jobs was in fact more extensive within the Bell Companies than within the nation as a whole.[8]

The jobs that women worked in were lower paying than the jobs men worked in even when they did the same work. The inside craft job of "framemen" was a male job in all the companies except Michigan Bell, where it was called "switchroom helper" and was a female job. When it finally concluded its affirmative action agreement with the government, AT&T had to give $500,000 in pay raises to the switchroom helpers at Michigan Bell to

bring their wages to the level they would have been paid had they been male framemen.[9]

The EEOC also accused AT&T of discriminating against blacks and other minorities. Of the 72,000 blacks employed in 1970, 80 percent were female. Black males were few and held the lowest-paying "male" nonmanagement jobs. There were extremely few blacks in management positions. Hispanics were likewise poorly represented in the workforces of those Bell companies located in areas of the country with high Hispanic populations.[10]

In 1971, as the EEOC and the company prepared for the hearings, they also began informal negotiations, encouraged by the administrative law judge, to find a basis for settling the case without formal proceedings. The negotiations continued on an intermittent basis throughout 1971 and 1972 as the hearings were conducted. During this period the Department of Labor issued Revised Order # 4. This was a set of rules to implement Executive Order 11246, issued by President Johnson in 1965. It required all federal contractors as a condition for retaining or acquiring federal contracts to take "affirmative action" to assure nondiscrimination in employment practices. The Executive Order assigned to the Secretary of Labor the responsibility of designing and enforcing rules to implement the Order. Revised Order # 4 contained rules which required contractors to create affirmative action plans containing goals and timetables for the hiring and upgrading of "underutilized" groups—minorities and women. The Department of Labor assigned to Government Services Administration (GSA) the authority to administer Revised Order # 4 in the telephone industry.

In the winter of 1972, AT&T submitted an affirmative action plan to GSA. Six months later, without consulting EEOC, GSA approved the plan. EEOC protested to the Solicitor of the Department of Labor, who set aside the GSA approval and joined EEOC in its negotiations with AT&T.[11]

EEOC had by this time filed charges against AT&T in three different federal courts. The hearings before the FCC still held open the possibility it would take regulatory action against AT&T. Moreover, the new participation of the Labor Department meant that AT&T's status as a federal contractor could be jeopardized unless it produced a satisfactory affirmative action plan. Faced with dim prospects of resisting successfully on three fronts, AT&T agreed to a consent decree in January, 1973, which was approved by the federal District Court in Philadelphia, one of the jurisdictions in which EEOC had filed charges. Without formally admitting any wrongdoing, AT&T agreed to undertake to increase the representation of women and minorities in job categories in which they were underrepresented and to compensate through back-pay and wage increases those who were putatively victims of its past discriminatory practices. In return, the government agreed to suspend its legal and administrative actions.

II. THE CONSENT DECREE

There were two elements to the agreement embodied in the January, 1973, consent decree. AT&T would first pay $15,000,000 in back-pay to 13,000 women and 2,000 minority men, and would make additional wage adjustments for 36,000 women and minorities.[12] As it worked out, the wage adjustments amounted to $30,000,000 the first year, for a total outlay of $45,000,000. (On March 30, 1974, AT&T and the government signed a second consent decree, which covered management personnel, calling for an additional $30,000,000 in back-pay and wage adjustments for 25,000 persons.)

Second, the company formulated a Model Affirmative Action Plan which altered its recruiting, transfer, and pro-

motion policies, and which set hiring and promotion "targets" or "goals" for fifteen job classifications. The ultimate minority goals for each Bell company were set in accordance with the minority ratio in the local labor force. The ultimate female goals were set at 38 percent for most job classifications in which they were underrepresented.[13] Accomplishment of these ultimate goals would result in proportional representation of minorities and women in all the job classifications in which they were underrepresented —that is, would result in minorities and women being employed in the same proportions to their numbers in the relevant labor force. The objective was "statistical parity."

To move toward the ultimate goals, yearly intermediate "targets" were formulated for each Bell company and each job classification by means of an elaborate formula. Based on estimations of yearly hiring and promotion opportunities in a classification, the current percentage of minorities or women in that classification, and the ultimate goal for that classification, yearly goals could be formulated.[14]

For example, suppose in job X at Central Bell 10 percent of the workers were female. Since the ultimate goal for females in X is approximately 40 percent (this is the level of female participation in the nation's workforce), the company was only at 25 percent of "full utilization" (proportional representation). By a special formula, this percentage was to be multiplied by a factor of 2 and the resulting percentage be the goal for female new hires for the year. If, for example, there were ten openings anticipated for the coming year in X, five of those hired would have to be women.

The hiring and promotion goals, consequently, required hiring and promotions at rates proportionately greater than the availability of women and minorities in the relevant labor pools or promotion pools. This was clearly expressed in the Model Affirmative Action Plan:

> The Equal Employment objective for the Bell System is to achieve, within a reasonable period of time, an employee profile, with respect to race and sex in each major job classification, which is an approximate reflection of proper utilization....
>
> This objective calls for achieving full utilization of minorities and women at all levels of management and nonmanagement and by job classification *at a pace beyond that which would occur normally*...[15]

An important feature of the Model Plan, which facilitated this accelerated hiring and upgrading, was provision for an "affirmative action override." In accord with its union contract, the company's promotion criteria called for "selection of the best qualified employee and for consideration of net credited service...."[16] Where employees were equally qualified, length of service was supposed to be decisive. The "affirmative action override" permitted (and required) both criteria—"best qualifications" and "longest service"—to be defeated whenever adhering to them did not allow the company to meet its goals (targets). In a supplemental order signed in 1976, the obligation of AT&T in regard to its affirmative action goals was expressed thus:

> ...to the extent any Bell System operating company is unable to meet its intermediate targets in [non-management] job classification 5-15 using these criteria [i.e., best qualified, most senior], the Decree requires that...selections be made from any at least basically qualified candidates for promotion and hiring of the group or groups for which the target is not being met....[17]

Thus, the consent decree and the Model Plan quite clearly envisaged the use of racial and sexual preferences. The intermediate targets or goals of the operating companies in the Bell System were

mandatory; and the companies could and must hire or promote less qualified and less senior persons over more qualified and more senior persons if this was what it took to achieve the intermediate targets.

Since the consent decree applied to 800,000 employees for six years, it is not hard to imagine that there were numerous instances in which employees or applicants were preferred over others because of their race or sex. It is difficult to establish exactly how frequently AT&T resorted to racial or sexual preferences. The company changed the way it defined "affirmative action overrides" during the duration of the decree, it avoided careful counting, and it never classified as overrides any preferences given in management jobs (classifications 1-4).[18]

Two observers report 28,850 overrides in 1973-74, although they differ on how many there were in 1975-76. The first claims there were about 12,000, the second that there were approximately 6,600.[19] A third observer reports 70,000 overrides during the four-year period.[20] It would probably be a reasonably conservative conjecture that over the full 1973-79 life of the consent decree, and counting both nonmanagement and management jobs, at least 50,000 times AT&T gave a racial or sexual preference in hiring or promoting someone. AT&T achieved 90 percent of its intermediate goals in 1974, 97 percent in 1975, and 99 percent thereafter.[21]

In January, 1979, the consent decree expired. AT&T retained most features of its program, aiming in the future to continue efforts toward the long-range goal of approximate proportional representation. It did, however, drop the affirmative action override from its repertoire of affirmative action tools.

III. RESULTS

As a consequence of the implementation of the Model Plan, considerable progress was made in increasing the representation of women and minorities in jobs from which they had been largely excluded in the past. For example, between 1973 and 1979 there was a 38 percent increase in the number of women employed in the top three job classifications (officials and managers), while there was only a 5.3 percent increase in the number of men. Women made significant strides in sales positions, increasing in numbers by 53 percent (a growth rate seven times faster than that of white males), and in inside crafts, increasing by 68 percent (white males were decreasing by 10 percent).[22] In the outside crafts, the number of women grew by 5,300 while the number of men declined by 6,700. Only in clerical positions did the number of women grow at a lesser rate than men.[23]

Blacks and Hispanic males also made gains in management and sales positions and inside crafts. In each case their growth rate exceeded the rate of total growth in those jobs.

Although women made important strides in status and mobility at AT&T, the total number of women employed actually declined between 1973 and 1979. At the end of 1972, AT&T employed 415,725 women (52.4 percent of all employees); at the beginning of 1979, it employed 408,671 women (50.8 percent of all employees). This overall decline was not inconsistent with the consent decree. The decree had two aims in regard to women. One was to move women in significant numbers into previously "male" jobs. The other was related: to break down the stereotype of "male" and "female" jobs at AT&T. Both aims were promoted by acting to increase the number of men in the administrative (i.e., secretarial), clerical, and operator jobs. This both worked against the stereotyping and allowed the company to significantly increase the share of women in other job categories without at the same time raising even higher their share of the total workforce.[24]

Two examples illustrate the steps AT&T took to break down the sex-segregation of earlier years. For one thing, the company made clerical positions entry level jobs for men. In 1973, 17 percent of men hired in the Bell companies entered through clerical positions, while 83 percent entered through craft positions. In 1979, 43.7 percent of men hired entered through clerical positions, while only 56.3 percent entered through crafts. Overall, the percentage of men in clerical roles grew from 5.9 percent to 11.1 percent.[25]

Secondly, the company made valiant efforts to increase the number of women in outside crafts. As a result of its efforts, by 1979 4.7 percent of outside craft workers were women, a 550 percent increase from 1973. This achievement was not without its difficulties or costs. The company inaugurated new pole-climbing courses, instituted new safety procedures, modified equipment for use by women, and recruited aggressively. Even so, the company was never faced with a superfluity of female applicants for outside jobs. There were high rates of female failure in the pole-climbing course, and high rates of attrition among those females who worked in the outside jobs. Accident rates for women were two to three times that of men.[26] In its new affirmative action program after the consent decree expired in 1979, AT&T decided to slow its integration of women into outside crafts.

IV. Costs and Benefits

The affirmative action program with its override provision generated unhappiness and lowered morale among white male employees, who viewed themselves as victims of "reverse discrimination and blocked opportunity." One survey indicated most white male employees were antagonistic toward the program.[27] It is easy enough to understand how perceptions of "reverse discrimination" could occur. In 1976, for example, fully two-thirds of all promotions went to women.[28] Instances in which the override resulted in very qualified and senior men being passed over in favor of inexperienced women doubtlessly occurred often enough to provide ample gripe material on the male grapevine. Thousands of grievances were filed within the company and there were two dozen reverse discrimination law suits.[29]

The most important law suits were by the major Bell union, the Communications Workers of America (CWA), which attempted without success to overthrow the affirmative action override.[30] In an unusual case, one AT&T worker, Daniel McAleer, did manage to win $7,500 in damages from the company as a result of his being passed over for promotion in favor of a woman. The court, which upheld his claim of reverse discrimination, explained:

> This is a sex discrimination case. Plaintiff ...was denied promotion by American Telephone & Telegraph Co. (AT&T). He was entitled to promotion under the provisions of a collective bargaining agreement but the job was given to a less qualified, less senior female solely because of her sex.[31]

The disgruntlement of male employees was not the only negative effect of the affirmative action program. One observer reported in *Fortune* that "two different telephone consultants...believe the consent decree had done some damage to AT&T's efficiency."[32] The decree resulted in some promotions of inexperienced and inadequately trained persons. There was some lowering of quality standards and the development of "double standards of discipline and performance."[33] Minorities and women were able to air grievances outside of regular channels, and supervisors were more reluctant to discipline or complain about women and minority workers. The supervisors' authority and power were eroded in other ways too, especially by the centralization of personnel decisions in the personnel offices. Previously, supervisors had considerable say about who got promoted.

The policy of forcing men to enter through clerical positions resulted in increased turnover, as did the efforts to increase the number of women in the outside crafts. There, the high attrition and accident rate of women probably resulted in some general decline in performance. However, overall turnover for all employees at AT&T appeared to have actually declined between 1973-1979.[34]

The affirmative action override, requiring the use of racial and sexual preferences, certainly contained the potential of pitting white against black, male against female. Racial and sexual hostility could have been inflamed. However, despite the widespread disgruntlement of white males with the affirmative action program, there appears to have been little adverse impact on employee relations.[35]

On the other hand, AT&T has reaped benefits from the consent decree. A company that employs 800,000 people has a voracious need for labor; and by virtually doubling its pool from which to fill its crafts, sales, and management jobs, the company has a richer source of talent to draw upon than before. Large numbers of qualified and ambitious minorities and women are now able to compete with white males for jobs, with a resulting increase often in the quality of those who win the competition.

Personnel departments, as a result of the need to monitor and manage the achievement of the affirmative action goals, have taken over much of the role in promoting and upgrading workers. Although a negative effect of this is erosion of the authority of supervisors, a positive effect is the greater objectivity and rationality that has been brought to the promotion process. The affirmative action plan and its goals have forced AT&T to be very much clearer about qualification and training standards for career advancement, and this has benefitted both company and workers.[36]

V. THE ISSUE POSED

That white male employees suffered lowered morale under the AT&T affirmative action program is not by itself morally significant. People can be disgruntled by changes which are perfectly legitimate or even morally mandatory. Whites, for example, might resist being supervised by blacks out of prejudice and hatred; or males might resent being bossed by perfectly qualified females. The disgruntlement of employees is more than just a management problem if it is based on *legitimate* grievances. In the case of the AT&T affirmative action program, there is no question that direct and explicit sexual and racial preferences were given in order to fill hiring and promotion goals. The representational aims of the affirmative action program could not otherwise have been accomplished. As a result, the expectations of achievement and advancement were frustrated for many persons because they turned out to be the wrong color or sex.

Is it reasonable or permissible to advance such representational aims by policies which select by race or sex? Aren't such policies unfair to some individuals? In an attitudinal survey taken in 1978, one AT&T worker offered this lament:

> One thing that really bothers me is moving up in the company. I am white, male, twenty-five. I am not a brain, but average. I have a lot of drive and want to get ahead. I have just been notified there is some kind of freeze which will last 3 or 4 months.

> [Note: frequently, when a goal couldn't be met, all promotions would be frozen until a person of the right sex or race could be found for the next slot.] In that time, if I am passed over, the company will go to the street. *This is not fair. I work for the company but my chances are less than someone on the street.*"[37]

One irony of the AT&T program was that this "unfairness" was not always confined to white males. As we have noted, a central feature of the consent decree was the aim that male participation in "female" jobs would increase just as female participation in "male" jobs increased. Thus, the Model Plan called for male hiring quotas in clerical jobs, with the ultimate goal of having 25 percent males in this category of jobs. (An informal goal called for 10 percent male operators.)[38] Affirmative action override thus was not applied only against white males; it was actually on occasion applied against women as well.

One AT&T employee, Bertha Biel, went to court when she was passed over for advancement so that a man could be selected. The court record tells the story:

> The employee, a female records clerk, on March 29, 1973 applied for a promotion to the position of operations clerk, a higher-paid job, when it became available. In January of 1973, however, the Company had conducted a work force analysis, required by the terms of the Title VII decree, and determined that males were underutilized in clerical positions. Under the decree the position of operations clerk falls into job class 11, a clerical job title which had traditionally been filled by females. The decree required the establishment of male hiring goals for this job class. In October 1973 the Company had one job class 11 opening to be filled for the remainder of the year. It had not met its intermediate goals for that year since no males had sought the opening. Accordingly, it filled its last opening for the year by hiring a male not previously employed by the Company.[39]

The court held against Bertha Biel and for the company. Thus, Bertha Biel could join the 25-year-old male worker's lament: *"This is not fair. I work for the company but my chances are less than someone on the street."*

On one level, it may seem a legal puzzle that a program like AT&T's which used sexual preferences against both men and women, as the occasion dictated, could be held by courts to be an appropriate expression of a law which says that it is an unlawful practice for an employer "to discriminate against any individual with respect to his compensation, term, conditions, or privileges of employment, because of such individual's race, color, sex, or national origin..." (Title VII, Civil Rights Act of 1964, 42 U.S.C. 2000 -2[2]). On another level, we are confronted with the question whether—judicial approval aside—the AT&T program was morally acceptable and an expression of a just social policy. Questions of fairness and justice were central to many of the complaints by AT&T workers and to the litigation by the unions. Likewise, decisions about the moral rightness (or at least moral tolerability) of the affirmative action program were made by management, judges, and government officials involved in its implementation. Moreover, the AT&T consent decree occurred in the midst of an ongoing public debate about the morality of "reverse discrimination."

NOTES

1. *EEOC* v. *AT&T,* 365 F. Supp. 1105 (1973), at 1108.

2. See *United States v. Allegheny-Ludlum Industries,* 11 FEP Cases 167 (1975); Phyllis A. Wallace, "What Did We Learn?" in Phyllis A. Wallace, ed., *Equal Employment Opportunity and the AT&T Case* (Cambridge, Mass.: MIT Press, 1976), p. 278.

3. Phyllis A. Wallace and Jack E. Nelson, "Legal Processes and Strategies of Intervention," in Wallace, ed., *Equal Employment Opportunity,* p. 243.

4. Ibid., p. 246.

5. 365 F. Supp. at 1109.

6. Wallace, *Equal Employment Opportunity,* p. 4; Judith Long Laws, "The Bell Telephone System: A Case Study," in Wallace, ed., *Equal Employment Opportunity,* pp. 160–61.

7. Laws, "Bell System," p. 154.

8. Ibid., p. 157.

9. Wallace and Nelson, "Legal Processes," p. 252; and Wallace, "The Consent Decree," in Wallace, ed., *Equal Employment Opportunity,* pp. 273–74.

10. Wallace, "Equal Employment Opportunity," in Wallace, ed., *Equal Employment Opportunity,* p. 258; Herbert R. Northrup and John A. Larson, *The Impact of the AT&T-EEO Consent Decree* (Philadelphia: The Wharton School, University of Pennsylvania, 1979), pp. 6–7 and tables pp. 41–65.

11. Wallace and Nelson, "Legal Processes," pp. 243–51.

12. Wallace, "Consent Decree," p. 272. The text of the decree is given on pp. 283–96.

13. Carol Loomis, "AT&T in the Throes of 'Equal Employment,'" *Fortune* 99 (Jan. 15, 1979), p. 47. The ultimate female goal for the outside crafts was set at 19 percent.

14. For details, see Northrup and Larson, "Impact," pp. 19–22.

15. FEP 431: 82. Emphasis added.

16. *EEOC* v. *AT&T,* 13 FEP Cases 392 (1976), at 402.

17. 13 FEP Cases at 402.

18. Loomis, "AT&T," p. 54. "All personnel executives interviewed testified that it [giving preference] has been both regular and often has been the only way the targets could be met." Northrup and Larson, "Impact," p. 57.

19. Loomis, "AT&T," p. 54; Northrup and Larson, "Impact," p. 14.

20. Jerry Flint, "In Bell System's Minority Plan, Women Get Better Jobs, But Total Number of Female Workers Drops," *New York Times,* July 5, 1977, C13.

21. Loomis, "AT&T," p. 50; Northrup and Larson, "Impact," p. 12.

22. Northrup and Larson, "Impact," pp. 25, 53, 55, 65.

23. Ibid., pp. 61, 59.

24. Since women compose about 40 percent of the U.S. labor force, they were already overrepresented—in gross numbers—at AT&T. The problem was not the lack of women employees, but the segregating of them.

25. Northrup and Larson, "Impact," pp. 59, 64.

26. Ibid., pp. 60–62; Loomis, "AT&T," p. 50.

27. Northrup and Larson, "Impact," p. 78.

28. Ibid., p. 80; Loomis, "AT&T," p. 54; Flint, "Bell System's Plan," p. C13.

29. 13 FEP Cases at 418; Loomis, "AT&T," p. 54.

30. See *EEOC* v. *AT&T,* 365 F. Supp. 1105 (1973); *EEOC* v. *AT&T* 506 F. 2d 735 (1974); *EEOC* v. *AT&T,* 13 FEP Cases 392 (1976).

31. *McAleer* v. *AT&T,* 416 F. Supp. 435 (1976), at 436.

32. Loomis, "AT&T," p. 57.

33. Northrup and Larson, "Impact," p. 76.

34. Loomis, "AT&T," p. 57; Northrup and Larson, "Impact," p. 68.

35. Northrup and Larson, "Impact," p. 79.

36. Ibid., pp. 68, 232; Loomis, "AT&T," p. 57.

37. Northrup and Larson, "Impact," p. 78. Emphasis added.

38. Loomis, "AT&T," p. 47; Northrup and Larson, "Impact," p. 58.

39. *Telephone Workers Union* v. *N.J. Bell Tel.,* 584 F. 2d 31 (1978), at 32.

Comment

Consider the evidence in 1971 for past discrimination by AT&T. The statistics on the numbers of women and blacks in various job categories are an important part of the evidence, but they prove nothing by themselves. What additional information makes, or would make, the charge of discrimination against AT&T morally compelling?

Consider separately the justifications for the two elements of the consent decree of January 1973: (1) back-pay and wage adjustments and (2) the Model Affirmative Action Plan. Was the government right to require both elements, or would only one have been preferable?

An advocate of nondiscrimination might criticize the consent decree for requiring AT&T to institute preferential hiring rather than to pursue a policy of nondiscrimination in the future. What would a policy of nondiscrimination require of AT&T? Try to specify in as much detail as possible nondiscriminatory qualifications for the various job categories. Consider, for example, whether length of service with the company is a discriminatory standard. Also try to specify what a nondiscriminatory policy of recruitment would be.

What are the best reasons for rejecting a policy of nondiscrimination? Would the fact that such a policy takes a long time to break sexual and racial stereotypes and to achieve a balanced workforce be a good reason? How do we decide how long is too long?

Next consider what is morally questionable about the affirmative action override instituted by AT&T. Which, if any, of the following effects of the override can you justify:

(1) bypassing more qualified men from outside the company;

(2) bypassing more qualified men for promotion from the inside;

(3) discriminating against women for clerical jobs;

(4) decreasing efficiency of service and increasing prices to consumers?

Some critics of preferential hiring argue that it is just to use affirmative action goals (employment targets based on predictions of how many women and minorities will be hired if practices are nondiscriminatory) but unjust to use quotas (places reserved for women and minorities regardless of their relative qualifications). Is the distinction between goals and quotas clear in the AT&T plan? Is the use of either, or both, morally justifiable?

The Appointment of an Acting Commissioner of Education

Eleanor Pelta

On June 15, 1979, Joseph Califano, Secretary of the Department of Health, Education and Welfare, announced the appointment of Marshall Smith as Acting Commissioner of Education, effective July 1. The announcement provoked a political storm. The Congressional Black Caucus charged Smith with racism for his role as researcher and "co-author" of Christopher Jencks' *Inequality: A Reassessment of the Effects of Family and Schooling in America.* Because of Smith's appointment, the Caucus threatened to withdraw their support for the new Cabinet-level Department of Education, which President Carter was eager to establish. Members of Vice President Mondale's staff approached Hale Champion, Under Secretary of HEW, urging him to ask Califano to rescind Smith's appointment. Before the appointment became effective, Smith himself asked Champion to have it withdrawn. Under instructions from the White House, Califano then offered the position to Mary Berry, a black woman serving as Assistant Secretary for Education in HEW. Berry served as the Acting Commissioner from July 1 to July 31, 1979.

Both Califano and Champion believed that Smith had been treated unfairly.

Copyright ©1981 by The Woodrow Wilson School, Princeton University. Reprinted by permission.

They thought that the Administration should have resisted the attacks on Smith's character, and in this case should not have let their policy goals take precedence over the merit principles that supported Smith's appointment. Califano said that he recognized that Presidents often have to subordinate their commitments to individuals to the larger goals of the government. In response to a similar incident in the Kennedy Administration, Robert McNamara had told Califano: "[w]here the President or one of his key objectives is concerned, none of us is important." But Califano adds that the "fact that I had since learned that McNamara was correct about the harsh realities of governing has never made it easier to accept the individual injustice of such situations."[1]

Early in 1979, Commissioner of Education Ernest Boyer told Califano he intended to resign, effective July 1, 1979, in order to become President of the Carnegie Foundation. Within the hierarchy of the Department, the Commissioner served as fourth in command in education. Although officially a lower position than that of the Assistant Secretary of Education, the job may have been operationally the most powerful post in education. Congressional statute vested it with significant authority. The Education Commissioner was the principal spokesman for the Administration, and chief administrator of the budget of the Office of Education. Aside from this financial responsibility, the Commissioner served as the line officer for the development and management of policy for the main federal programs in education.

Although the office of Commissioner has no formally prescribed qualifications, the person who occupies the office, it was generally acknowledged, should have (at least) a thorough knowledge of issues and policies related to education, and a strong capability for administration. Since one of HEW's goals was to increase management effectiveness in the Commissioner's office, specifically in regard to funding of education programs, Califano and his associates sought an Acting Commissioner who would be both a skilled manager and an able policy planner in the area of federal financing of elementary, secondary, and higher education.[2] Decker Anstrom, Associate Director of the White House Personnel Office at the time, added that the Acting Commissioner would also be responsible for the approval of certain state educational programs, would be a major participant in the development of the 1981 proposed budget, and would be involved in awarding of discretionary grants. Finally, he or she would be a central figure in effecting a smooth transition when the Office of Education became a Cabinet-level Department of Education.[3]

When Boyer announced his resignation, the proposal for a Cabinet-level Department of Education was still pending in Congress. Carter and Mondale were both deeply committed to the creation of the Department. Califano and White House personnel aides preferred to fill the interim position of Acting Commissioner with an insider from HEW because the appointment of an outsider might have given Congress the impression that HEW was grooming a Secretary for the new Department. Califano, Champion, and White House aides wanted to avoid this impression by choosing a replacement who could not be perceived as a potential Secretary. They hoped in this way to ensure that the pending legislation would be discussed in Congress on its merits rather than as an issue of political patronage.

By late March of 1979, Califano had narrowed the choice to two candidates: Thomas Minter, Deputy Commissioner in charge of Elementary and Secondary Education, and Marshall Smith, Assistant Commissioner of Education for Policy Studies. Califano considered Minter to be the more experienced administrator. The fact that Minter was black was also a factor in his favor in Califano's view. The White House had, on several occasions, communicated concern over the poor affirmative action record of HEW and had actively encouraged Califano to increase the number of minority appointments within the Department.[4]

Marshall Smith had been a special assistant to Commissioner Ernest Boyer. He had helped to develop the elementary and secondary education legislation for the Department, and was also directly involved in the area of legislation for higher education, which would be the focus of much attention during the rest of the 96th Congress.[5] As an academic policy analyst, Smith had avoided any political ties, and would not be perceived as a potential Secretary of Education.

According to Champion, the general consensus within the Department was that Smith was the ablest candidate for the position. He was, in Champion's words, the "best-balanced guy" in management and policy-making. Richard Beattie, who at the time was moving from the position of Califano's Executive Assistant to that of HEW general counsel, adds that those involved in the appointment were reluctant to appoint Minter for fear of creating a gap in the administration of important programs in elementary and secondary education.

Califano later implied that he felt that both Minter and Smith would perform equally well as Acting Commissioner. He said that he was "leaning toward Minter largely because Carter was so intent on putting more blacks and other minorities in jobs at HEW." The decisive factor favoring Smith, according to Califano, was the preference expressed by two White House personnel aides, Arnie Miller and Harley Frankel, at a meeting in late March with Califano's executive recruiter, Peter Bell.[6]

From the perspective of the White House Personnel Office, however, Califano's account of the decision to appoint Smith is incomplete. The White House thought that Califano should have consulted the President more closely on the appointment of an Acting Commissioner. According to Decker Anstrom (whose area of responsibility as Associate Director of the White House Personnel Office included presidential appointments in Education), the usual procedure for such an appointment included several meetings between the Personnel Office and the Cabinet department, extensive reference checks on candidates, and meetings with interested parties on Capitol Hill, including lobbyists. Anstrom recalls that the Personnel Office considered among its candidates for Acting Commissioner not only Minter and Smith, but many other senior officials, including Berry and Champion. Officials in the Personnel Office investigating the potential candidates wanted above all to choose an Acting Commissioner who did not endanger an important component of the President's domestic policy—his proposal for the new Department of Education.

Anstrom suggests that Califano needlessly abbreviated the appointment procedure. Instead of the typical series of discussions, he conducted only one brief conversation in which only the names of Minter and Smith were mentioned, and then suddenly announced the appointment of Smith. While Anstrom has no doubt that Smith was at the time the consensual choice at HEW, he felt that Califano's brief and incomplete communication with the White House on this appointment had precluded a full discussion of the qualifications of all the candidates.[7]

The White House Personnel Office explains the appointment of Smith within the broader perspective of the relationship between Secretary Califano and the White House. Smith recalls at the time of his appointment that there was "a clear tension within the department, with... the President about to fire Califano."[8] Although neither Califano nor any member of HEW knew of the President's intentions at this early date, the relationship between Califano and Carter in 1979 was, in Decker Anstrom's words, "bad at best."[9] Anstrom attributes a great part of this friction to Califano's tendency to make political appointments without fully consulting the White House. Califano often only talked to the President or his aides, Anstrom says, after he had already made his choice. To those in the White House Personnel Office, Smith's appointment was another "turf" battle with Secretary Califano.[10]

In addition, there was an ongoing struggle between HEW and the White House over the issue of affirmative action appointments. Califano recalls that President Carter continually objected to the appointments of white males to HEW positions. In several notes and conversations, Carter had expressed his displeasure with what he termed "the worst affirmative action record in my administration." Califano believed that Carter's "desire was to appease constituencies as much as to satisfy a fundamental commitment to civil rights."[11]

Anstrom confirms that the White House thought Califano insensitive to the affirmative action goals of the administration. The White House was constantly pressing Califano to appoint more women and minorities to senior positions at HEW. From the President's perspective, the appointment of Smith, and the stand taken by Califano and Champion after the controversy broke, appeared to be a "complete thumbing of [their] nose at the White House, specifically at a time when it endangered the President's [Education] legislation."[12]

Califano announced Smith's appointment just before leaving for China on a Presidential mission. That weekend (June 16-17), Vice President Mondale heard from Parren Mitchell, a Democrat from Maryland and Chairman of the Congressional Black Caucus.[13] Mitchell strongly opposed Smith's appointment because Smith had been involved in the research for a book which, Mitchell alleged, was racist. Smith had been a researcher and statistical consultant for Christopher Jencks' *Inequality: A Reassessment of the Effect of Family and Schooling in America.* Smith is also listed as "co-author." The book tries to demonstrate that the "traditional strategies for equalizing individual earning power" have not been successful.[14] The great gap in income between blacks and whites cannot be attributed to differences in their schooling, "since differences between schools seem to have very little effect on any measurable attribute of those who attend them."[15] The book also claims that desegregation did little to increase the relative performance of black children in school. Research for *Inequality* was a collaborative effort involving a team of seven assistants (of whom Smith was one). But in the Preface to the book, Jencks assumes sole responsibility for the interpretation of the facts:

> This interpretation is not a collective effort.... The present text was written by Christopher Jencks. It embodies his prejudices and obsessions, and these are not shared by all the co-authors.[16]

Both before and after his work on *Inequality,* Smith himself had written several articles supporting desegregation and federal funding for compensatory education.

Smith recalls that Mitchell, with whom he had spoken at the time, saw *Inequality* as a "negative book." Smith thought that Mitchell had probably not read *Inequality,* but had armed himself with a list of quotations taken out of context, gathered by a member of his staff. In Smith's view, the book became a symbol of racism primarily to people who had not carefully analyzed it.[17]

Califano later wrote that Mitchell wanted Mary Berry to be Acting Commissioner, and eventually first Secretary of the Department of Education.[18] Although the position of Acting Commissioner was not necessarily a step toward the post of Secretary of Education, some observers might have perceived it as such, because of the public visibility of the Commissioner. Califano implies that Mitchell used the charge of racism to press for the appointment of a black to that position. A *New York Times* editorial in June claimed: "The Black Caucus members preferred Mary Berry, hoping that she would thus gain the inside track for Secretary of Education if Congress finally agrees to make it a separate Cabinet department."[19] The Caucus did not suggest that Minter was an acceptable alternative to Berry.

Champion, who bore much of the pressure of the controversy while Califano was in China, believes that Jencks' book was the primary factor behind Mitchell's opposition: "The truth of the matter was that Jencks' book came out with conclusions that the black community didn't like."[20] According to Champion, the Black Caucus would have been satisfied with the appointment of a white candidate, as long as it was not Smith. Decker Anstrom suggests that the members of the Black Caucus were concerned about HEW's poor hiring record on affirmative action under Califano's leadership. In Anstrom's opinion, the Caucus' opposition to Smith was motivated by a genuine concern over Jencks' book, but magnified by continuing frustration over the lack of minority appointments at HEW.

The Office of the Vice President was an appropriate place for Congressman Mitchell to lodge his objection. Mondale had a strong relationship with the Black Caucus, as well as a deep commitment to improving American education, a goal to which he had devoted much of his time as a Senator. Califano recounts that the Department of Education bill was Mondale's "crusade": it was "the only campaign pledge that unmistakably bore his name as well as Carter's, the symbol of his profound dedication to education in contrast with Edward Kennedy's commitment to health."[21]

Mitchell threatened to go on the floor of the House and withdraw his support from the Department of Education bill if Smith's nomination was not rescinded.[22] According to a source familiar with these events, White House aides who were "counting votes" were seriously worried about Mitchell's threat because they believed that the Black Caucus could swing a significant number of votes.[23] Califano also observes that other members of the Administration

feared Mitchell's threat, since several black leaders, including Shirley Chisholm, had already expressed serious doubts about creating a Department of Education. Among the reasons for these doubts Califano notes that

> ...they considered it critical to keep the liberal, labor-backed programs in a single department so the lobbying efforts of individual groups would reinforce one another. They also feared, as I did, that putting the civil rights effort under the top education official, rather than independent of that official as it was at HEW, would soften enforcement.[24]

Champion, however, believed that Mitchell's denunciation of the bill would have had little or no effect upon the House vote: "The fear that it would not pass was a misinterpretation on the part of the White House."[25] Yet, some time after the Smith controversy, Mondale requested that Califano phone twenty-five representatives who were undecided or opposed to the bill, in order to convince them to approve it. And in the end, the bill passed the House by only four votes, 210 to 206.[26]

Smith nevertheless believed that Mondale or his aides had not reacted well to Mitchell's charges—he called it a "knee-jerk reaction." The Monday or Tuesday after Mitchell's call to the Vice President's office, Bert Karp and Marty Kaplan, two of Mondale's aides, called Smith and asked him to withdraw. Smith believes that this phone call came at the request of Mondale himself. Indeed, according to Califano, Mondale called Champion at some point during the week of June 16 to request, on behalf of the President, that Smith's nomination be withdrawn.[27]

To Califano and Champion, the Vice President viewed the controversy over Smith's appointment simply as an obstacle to an important goal of the administration. Describing the June 25 meeting between Champion and Mondale, Califano quotes Champion as remarking that Mondale "doesn't care about anything except the Department." Califano also notes that Mondale did not see a threat to academic freedom implicit in the withdrawal of Smith's appointment.[28] Champion recalls that he did not think at the time that the Department of Education bill was as important as did the White House: "It was a question of the failure of a bill versus the damage done to an individual; a standard of what one did in the interest of a piece of legislation."[29]

When the controversy came to the attention of Mondale's staff, the issue was not which candidate was "best-qualified." Stuart Eizenstat, Presidential Adviser on Domestic Policy and Affairs at the time, suggests that there were two major factors in the decision to ask for Smith's withdrawal: the general uneasiness over a "political storm" at an inopportune time; and the concern over the impact of the appointment upon a block of votes potentially key to the passage of the legislation.[30]

According to Eizenstat, the appointment of a black to the position of Acting Commissioner was not a fundamental goal of the Vice President's staff. Nor was Mary Berry, who was eventually appointed Acting Commissioner, a particular favorite of the White House. The suggestion to appoint Berry instead of Smith may have originated with members of the Black Caucus. Spencer Rich, the reporter who covered these events for the *Washington Post*, says that Berry "was being groomed" for the position of first Secretary of Education by the Black Caucus.[31] Califano also suggests that Parren Mitchell had the appointment of Berry in mind when he made the charges of racism against Smith.

But Decker Anstrom challenges the claim that Mondale's office disregarded the candidates' qualifications. He reports that Berry's qualifications had previously been considered during the appointment process. According to Anstrom, Berry was the best-qualified candidate for the job of Acting Commissioner.[32] The Vice President's staff was acquainted with Berry; she had worked with the staff on the proposal for the Department of Education. Marshall Smith also believes that Mondale's staff took qualifications into account, and he suggests that "if the Carter Administration was concerned with symbolically having a black for the job, that would legitimately be a consideration."[33]

In Califano's absence, Champion acted as Califano's agent in discussions with the White House during the controversy. Champion at first resisted the pressure from Mondale's office, refusing to remove Smith until he was able to speak directly with the President.[34] Champion felt that Mitchell's charges were an attack on academic freedom, and that

> [t]his type of anti-intellectual message was dangerous to send, especially through HEW.... The withdrawal of the Smith appointment would have been equivalent to a public acknowledgement that the allegations against him were true, and they weren't. The whole thing seemed like an over-reaction to a heated argument in Congress.[35]

Califano quotes Champion as referring to "McCarthyism" implicit in the controversy, and recounts Champion's reluctance to withdraw Smith's appointment even after a telephone conversation and a personal meeting with Mondale.[36] Califano and Champion both claim that they never actually withdrew Smith's name; the final decision came from Smith himself.[37]

The choice Smith faced was whether to withdraw immediately, or wait to see what turn the controversy would take. At one point, Smith recalls, he asked himself whether he should "stonewall it." But he felt that this could hurt Califano's already fragile relationship with the White House, and decided to withdraw his appointment. Smith felt that Mitchell's concerns, while misperceptions, were "fair game" in a political debate. It was the "knee-jerk" reaction of the Vice President and request for withdrawal by the White House that bothered him, not the fact that his academic opinions had been challenged. He assumed that the White House had enough sense not to disregard totally his career and legitimate academic reputation.[38]

From the perspective of aides in the White House Personnel Office, HEW officials were trying to protect Smith as part of another struggle over "territory" in the appointment process. Anstrom emphasizes the need to see the Smith controversy within the broader pattern of tension between Califano and the White House: the fight about Smith amounted to a "show-down" over who would control appointments. Any injustice done to Smith, the possible damage to his reputation and career, was, according to Anstrom, only a secondary consideration for those in charge at HEW.[39] As Smith himself suggested, he was "a minor casualty of a much larger situation."[40]

It is possible that Califano's position on Smith's appointment was partly influenced by his view of the Department of Education bill. Califano believed that keeping Health, Education and Welfare in a unified Cabinet Department would continue to be essential to the success of many important social programs.[41] He also felt that a separate Department of Education would be too vulnerable to lobbying by special interest groups and to Congressional intervention. Califano had urged President Carter in a memo of November 1977 to reject the idea of a Cabinet-level Department of Education.

Yet the allegation that Califano deliberately used the Smith controversy to try to sabotage the bill is challenged by several people. Richard Beattie, Califano's executive assistant at the time, believes that "with Califano, it was a matter of principles; [his] personal opinion of the [Education] Department was irrelevant. His resistance to the pressure had to do with his feeling that this charge of racism was an outrage."[42] *Post* reporter Rich also doubts the validity of the allegation, pointing to the swiftness with which HEW capitulated to the pressure from the Black Caucus and Mondale's office.[43] Even Stuart Eizenstat believes that Califano and Champion resisted the demands for so long because they genuinely felt that the allegations against Smith were not well-founded, not because they were opposed to the legislation.[44]

Mary Berry was appointed Acting Commissioner on June 26, one day after Smith officially withdrew. News of Smith's withdrawal became public on June 27.

Was Smith offered any compensation for losing the appointment? Califano suggests that Mondale's office offered Smith a major position in the new Department of Education, but Smith declined the offer.[45] Smith says that he received no explicit offer of a post, only hints of one, since the legislation had not yet passed the House.[46] Califano recounts a meeting with Mondale which took place on July 9, two days after Califano returned from China. During this meeting, Califano expressed a concern over how Smith was treated, and suggested that he be designated Acting Commissioner after Berry's thirty-day term ended. (By law, the Assistant Secretary of Education could not occupy the Commissioner's post for more than thirty days.) But no action was ever taken on Califano's suggestion.[47]

What was the role of the President in the withdrawal of the Smith appointment? Carter evidently took little if any part in the initial choice of Smith. What role the President played in the withdrawal of the offer is less clear. Califano notes that in his conversation with Champion, Mondale "pointedly" remarked that he was speaking on behalf of the President in asking for Smith to step down.[48] According to Eizenstat, however, Carter was not directly involved in Smith's withdrawal. Carter had only peripheral knowledge of the controversy, though he agreed with the decision to ask for the withdrawal.[49] Anstrom recalls that Carter was directly involved in the appointment and approval of Berry.[50] Califano confirms that he announced Berry's appointment on instructions from the White House.[51]

What considerations should have influenced Califano, Mondale, and the President in choosing an Acting Commissioner of Education? Some participants in these events argued that the appointment should have been determined solely on the basis of the professional qualifications of the candidates. Richard Beattie expressed such a view:

> The reaction of the Vice President's office was terrible government. The Vice President's office should have stood up and said to the Black Caucus that the appointment of the Commissioner should have nothing to do with the passage of the bill....[52]

A *New York Times* editorial concurred, charging the Vice President's office with "cruel tactics."[53]

But others closely involved with the process insisted that Califano should have given more consideration to the policy objectives of the administration. As one participant put it, there is "no distinction between personal qualifications and political considerations. We're dealing with political realities — everything involves appropriate compromises. Nothing is removed from politics; everything is subject to political review. Ideally, we would hope that there would be a mixture of personal qualifications and political advantage in a political appointment."[54]

The participants in these events not only took different views of this "mixture," but they also interpreted the "political advantage" in different ways. Was withdrawing Smith's appointment an attempt to reassert the President's authority in personnel decisions, an effort to strengthen the political power of Mondale, a move to save the proposal for a Department of Education, or a way to advance affirmative action in the federal government? To some, it was all of these. To others, it was a simple injustice.

A NOTE ON THE CANDIDATES*

Marshall Savidge Smith was born September 16, 1937. He received his B.A. from Harvard College in 1960 and an Ed.D. from Harvard Graduate School in 1970. Prior to 1979, his work experience included Assistant Commissioner for Policy Studies in the U.S. Office of Education (1977–79); Associate Director of the National Institute of Education (1976–77); Project Director for the National Evaluation of Head Start (1971–73); instructor, assistant, and associate professor at the Harvard Graduate School of Education (1966–76); and computer programmer and systems analyst for the Raytheon Company (1959–62). He has also served as a consultant to the Boston School Department and the U.S. Civil Rights Commission, and on the

---

*Prepared with the assistance of Mike Comiskey.

Board of Directors of the Huron Institute, the Community Learning Center (Cambridge, Mass.), and the Institute for Research on Teaching (Michigan State). Smith has coauthored two books: C. S. Jencks et al., *Inequality: A Reassessment of the Effect of Family and Schooling in America* (1972); and P. J. Stone et al., *The General Inquirer: A Computer Approach to Analysis* (1967). He has authored or coauthored more than ten scholarly articles on topics ranging from equality of educational opportunity to experimentation in educational policy and computer programming in the social sciences. Between 1970 and 1973, he wrote a report on Project Head Start commissioned by HEW; one on the design of an impact study of Day Care and one for the U.S. Office of Economic Opportunity on financing elementary education by vouchers.

Smith is now Director of the Wisconsin Center for Education Research and Professor of Educational Policy Studies and Educational Psychology at the University of Wisconsin.

Thomas Kendall Minter was born June 28, 1924. He received his B.S. from New York University in 1949, an M.A. from NYU in 1950, an S.M.M. (Master of Sacred Music) from the Union Theological Seminary in 1950, and an Ed.D. from Harvard in 1971. Prior to 1979, his work experience included Deputy Commissioner for Elementary and Secondary Education in the U.S. Office of Education (1977–79); Superintendent of Wilmington Public Schools (1975–77); Superintendent of District 7 of the School District of Philadelphia (1972–75); Director of the Pennsylvania Advancement School (1970–72); Administrative Assistant to the Superintendent of Schools in Pennsylvania (1968–70); and Administrative Assistant to the Director of

Field Services in Boston (1967–68). Minter taught for eleven years at the junior and senior high school levels (1955–66) and four years as instructor at Maryland State Teachers College (1949–53). He has also served as a consultant to the Human Resources Administration (New York), the National Alliance of Black School Educators, the National Ed.D. Program for Educational Leaders, the Superintendent of Schools in Portland, and Research for Better Schools. He was a member of the Carter-Mondale Transition Planning Group (1976). He was a long-standing member of the Association for Study of Afro-American Life and History, the NAACP, Phi Delta Kappa Honorary Educational Fraternity, and Phi Mu Alpha Honorary Music Education Fraternity. He has authored several unpublished studies of school desegregation and community control of urban schools.

Minter is now Dean of Education at Lehman College in New York City.

Mary Frances Berry was born February 17, 1938. She received her B.A. from Howard University in 1961, an M.A. from Howard in 1962, a Ph.D. from the University of Michigan in 1966, and a J.D. from Michigan in 1970. She was admitted to the Washington, D.C., Bar Association in 1972. Prior to 1979, her work experience included Assistant Secretary for Education in the Department of Health, Education and Welfare (1977–79); Chancellor and Professor of History and Law at the University of Colorado (1976–77); Director and Provost of the Division of Behavioral and Social Science at the University of Maryland (1972–74); and Acting Director of Afro-American studies at Maryland (1970–72). Prior to 1970, she taught on the faculties of Eastern Michigan University and Central Michigan University, and served on the

Board of Directors of the Metropolitan Washington Housing and Planning Association. She has also served as a consultant to the Department of Housing and Urban Development, the Department of Health, Education and Welfare, and the U.S. Civil Rights Commission. She has been on the Board of Directors of the Afro-American Bicentennial and Corporate Chairperson of the Maryland Commission on Afro-American and Indian History and Culture. She is a member of the National Academy of Public Administration, the Organization of American Historians (Executive Board 1974–77), and the Association for the Study of Afro-American Life and History (Executive Board 1973–76).

Berry has authored three books: *Black Resistance/White Law* (1971); *Military Necessity and Civil Rights Policy* (1977); and *Stability, Security and Continuity: Mr. Justice Burton and Decision-making in the Supreme Court, 1945–58* (1978). She also authored or coauthored several scholarly articles on Afro-American history.

Berry is now Professor of History and Law and a senior fellow at the Institute for the Study of Educational Policy at Howard University, and a member of the U.S. Civil Rights Commission.

NOTES

1. Joseph A. Califano, Jr., *Governing America* (New York: Simon and Schuster, 1981), p. 289.

2. Interview with Hale Champion, July 7, 1982.

3. Interview with Decker Anstrom, Aug. 2, 1982.

4. Califano, *Governing America*, p. 229.

5. Ibid., p. 287.

6. Ibid.

7. Interview with Anstrom, Aug. 2, 1982.

8. Interview with Marshall Smith, July 8, 1982.

9. Interview with Anstrom, Aug. 2, 1982.

10. Interview with Anstrom, Aug. 2, 1982.

11. Califano, *Governing America*, pp. 229–30.

12. Interview with Anstrom, Aug. 2, 1982.

13. Interview with Smith, July 8, 1982.

14. Christopher S. Jencks, *Inequality: A Reassessment of the Effect of Family and Schooling in America* (New York: Basic Books, 1972), p. 12.

15. Ibid., p. 8.

16. Ibid., p. v.

17. Interview with Smith, July 8, 1982.

18. Califano, *Governing America*, p. 287.

19. Editorial: "Education Disgraced," *New York Times*, June 28, 1979, p. A18.

20. Interview with Champion, July 7, 1982.

21. Califano, *Governing America,* p. 292.

22. Ibid., p. 287; Interview with Smith, July 8, 1982.

23. Interview with anonymous source, July 12, 1982.

24. Califano, *Governing America,* pp. 287–88.

25. Interview with Champion, July 7, 1982.

26. Califano, *Governing America*, p. 291.

27. Ibid., p. 288.

28. Ibid., pp. 288–89.

29. Interview with Champion, July 7, 1982.

30. Interview with Stuart Eizenstat, July 24, 1982.

31. Interview with Spencer Rich, July 24, 1982.

32. Interview with Anstrom, August 2, 1982.

33. Interview with Smith, July 8, 1982.

34. Califano, *Governing America*, p. 288.

35. Interview with Champion, July 7, 1982.

36. Califano, *Governing America*, pp. 288–89.

37. Interview with Champion, July 7, 1982; Califano, *Governing America*, p. 290.

38. Interview with Smith, July 8, 1982.

39. Interview with Anstrom, Aug. 2, 1982.

40. Interview with Smith, July 8, 1982.

41. Califano, *Governing America,* pp. 278–81.

42. Interview with Richard Beattie, July 26, 1982.

43. Interview with Rich, July 24, 1982.

44. Interview with Eizenstat, July 24, 1982.

45. Califano, *Governing America*, p. 290.

46. Interview with Smith, July 8, 1982.

47. Califano, *Governing America,* p. 291.

48. Ibid., p. 288.

49. Interview with Eizenstat, July 24, 1982.

50. Interview with Anstrom, Aug. 2, 1982.

51. Califano, *Governing America*, p. 290.

52. Interview with Beattie, July 26, 1982.

53. Interview with anonymous source, July 12, 1982.

54. Ibid.

Comment

The goals of equal opportunity and affirmative action are mixed in this case—as in many high-level appointments—with other political considerations that public officials commonly accept as legitimate. If you were in Califano's position, how would you have decided whether to support Thomas Minter or Marshall Smith? Consider, first, the qualifications relevant to the social function of the job. Was Minter's race a qualification? Then try to decide whether Califano should have taken into account other factors that are not, strictly speaking, qualifications. If race is not a qualification, should it make a difference in any case? What consideration, if any, should Califano have given before making his decision to the effect of this appointment on the prospects of the Department of Education bill?

Once Califano announced the decision to appoint Smith, how should he, Champion, and Mondale have responded to the protests by the Black Caucus against the appointment? If, as Champion suggested, "it was a question of the failure of a bill versus the damage done to an individual," should the bill or the individual have been sacrificed? In answering this question, try to establish precisely what damage was done to Smith. What consideration was he owed before and after being informed of the decision to offer him the appointment? To some, the fact that the job was a political appointment rather than a civil service position meant that the normal standards of fair treatment for individuals should be compromised. What compromises, if any, would you justify in this and similar situations?

After examining the decisions that Califano made at each step in this case, you might also consider the processes that he used to make those decisions. Quite apart from whether his decisions were good ones is the question of whether the procedures he used to arrive at those decisions were morally the best ones. Had Califano consulted more extensively with the Personnel Office, would he have been bound to accept their preferred candidate? Would such consultation have made his final decision more justifiable had he continued to disagree with the Vice-President's choice?

Recommended Reading

Michael Walzer's *Spheres of Justice* (New York: Basic Books, 1983), pp. 129–64, is one of the few works that includes a detailed discussion of principles governing the distribution of jobs in a just society. Judith Jarvis Thomson defends preferential hiring when candidates are equally qualified in "Preferential Hiring," in Marshall Cohen et al. (eds.), *Equality and Preferential Treatment* (Princeton, N.J.: Princeton University Press, 1977), pp. 19–39. Robert Simon criticizes Thomson's limited defense in "Preferential Hiring: A Reply to Judith Jarvis Thomson," in *Equality and Preferential Treatment*, pp. 40–48. George Sher considers whether preference may be given to a candidate who is less than the best qualified person for a job in "Justifying Reverse Discrimination in Employment," in *Equality and Preferential Treatment*, pp. 49–60. See also Alan Goldman, "Affirmative Action," in *Equality and Preferential Treatment*, pp. 192–209; and Robert Amdur, "Compensatory Justice: The Question of Costs," *Political Theory*, 7 (May 1979), pp. 229–244. Robert Fullinwider provides a clear summary of the principal arguments on both sides of the controversy in *The Reverse Discrimination Controversy* (Totowa, N.J.: Rowman and Littlefield, 1980).

8 Liberty and Paternalism

Introduction

Paternalism is interference with a person's liberty with the aim of promoting his or her own good. John Stuart Mill rejected paternalism absolutely: "because it will be better for him to do so" or "because it will make him happier" never justifies restricting the liberty of a sane adult. Yet most people value other goods, such as health and happiness, along with liberty. And sometimes they can secure these goods, or their future liberty, only if society restricts their present freedom of choice. When Mill considers specific examples where important interests other than liberty are at stake, he abandons his absolutist prohibition against paternalism. He defends preventing someone from crossing an unsafe bridge and approves outlawing slavery based on voluntary contract.

Recognizing that some people always and all people sometimes are incapable of exercising liberty, many contemporary political theorists accept an even broader range of paternalistic restrictions on adult behavior than Mill did. They would favor, for example, banning the use of harmful drugs and requiring the use of seat belts and motorcycle helmets. Others, condemning the rapidly growing intrusion of government into the lives of citizens, defend Mill's explicit absolutism. The controversy in political theory parallels the challenge of paternalism in contemporary politics: can government protect the welfare of its citizens without denying their claims to freedom?

We might begin to meet this challenge by justifying paternalistic intervention only if it satisfies these criteria: (1) the decisions it restricts are already unfree; (2) the intervention is minimally restrictive in time and effect; (3) the person whose freedom is restricted could accept the goal of the intervention were his or her decisions unimpaired. But to state these criteria is not to solve the problem of paternalism, especially as it arises in public policies that affect many people and have uncertain consequences. When are the decisions of a group of people unfree? How limited must an intervention be (and how limited can it be while still being effective)? In what sense must the affected individuals accept its purposes? Must they all accept it or only a majority?

"Legalizing Laetrile" illustrates each of these problems in deciding whether a paternalistic policy is justifiable. New Jersey legislators and public health officials disagreed about whether cancer patients exercise free choice in deciding to

195

use Laetrile. They differed over what is the least restrictive yet effective means of protecting patients against medical fraud. And they offered competing accounts of what people who use Laetrile really want: an effective cure for cancer, psychic comfort, or both.

Paternalism in public policy raises not only the problem of a hard choice among competing goods, but also a dilemma of process: who has the authority to make paternalistic decisions and by what procedures should they make them? We may agree that the policy is correct, but criticize the way it was made. In this case, our answer to the question of whether citizens should be free to use Laetrile still leaves open a series of questions concerning the process by which the decisions about Laetrile were made. Did the legislators who voted for legalization in the hope and expectation that the Department of Health would delay effective passage of the bill act ethically? Once the Laetrile law was passed, did Department of Health officials act correctly in interpreting the law as they did and in enforcing the guidelines for testing and manufacturing the drug as strictly as the law permitted?

To answer these questions, we must consider the moral duties of legislators and bureaucrats in a democracy. In one theory of democracy, attributed to Joseph Schumpeter, the only moral duty of politicians is to preserve the institutional arrangements that make possible the ongoing competitive struggle for the people's vote. A second democratic theory, associated with Mill, offers a more demanding ideal of representation, which would hold legislators accountable for particular policies. Because legislators wield so much power over so many people, we can insist that they give citizens sufficient information to assess their decisions, especially on salient and controversial issues such as legalizing Laetrile.

Legalizing Laetrile
Marion Smiley

Laetrile (also known as vitamin B-17, or Amygdalin) is a derivative of the apricot pit and has been promoted during the last twenty-five years as a cure, treatment, or prophylaxis for cancer. It has also been promoted as a treatment for red blood cell deficiencies, for sickle-cell anemia, for various parasitic diseases, and for arthritis. In 1963 the FDA banned the use of Laetrile on the grounds that Laetrile is not *effective* in the treatment of either cancer

Copyright © 1980 by the Woodrow Wilson School, Princeton University. Reprinted by permission.

or other health problems. Despite the ban, public support for Laetrile grew. In 1977 the FDA conducted further tests on Laetrile and reaffirmed its ban. Although the Supreme Court in 1979 sanctioned in certain respects the FDA's authority to ban Laetrile, the controversy has not been finally resolved. Moreover, the issues raised in the controversy go beyond the matter of Laetrile and are likely to arise in other instances of government regulation in the future. This case study describes the history of the FDA's involvement in the regulation of Laetrile; summarizes the scientific and ethical arguments that have been offered by the proponents and opponents of the drug; and provides an account of the controversy as it evolved in the state of New Jersey.

LAETRILE AND THE FDA

Dr. Ernest Krebs, Sr., who discovered Laetrile in 1920, at first considered it to be too toxic for use in the treatment of cancer. In 1937, Dr. Krebs' son, Ernest Krebs, Jr., "purified" the drug to meet his father's standards of toxic safety, and shortly thereafter, father and son went into the Laetrile business together.

According to Krebs, Jr., cancer cells contain a large amount of an enzyme that releases cyanide from Laetrile. Once released, this cyanide supposedly kills the cancer cells. Laetrile would not kill the normal cells as well, Krebs claimed, because normal cells do not contain nearly so much of the cyanide-releasing enzyme as do cancer cells.

Although the FDA never shared Krebs' view of apricot pits, the agency took no legal measure against the proponents of Laetrile until 1962. The FDA in that year charged Krebs, Jr., with violating the new drug provisions of the Federal Food, Drug and Cosmetic Act; the law provided for the first time that all drugs approved by the FDA must be effective, as well as safe. After many unsuccessful attempts to obtain FDA approval of Laetrile as a drug, Mr. Krebs, Jr., claimed that Laetrile was not really a *drug* but instead was a vitamin. He argued that Laetrile was vitamin B-17, the very vitamin needed to prevent and treat cancer (cancer itself now being conceived of as a disease of vitamin deficiency). The advantage of promoting Laetrile as a vitamin was that in this form it would be exempt from the FDA's drug laws.

In early 1974, the FDA took legal action against two vitamin B-17 products, Aprikern and Bee-Seventeen; the FDA maintained that even if Laetrile were a vitamin, it would also still be a drug and therefore susceptible to FDA drug regulation. In 1975 a federal court judge in California held that vitamin B-17 was not even a vitamin, and he placed the manufacturers of Aprikern and Bee-Seventeen under permanent injunction. In 1976 a federal court judge in New Jersey went a step further and concluded that the promotion of vitamin B-17 products constituted a "fraud on the public" and was therefore to be prohibited.

In response to these legal actions, the proponents of Laetrile changed their account of the nature of Laetrile, or vitamin B-17. Proponents of Laetrile for the most part no longer advertise vitamin B-17 as an independent cure for cancer. Instead, they offer vitamin B-17 as part of a more general regimen that often includes large doses of vitamin C, enzymes of various sorts, and sometimes even transcendental meditation. Furthermore, the proponents of Laetrile do not currently claim that it can cure cancer. Instead, they argue that it can prevent cancer or control it.

On April 8, 1977, Laetrile proponents were successful in a case involving *Mr. Glen L. Rutherford et al.* v. *The United States of America et al.* in the U.S. District Court for Western Oklahoma. Judge Luther Bohanon ruled that any cancer patient certified by affidavit to be terminally ill should be allowed to use Laetrile. On May 10, 1977, Judge Bohanon issued a subsequent order specifying both the format of the affidavit to be used and the amount of Laetrile that each patient may import.

In opposition to Judge Bohanon's orders, the FDA on August 5, 1977, ruled once again against the use of Laetrile. Donald Kennedy, Commissioner of the FDA, based his decision to keep Laetrile off the market on both scientific and ethical arguments. First, he argued, qualified experts still do not recognize Laetrile as a safe and effective drug. He further argued that doctors who deal with cancer patients find that the patients turn to legitimate therapy too late, having delayed while trying Laetrile. Furthermore, he observed, another substantial group of cancer victims avoids effective treatment altogether and uses Laetrile instead.

Addressing himself to the "freedom of choice" issue, the Commissioner argued that "the very act of forming a government necessarily involves the yielding of some freedoms in order to obtain others." Applying this principle to the Laetrile issue, he wrote:

> ...in passing the 1962 amendments to the Food and Drug Act—the amendments that require a drug be proved effective before it may be marketed—Congress indicated its conclusions that the absolute freedom to choose an effective drug was properly surrendered in exchange for the freedom from danger to each person's health and wellbeing from the sale and use of worthless drugs.[1]

In response to the FDA ruling, Judge Bohanon in December of 1977 permanently enjoined the FDA from interfering with the use of Laetrile. The FDA appealed to the Supreme Court and, on June 18, 1979, the Supreme Court overturned Judge Bohanon's decision. The Court argued that Congress had included the safety and effectiveness clauses in the federal Food, Drug, and Cosmetic Act in order to protect all citizens—including the terminally ill. The concept of safety, it maintained, is not without meaning for terminal patients: "a drug is unsafe for the terminally ill, as for anyone else, if its potential for inflicting death or physical injury is not offset by the possibility of therapeutic benefit." Furthermore, "the effectiveness of a drug does not necessarily denote capacity to cure; in the treatment of any illness, terminal or otherwise, a drug is effective if it fulfills, by objective indices, its sponsors' claim of prolonged

life, improved physical conditions, or reduced pain."[2]

LAETRILE AND THE
SCIENTIFIC ARGUMENTS

Several major studies have tested Laetrile's effectiveness, and virtually all of them have concluded that Laetrile is useless in the treatment of cancer. In 1953, the Cancer Commission of the California Medical Association found Laetrile to be completely ineffective as a cancer cure. Ten years later, when the California Department of Health reported to the public that Laetrile was ineffective in the treatment of cancer, California banned the drug. That same year, the *Canadian Medical Association Journal* reported that two formulations of Laetrile—one an American product, the other produced in Canada—were completely ineffective in the cure of cancer. The Canadian study itself inspired further testing of Laetrile. Between 1957 and 1975, the National Cancer Institute tested Laetrile on five different occasions and concluded on each occasion that Laetrile was useless in the treatment of cancer. Likewise, between 1972 and 1976, the Sloan-Kettering Institute in New York City reached similar conclusions in thirty-seven separate tests of Laetrile.

Whereas these earlier studies generally showed only that Laetrile is ineffective, more recent work has suggested that the drug may be unsafe as well. Recent animal experiments have shown Laetrile to be potentially toxic because of its cyanide content. Furthermore, at least thirty-seven cases of poisoning and seventeen deaths have resulted from the use of Laetrile by humans. Dr. Joseph F. Ross, Professor of Medicine at the UCLA School of Medicine, testified at the July 12, 1977, Senate Hearing on Laetrile that when released in the gastrointestinal tract, the cyanide content of Laetrile interferes with the body's ability to use oxygen, and hence can produce cyanosis, dizziness, stupor, coma, nausea, vomiting, shock, or death. Dr. Robert C. Eyerly, Chairman of the Committee on Unproven Methods of Cancer Management, maintains that the presence of Laetrile in American society poses a danger for children. According to Dr. Eyerly, the ingestion of five capsules of Aprikern or two packets of Bee-Seventeen can be fatal to a child.

Scientific evidence in *support* of Laetrile's safety and effectiveness has been rare. Two scientific papers are sometimes cited in support of the drug. The first paper, however, has been criticized by a committee of university biochemists, who found in the paper twenty-five statements based on erroneous facts or false assumptions. The second paper has had a better reception in scientific circles. But its author, Dr. Harold Manner of Chicago's Loyola University, cautioned the Senate Committee against accepting his conclusions until the results upon which he based those conclusions could be replicated.

Laetrile and the Argument from Free Choice

Many proponents of the drug in recent years have chosen to defend the use of Laetrile on ethical or political grounds. They argue that to restrict the use of Laetrile is to violate the individual's right to free choice in medical treatment. The group that has become the most powerful supporter of this position is itself called the Committee for Freedom of Choice in Cancer Therapy. In 1978, it claimed to have 450 chapters and 23,000 members. Other groups which have come to the support of Laetrile include the International Association of Cancer Victims and Friends, the Cancer Control Society, and the National Health Federation — all alleged to be right-wing organizations, some with the backing of the John Birch Society.

While the position of these groups is essentially that individuals should have the right to choose their own medical treatment, the groups differ on how extensive such a right to choose should be. Some believe that individuals should be able to obtain any drug that they themselves wish to use — regardless of whether that drug may have been deemed unsafe or ineffective. Other more moderate proponents of Laetrile agree that the safety clause should be retained in its present form, but argue that instead of banning drugs found to be ineffective, the FDA should require manufacturers to print a "statement of ineffectiveness" on the label of, say, every bottle of Laetrile tablets sold over the counter or by prescription. Still other Laetrile supporters think that the drug should be dispensed by prescription only. Finally, some supporters maintain merely that Laetrile should be prescribed only to patients who have been certified "terminally ill."

The supporters of the legalization of Laetrile do not all favor the use of Laetrile itself. Many believe that Laetrile is a fraud but that it should still be legalized. Laetrile should be legalized, they argue, because its prohibition constitutes a violation of individuals' right to free choice. Representative Steven Symms, Republican from Idaho, expresses some of the antipaternalist perspective that underlies this view:

> Freedom is the issue. The American people should be allowed to make their own decisions. They shouldn't have the bureaucrats in Washington, D.C. trying to decide for them about what is good and what is bad, as long as it is safe....
>
> The FDA is typical of what you get in regulatory agencies — a very protective mentality by bureaucrats who want to protect their own jobs and their own positions. It's easier for them to say "No" to a product — Laetrile or anything else — than it is to say "Yes." The FDA is simply not faced with the urgencies of patient care....
>
> Stringent drug regulation for society as a whole limits therapeutic choice by the individual physician, who is better able to judge

risks and benefits for the individual patient.[3]

Similarly, Robert Bradford, president of the Committee for Freedom of Choice in Cancer Therapy, testified:

> The FDA must get off the backs of physicians, cancer patients, and ourselves. What, in the name of humanity, is the agency doing? Whom does it represent? Surely, not the people....
> Rest assured, gentlemen, that the people demand Laetrile, and they are going to have it, whether Big Brother likes it or not.[4]

What do "the people" think about drug regulation and Laetrile? Cambridge Reports, Inc., surveyed consumer attitudes concerning drug regulation. One of the questions asked was:

> Some people say companies should tell us in plain English what the possible dangers are in a product, as they do on cigarette packages, and then leave it to us, as individual consumers, to decide whether or not we want to use the product. Would you agree or disagree?[5]

Eighty-two percent of the respondents agreed, 9 percent answered that they were unsure, and 9 percent disagreed. In a study more directly related to Laetrile, a Harris Poll indicated that Americans oppose the ban on Laetrile by a 53 to 23 percent margin.[6]

The proponents of Laetrile repeatedly invoke the individual's right to free choice in medical treatment, including the right to choose foolishly. As one individual in favor of legalizing Laetrile wrote:

> If the people want to use unapproved or home remedies it is their right to do so. If they want to delay conventional and possibly life-saving treatment then it is their right to do so, foolish and tragic as it might be.[7]

The FDA and most of the medical profession disagree with this position. They argue that the legalization of Laetrile will actually *decrease* the opportunities for free choice. In the first place, they maintain that the choice of a product (medical or otherwise) is not a *free* choice if the product in question is a fraud. In the words of one high-ranking FDA official:

> Laetrile is the most unattractive kind of fraud. It is making some people very rich on the basis of promises that, according to all available evidence, are false, and are known by many of the proponents of Laetrile to be false. The major promoter has a very seamy record and there are hints of ties to right-wing paramilitary groups in the case of the Wisconsin operation.[8]

In the second place, they argue that choices made under extreme emotional stress are not really free. Cancer patients and their families are often forced to make choices when they are under such emotional stress, and these choices, therefore, cannot be considered wholly free. Moreover, they argue that choices made under emotional stress—if unwise—can in effect decrease the possibilities for free choice in the future.

The opponents of Laetrile further insist that, whether toxic or not, Laetrile is unsafe simply because it is ineffective. As Dr. Daniel S. Martin, research associate of the Institute of Cancer Research of Columbia University, has stated:

> [N]o worthless drug is without harm; a patient's choice of Laetrile, to the extent that such a choice delays or interferes with swift diagnosis and prompt effective treatment, is potentially fatal.[9]

Dr. Martin cites a number of cases (documented by the American Cancer Society) in which patients with treatable cancer abandoned conventional therapy for Laetrile. By the time these patients realized that Laetrile was not working, their chances for recovery were either poor or nil. Summarizing and broadening the position of the opponents of the legalization of Laetrile, Arthur A. Checchi writes:

It is in the public interest for legislators to leave basic decisions concerning the safety and efficacy of specific products to experts who are qualified to make such judgments rather than to laymen who are not....

In debating special legislation for products such as Laetrile, we must consider who are the likely purchasers and users of the questionable products: it is the desperate with serious diseases not entirely treatable by recognized procedures; and unfortunately, there is a growing group of people in our society which distrusts the government, big industry and our scientific institutions....

There can be Freedom of Informed Choice only where the persons making the judgment have the basic training and understanding of the issues to make that choice. That person must be qualified. Unfortunately, the average person is not....

The gullible, like children, should be protected from those who exploit them.[10]

LAETRILE IN NEW JERSEY

While the interstate manufacture of drugs comes under the jurisdiction of the FDA, the control of the intrastate manufacture of drugs falls to the regulatory agencies of each state. Hence, when a New Jersey company announced its plans to manufacture Laetrile in the state of New Jersey, the New Jersey Commissioner of Health became responsible for deciding whether these plans could be carried out. The responsibility was an unusual one for the Commissioner since drugs are rarely manufactured on an intrastate basis. Furthermore, since the New Jersey State Department of Health never had to review new drugs before, the state never bothered to revise the New Jersey drug law in accordance with the changes the federal drug law made in 1962. Unlike its federal counterpart, the New Jersey drug law requires that a new drug be examined only for its safety, not for its efficacy.

The situation posed a dilemma for the Commissioner, Dr. Joan E. Finley. On the one hand, she strongly believed that Laetrile should not be allowed on the market (agreeing with the FDA that if a drug were to be allowed to be sold, it should first be proved effective as well as safe). On the other hand, she was forced by New Jersey law to examine Laetrile only for its safety.

Without waiting for the Commissioner's decision on Laetrile, three New Jersey State Assemblymen on May 2, 1977, introduced a bill to legalize Laetrile. The bill, A-3295, introduced by Assemblymen Gregario, Deverin, and Karcher, read:

1. No duly licensed physician shall be subject to any penalty or disciplinary action by any state agency or private professional organization solely for prescribing, administering or dispensing amygdalin, also known as Laetrile or Vitamin B-17, to a patient who has made a written request for such substance.... [The form on which the request is made must include the statement] "Amygdalin has not been approved as a treatment or cure of cancer by the United States Food and Drug Administration.... Neither the American Cancer Society, the American Medical Association, nor the Medical Society of New Jersey recommends use of Amygdalin (Laetrile) in the treatment of any malignancy, disease, illness or physical condition.... There are alternative recognized treatments for the malignancy, disease, illness or physical condition from which I suffer which he [my doctor] has offered to provide...."

2. No duly recognized pharmacist shall be subject to any penalty or disciplinary action...for dispensing amygdalin...labelled with the following statement: "Amygdalin has not been approved as a treatment or cure of any malignancy, disease, illness or physical condition by the United States Food and Drug Administration."

3. No health care facility or employee thereof may restrict or forbid the use of, refuse to administer, or dispense amygdalin, when prescribed by a physician....

4. No person shall be held liable to any civil or criminal penalty solely for the manufacture...interstate commerce in this state of amygdalin....

5. The State Department of Health shall maintain records concerning the use of the substance amygdalin...and shall make periodic studies concerning the efficacy of such substances in the treatment of cancer.[11]

Debate on the bill lasted only two days. Arguing against the bill, the Commissioner insisted that the New Jersey drug law is "archaic" and that it should be changed to include some requirement for effectiveness; this change would prohibit drugs such as Laetrile from making their way onto the market.[12] Also testifying against Laetrile were representatives of the FDA and the Public Health Council of the State of New Jersey.

Most of those testifying, however, supported the legalization of Laetrile. One group testified on behalf of friends and relatives who had cancer and who had allegedly been helped by Laetrile or who now sought the "right to hope" that it supposedly provides. Assemblyman Gregario himself fell into this category; he described at length his father's bout with cancer and his own decision to take Laetrile as a preventative treatment for cancer. Then there were representatives from the Committee for Freedom of Choice and Options, Inc. Both of these representatives stressed the individual's right to freedom of choice in medical treatment and the ever-increasing intrusion of government into the lives of citizens.[13]

Outside the hearing room, several members of the federal and state health agencies argued that only they were capable of deciding whether individuals should be allowed to use Laetrile. Many state legislators and assemblymen maintained, on the contrary, that only individuals by themselves or through their legislators were competent to make such decisions.

Donald Foley, Deputy Commissioner of Health for the State of New Jersey and the department official chiefly responsible for drug regulation in the state, argued that his department should have the authority for decisions concerning the legalization of Laetrile. First of all, he argued, "drugs differ from mere commodities; they are life-saving and life-endangering; and therefore decisions concerning them should be made by those who can best judge them." Second, "the public isn't as informed as they think they are. They're not dumb, but when they read the label they don't understand what they read. They don't know chemistry." Third, individuals with cancer are under emotional stress and therefore cannot always act in a rational manner when choosing their medical treatment. According to Foley, "some of them are in such an emotional state that if you told them that they would be cured if they jumped off the Brooklyn Bridge, they would jump. This is what we want to stop."[14]

Many of the scientists and pharmacists in the Health Department favored giving individuals more free choice than Foley's position permitted. But even they agreed with Foley that the department itself should regulate the use of Laetrile.[15] Thomas Culkin, a department pharmacist concerned with the Laetrile issue, articulated a typical middle position between free choice and government regulation. While he agreed that "individuals must be allowed free choice if they are to be considered adults," he argued that "to talk about freedom without also talking about the regulation of those who might take advantage of that freedom is foolish.... This is one reason why the safety clause of our regulations is so important." He continued, "If Laetrile is proven safe, individuals should be able to use it if they want to." In this instance, the "state's job should be one of educator and not father."[16]

Many state legislators went further than Culkin in their commitment to free choice: "only the individual can know what is really good for himself" and "while the Health Department is certainly necessary up to a point [to ensure safety], beyond that point it starts to get in the way of the individual's ability to function."[17] Legislators also warned of the general tendency of bureaucracies to stifle medical innovation. As one assemblyman commented on the FDA, "It is not their fault, they just have so much to deal with that it takes them twenty years to get to a drug which could have saved thousands of lives by then.... If the drug is safe, why not let people use it and then we'll find out whether it's effective or not."[18]

On January 10, 1978, the bill to legalize Laetrile passed by a wide margin in both houses. Governor Byrne signed the bill one day later, stating that

> I recognize that the drug Laetrile is not a proven cure for cancer. Clearly, it is no more than a source of psychic comfort to cancer patients.... Yet I do not believe that people should be deprived of its use; and I have faith in the medical profession that it will not be abused and that cancer patients will be advised of proven and recognized cancer treatment methods.[19]

Asked why the Laetrile bill passed so easily, health officials and legislators cited in addition to the ideological and emotional factors discussed above, several more purely political factors. First, the bill came up for a vote at the very end of the legislative session, when almost everyone was fatigued and eager to go home. Second, political bargaining had taken place; some legislators voted for the Laetrile bill only to ensure support for their own bills that would be voted on later.

A third reason for the bill's relatively easy passage, also revealed by interviews, is that several legislators knew all along that, regardless of whether or not the bill were enacted, Laetrile almost certainly could not be manufactured in New Jersey for at least seven or eight years. The legislators knew that the New Jersey Department of Health had the intention and the authority to prolong the procedure for testing the safety of Laetrile. For at least a few legislators, the prospect of an eight-year period during which Laetrile would not be allowed on the market was sufficient to overcome any qualms they had about voting for the Laetrile bill.

Laetrile in New Jersey, according to Deputy Commissioner Foley, is "in hold, and will be for at least seven or eight more years to come...until we can prove it is safe enough for the people of New Jersey." Some people contend that the Department of Health is merely stalling. Foley disagrees, but adds that "although we are not stalling (it's simply that testing takes a long time and we have a backload), I think that the seven or eight years it will take to complete the Laetrile tests may be enough time for people to come to their senses.... Hopefully by then they will have taken it upon themselves to vote down Laetrile."[20]

IMPLEMENTING THE LAETRILE LAW

The state Health Department delegated to its Bureau of Drugs the responsibility for implementing and enforcing the Laetrile Act.

The state official who is the Director of the Bureau of Drugs is a nationally recognized scientist and administrator. He has published many professional articles concerning drugs, and has recently been elected president of a multistate health association. Because of his professional stature, any Laetrile actions he takes may be followed by other officials in states that have Laetrile laws.

The Director, on the basis of the available scientific evidence, emphatically believes that "Laetrile is not only worthless in the treatment of cancer, but that it is a health fraud; and worse still, citizens in the state are foregoing conventional cancer treatment in favor of Laetrile with fatal results."

The Laetrile Act did not change any existing drug laws in the state. The old state drug law does have a safety requirement for intrastate "new drugs." However, this part of the law has not been enforced in over twenty years because the FDA safety regulations were applied in the state. These regulations require an extensive animal work-up on the toxicity and toxicology of all new drugs prior to distribution in interstate commerce. The extent of *just* intrastate use of a drug is illustrated by the Director's comment that "he can only remember during the past twenty years, only two requests for state approval of a new drug...and in both cases he convinced the applicant not to apply."

However, two applications have recently been received by the Division of Drugs for approval to manufacture Laetrile in the state. One application is from a chemical company which has found a method to synthesize Laetrile. The other application is from a company in Mexico which is currently manufacturing the drug and wishes to set up a subsidiary plant in the state. Both companies have followed up their initial requests with phone calls and letters.

Prior to any definitive response to the two manufacturers, the state Director of the Bureau of Drugs has, with the *concurrence* of the Health Commissioner, promulgated, *without public hearings,* regulations under the existing "old" state drug laws pertaining to the safety of intrastate new drugs. In essence, the state has adopted by reference the FDA regulations pertaining to safety requirements of new drugs.

In order to satisfy the very strict "safety tests" regulations, a sponsor would have to initiate a complete animal study which could take several years and cost several hundred thousand dollars. "In effect," the Director said, "even if a company were to

do this, the approval and legal use of Laetrile in the state could be delayed from three to eleven years. The FDA experience is that it takes an average of seven to eight years for a 'new drug' to be approved."*

The Director, under the quality control authority of the Laetrile Act, has also, with the concurrence of the Health Commission and without public hearings, adopted by reference the Good Manufacturing Practices (GMPs) regulations of the FDA.

These regulations require that Laetrile manufacturers have *adequately* equipped facilities, *adequately* trained technical and professional personnel, the *necessary* analytical controls and *adequate* record keeping methods. Laetrile not manufactured under conforming methods or in conforming facilities is considered adulterated and will be seized and destroyed by the state.

These GMP regulations rigidly interpreted could also further delay the distribution of Laetrile in the state.

The Director has said that the Health Department interprets the legislative intent as requiring safety testing. He commented, "The legislature is aware of both of these new regulations but, as of yet, is not cognizant of the FDA experience in terms of granting 'new drug' approval (the average of seven to eight years it takes) or the state intention 'literally' to enforce GMPs on Laetrile manufacturers if and whenever necessary."

The Department's actions, the Director has stated, have been taken in effect "so that the state will have time to realize that Laetrile is a most dangerous hoax and health fraud and will repeal the law." In the meantime, he believes that "lives will be saved by conventional cancer treatments rather than lost because of Laetrile."[21]

---

*This time frame also includes satisfying the efficacy requirements for new drugs which may require two to three years of testing.

NOTES

1. HEW Release, Aug. 4, 1977.

2. *U.S.* v. *Rutherford,* 61LEd 2d 68, 99 S Ct (1979).

3. Representative Steven Symms, quoted in *U.S. News and World Report,* June 13, 1977, p. 51.

4. Arthur A. Checchi, "The Return of the Medicine Man: The Laetrile Story and the Dilemma for State Legislators," *Association of Food and Drug Officials Quarterly Bulletin,* April 1978, p. 94.

5. Cambridge Reports, Inc., 1978.

6. Lewis Harris, *The Harris Survey* (New York: Chicago Tribune-New York News Syndicate, 1977).

7. Editorial, *Buffalo Courier Express,* June 15, 1977.

8. Interview with anonymous official.

9. Dr. Daniel S. Martin, *Philadelphia Inquirer,* Feb. 12, 1978.

10. Checchi, "Medicine Man."

11. Assembly Bill No. 3295 introduced May 2, 1977, with Senate Committee amendments adopted on Jan. 10, 1978.

12. New Jersey State Assembly Hearing on A3295, New Jersey State Document 974.90 N222 1977, p. 3.

13. Ibid., pp. 6–40.

14. Interviews with Donald Foley, Dec. 7, 1978, and Jan. 11, 1979.

15. Interviews with New Jersey Department of Health administrators, scientists, and pharmacists, Jan. 8 through Jan. 16, 1979.

16. Interview with Thomas Culkin, Jan. 10, 1979.

17. Interviews with New Jersey state legislators, Jan. 8 through Jan. 16.

18. Ibid.

19. Governor Brendan Byrne, quoted in the *Trenton Times,* Jan. 11, 1977, p. 2.

20. Interview with Donald Foley, Jan. 11, 1979.

21. The preparation of this case benefited greatly from the work of Robert Rich.

Comment

This case is best analyzed, first, by deciding whether the legislators voted for the best policy and, second, by judging the process by which they and Department of Health officials legalized Laetrile but delayed its approval.

The first step in judging the content of the decision to legalize Laetrile is to decide whether the legislature's explicit policy was paternalistic. Avoid the common tendency to describe all cases of justified paternalism as nonpaternalistic. Mill, for example, denies that intervention in the case of the person crossing the unsafe bridge is paternalistic "for liberty consists in doing what one desires, and he does not desire to fall into the river." But if the person wants to cross the bridge and if we thwart his desire in order to save his life, then our intervention is paternalistic. Determining whether a restriction on freedom is paternalistic therefore must be separated from the question of whether the restriction is justified.

Also, be careful not to conflate the problems of paternalism and democracy by labeling any democratic decision paternalistic simply because its effect is to limit the freedom and protect the interests of a minority. A law whose purpose is to satisfy the preferences of a democratic majority may not be paternalistic if, for example, its purpose is to restrict the majority's freedom. Was the ban on Laetrile such an instance?

Was the decision to make Laetrile available only by prescription the best one? Consider the major alternatives available to the legislature: permitting the sale of Laetrile over the counter, with or without mandatory labeling; and banning its production and sale, with or without exceptions for the terminally ill.

What policy should someone support who, like Representative Symms, believes that "freedom is the only issue"? What restrictions on the availability of Laetrile are necessary and sufficient to create free choice?

If you have doubts about the absolute value of freedom, even of informed choice, you will consider paternalistic alternatives to the free market. The policy explicitly endorsed by the legislature does not leave the choice up to the market: doctors stand between buyers and sellers. May we assume, as Symms seems to, that by permitting doctors to prescribe Laetrile, patients are free to choose among therapies by choosing among doctors?

Are claims that cancer patients cannot understand the choice among the therapies and suffer from severe emotional stress sufficient to justify a complete ban on Laetrile? Is it plausible to maintain that those whose freedom is restricted by a ban nevertheless accept the goal of governmental intervention or would accept it if their decision-making faculties were not impaired?

In judging the process by which the Laetrile policy was enacted and implemented, keep in mind the distinction between content (was the right policy adopted?) and method (was it adopted rightly?). The legislators had democratic authority to determine the policy on Laetrile. Are there any grounds for criticizing how they made their decision? Consider whether citizens who supported (or opposed) the legalization of Laetrile had sufficient means for holding their representatives accountable.

Suppose a legislator reasoned as follows: "I will vote for legalizing Laetrile because I am reasonably sure that even if the law is passed, Laetrile will not be marketed for at least seven years. If I vote against legalization, I will probably lose the next election to Joe Smith whom I know to be incompetent and corrupt. Therefore, it is in the public interest, as well as my own, to concede to my opponents on this issue, despite the fact that I firmly believe that their position is wrong." The legislator votes for legalization and it passes by one vote. Evaluate his action.

Bureaucratic discretion in this case, as in many others, is great. Here it allows officials of the Department of Health and Bureau of Drugs to act on their own moral judgments concerning Laetrile. If the Bureau of Drugs can test Laetrile for safety in less than seven or eight years, should it act as quickly as possible, or should it draw the testing period out as long as is legally possible in deference to the intent of those legislators with whom the director morally agrees? To what extent should Foley assume some of the same duties as legislators when he makes (rather than simply implements) policy? If Foley has a duty of accountability like a legislator, what would that duty require of him in this case?

Recommended Reading

The classic source on paternalism is Mill's *On Liberty*, Introductory, chapters 4 and 5. For modern discussions, see Gerald Dworkin, "Paternalism," *Monist* 56 (1972), pp. 64–84, reprinted in R. Wasserstrom (ed.), *Morality and the Law* (Belmont, Calif.: Wadsworth, 1971); John Rawls, *A Theory of Justice* (Cambridge, Mass.: Harvard University Press, 1971), pp. 248–50; and D. F. Thompson, "Paternalism in Medicine, Law and Public Policy," in D. Callahan and S. Bok (eds.), *Ethics Teaching in Higher Education* (New York: Plenum, 1980), pp. 245–73.

On the ethics of democratic representation, Mill is, once again, a good place to start. See his *Considerations on Representative Government* (Indianapolis: Bobbs-Merrill, 1958), chapters 5–8, 12, and 15. Compare Joseph Schumpeter, *Capitalism, Socialism and Democracy* (New York: Harper and Row, 1975), pp. 240–83. Hanna Fenichel Pitkin, *The Concept of Representation* (Berkeley: University of California Press, 1972), chapters 7–10, is a useful commentary.

9 Liberty and Life

Introduction

The idea that all persons have a right to life commands widespread support in this country. But what beings possess this right is one of the most divisive questions of our recent political history. The "pro-life" movement defends the fetus's right to life while "pro-choice" groups defend a woman's right to abortion. They disagree on questions of both personal morality (whether having an abortion is moral) and political morality (whether abortion should be legal).

The structure of the pro-life argument is:

The fetus is a person.

It is wrong to kill a person (except in self-defense).

Abortion is therefore wrong (unless a mother's life is at stake).

It should therefore be illegal.

The typical pro-choice argument has a parallel logic supporting the opposite conclusion:

The fetus is not a person, but is part of a woman's body and significantly affects her life.

A woman has a right to control her own body and life.

Abortion therefore is a woman's right.

It should therefore be legal.

The two sides are divided by fundamentally different perceptions of what a fetus is, perceptions that seem impervious to change by rational argument. Each views the perception of the other as "not simply false, but wildly, madly false—nonsense, totally unintelligible and literally unbelievable" (Roger Wertheimer). While philosophers may not even in principle succeed in resolving this controversy, they can hope to make a more modest contribution. They may be able to show that the premises of each side support less extreme conclusions on the level of both personal and political morality.

Some philosophers have argued that even if the fetus is a person, its death may be justifiable. Self-defense is not the only justification for letting an innocent person die. One is not obligated to save an innocent person at great personal sacrifice if one is not otherwise responsible for the person's situation. On this view, the basic premise of the pro-life position leads to a less absolutist stance against abortion. Other writers have suggested that even if abortion is wrong at the level of personal morality, it may still be right for a liberal state to legalize it when the public is so divided over its morality.

Philosophers also have criticized the internal logic of the extreme pro-choice position. They have argued that the right of a woman to control her body is not absolute: it does not include the right to destroy for trivial reasons what is admittedly a potential life. And the pro-choice position is not, as its proponents often argue, neutral as a political morality. Giving all women a choice between having and not having an abortion is still, for those who believe that the fetus is a person, giving women the right to kill innocent people. To the pro-life advocates this choice is immoral, just as for those who do not believe that the fetus is a person, outlawing abortion is immoral because it restricts a woman's right to control her own body and her freedom more generally.

The political morality of abortion is complex because no policy can be morally neutral, and neither side can rationally convince the other of the moral superiority of its position. Political philosophers have suggested several ways of dealing with situations of this kind. One is to consider a compromise that is fair to both sides, though not fully satisfying the moral claims of either. Another is to find a method of decision-making that is procedurally fair, even if its results favor one side of the moral controversy. Despite the vast literature on abortion, neither of these alternatives has been examined with sufficient care.

The case in this section adds another complication to an already difficult political issue. Given that abortion is now legal in this country under most circumstances, should the government subsidize abortions for poor women? Most people who believe that abortion is a woman's right also argue that the government should subsidize it for poor women. But critics point out that having a right to free speech, for example, does not obligate the state to provide anyone with a subvention for publication. Most pro-life advocates argue that, even if the law permits some women to obtain abortions, there is no reason for the government to subsidize the taking of innocent lives. Yet some who believe that abortion is morally wrong dissent from this view on grounds that the exercise of legal rights should not be effectively withheld from the poor. Califano's account of his position while he was Secretary of the Department of Health, Education and Welfare raises yet another issue in political ethics: what should a public official do when the policy he may be instructed to enforce violates his own moral principles?

Abortion

Joseph A. Califano, Jr.

The abortion issue marked my initiation by public controversy as Secretary of Health, Education, and Welfare.

It was certainly not the issue I would have chosen to confront first. The abortion dispute was sure to make enemies at

From *Governing America* by Joseph Califano, Jr. Copyright © 1981 by Joseph Califano, Jr. Reprinted by permission of Simon & Schuster, Inc.

the beginning of my tenure when I particularly needed friends; guaranteed to divide supporters of social programs when it was especially important to unite them; and likely to spark latent and perhaps lasting suspicions about my ability to separate my private beliefs as a Roman Catholic from my public duties as the nation's chief health, education, and social service official.

The issue whether Medicaid should fund abortions for poor women was more searing than many I faced, but it was quintessentially characteristic of the problems confronting HEW. The abortion dispute summoned taproot convictions and religious beliefs, sincerely held and strenuously put forth by each side, about the rights of poor people, the use of tax dollars, the role of government in the most intimate personal decisions. The pro- and anti-abortion forces each claimed that the Constitution and the American people were on its side, and each truly believed that it was protecting human life. Wherever those forces struggled to prevail—in the courts, the Congress, the executive regulatory process, the state legislatures, and city councils—there were HEW and its Medicaid program. And there was no neutral ground on which HEW or its Secretary could comfortably stand, for any decision—to fund all, or none, or some abortions—would disappoint and enrage millions of Americans who were convinced that theirs was the only humane position.

The controversy exposed me to the world of difference between being a White House staffer—however powerful—and being a Cabinet officer, out front, responsible not only to the President as an advisor but also to the Congress and the American people. It was one thing to be Lyndon Johnson's top domestic policy advisor crafting Great Society programs, but not accountable to the Congress and not ultimately responsible. It was quite another to be the public point man on an issue as controversial as federal financing of abortions for poor people.

Lyndon Johnson had held his White House staff on a particularly short leash. We spoke only in his name—explaining what he thought, how he felt, what his hopes and objectives for America were. "The only reason Hugh Sidey [of *Time*] talks to you is to find out about me, what

I think, what I want. He doesn't give a damn about you," Johnson so often told us, "so you make sure you know what I think before you tell him what you think I think." Indeed, during my lengthy press briefings on new legislative programs, as Johnson read early pages of the instantly typed transcript in his office, he sometimes sent messages to me to correct statements or misimpressions before the briefing ended.

Cabinet officers, of necessity, function with less detailed and immediate presidential guidance. It goes with the territory for a Cabinet officer to put a little distance between himself and the President, particularly on such controversial issues as abortion. Presidents expect, as they should, that their Cabinet officers will shield them from as much controversy as possible so that precious presidential capital can be spent only for overriding national objectives the President selects.

Jimmy Carter first talked to me about abortion when we lunched alone in Manchester, New Hampshire, in early August 1976. He expressed his unyielding opposition to abortion and his determination to stop federal funding of abortions. He asked me to work with Fritz Mondale to make his views known to the Catholic hierarchy and influential lay Catholics. Mondale was using his Minnesota friend Bishop James Rausch, who was then the general secretary of the National Conference of Catholic Bishops, to get Carter's view across, and Charlie Kirbo would be quietly communicating with Terence Cardinal Cooke in New York, but Carter said he wanted a "good Catholic" to spread the word of his strong opposition to abortion. I was impressed by the sincerity and depth of Carter's views on abortion and I found his determination to get credit for those views politically prudent in view of the inevitable opposition his position would incite. It later struck me that Carter never asked my views on the subject, and I never expressed them. Our conversation simply assumed complete agreement.

The assumption was well grounded. I consider abortion morally wrong unless the life of the mother would be at stake if the fetus were carried to term. Under such tragic and wrenching circumstances, no human being could be faulted for making either choice, between the life of the mother and the life of the unborn child. Those are the only circumstances under which I considered federal financing of abortion appropriate.

During the 1976 presidential campaign, I never had to reconcile my beliefs as a Catholic about abortion with any potential duty to obey and execute the law as a public servant. In promulgating Carter's view, like any proponent of a presidential candidate, I took as a given his ability to translate that view into law or public policy. Since my conversations were with those who opposed abortion, no one asked me what Carter would do if the Congress enacted a different position into law.

In talks with Monsignors George Higgins and Francis Lally, and others at the Catholic Conference, I sought to convince them that Carter shared their view. Higgins was an old friend from the Johnson years and he helped get Carter's position better known in the Catholic community. But Higgins confided that nothing short of a firm commitment to a constitutional amendment outlawing abortion would satisfy the conservative elements of the Catholic hierarchy. When I reported this to Mondale, he expressed doubt that Carter would — or should — go that far, particularly since in January 1976 he had said he did "not favor a constitutional amendment abolishing abortion." I agreed.

Eventually, in response to the numerous questions on abortion during the campaign and after a meeting with Catholic bishops in Washington on August 31, 1976, Carter said that he had not yet seen any constitutional amendment he would support, but he "would never try to block . . . an amendment" prohibiting abortions. He added pointedly that any citizen had the right to seek an amendment to overturn the Supreme Court's 1973 *Roe* v. *Wade* decision, which established a woman's constitutional right to have an abortion, at least in the first trimester of pregnancy.

In November 1976, after the election, as Mondale, Tip O'Neill, and other friends reported conversations in which Carter or his close advisors such as Jordan and Kirbo were checking on my qualifications, it became clear that I was a leading candidate for the HEW post. Then, for the first time, I had to focus on the depth of my personal religious belief about abortion: As Secretary of Health, Education, and Welfare, would I be able, in good conscience, to carry out the law of the land, even if that law provided for federal funding of all abortions? I asked myself that question many times before others began asking it of me.

Both my parents are devoutly religious Catholics. Their influence and my education at St. Gregory's elementary school in Brooklyn, at the Jesuit high school Brooklyn Prep, and at the College of the Holy Cross had provided me not only with some intellectual sextants but with a moral compass as well. Like many Catholic students and young lawyers in the 1950s, I had read the works of John Courtney Murray, a leading Jesuit scholar and philosopher. His writings on the rights and duties of American Catholics in a pluralistic society and the need to accommodate private belief and public policy were guides for liberal Catholics of my generation. But even with this background, it was an exacting task in modern America to get clarity and peace in my private conscience while satisfying the legitimate demands of public service and leadership.

The abortion issue never came up in the Johnson administration. But family planning, even the aggressive promotion of the use of contraceptives to prevent pregnancy as a government policy, was an issue I had confronted in those years. President Johnson was an ardent proponent of birth control at home and abroad. He repeatedly rejected the unanimous pleas of his advisors from Secretary of State Dean Rusk to National Security Advisor Walt Rostow to ship wheat to the starving Indians during their 1966 famine. He demanded that the Indian government first agree to mount a massive birth control program. The Indians finally moved and Johnson released the wheat over a sufficiently extended period to make certain the birth control program was off the ground.

Johnson spoke so often and forcefully about birth control that the Catholic bishops denounced him publicly. He sent me to try to cool them off. Working discreetly with Monsignor Frank Hurley, then the chief lobbyist for the Catholic Conference in Washington, we reached an uneasy off-the-record truce: If LBJ would stop using the term "birth control" and refer instead to the "population problem," which allowed increased food production as a possible solution, the bishops would refrain from public attacks on him. Johnson agreed, and spoke thereafter of "the population problem" — but with equal if not greater vigor.

During my years with Lyndon Johnson, and the legislative fights to fund family planning services through the Public Health Service and the War on Poverty, I had to relate my private conscience to public policy on family planning. The alternatives of teen-age pregnancy, abortion, mental retardation,

poverty, and the like were far worse than providing access to contraceptives; to expect all citizens to practice premarital celibacy or all married couples to use the rhythm method was unrealistic in America's increasingly sexually permissive society. I was able to reconcile my private conscience with public policy. I concluded that it made sense for government to fund family planning programs that offered and even encouraged artificial birth control. I had no moral qualms about such a policy in a pluralistic society so long as it respected individual dignity and religious belief. The Catholic bishops disagreed with Johnson. But among theologians there was a great diversity of opinion about the moral propriety of birth control in various personal situations; I inclined to the more liberal position.

Abortion was a far more difficult issue. Here I faced my own conviction that abortion was morally wrong except to save the life of the mother, that medically unnecessary abortions offended fundamental standards of respect for human life. It is one thing temporarily to prevent the creation of a human life; quite another level of moral values is involved in discarding a human life once created. With abortion, I had to face direct conflict between personal religious conviction and public responsibility.

I was to learn how difficult it would be to preserve the precious distinction between public duty and private belief. Setting forth my own and the President's view of appropriate public policy on federal funding of abortion, putting the issue in perspective, relating it to considerations of fairness, and striving to separate my own personal views from my responsibilities as a public official once the Congress decisively acted on the legislation were to be matters of enormous complexity and lonely personal strain. Whatever inner strength I mustered from my own religious faith, the public anguish would not be eased by the fact that I was the only Catholic in the Carter Cabinet.

The anti-abortion, right to life groups and the pro-abortion, freedom of choice organizations had turned the annual HEW appropriations bill into the national battleground over abortion. The issue was whether, and under what circumstances, HEW's Medicaid program to finance health care for poor people should pay for abortions. It would be debated and resolved in the language of the HEW appropriations law, and the regulations implementing the law. This made the Secretary of HEW an especially imposing and exposed figure on the abortion battlefield.

With the Supreme Court's *Roe* v. *Wade* decision in 1973, HEW's Medicaid program promptly began funding abortions for poor women as routinely as any other medical procedure. By 1976, estimates of the number of HEW-funded abortions ranged as high as 300,000 per year. The furies that the *Roe* decision and its impact on HEW's Medicaid program set loose turned abortion into a legal and political controversy that the courts and the Congress would toss at each other for years. The federal financing of an estimated 300,000 abortions set off an emotional stampede in the House of Representatives in 1976, led by Republican Representative Henry Hyde of Illinois, and reluctantly followed by the Senate, to attach a restriction to the 1977 HEW appropriations bill prohibiting the use of HEW funds "to perform abortions except where the life of the mother would be endangered if the fetus were carried to term."

Before the restriction took effect, pro-abortion groups obtained an injunction from Federal District Judge John F. Dooling in Brooklyn, blocking its enforcement until he could decide whether the

Supreme Court decision in *Roe* v. *Wade* established an obligation of the federal government to fund abortions, as a corollary to the right to have them performed.

Whatever the courts ultimately ruled, the abortion issue would continue to be a volatile inhabitant of the political arena. Sincerely held as I believe it was, Carter's stand was also a critical part of his election victory. Betty Ford's strong pro-abortion views and Gerald Ford's ambivalence were thought by Carter to have hurt the Republican candidate.

But Carter's appointment of pro-abortionist Midge Costanza as a senior White House aide and his strong support of the Equal Rights Amendment and other feminist causes gave women's groups some hope that his position would be softened. The pro-lifers were suspicious because Carter's colors blurred on the litmus test of supporting a constitutional amendment outlawing abortion. With pro- and anti-abortion advocates poised to battle for the mind of the administration, I prepared for my confirmation hearings on January 13, 1977.

From my religious and moral convictions, I knew my conscience. From my training at Harvard Law School and my life as a lawyer and public servant, I knew my obligation to enforce the law. But on the eve of becoming a public spokesman for myself and the administration, I sought the reassurance of double-checking my moral and intellectual foundation. I consulted an extraordinary Jesuit priest, James English, my pastor at Holy Trinity Church in Georgetown. He came by my law office on the Saturday morning before the confirmation hearing. He sat on the couch against the wall; I sat across the coffee table from him. I told him I wanted to make one final assessment of my ability to deal with the abortion issue before going forward with the nomination. If I could not enforce whatever law the Congress passes, then I should not become Secretary of Health, Education, and Welfare.

Father English spoke softly about the pluralistic society and the democratic system, in which each of us has an opportunity to express his views. Most statutory law codifies morality, he noted, whether prohibiting stealing or assault, or promoting equal rights, and the arguments of citizens over what the law should be are founded in individual moral values. He said that my obligation to my personal conscience was satisfied if I expressed those views forcefully.

I postulated a law that any abortion could be funded by the federal government, simply upon the request of the woman. He said that so long as I tried to pursue the public policy I believed correct, then I was free — indeed, obliged if I stayed in the job — to enforce that permissive law. I was relieved, comforted by his quiet assurance. As I thanked him for coming by, he mentioned an expert in this field, Father Richard McCormick, a Jesuit at the Kennedy Institute of Bioethics at Georgetown, whose advice I might find helpful.

On the following Monday evening, January 10, representatives of the National Women's Political Caucus sat on the same red couch Father English had occupied. It was the most intense of a series of meetings with various special interest groups.

As the women filed through the door to my office, I shook hands with each one. Their eyes seemed cold and skeptical, and reflected deep concern, even when they smiled. The warm welcome with which I greeted them masked my own foreboding about the imminence of the clash on abortion.

The discussion began on common ground: the failure of the Nixon and Ford administrations to enforce laws prohibiting sex discrimination. One after another, the representatives of each group

in the women's political caucus attacked the enemy: discrimination in the Social Security system (in terms far more forceful than Jimmy Carter's quaint accusation that the benefit structure encouraged senior citizens to "live in sin"), in the federal income tax system, and on the nation's campuses. Most mentioned female appointments at HEW, but since they knew I was searching for qualified women, they did not linger on the personnel issue. Margot Polivy, a tough and talented attorney litigating to eliminate discrimination in women's athletics, pressed her case for HEW enforcement of Title IX, the law prohibiting sex discrimination at educational institutions that receive federal funds.

I shared most of the views the women expressed on these subjects and they knew it. When are they going to stop circling their prey, I thought, and ask about abortion?

Dorothy Ross, a committed feminist who had been helping me recruit for HEW jobs, was seated at my left. She had told me abortion would be the key topic and I wanted to get it over with. Then one of the women put the question: "What's your view on abortion?"

I had decided to make my view unmistakably clear. It was important to state my position on abortion before the Senate confirmation hearings. No senator should be able to claim that his vote was cast for my confirmation without knowing my view on this subject. But in the tension of the moment, it was not easy or pleasant to get the words out.

"I believe abortion is morally wrong," I said softly and firmly. "That is my personal belief."

There was a brief moment of breathtaking at the depth of conviction in my voice. Then the women responded.

"Would you deny federal funds for abortion?" one woman angrily asked.

"I oppose federal funding for abortion." The circling was over. The questions were accusations called out like counts in an indictment.

"The Supreme Court gives a woman a right to an abortion. You would deny that right to poor women?"

"You'd deny a woman her constitutional right?"

"How can you be a liberal and hold such a view?"

"Suppose the woman's life is at stake?"

"What about rape or incest?"

"Suppose the child would be retarded, a vegetable?"

"Are you going to impose your religious views on HEW?"

The questions came with such furious vehemence that I had to interrupt to respond.

"Look," I said, "I have no intention of imposing my personal view on anybody. I am prepared to enforce the law, whatever it is."

"But how could you possibly," one of the women asked, "when you have such strong personal views, such religious commitment?"

"There's nothing wrong with religious commitment," I fired back, "and nothing about it prevents me from enforcing the law."

The women made no attempt to disguise their anger or their suspicion. I wanted to end the meeting before it further deteriorated. The subject was even more volatile than I had anticipated. I was shaken by the obvious depth and genuineness of their emotional and intellectual conviction, and the difficulty of some of the questions they had raised. But there was nothing to be gained by heated exchanges. If there were no other matters on their minds, I suggested we conclude the meeting. They were just as anxious as I to cut off discussion: they, out of a desire to report to their colleagues and plan strategy; I, out of relief.

The parting was superficially amicable, but the battle lines had been drawn. Washington's feminist network buzzed with reports of the meeting throughout that evening and the next day. Late that Tuesday afternoon I was told that the women's groups would attack my nomination on the basis of my stand on abortion.

By Wednesday, the day before my confirmation hearing, the National Abortion Rights Action League had asked to appear, on behalf of fourteen groups which supported federal funds for abortion, before both Senate committees scheduled to hear me testify on my nomination.

As I drove to my office early on Thursday morning, the radio news broadcasts were announcing that Senator Robert Packwood of Oregon, a staunch proponent of Medicaid-funded abortions and member of the Finance Committee which had jurisdiction over my nomination, would question me closely on abortion and might well oppose my nomination unless I changed my reported views.

I needed a much more sophisticated grasp of the political code words on abortion. I knew my own position, but the Senate hearing rooms of Washington were paneled and carpeted with good intentions and clear views ineptly expressed by well-meaning witnesses. I wanted to be sure I could maneuver through the verbal and emotional minefield of pro- and anti-abortionists. It was imperative for those in the abortion controversy, from Cardinal Cooke to National Abortion Rights Action League Executive Director Karen Mulhauser, to understand the words I spoke as I meant them, and I wanted to be confident that I knew what they would hear when I spoke. Far more careers have been shattered in Washington because of what people say than because of what they do—and far more often through words spoken by inadvertence or ignorance than by design.

As I parked my car, I recalled Father English's recommendation of Father Richard McCormick as an ethicist well versed in the abortion controversy. I called him as soon as I got to the office. I told him I had only a few minutes before leaving for the Senate hearing. I quickly reviewed the old ground with him, the obligation to enforce a law contrary to my personal view. Then I moved to some of the harder questions, about pursuing a public policy for our pluralistic country that differed from my personal beliefs.

"What about rape and incest? In terms of public policy, it seems to me that when a woman has been the victim of rape or incest, a case can be made to permit an immediate abortion."

"First of all," McCormick responded, "the woman may be able to solve the problem if she acts fast enough without even getting to an abortion. Even after fertilization but before implantation in the uterus, there are things like twinning and possible recombination of fertilized eggs. These things create doubt about how we ought to evaluate life at this stage. It may take as long as fourteen days for the implantation process to end."

"Do you mean that from an ethical point of view, you don't see any abortion problem for up to two weeks?" I asked.

"I mean there are sufficient doubts at this stage to lead me to believe it may not be wrong to do a dilation and curettage after rape. It's very doubtful that we ought to call this interruption an abortion. Absolutist right to life groups will still complain. But serious studies support this. The pro-abortionists feel very strongly about rape and incest."

"Suppose the doctor says the child will be retarded, or severely handicapped physically?"

"That is a much more difficult question. The Church would not permit an abortion, and the right to life and pro-abortion groups feel deeply here," McCormick replied.

"And what about some severe or permanent damage to the mother's health short of death?"

"That's another tough question in public policy terms. The Church would oppose abortion."

"Well, it's going to be an interesting morning," I mused aloud.

McCormick summed up rapidly. "You should always keep in mind three levels of distinction here. First, there is the personal conscience and belief thing. Second, there is what the appropriate public policy should be in a pluralistic democracy, which could be more liberal on funding abortions than one would personally approve as a matter of conscience or religious conviction. Actual abortion for rape and incest victims might be an example here. And third, there is the obligation of the public official to carry out the law the nation enacts."

"So I could pursue a policy for the country that funded abortion for rape and incest victims even though the Church — and I as a matter of personal and religious conviction — opposed abortion under those circumstances."

"Yes, you could."

I thanked him and rushed out of the office to my confirmation hearing.

I had to walk past a long line of people waiting to get into the standing-room-only Senate Finance Committee room in the Dirksen Building. Inside the door I had to weave through spectators and climb over legs to get to the witness table. The lights of all three networks were on me, sporadically augmented by clicking cameras and flashing bulbs from photographers sitting and kneeling on the floor in front of me. Seated behind their elevated and curved paneled rostrum, the committee members and staff looked down at me.

The hearing began promptly at 10:00 A.M. After fifteen minutes in which I made a brief opening statement and received some generous praise from Chairman Russell Long, Senator Packwood began:

"Mr. Califano, you know I have some strong feelings about abortion.... What is your personal view on abortion?"

The cameras turned on me.

I began by expressing my recognition of the difficulty of the abortion issue and the sincerity and depth of feeling on all sides. I noted that Carter and I shared identical views on the subject, although we came from quite different religious, cultural, and social backgrounds. I then set forth my views:

"First, I personally believe that abortion is wrong.

"Second, I believe that federal funds should not be used for the purpose of providing abortions.

"Third, I believe that it is imperative that the alternatives to abortion be made available as widely as possible. Those alternatives include everything from foster care to day care, family planning programs to sex education, and especially measures to reduce teen-age pregnancies.

"Finally, we live in a democratic society where every citizen is free to make his views known, to the Congress or to the courts. If the courts decide that there is a constitutional right in this country to have an abortion with federal funds, I will enforce that court order. If the Congress changes its mind and amends the statute which it has passed, or passes other laws which direct that funds be provided for abortion, I will enforce those laws. I will enforce those laws as vigorously as I intend to enforce the other laws that I am charged with enforcing if I am confirmed, including laws against discrimination

against women on the basis of sex in Title IX, the Title VI laws."

Packwood pressed: "You are opposed and would be opposed to federal funds for abortions under any circumstances... if the life of the woman is jeopardized, if the fetus is carrying a genetic disease?" I testified I did not oppose federal funding of abortion where carrying the fetus to term endangered the life of the mother. That was not as far as Packwood wanted me to go.

Packwood continued: "What I am really interested in, Mr. Califano, what I would hope is that your feelings as a person would not interfere with the law, the enforcement of the laws." I assured him that my personal views would not interfere with my enforcement of the law.

Packwood asked what my recommendation would be for legislation in the future. The same as Carter's, I responded. "We would recommend that federal funds not be used to provide abortions" in Medicaid or any other program.

Packwood's first-round time was up. The tension in the room eased a little as other senators asked questions on Social Security, balancing the budget, eliminating paperwork, busing, race discrimination, a separate department of education, Medicare and Medicaid management, handicapped rehabilitation programs, fraud and abuse in the welfare program, older Americans, alcoholism, and other matters prompted by special interest constituencies and the concerns of Americans that HEW intruded too deeply in their lives. The ever-present staffers whispered in senators' ears and passed their slips of paper from which senators read questions.

Texas Senator Lloyd Bentsen tried to lighten the atmosphere as he began: "Mr. Chairman, I am very pleased to see Mr. Califano here. I have known him for many years and have had a great respect for his ability, intelligence, integrity, and judgment—until he took this job." The room burst into laughter.

At about noon, it was Packwood's turn again. When our eyes engaged, it was a signal for all the buzzing and rustling in the room to stop. As I expected, he went right to abortion, asking how I would change the law if I had the power to do so. I told him that President Carter and I would support the ban on the use of federal funds for abortions except where the mother's life was at stake. "That is the position...of the Carter administration," I concluded, quoting from one of the President-elect's campaign statements.

Packwood felt so strongly about the issue his face went florid with anger.

I thought for an instant about raising the issue of rape and incest, but immediately decided against it. This abortion controversy would be with me and the President for a long time and I didn't want to go any further than absolutely necessary without careful thought.

With his blue eyes blinking in disbelief, Packwood's voice rose: "If you had a choice...your recommendation would be that no federal funds will be used for those two hundred and fifty or three hundred thousand poor women, medically indigent, mostly minorities, who could not otherwise afford abortions?"

I reiterated: that would be my recommendation and the position of the administration. When I expressed the need to provide alternatives to abortion, Packwood interrupted: "How do you deal with teen-age pregnancies once the teen-ager is pregnant?" I said we needed more sensitive, decent human alternatives, treating the pregnant teen-ager as a person, letting her remain in school or continue her education in a home. I also recognized the need for better sex education and more effective family planning programs.

Packwood expressed support for all such programs. Then, his voice again rising, he said, "What we are saying, as far as the Carter program goes, with all the planned parenthood facilities, all the homes for unwed mothers, all the decent facilities to take care of them, if that woman wants to have an abortion and is poor and cannot afford it, tough luck." The last two words came out in angry disgust.

I could hear the whir of the television cameras.

"Senator, what I am saying is that we should reduce these cases to the greatest extent possible."

Packwood repeated for the television evening news: "Still, tough luck, as far as federal help is concerned."

I noted that "The federal government is not the only source of all funds," and private organizations were free to finance abortions. I then reminded Packwood that the administration position "is what the Congress has said in the Hyde amendment. The Senate and the House...voted for that amendment last year."

He asked whether the administration would oppose funding abortions in a national health insurance program. I said it would.

Packwood shook his head in apparent despair. We come to this issue from such different premises, I thought. To him, it is unfair for the government not to fund abortions for poor women when the Supreme Court has established a constitutional right to an abortion in the first trimester. To me, there is no question of equity. I thought abortion was wrong for women who could afford it unless the life of the mother was at stake, so I had no misgivings on grounds of equity in opposing the use of public funds to pay for abortions for poor women, as a matter of statutory law. Where the life of the mother was endangered, I favored public funding of abortions for the poor. The constitutional right to an abortion in the first trimester did not, in my mind, carry with it the right to public funding. The Constitution guarantees many precious rights—to speak and publish, to travel, to worship—but it does not require that the exercise of those rights be publicly funded.

Packwood cited Carter's hedging during the campaign and asked about a constitutional amendment to reverse the Supreme Court decision striking down state abortion laws. I responded that I opposed any constitutional amendment on abortion. "We run to the Constitution to stop busing, we run there on prayers in schools. We have to stop running to the Constitution to solve all of our problems." Packwood, still unsatisfied, had no further questions.

As the television crews disassembled their cameras, Senator Harry Byrd launched an attack on HEW's interference in local schools with excessively detailed civil rights questionnaires, and asked me about my support for voluntary charitable organizations.

The hearing before the Senate Finance Committee lasted so long that I had less than an hour before the Senate Committee on Labor and Public Welfare session began early in the same afternoon. Within fifteen minutes of its start, Senator Jacob Javits of New York asked about my ability to carry out the law, in view of my personal beliefs. I told Javits I had no qualms of conscience about my ability to enforce the law, "whatever the law is."

After a two-and-one-half-hour interlude of questions on civil rights enforcement, the isolation of HEW from the rest of the nation, welfare reform, busing, museums, education funding, biomedical research, national health insurance, conflicts of interest, animal testing of drugs, lack of coordination among Cabinet departments, and HEW's unresponsiveness to state and local government,

Maine Democratic Senator William Hathaway returned to abortion. He characterized my position as being "morally and unalterably opposed to abortion," and then asked: "Does this mean that your convictions are so strong that if Congress should enact a law, whether it is national health insurance or whatever, that did provide federal funds for abortion, that you would recommend to President Carter that he veto such legislation?"

I hedged to get time to answer this unexpected question. I had never discussed this situation with Carter and I did not want to box the President in by simply saying I would or would not recommend a veto. "I do not think President Carter, in terms of his own views, needs my advice on whether to veto that legislation."

As Hathaway pressed, asking what I would recommend if Carter sought my advice and how active a role I would take, I decided to finesse the question. "I cannot answer that question. Laws come over with lots...of provisions in them, and whether one provision is of such overriding importance in terms of the national administration's policy that the bill ought to be vetoed...is something very difficult to judge in the abstract." There was no way I would judge this issue now.

Hathaway sensed what I was thinking and helped out by noting the difference between a national health insurance program that the administration wanted with abortion funding being the only unwelcome provision and a bill that simply provided federal funds for abortion.

He then asked whether I would lobby the Congress against legislation which permitted federal funds to be spent for abortion. I told him that the administration would lobby against such legislation.

Hathaway expressed concern about anyone forcing his religious or other beliefs on the public, citing as examples a Christian Scientist HEW Secretary who did not believe in modern medicine, or a vegetarian Secretary of Agriculture who did not believe food stamps should be spent for meat. I responded firmly that if I had the slightest hesitation about enforcing whatever law the Congress passed, I would not be sitting in front of him.

Hathaway didn't question that. His concern was that no individual "should enforce his particular religious or moral beliefs into the policy-making area." I responded that "the Congress had made a judgment last year that restricting federal funds for abortions was a matter appropriate for legislation." As to my personal views, I was expressing them so every senator who had to vote on my confirmation would know them.

Unlike the exchange with Packwood, the exchange with Hathaway ended on a conciliatory note. He appreciated my candor and hoped that I would maintain an open mind during the course of the debate on abortion.

But neither the press nor the American public was prepared for any conciliation on this issue. Before I had departed the hearing room the first of some 6,473 letters and telegrams and hundreds of phone calls, unyielding on one side or the other, began arriving at my office. That evening, the *Washington Star*'s front page headlined: ANGRY SENATOR BLASTS CALIFANO ON ABORTION. The story featured Packwood's questioning and his "tough luck" comment. It did report my commitment to enforce the law vigorously, and it questioned an assumption that Packwood and Hathaway had made—that the woman's right to an abortion established in *Roe* v. *Wade* implied a right to federal funds to pay for the procedure. Earlier in the week, during oral arguments before the Supreme Court on pending abortion cases, several Justices had questioned any such right to funds. There were indications that the Court would throw the scalding issue back into the legislative-

executive political process. That possibility only enhanced the significance of my views—and President Carter's.

That evening Carter telephoned me: "How did the testimony go today?"

"All right, I think, Mr. President," I responded hesitantly. "I hope I didn't create any problems for you."

"What did they ask you about?"

"Most of the questions were on your campaign promises, like welfare reform and national health insurance, and then typical special interest questions about HEW's constituencies and busing. I testified for seven hours. But the fireworks came in the thirty minutes of questioning about abortion."

"I saw what you said in the paper and on television. You hang tough. You're saying the right things."

"Thank you, Mr. President."

In public comments outside the hearing, Packwood expressed deep concern and anger. Javits predicted a long and contentious struggle over the issue. And Karen Mulhauser of the National Abortion Rights Action League said it was "unthinkable" that a leading civil rights attorney "would openly discriminate" against indigent women. "We really didn't know until this week how extreme Califano's views were," she added. The lead editorial in the *Washington Post*, my former law client, was headed "Mr. Califano on Abortion," and took after me and my new boss: "The fact that each man reached this conclusion as a matter of personal conviction makes the conclusion itself no less troubling. For, personal or not, the effect of their common position would be to deny the poor what is available to the rich and not-so-rich. To argue as they do, that the emphasis should be on other medical services and/or pregnancy services does not address this inequity."

On Inauguration Day, January 20, 1977, the new President sent the nominations of the nine Cabinet members-designate whose hearings were completed to the Senate for confirmation. Eight were swiftly confirmed. Senator Packwood denied the Senate the necessary unanimous consent to consider my nomination that day.

Majority Leader Bob Byrd called my nomination to the Senate floor on January 24. Packwood was vehement. He said I held my views so passionately, so vigorously, that "I think it is impossible that Mr. Califano will be able to fairly administer the laws involving abortion, assuming that the Supreme Court says women... continue to have a right to an abortion, and that they continue to have a right to federal funds to help them."

Javits shared Packwood's view favoring federal funds for abortion, but he felt my qualifications in other areas merited my being confirmed. Other Republicans, from Senate Minority Leader Howard Baker to arch-conservative Carl Curtis, the ranking minority member of the Finance Committee, supported the nomination. The debate was brief, the vote 95 to Packwood's 1. Strom Thurmond was the first to phone to tell me of the Senate confirmation and congratulate me.

I called to thank each senator who had spoken on my behalf. Then I thought about Packwood. I felt that he had been petty in holding my nomination up four days, and that there had been an element of grandstanding in it. However, I had to accept the fact that his beliefs on abortion were as sincerely held as mine. From his point of view, putting that extra spotlight on me may have provided a little insurance that I would be careful to enforce a law that funded abortions more widely than I considered appropriate. I had been confirmed overwhelmingly, and I had to deal with him as a member of the Senate Finance Committee that had jurisdiction over such key HEW programs as Social Security, Medicare, Medicaid, and

welfare. I swallowed a little hard and called him: "Bob, I understand your view on abortion. But I'm now Secretary and you and I agree on virtually every other social issue. I hope our differences on abortion won't prevent us from working together." Packwood, clearly surprised, thanked me for the call.

In a *New York Times* editorial on January 31 condemning my position on abortion, one element struck me as amusing: "Mr. Califano's statement in one sense represents his personal opposition to abortion. In another sense, it is a free political ride, earning credit for the administration from abortion foes without his having any real decision to make. It was Congress, though sharply split, which last fall decreed the ban on Medicaid funds for abortions. It is the courts, now scrutinizing that ban, which will decide. And Mr. Califano has pledged, as he must, to carry out the orders of the courts." I could understand the point of the editorial, but I hardly considered my experience before the Senate committees a free ride.

The abortion issue would track me for most of my term as HEW Secretary. I shortly discovered that, like Champion and Shanahan, few, if any, of my colleagues at HEW shared my view or the President's on abortion. Everyone in the top HEW management who expressed his opinion disagreed with mine. Only at the Christmas open house, when they streamed through my office to shake hands and have a picture taken, would HEW employees—mostly the blacks or Catholics—whisper, "Don't let them kill those black babies," or "God bless you for your stand against abortion."

The same was true at the White House. A few staff members, such as Midge Costanza, were publicly outspoken in favor of federal funding for abortion. Shanahan called me on July 15, 1977, and said she was going to a meeting at the

White House, set up by Midge Costanza to organize the women in the administration to urge Carter to change his position on abortion. Shanahan said they might draft a petition asking to see Carter and setting forth their views. I was incredulous that a White House staffer would organize such a meeting. I had no question about Shanahan's loyalty, but was appalled at Costanza's judgment and seriously questioned her loyalty to Carter. Two of the other top appointees at HEW, Assistant Secretary for Human Development Services Arabella Martinez and Assistant Secretary for Education Mary Berry, also went to the meeting.

A story was in the *Washington Post* on the morning following the Friday afternoon meeting. Jody Powell called Shanahan at about 11:00 A.M. "I just wanted to find out what right you all think you had to have a meeting like that in the White House?" Before Shanahan could respond, he answered, "No right, none at all."

"We have a right to express our views," Shanahan began.

Powell snapped, "At least General Singlaub [who disagreed with the President's policy in Korea] resigned. I can respect him."

"I did not give up my First Amendment rights when I joined the administration," Shanahan shot back.

Powell was incensed. "Most of these turkeys wouldn't have a job if it weren't for the President."

Shanahan spoke firmly, in the tense, modulated tone her voice often assumed when all her energy was devoted to maintaining her composure: "These women left damn good jobs to join the administration. Most are better qualified than men who got jobs of the same rank."

"Not you, Eileen, I don't include you," Powell responded defensively to the former economic correspondent for the *New York Times*, "but these turkeys

would not have jobs if the President hadn't given them one."

When Shanahan told me about this conversation later that afternoon, she was still trembling with indignation and rage. Fortunately, she found great satisfaction in her work and she and I had developed a relationship of sufficient respect that she decided not to resign.

I assumed Carter would be enraged when he heard about the women's meeting—and he was, privately, and at the Cabinet meeting on Monday, July 18. "I don't mind vigorous debate in the administration. As a matter of fact, I welcome it," Carter said, "but I do not want leaks to the press or attacks on positions we've already established. If the forty women had listened to my campaign statements, they should know my position." Carter then contrasted Commerce Secretary Juanita Kreps and HUD Secretary Pat Harris with the group of women who met with Midge Costanza. Kreps raised her hand to speak. The President recognized her. In her soft-spoken, polite, and respectful manner, she said: "Mr. President, I appreciate the intent of your comment about me and I, of course, am loyal to you as we all are." What well-chosen words, I thought. "But"—Kreps paused to make certain we were all appropriately postured on the edge of our Cabinet chairs—"you should not take my absence from the meeting of the women as an indication of support for the administration's position on abortion."

Carter seemed somewhat surprised, not at Kreps's position, but at the quiet firmness with which she expressed her view in front of the Cabinet and the "barber shop" patrons (as I sometimes thought of the crew of aides and note-takers that sat against the wall in the Cabinet Room). From across the Cabinet table, Pat Harris promptly agreed with Kreps, but promised to keep her views within the official family. The President, so uncomfortable that he almost sounded defensive, indicated he was of course not talking about "Juanita and Pat," and reiterated his desire for "full debate," but he insisted on "complete loyalty" once an administration decision was made.

When the President walked in to begin the Cabinet meeting two weeks later, on August 1, the first Costanza had attended after her women's meeting, he put his arm around her, kissed her, and said, "Nice to see ya, darlin.'"

Whatever distance the President wanted from me on other policies, like school integration, the anti-smoking campaign, or Social Security cuts, he held me at his side whenever he spoke of abortion: during a March 1977 Clinton, Massachusetts, town meeting and on a Los Angeles television show in May 1977 ("Joe Califano, who is Secretary of HEW, feels the same way I do against abortions"); in Yazoo City, Mississippi, in July 1977 ("...the Secretary of HEW agrees with me completely on this issue..."); at a Bangor, Maine, town meeting in February 1978 ("Joe Califano, who is head of HEW, is a very devout Catholic.... I happen to be a Baptist, and his views on abortion are the same as mine"); with college and regional editors and at general press conferences.

There were demonstrations, first in front of the building where my law office was located, then at the corner of Independence Avenue and Third Street, S.W., where the HEW headquarters and my offices were. The demonstrations, always peaceful but with increasingly sensational placards during 1977, were, as I looked out my window, a constant reminder of the potential of this issue to consume my energies to the detriment of other programs. A week after my confirmation, on January 31, 1977, Karen Mulhauser led a contingent of marchers from the National Abortion Rights Action League, carrying signs ("Califano

Will Enslave Poor Women") that, however overdrawn they seemed to me, conveyed how many Americans felt. Coupled with the personal turmoil the issue stirred in several key managers I had recruited, both men and women, I decided it was imperative to set an overall tone and strategy from the beginning.

I was a bureaucratic child of the 1960s, acutely sensitive to the potential of an issue that touches on human life to kindle a consuming movement — as the military draft fueled the anti-Vietnam War movement. On abortion, the issue was life itself: If we all believed that life began at the same time, there would be no debate on abortion. If all citizens believed life begins at the moment of conception, then they would consider it intolerable for their national government to permit, much less fund, abortion because it involves the elimination of life. If, however, the body politic unanimously believed that life does not begin until the second or third trimester, or that there is no life until the fetus can be viable separate from the mother's body, then it would offend social justice for the government of such a single-minded people not to fund abortions for the poor when rich and middle-class women could easily obtain them to avoid serious illness or the later creation of retarded or physically handicapped life. However, the American people are far from unanimous in their view of when life begins; indeed, disagreement on that issue has been so strong it spawned as bitter a social and political dispute as the 1970s produced.

I concluded that it was not sufficient simply to express my view clearly and consistently, but that it was also essential to communicate the certainty with which I held it. Any hedging would only encourage those who disagreed to hope for a change that would not be forthcoming, and those who agreed to take steps to stiffen my resolve. By repeatedly and clearly setting forth my position, I could perhaps deflect the resources of some of the pro- and anti-abortion partisans to other targets they felt they had the opportunity to influence or the need to bolster.

My second conclusion was that I must do all I could to avoid unnecessary provocation. My obligation was to keep some measure of political decorum in this emotional debate. I did not have the luxury of an outside antagonist to be flip or hyperbolic. I refused to see or speak before pro-life groups who wanted to give me awards or roses, and I tried (not always with success) to avoid crossing picket lines or confronting demonstrators directly. In 1977, this involved going to a lot of places through the back door.

I had to display a calm and reasoned approach because of my obligation to enforce whatever law the Congress ultimately passed or the courts eventually declared constitutional. On this issue, above all, it was not enough for me to be fair; it was critical for the interested people to perceive they were being fairly treated.

Maintaining a sense of integrity was important not only to the public, but to the professionals in the department. HEW's Center for Disease Control was charged with the surveillance of communicable diseases. Most commonly identified with monitoring and reporting on influenza or other communicable diseases, the center was also responsible for surveillance of abortions and abortion-related deaths in the United States. In October 1977, at the peak of the legislative debate over Medicaid funding for abortion, there were reports that an Hispanic-American woman had checked into a McAllen, Texas, hospital with complications from an abortion improperly performed in Mexico. There were allegations that the woman was covered by Medicaid and had been told by a Texas doctor that if she had only come a few weeks earlier, she would

have been eligible for Medicaid funding for an abortion, but now the law prohibited it. The woman died within a few days of being admitted to the hospital.

I called Bill Foege, whom I had recently appointed director of the center, and asked him to check out the reports. He came to Washington and nervously told me that while it was difficult to establish the facts because the woman might have gone to Mexico to keep the abortion secret, she had received two Medicaid-funded abortions before the Hyde amendment took effect. "So we may have a confirmed death from an abortion improperly performed on an otherwise Medicaid-eligible woman," Foege said, resting his paper on his lap as though trying to produce relief from a tension that still persisted.

I studied him silently for a moment and then realized that he was concerned about my view of the center's role in keeping abortion statistics.

"Look," I said, "you must understand this: I want you to keep statistics as accurately as you can, to investigate as meticulously as you can. Our obligation —whatever my views—is to set the facts before the Congress and the people. Particularly on an issue like this, we must maintain the integrity of HEW's data. The only way to deal with an issue this hot is to be accurate."

His face brightened in relief. "That's just the way I feel," he said.

While I could not predict the route or timetable, I sensed that the abortion issue was inexorably headed for my desk. On June 20, 1977, the Supreme Court decided in *Beal* v. *Doe* and *Maher* v. *Roe* that the federal government had no constitutional obligation to fund discretionary abortions that were not medically necessary. Like so many ardently awaited Supreme Court decisions, this one created as much controversy as it resolved. The Court had cleared the way to having the Hyde amendment go into effect, thus restricting Medicaid funding to abortions where the life of the mother would be endangered if the fetus were carried to term. The Court had also moved the debate back into the political arena, to the floors of the House and Senate and the HEW regulatory process.

I asked my staff to prepare a guideline to implement the Hyde amendment. Judge Dooling in Brooklyn would now have to withdraw his order blocking enforcement of that amendment and I wanted to be ready to issue the necessary instructions the same day the judge acted. Any delay would only give the pro- and anti-abortionists more time to demonstrate. If I could act immediately, there would be only one day of newspaper and television coverage.

As we planned to move as quickly and quietly as possible, the President was hit with a question about the Supreme Court decision at his July 12 press conference. I was signing routine mail, casually watching the televised conference, when Judy Woodruff of NBC News caught my attention with a question asking how "comfortable" the President was with the recent Supreme Court decision "which said the federal government was not obligated to provide money for abortions for women who cannot afford to pay for them." The President reiterated his view that "I would like to prevent the federal government financing abortion."

Woodruff followed up: "Mr. President, how fair do you believe it is then that women who can afford to get an abortion can go ahead and have one and women who cannot afford to are precluded?"

In an echo of a statement by John Kennedy, the President answered, "Well, as you know, there are many things in life that are not fair, that wealthy people can afford and poor people can't. But I don't believe that the federal government

should act to try to make these opportunities exactly equal, particularly when there is a moral factor involved."

I had been leaning back in my chair and almost went over backward. I was stunned at the President's response. It was clear to me that he had no idea of the bitter reaction his comment would incite. It couldn't have been deliberate. At worst, it was an on-the-spot, clumsy attempt to appeal to fiscal conservatives and right-to-lifers; at best it was an inept, off-the-top-of-his-head answer to a question for which he was not prepared. Within an hour Eileen Shanahan was in my office, tears of anger welling in her eyes, to tell me that the press wanted my comment on the President's "life is unfair" remark. "None, none, none," I said.

The only person who told me she agreed with the comment of the President was Eunice Kennedy Shriver, who wrote me on July 15: "In terms of the equity argument, I think the President's answer is satisfactory." It was one of the few times I can recall disagreeing with the political judgment of this extraordinary woman. She had become and remained a dedicated and politically persistent participant in the abortion controversy, an energetic opponent of federal funding.

In July, unknown to the public, to most of the antagonists prowling the halls of Congress with roses and hangers and, indeed, to most congressmen and senators, a secret compromise remarkably close to the agreement the House and Senate would reach in December was beginning to take shape in the mind of Eunice Kennedy Shriver. She called me, as she was undoubtedly calling others, in the middle of the month, three weeks after the Supreme Court tossed the issue back to the Congress. She had "some language that might be acceptable to both the House and Senate" and end the widespread access to abortion. "We've got to face the rape and incest argument, don't you think?" And, spraying words in her staccato Massachusetts accent, she added: "We also have to deal with serious damage to the mother – physical damage, not this fuzzy psychological stuff."

Eunice read me some language and concluded, "I'm sending this over to you, personally and confidentially, and you can use it as your own."

Just as I was about to hang up, she added, "And Joseph, when we get over this, we need a teen-age pregnancy bill. I'm getting Teddy to introduce it and I want the two of you to work together on it." Eunice was working on a bill to fund centers to help teen-agers who were pregnant (she was so well connected within HEW that I got her revision of my draft testimony in support of the bill before I even received the draft from the departmental staff). Impressed by a Johns Hopkins program that helped teen-agers deal with their babies and avoid having more, she wanted to duplicate it around the nation. But even there she stood firmly on abortion. When the teen-age pregnancy bill was being considered in 1978 and HEW Deputy Assistant Secretary Peter Schuck was quoted as saying states might give funds to clinics providing abortions if they were providing services to pregnant teen-agers, Eunice sent me a strong letter: "I certainly have not worked on this bill for three years under the assumption that abortion services would be provided under the bill. . . . I will not continue, quite frankly, if abortion services are permitted under this legislation." Due in large measure to her lobbying on the Hill, when the bill was eventually enacted, no abortion services were funded under it.

The confidential proposal Eunice Shriver sent me suggested modifying the Hyde amendment to prohibit the use of funds to perform an abortion, except in cases of rape or incest, where necessary to save the life of the mother, or where the

mother has an organic disease that would cause grave damage to her body if the pregnancy were continued to term. Under her proposal, she estimated that only a thousand to fifteen hundred abortions per year would be performed under Medicaid, mainly involving mothers with severe heart or kidney disease or severe diabetic conditions. "I am told," her letter concluded, "that 80 percent of the abortions performed under Medicaid would be eliminated by this language."

There were few takers for the Shriver compromise in July, but before the abortion legislation saga ended in December 1977, the House and Senate would agree on language reflecting her influence and access to key members.

On August 4, 1977, Judge Dooling reluctantly lifted his injunction against enforcing the Hyde amendment. Within hours, I announced that HEW would no longer fund abortions as a matter of course, but would provide funds "only where the attending physician, on the basis of his or her professional judgment, had certified that the abortion was necessary because the life of the mother would be endangered if the fetus were carried to term."

The House and Senate Conferees' report on the Hyde amendment approved funding for termination of an ectopic (fallopian tube) pregnancy, for drugs or devices to prevent implantation of the fertilized ovum on the uterus wall, and for "medical procedures for the treatment of rape or incest victims." I had asked Attorney General Griffin Bell to interpret that language. His opinion concluded that the Hyde amendment and the quoted language prohibited funding abortion for rape or incest (unless the life of the mother was threatened), but permitted funding for prompt treatment before the fact of pregnancy was established.

On the same day Judge Dooling lifted his injunction and I issued my guidelines under the Hyde amendment to the 1977 HEW Appropriations Act, the Senate voted by a lopsided 60 to 33 to permit payment for abortions under a broad "medically necessary" standard in 1978. Earlier that week the House had voted 238 to 182 to retain the strict Hyde amendment language.

And on that same August 4th day, the Defense Department revealed that it had funded 12,687 abortions at military hospitals between September 1, 1975, and August 31, 1976. The Pentagon policy was to fund abortions for members and dependents for reasons of physical and mental health. The *Washington Post* story reporting military abortion statistics also noted that federal employees were entitled to abortions under the general health plans, but no records were kept of the number of abortions performed for them and their dependents.

In this state of chaos and division, the House and Senate left Washington for their August recess. When the Congress reconvened in September, high on its agenda was the House and Senate Conference on the Labor-HEW appropriations bill.

There are two ways to block federal funding of a particular activity otherwise authorized. One is to pass a statute that prohibits the federal government from acting. Such legislation must be referred to the authorizing committees of the Senate and the House; normally those committees would be required to hold hearings and report the legislation before it was eligible for consideration on the floor. That can be a long and tedious process—with no certainty that the legislation will ever get to the floor of both Houses for a vote. The authorizing committee can block consideration by simply holding the bill.

The other way to block federal funding for a specific purpose is through the appropriations process, either by not providing funds, or by attaching a rider to an appropriations bill, stating that none of the appropriated funds can be spent for the proscribed activity. The appropriations rider has the same practical force as authorizing legislation, and it offers a significant advantage to legislators: Each year the appropriations bills for the executive departments must be reported by the appropriations committees and acted on by the Congress if government is to continue functioning. The disadvantage is that, unlike substantive, authorizing legislation, the appropriations rider comes up for review each year.

Until the mid-1960s, there were few such riders. By and large, House and Senate parliamentarians ruled them out of order because "substantive legislation" was not permitted on appropriations bills. But as the government funded more activities, the lines between substantive legislation and limits on the uses of federal funds became increasingly hard to draw. The more controversial the activities funded by the appropriations bill, the more frequent the attempt to restrict spending by riders.

No bill attracted more politically aggressive, true-believing interest groups than the annual HEW appropriations bill. It had become honey for a host of political bees: riders prohibiting loans or grants to students who crossed state lines to incite to riot (a hangover from the Vietnam War), forbidding the use of funds for busing, limiting the use of funds to obtain civil rights enforcement information from schools. Senator Warren Magnuson, Chairman of the Senate Appropriations Committee, told me during my first month in office, "Joe, you won't recognize the appropriations hearing for HEW. It has attracted the Goddamnedest collection of kooks you ever saw. We've got to stop all these riders. Make them go to the authorizing committees." But Magnuson's outburst was to prove nothing more than exasperated hope. For during the fall of 1977, he would be involved in the bare-knuckled, prolonged fight over the abortion rider on the HEW appropriations bill.

Some facts about abortions also helped inflame the issue. In 1975, the nation's capital had become the first city in America where abortions outnumbered births. As the congressional recess ended in September 1977, the District of Columbia government revealed that in 1976, legal abortions obtained by District residents totaled 12,945 — an unprecedented one-third more than the city's 9,635 births. And 57 percent of the abortions — 7,400 — were paid for by the Medicaid program before the Hyde amendment went into effect on August 4. The high abortion rate in Washington, D.C., reflected the nationwide abortion rate among blacks, which was double that among whites.

With the Congress returning to Washington, the pro-abortionists moved to counter the right to life roses. On September 7, pro-abortion leader Karen Mulhauser announced a campaign to mail coat hangers to Representative Daniel Flood, the Pennsylvania Democrat who chaired the HEW appropriations subcommittee, and other anti-abortion members.

The first meeting of the House and Senate all-male cast of conferees on September 12 broke up almost as soon as it started. Magnuson and Massachusetts Republican Senator Edward Brooke (who, like Packwood, strenuously fought to fund abortions under Medicaid) vowed that they would not return to the conference table until the House voted on the Senate version of the abortion rider. House Committee Chairman Flood initially refused. But, under pressure from his colleagues who feared that funds for important HEW programs and paychecks for federal employees would be inter-

rupted if no appropriations agreement were reached, Flood took the Senate proposal to fund abortions where "medically necessary," to the House floor. On September 27, the House overwhelmingly rejected the Senate language, 252 to 164.

Then Flood took Magnuson up on his earlier commitment to compromise if the House would first vote on the Senate language. But Magnuson was not prepared to give much and House conferees ridiculed his attempt to cover genetic disease, with statements that his suggestion would permit abortions where the child had a blue and brown eye. At one point Magnuson proposed limiting funding to situations where the life of the mother was at stake, cases of rape or incest, and situations involving "serious permanent health damage." When I heard about his proposal, I suspected the fine hand of Eunice Shriver. But Flood's initial reaction was scathing. "You could get an abortion with an ingrown toenail with that Senate language," and it went nowhere.

After House Speaker Tip O'Neill complained that only pro-abortionists Magnuson and Brooke attended the conference for the Senate, thus making compromise near-impossible with the dozen House members usually present, more Senate conferees went to the meetings. The conversation became more civil, but the conferees were no closer to agreement as September 30, the end of the fiscal year and the end of HEW's authority to spend money, arrived.

Up to that point I had decided to stay out of the congressional fight over abortion. The administration view was well known. The President did not want to be part of any compromise that was more permissive than his anti-abortion campaign statements. It was one thing to carry out whatever law the Congress passed, quite another to take an active role in easing the restriction. Carter was committed to the former; he wanted no part of the latter.

Popular sentiment, reflected in the polls, was with the strict House view, and many pro-abortionists realized that. On October 6, for example, Norman Dorsen, head of the American Civil Liberties Union, in opposing a constitutional convention, cited his concern that a nationwide convention might be used to outlaw abortion completely. With that kind of popular support, the House was likely to hold to the strict limits on federal funding for abortions that Carter favored.

Moreover, my conversations with members of Congress had led me to the conclusion that I could be of little, if any, help in drafting the substance of an eventual compromise. Abortion was such a profoundly personal issue that neither I nor a President who, during his first nine months of office, had already lost a good deal of respect on the Hill, would have much influence with individual members.

Only once had I come close publicly to entering the debate during this time. I understood the depth of conviction and humane values that motivated most abortion advocates, but I was deeply offended by the cost-control, money-saving argument pushed by the staunchly pro-abortion Alan Guttmacher Institute, the research arm of the Planned Parenthood Federation of America. In late September, the Institute published a report claiming that the Hyde amendment would cost the public at least $200 million, for the first year of their life, to take care of children who could have been aborted under Medicaid. I wanted to denounce this kind of argument in severe terms: it was appallingly materialistic and represented a selfish failure to confront moral issues as such. But in the interests of being firm yet not provocative, I waited until I was asked about it at a press conference to express my views, and then did so in muted tones.

Now, however, I had to get into the congressional fight. On October 1, I was compelled to eliminate all hiring and overtime and virtually all out-of-town travel by HEW's 150,000 employees. I also warned that they might receive only half their pay in mid-October unless the House and Senate resolved the appropriations fight over abortion. It was, so far as we could tell, unprecedented at the time for a department to have no authority to operate or spend money after the first of the new fiscal year.

Despite the situation, the conferees again failed to reach agreement on October 3, and postponed any further action until October 12, after the Columbus Day recess. That postponement jeopardized beneficiaries of HEW programs and the pay of Department employees. Across the nation, state rehabilitation agencies for the handicapped were running out of money to process claims for Social Security disability benefits; New York State would be unable to meet its payroll for employees to process disability determinations; Texas intended to furlough 612 employees on October 12; Idaho would have no money for its nutrition and community services programs for the aged.

I called Tip O'Neill and Bob Byrd on October 10th, and asked them to try to break the abortion deadlock in order to avoid severe human suffering. The next day I sent them a letter and made it public. It was, the letter charged, "grossly unfair to hold the vulnerable people of our nation and thousands of federal and state employees hostage" in the congressional dispute over the use of federal funds for abortions. If the Congress could not agree on abortion language, I urged them to pass a Continuing Resolution to give me authority to spend in early 1978 at the end-of-1977 level in order to continue HEW programs that people depend on each day. The Senate opposed a Continuing Resolution because it would also keep the Hyde amendment in effect.

I sent telegrams to the state governors alerting them to imminent funding terminations so they would press their congressmen and senators to act. I asked Labor Secretary Ray Marshall to tell the Congress and the public of the dangers of continuing to hold up 1978 funding, since his department's appropriations were tied to the HEW bill. Marshall announced that further delay could force many states to stop processing unemployment insurance claims and halt federally funded job and health safety programs. At my suggestion, President Carter told the congressional leadership on the morning of October 12 that, while we all recognized what an emotional issue abortion was, the paychecks of federal employees should not be held up while Congress tried to resolve it. House Appropriations Committee Chairman George Mahon warned of "chaos in some parts of our government." By October 13, after wrangling with each other and some spirited debate on the House floor, both legislative bodies passed a Continuing Resolution to provide funds for fifteen days until the end of the month.

On Sunday, October 16, I was scheduled to appear on the ABC-TV program *Issues and Answers*. On the Saturday morning preceding the program, I called the President to review the administration's position on abortion. The President said that his position had not changed since the campaign.

"One issue in sharp dispute is how to handle victims of rape or incest," I said, asking whether he objected to funding abortions for rape or incest victims and referring to his July 12, 1977, press conference. There Carter had said that the federal government "should not finance abortions except when the woman's life is threatened or when the pregnancy was the result of rape or incest. I think it ought to be interpreted very strictly."

I asked the President whether his "very strictly" interpretation was related to the dispute between House and Senate conferees over medical procedures short of abortion for rape or incest performed shortly after the act, as distinguished from outright abortion. Carter said he was unaware of the dispute, but wanted to stay out of it. I said that it might not be possible for me to do that. Then leave the administration position ambiguous on this issue, he suggested. "Above all I want people to understand I oppose federal funding for abortion in keeping with my campaign promise."

The words had the texture of the three dimensions that came into play when Carter discussed abortion with me: his deep personal belief, his sense (particularly in the first year) that he would violate some sacred trust if he did not adhere to his campaign statements, and his insistence on getting the political plusses out of issues that had such significant political minuses as well.

ABC White House correspondent Sam Donaldson asked the first question on the program the next day: What was the administration's position on abortion? I recited the administration position opposing federal funds for abortions "except where the life of the mother is endangered if the fetus were carried to term, or for treatment as a result of rape or incest."

After Bettina Gregory asked about teen-age pregnancy, Donaldson pressed for precision on the issue of rape or incest. "The House position...would not even allow abortions to be financed in the case of rape or incest, unless someone comes forward and it can be established that there is not yet a pregnancy that has been medically found. Is that reasonable?"

Trying to satisfy the President's desires, I responded: "In the case of rape or incest, you would assume that the individual would come promptly for treatment and that is a matter of several days. Doctors and experts disagree on it. It can be days or a couple of weeks."

Donaldson noted that the House would allow a dilation and curettage only where an abortion was not involved, and asked if I agreed. I hesitated, then in pursuit of the President's overriding objective to be anti-abortion, responded: "Yes, that is the way I feel; that is the way the President feels. He made that clear during the campaign repeatedly, as you are well aware, covering him during the campaign."

I then recalled my own desire to cool the debate, and added: "This is a very difficult issue; it is a very complex issue; it is a very emotional issue. There are strong feelings on all sides. I think in terms of the nation as a whole what is important is that this issue is being debated in every state in the union...in city after city. The way to reach a consensus in a democracy is to have people talk about it, where they live; and that is happening now in this country...the issue should be debated in more places than in the House and Senate."

When the Continuing Resolution ran out on October 31, House and Senate conferees agreed to language which would permit federal funding for abortion in cases of rape, including statutory rape of minors, or incest, where a prompt report was made to appropriate authorities. They were still split over Senate language which would permit abortions "where grave physical health damage to the mother would result if the pregnancy were carried to term." By the next day, however, the House conferees wanted only forced rape covered. The Senate conferees were furious, and the conference broke up in acrid charges of bad faith. This skirmish marked the first time the House conferees had agreed on abortion, as distinguished from treatment before the fact of pregnancy was established, in

any rape situation. Nevertheless, with their conferees unable to agree, the House and Senate voted another Continuing Resolution, giving members a three-week respite from the issue until December 1.

But there was no respite from the demonstrations. Without fail, during the week pickets marched outside HEW. The signs got more vivid; the crude printing crueler. There were the color pictures from *Life* magazine and the roses and hangers, which had become calling cards for the protagonists. The rhetoric was increasingly sprinkled with harsh accusations of "murder" by each side—of killing unborn children by Medicaid abortion, or poor mothers by back-alley abortion. Some placards accused me of being a "murderer of poor women."

Wherever I went, pickets greeted me. When I spoke in Oregon at a Democratic political fundraiser, several hundred demonstrators from both sides paraded outside the Hilton Hotel. The Oregon Legislative Emergency Board was scheduled to decide in ten days whether to replace lost federal abortion funds with state money. The pro-abortionists angrily accused me of trying to inject my own views into the Oregon fight, which I had not heard of until arriving in Portland.

The sincerity of the Oregon demonstrators and others like them took its toll on me: earnest pleas of both sides were moving. None of the lighthearted sidebars that accompanied most demonstrations— even some during the Vietnam War— were present during pro- and anti-abortion rallies. When I avoided demonstrators by going out a side entrance, as I did that evening in Oregon, I felt like a thief in the night, denying these committed marchers even the chance to know they had been at least heard, if not heeded.

The most vehement demonstration took place in New York City's Greenwich Village on Saturday afternoon, November 12. It was my most draining emotional experience over the abortion issue.

New York University President John Sawhill invited me to receive NYU's University Medal. The award ceremony was to consist of a brief talk and an extended question and answer period. As the day approached I was told that pro-abortionists planned a major demonstration. When I arrived at the NYU Law School in Washington Square, there were several thousand demonstrators. They were overwhelmingly pro-abortion; the handful of right-to-lifers there said they had heard of the demonstration only the evening before and had no chance to mobilize their supporters. Bella Abzug reviled the "white-male dominated White House." Speaker after speaker attacked me for "imposing my Roman Catholic beliefs on poor women." "Our bodies, ourselves," protesters chanted to the beat of a big drum. "Not Califano's."

The crowd was so large and noisy, I could hear it clearly when I entered the law school around the block from the demonstrators. As I reached the back entrance, ACLU Chairman Norman Dorsen, a friend of twenty-five years, greeted me with a broad smile on his face. "It took Califano to bring the sixties back to NYU," he cracked. We all chuckled at that welcome, which broke the tension for the next few minutes.

When Dorsen, who was to moderate the question and answer period, Sawhill, and I entered the auditorium, my right arm and hand were in a cast, held by a sling, due to an operation on my thumb the week before. The auditorium was crushingly overcrowded. Every seat was taken; every inch of wall space lined with standees. The antagonism of the audience was so penetrating I could physically feel it as I sat on the elevated stage. Even the cast on my arm will evoke no sympathy here, I thought.

Sawhill spoke first about me. He then turned to give me the medal. As I rose to receive it, the last row of the audience unfurled a huge pro-abortion banner across the back of the auditorium. Fully half the audience stood and held up hangers, many with ends that had been dipped in red nail polish. When the medal was presented, at least a hundred people in the audience turned their backs to me. Many of them remained in that position throughout the entire ninety minutes of my speech and the question and answer session that followed.

The question period was largely devoted to abortion, with many emotional statements and speeches. None, however, struck me more forcefully than that of an intense woman who picked up on a comment I had made earlier that year. On the Sunday, March 20, NBC program *Meet the Press,* Carol Simpson had queried me at length on abortion and the adequacy of the administration program for alternatives to abortion. In the course of one extended response, I observed: "I have never known a woman who wanted an abortion or who was happy about having an abortion. I think it is our role to provide for those women the best we can in terms of family planning services, of day care centers for their children, of health, and prenatal services to make sure children are born healthy, and all the decent things in life that every child in this country deserves, whether it is health care or a clean home or a decent schooling, and we will do our best to do that."

To my left, about halfway down the aisle in the NYU auditorium, a woman rose to the microphone. Her head was tilted sideways, her eyes spilled over with anger, even hatred. "Look at me, Mr. Califano," she shouted with defiant emotion. "I want you to see a woman who wanted an abortion. I want you to see a woman who was happy at having an abortion. I want you to see a woman who had an abortion two weeks ago and who intends to have another abortion."

The room fell into total silence as the tone of her voice became that kind of gripping whisper everyone can hear even when they don't want to: "I want you to go back to Washington knowing that there are women who are happy who have had abortions, knowing that there are women who want abortions. I don't ever want you to make a statement like the one you made saying that you have never known a woman that wanted to have an abortion or never known a woman who was happy about having an abortion. You have now met one."

So draining was the emotional experience at NYU, that afterward, when I got into the car to Kennedy Airport to depart for England, Germany, and Italy to look at national health programs — my first trip abroad as Secretary of HEW — I instantly fell asleep and did not wake up until the driver shook me to say we had arrived at Kennedy.

The abortion issue followed me to Europe. There were questions in England and the Italians were in the midst of their own volatile parliamentary debate on the issue. The latent suspicion of my Catholicism again surfaced in Rome. Immediately after my audience with Pope Paul VI, several reporters called at the Hassler Hotel to see if the Pope talked to me about abortion. He had not mentioned the issue. His focus was on the failure of the food-rich nations such as the United States to feed the world.

I returned to Washington on Thanksgiving eve. I knew the abortion issue would erupt again when the latest Continuing Resolution expired. But I was not prepared for the news the *Washington Post* brought me on the Sunday after Thanksgiving. Connie Downey, chairperson of an HEW group on alternatives to abortion, had written a memo express-

ing her views to her boss, Assistant Secretary of Planning and Evaluation Henry Aaron. The *Post* headlined the most sensational portion of an otherwise typical HEW memo: TASK FORCE HEAD LISTS SUICIDE, MOTHERHOOD, AND MADNESS: ABORTION ALTERNATIVES CITED IN HEW MEMO.

The memo, written more than four months earlier on July 18, contained this paragraph: "Abortion is but one alternative solution to many of the problems... which may make a pregnancy unwise or unwanted.... It is an option, uniquely, which is exercised between conception and live birth. As such, the literal alternatives to it are suicide, motherhood, and, some would add, madness...."

The memo had never reached me, but its leak provided a dramatic reminder of the potential for turmoil within HEW and raised the curtain on the final act between the House and the Senate on the fiscal 1978 HEW appropriations bill.

Returning from Thanksgiving recess, the House leadership was determined to press for a compromise. They did not want the Christmas checks of federal employees to be short. Appropriations Committee Chairman Mahon called me on November 29 to say he had decided to take the leadership completely away from Flood, who ardently opposed federal funds for abortion. "He's just implacable on the subject," Mahon said, distraught. "I'm retiring, but this kind of conduct is a disgrace to the House. We all look asinine."

In secret negotiations with Senator Brooke, Mahon eventually produced the compromise on December 7. The House voted twice within less than four hours. The first time members rejected a Mahon proposal and voted 178 to 171 to stand by their strict position against all funding for abortions except those needed to save the mother's life. Minutes later, Mahon, dejected but determined, won speedy approval of new language from the Rules Committee and rushed back to the House floor. The House reversed direction and adopted the new and relaxed standard, 181 to 167. Within two hours, with only three of its hundred members on the floor, the Senate acceded to the House language and sent the measure to President Carter for his signature.

Under the measure, no HEW funds could be used to perform abortions, "except when the life of the mother would be endangered if the fetus were carried to term, or except for such medical procedures necessary for the victims of rape or incest, when such rape or incest has been reported promptly to a law enforcement agency or public health service; or except in those instances where severe and long-lasting physical health damage to the mother would result if the pregnancy were carried to term when so determined by two physicians."

Senator Brooke described the outcome as "not really acceptable to either side, but it makes some progress." Representative Hyde said that the measure "provides for the extermination of thousands of unborn lives." Senator Javits called the action "a major victory for women's rights." ACLU Chairman Dorsen characterized it as "a brutal treatment of women with medical needs for abortion." Any relief I felt at seeing at least some resolution was lost in the knowledge that the protagonists would rearm to battle over the regulations I had to issue.

As soon as President Carter signed the $60 billion appropriations bill on December 9, it landed on my desk, for the final provision of the compromise language stated: "The Secretary shall promptly issue regulations and establish procedures to ensure that the provisions of this section are rigorously enforced."

The antagonists turned their attention to me. Magnuson and Brooke wrote and called with their permissive interpretation. Robert Michel, ranking Republican on the Appropriations Committee, wrote with his strict view. Dan Flood called and other members — and their even more aggressive staffs — pressed for their interpretation of words such as "medical procedures," "promptly reported," "severe and long-lasting physical health damage," and "two physicians."

There was no way in which I could avoid becoming intimately involved in making key decisions on the regulations. I decided personally to read the entire 237 pages of self-serving and often confused congressional debate and to study the ten different versions of this legislation that were passed by either the House or the Senate.

To assure objectivity, to balance any unconscious bias I might harbor, and to reduce my vulnerability to charges of personal prejudice, I assigned the actual regulation writing to individuals who did not share my strong views about abortion and, more importantly, who stood up for their own views and did not hesitate to tell me when they thought I was wrong. The bulk of the work was done by Richard Beattie, the Deputy General Counsel of HEW, and HEW attorneys June Zeitlin and David Becker, all of whom opposed any restrictions on federal funding of abortions. I also asked the Attorney General to review independently the regulations we drafted at HEW. Once they were in effect, I would establish a detailed auditing system to assure compliance and fulfill the congressional mandate "to ensure that the provisions of this section are rigorously enforced."

Finally, I decided not to consult the President about the regulations. Carter had enough controversial problems on his desk without adding this one. My responsibility under the Constitution and under our system of government was to reflect accurately the law passed by the Congress. Neither Carter's personal views nor mine were of any relevance to my legal duty to ascertain what Congress intended and write regulations that embodied that intent.

In pursuit of my overall goal of cooling the temperature of the debate, I wanted to issue the regulations more "promptly" than anyone might expect. Not relying solely on my own reading of the congressional debates, I asked the lawyers for a thorough analysis of the legislative history. We then spent hours discussing and debating what the Congress intended on several issues, frustrated by the conflicting statements in the congressional record. We determined that for rape and incest victims, the term "medical procedures" as used in this new law now clearly included abortions; that a "public health service" had to be a governmental, politically accountable institution; that short of fraud we should accept physicians' judgments as to what constituted "severe and long-lasting physical health damage"; that the two physicians whose certification was required must be financially independent of each other; and that the rape or incest victim need not personally make the required report to public authorities. We resolved a host of other issues as best we could against the backdrop of the heated and confusing congressional debate. They were wearing days, because I felt the law was too permissive, and its provisions were in conflict with my own position. I revisited many decisions several times, concerned, on overnight reflection, that I had bent too far to compensate for my personal views and approved inappropriately loose regulations, or that I was letting my personal views override congressional intent.

By far my most controversial determination was to define "reported promptly" in the context of rape and incest to cover a sixty-day period from the date of the incident. Even though the Attorney General found the judgment "within the permissible meaning of the words within the Secretary's discretion," there was a storm of controversy over this decision.

There were widely varying interpretations on the floor of the House and the Senate. Most of the legislative history on the Senate floor was made by pro-abortion Senators Magnuson and Brooke. They spoke of "months" and "ninety days" to make the period as long as possible. On the House side, Mahon and other proponents of the compromise spoke of "weeks" and "thirty days" as they cautiously maneuvered this difficult piece of legislation to passage. On the floor of Congress, pro- and anti-abortionists could express their views and protect their constituencies. But I had to select a number of days and be as certain as possible that it would stick.

After extensive internal discussion and spirited argument within the department, I concluded that a sixty-day reporting period was within the middle range of the various time limits mentioned in the debates. The dominant issues during debate were access to abortions and prevention of fraud. The sixty-day period was long enough for a frightened young girl or an embarrassed woman who might not want to report a rape or incest, or one in shock who psychologically could not, to learn whether she might be pregnant and to make the report to public authorities. Sixty days was also prompt enough to permit effective enforcement of the law.

I was ready to issue the regulations during the third week of January 1978. On Monday, January 23, the annual March for Life to protest the 1973 Supreme Court abortion decision was scheduled to file past HEW en route from the White House to the Capitol. I decided to delay issuing the regulations until later in the week. The participants were outraged at the House-Senate compromise. As march leader Nellie Gray saw it, "The life issue is not one for compromise and negotiation. Either you're for killing babies or you're against killing babies."

I issued the regulations on January 26. Attorney General Bell concluded that they were "reasonable and consistent with the language and intent of the law." The *New York Times* editorialized that I had "done [my] duty.... He has interpreted the nation's unfair abortion law fairly.... On several controversial issues Mr. Califano and his lawyers have performed admirably, hacking their way through a thicket of ambiguities in the law that passed a bitter and divided Congress in December after months of heated debate."

The right to life lobby disagreed. Thea Rossi Barron, legislative counsel for the National Right to Life Committee, called the regulations an example of "a rather blatant carrying out of a loophole to allow abortion on demand." The pro-life groups were particularly disturbed about the sixty-day reporting period for victims of rape or incest. But the most severe critic of that provision was Jimmy Carter.

In testifying before the House Appropriations Committee on the morning of February 21, 1978, less than a month after issuing the regulations, Chairman Flood and Republican Robert Michel pressed me to provide an administration position on tightening the restrictions on abortion.

I called the President during the luncheon break. The President wanted the reporting period for rape or incest shortened. He was "not happy" with the sixty-day time period in the regulations. "I believe such instances are reported promptly," he said coolly.

I told him that the sixty-day period was my best judgment of what Congress in-

tended in the law. Carter "personally" believed sixty days permitted "too much opportunity for fraud and would encourage women to lie."

"But what counts is what the congressional intent is," I argued.

The President then said he thought the regulations did not require enough information. He particularly wanted the doctor to report to Medicaid the names and addresses of rape and incest victims. The President was also inclined to require reporting of any available information on the identity of the individual who committed the rape or incest. Carter said, "Maybe some women wake up in the morning and find their maidenhead lost, but they are damn few. That actually happened in the Bible, you know."

"Perhaps we can tighten the reporting requirements," I responded, somewhat surprised at his Biblical reference. "Do you have any strong feelings on the legislation itself?"

Carter expressed some strong feelings: "I am against permitting abortions where long-lasting and severe physical health damage might result. I think that might permit too much of a chance for abuse and fraud. I want to end the Medicaid mills and stop these doctors who do nothing but perform abortions on demand all day."

When I testified that afternoon, I gave the House Appropriations Subcommittee some indication of the administration's views and agreed to submit a letter with the administration's position the next day.

After preparing a draft, I called the President and reviewed my proposed letter for the committee word by word. The letter set the administration position as stricter than the December compromise of the Congress. The administration opposed funding abortions in situations involving "severe and long-lasting physical health damage to the mother." The President and I compromised on the rape and incest paragraph: "In the case of rape or incest, we believe that present law requires the sixty days specified in the regulation as the period Congress intended for prompt reporting. In order to reduce the potential for fraud and abuse, it may be advisable to reduce that period to a shorter period of time."

Just as he was hanging up the phone, Carter again directed me to tighten the reporting provisions on rape and incest. "I want rules that will prevent abortion mills from simply filling out forms and encouraging women to lie."

I changed the regulations to require that the names and addresses of both the victim and the person reporting the rape or incest, and the dates of both the report and the incident, be included in the documentation for Medicaid funding. This change drew immediate fire from the National Organization for Women's National Rape Task Force, but it was well within my discretion under the law and consistent with the congressional intent.

Yet the President was still not satisfied. He wanted the sixty-day reporting period shortened, regardless of congressional intent. He raised the issue again two months later at the Camp David Cabinet summit of April 17, 1978, sharply criticizing "the regulations HEW issued on abortion" among a series of actions by Cabinet officers with which he disagreed.

The concern of the President and others that the regulations were too loosely drawn in the rape and incest area has not turned out to be justified. During the first sixteen months under the law and regulations, until shortly before I left HEW, only 92 Medicaid abortions were funded for victims of rape or incest. The overwhelming majority of Medicaid-funded abortions—84 percent of 3,158 performed—were to save the life of the

mother; 522 were to avoid severe and long-lasting health damage to the mother. Eunice Shriver's estimate of 1,000 to 1,500 Medicaid-funded abortions each year was not too far off, particularly when compared with the 250,000 to 300,000 abortions estimated to have been performed annually under Medicaid in the absence of any funding restrictions.

I came away from the abortion controversy with profound concern about the capacity of national government, in the first instance, to resolve issues so personal and so laced with individual, moral, and ethical values. The most secure way to develop a consensus in our federal system is from the bottom up. But once the Supreme Court established a woman's constitutional right to an abortion against the backdrop of federally funded health care programs, the issue was instantly nationalized. As each branch acted—the Congress with the Hyde amendment, the executive with its regulations, and the Supreme Court in its opinions—the mandates from the top down generated as much resentment as agreement. This is true even though, by 1978, many states had more restrictive provisions on abortion funding than the national government.

In 1978, the Congress extended abortion funding restrictions to the Defense Department budget. In 1979, it applied an even stricter standard to both HEW and Defense appropriations, by eliminating funding in cases of long-lasting physical health damage to the mother, thus funding abortions only when the life of the mother is at stake or in cases of rape or incest, as Carter and I proposed for HEW in February 1978. The Supreme Court in the *McRae* case upheld the constitutionality of the Hyde amendment in June of 1980, concluding that the right to an abortion did not require the government to provide the resources to exercise it and that the Congress could restrict the circumstances under which it would pay for abortions. Months later, the Senate and House agreed to place tighter restrictions on Medicaid funding of abortions. Under the 1981 appropriations legislation, such funding is permitted only where the mother's life is at stake, in cases of rape reported within 72 hours and in cases of incest. That legislation permits the states to be even more restrictive; they are "free not to fund abortions to the extent that they in their sole discretion deem appropriate." Similar language was attached to the Defense appropriations bill.

Conforming the Defense and HEW appropriations bills provides the same standards for most of the federal funding arena. So long as the Congress acts through the appropriations for each department, however, rather than by way of across-the-board authorizing legislation, there will be inconsistencies. Even within HEW, the abortion funding policy has been a quilted one. The restrictions do not apply to disabled citizens whose health bills are paid by Medicare, because that program is financed out of Social Security trust funds, not through the HEW appropriations bill. Nor do the funding limits apply to the Indian Health Service; though administered by HEW, funds for the Indian Health Service are provided in the Interior Department appropriations bill. The Congress has begun to move to prohibit the use of federal funds to pay for abortion through federal employee health insurance. The inevitable challenges in court to new restrictions and the recurrent debate in the Congress assure continuing turmoil and controversy over the abortion issue.

In personal terms, I was struck by how infinitely more complex it was to confront the abortion issue in the broader sphere of politics and public policy in our pluralistic society than it had been to face it only as a matter of private conscience. I found no automatic answers in Christian theology and the teachings of my church to the vexing questions of public policy it raised, even though I felt secure in my personal philosophical grounding.

I was offended by the constant references to me as "Secretary Califano, a Roman Catholic" in the secular press when it wrote about the abortion issue. No such reference appeared next to my name in the stories reporting my opposition to tuition tax credits favored by the Catholic Church or my disputes with the Catholic hierarchy on that issue.

I was dismayed by the number of Catholics and diocesan papers that attacked me for the regulations I issued on abortion. Their attack so concerned Notre Dame president Father Theodore Hesburgh that he urged me to speak about the conscience and duty of a Catholic as a public official at the commencement in South Bend in 1979. The assumption of many bishops that I could impose my views on the law passed by the Congress reflected a misunderstanding of my constitutional role at that stage of the democratic process. As it turned out, like the President's, their assumption that the sixty-day reporting period for rape or incest constituted a legal loophole was as ill-founded in fact as it was in law.

Throughout the abortion debate, I did —as I believe I should have—espouse a position I deeply held. I tried to recognize that to have and be guided by convictions of conscience is not a license to impose them indiscriminately on others by one-dimensionally translating them into public policy. Public policy, if it is to serve the common good of a fundamentally just and free pluralistic society, must balance competing values, such as freedom, order, equity, and justice. If I failed to weigh those competing values— or to fulfill my public obligations to be firm without being provocative, or to recognize my public duty once the Congress acted—I would have served neither my private conscience nor the public morality. I tried to do credit to both. Whether I succeeded is a judgment others must make.

Comment

Father McCormick helpfully identifies three levels of moral questions about abortion: (1) the personal morality of having an abortion, (2) the political morality of legalizing and funding abortion, and (3) the obligations of public officials in carrying out the law. We cannot ignore the first level of personal morality in considering our positions on public policy and the obligations of public officials, but this case focuses on the second and third levels.

Begin with the issue of public policy—whether the government should fund abortions for poor women. Note Califano's responses to a representative from the National Women's Political Caucus: "I believe abortion is morally wrong," and "I oppose federal funding for abortion." Must the second position necessarily follow from the first? Senator Packwood and Judy Woodruff both suggest that it would be unfair for the government not to fund abortions for the poor as long as they are legal. They thereby attempt to separate the question of whether abortion should be legal from the question of whether the government should subsidize abortion for poor women once it is legal. Assess the responses of Califano and Carter to this defense of federal funding on grounds of fairness. Is there any principle other than fairness that would favor funding?

One philosopher has suggested that legalizing abortion but not subsidizing it is a fair compromise between the pro-life and pro-choice positions, although it completely satisfies the moral claims of neither. If a compromise is the best solution to the public policy question, are these the right terms?

Consider next the question of whether Califano was correct in thinking that he could act responsibly in public office while personally opposing abortion. Did he use the correct standard—willingness to enforce whatever law Congress passes—in deciding to accept the position? Having accepted the position, did Califano act properly in office? Consider the ways in which his opposition to abortion might have affected his conduct in office, including his public statements. Was he justified in interpreting the intent of Congress as he did in writing HEW regulations on funding abortion? Should he have compromised with the President on the paragraph concerning rape and incest?

The moral conflicts Califano faced might have been even more difficult had Congress instructed HEW to fund abortions through Medicaid. Would Califano then have been justified in doing anything to oppose such a policy? Had Califano been committed to the position that poor women have a right to subsidized abortion, what should he have done in the face of congressional action to the contrary?

Recommended Reading

Most of the philosophical literature focuses on the personal morality of abortion. A good place to start is a widely discussed article by Judith Jarvis Thomson, "A Defense of Abortion," in Marshall Cohen et al. (eds.), *The Rights and Wrongs of Abortion* (Princeton, N.J.: Princeton University Press, 1974), pp. 3–22. John Finnis, "The Rights and Wrongs of Abortion," in *The Rights and Wrongs of Abortion*, pp. 85–113, takes issue with Thomson's qualified defense of abortion. See also Steven L. Ross, "Abortion and the Death of the Fetus," *Philosophy and Public Affairs*, 11 (Summer 1982), pp. 232–45; and L. W. Sumner, *Abortion and Moral Theory* (Princeton, N.J.: Princeton University Press, 1981).

On the question of what the government's position on abortion should be, see Roger Wertheimer, "Understanding the Abortion Argument," in *The Rights and Wrongs of Abortion,* pp. 23–51; and George Sher, "Subsidized Abortion," *Philosophy and Public Affairs*, 10 (Fall 1981), pp. 361–72. A utilitarian case in favor of legalizing abortion and a critique of other approaches is in Jonathan Glover, *Causing Death and Saving Lives* (New York: Penguin Books, 1977), chapters 4, 9–11.

Philip Abbott criticizes the way philosophers have treated the abortion issue in "Philosophers and the Abortion Question," *Political Theory,* 6 (Aug. 1978), pp. 313–36. Roger Wertheimer, "Errata: A Reply to Abbott," *Political Theory,* 6 (Aug. 1978), pp. 337–44, responds. In light of this debate, Amy Gutmann examines what moral philosophy can contribute to resolving political problems such as abortion in "Moral Philosophy and Political Problems," *Political Theory,* 10 (Feb. 1982), pp. 33–48.